The Hatchet and the Plow

The Life and Times of Chief Cornplanter

William W. Betts, Jr.

iUniverse, Inc.
Bloomington

iUniverse books may be ordered through booksellers or by contacting:

iUniverse
1663 Liberty Drive
Bloomington, IN 47403
www.iuniverse.com
1-800-Authors (1-800-288-4677)

ISBN: 978-1-4502-6713-7 (sc)
ISBN: 978-1-4502-6714-4 (hc)
ISBN: 978-1-4502-6715-1 (ebook)

Library of Congress Control Number: 2010915441

Printed in the United States of America

iUniverse rev. date: 12/1/2010

Contents

Preface		ix
Acknowledgments		xi
Order Of Events		xv
Prologue		xix
Chapter I:	Ganawaugus and the Stinking Water	1
Chapter II:	Gaiantwaka	14
Chapter III:	"None of Our Business"	22
Chapter IV:	The Border Wars	35
Chapter V:	Iroquois Take Up the Hatchet	46
Chapter VI:	Wyoming	66
Chapter VII:	The Sullivan Campaign	75
Chapter VIII:	The Mohawk Valley	107
Chapter IX:	The 1784 Fort Stanwix Treaty	113
Chapter X:	Philadelphia and New York City	130
Chapter XI:	Fort Harmar	138
Chapter XII:	Thomas Mifflin and George Washington	144
Chapter XIII:	Home Again	165
Chapter XIV:	War in the West	180
Chapter XV:	John Adlum at Cornplanter Town	216
Chapter XVI:	Fallen Timbers	230
Chapter XVII:	The Canandaigua Treaty	245
Chapter XVIII:	Cornplanter Town	256
Chapter XIX:	The Big Tree and the Sawmill	270
Chapter XX:	The Quaker Mission	280
Chapter XXI:	Handsome Lake and Red Jacket	303
Chapter XXII:	The War of 1812	319
Chapter XXIII:	Last Years	325

Afterword	351
Image Credits	363
Works Consulted	365
Notes	379
Index	407

for Jane

whose great, great, great, great grandfather launched a few cannon balls at Chief Cornplanter

Preface

Throughout the long War for Independence and for many years afterwards, the most prominent of the Native American Indians (excepting only the Mohawk Joseph Brant) was the Seneca chieftain known to the British as Captain O'Beal and to the Americans as Cornplanter. Although a half-breed, he never thought himself anything but an Indian. He never learned to speak English, or to read or write English. And he regularly fostered the impression that he was not understanding much of the English he was hearing. He did sport a bit of the white man's beard in his dotage; but he wore deerskin moccasins until his dying day.

Allied with the British, he fought fiercely through most of the Revolution in what he had been persuaded was the best chance for his people to hold on to the land they had occupied for centuries. At the close of the long war he worked tirelessly and earnestly for accommodation, participating in the treaty sessions by which the lands of his people passed steadily to the European settlers. In his middle years he urged his people to adjust to the ways of the white man, which meant schools, and a formal government, and the plow and the sawmill.

But his last years were tormented by the bitterness which results from disappointment, disillusionment, and betrayal. He closed out his life in a pained rejection of everything associated with the white people. He turned away from the religious views espoused by the Quakers, by the Congregationalists, by the Presbyterians. His devotion was to Nauwenneyu, the Great Spirit. To the very end he could not speak for any length of time without expressing reverence for Nauwenneyu.

He lived a very long life, and as it is regularly with the energetic and passionate life, Cornplanter's was a turbulent one. It had its highs and its lows. It included some ugly moments, but it had its glory days as well. In the end, it has to be considered a life of achievement. It figured dramatically and consequentially in the birth of a nation, and it attended the surrender of an ages-old civilization. It is not too much to say that the course of history would have been much, much different had not this warrior been born of an Indian woman in Ganawaugus 260 years ago.

In the course of this long life Cornplanter enjoyed close associations with many of the principals of the early American history: George

Washington, General Anthony Wayne, Colonel Thomas Proctor, General Arthur St. Clair, General William Irvine, Timothy Pickering, General Henry Knox, the financier Robert Morris, the Tories Colonel John Butler and son Walter Butler, the first Governor of Pennsylvania, Thomas Mifflin, and the first Lieutenant Governor of Upper Canada, John Graves Simcoe. He experienced meaningful relationships with David Mead, the founder of Meadville, Pennsylvania, and with Reverend Timothy Alden, the founder and President of Allegheny College. He stood foremost among the Iroquois chieftains, Joseph Brant, Red Jacket, Old Smoke, Kayahsotha, Sagwarithra, Handsome Lake, Little Beard, and Farmer's Brother.

Of course he was never to know how very large a role history would accord him in accounting for the emergence of the United States of America.

The monument that has been erected for his grave site is as much a monument to the tragic fate of the Native American Indians and to the birth of a new nation as it is to the memory of the single Seneca Indian chief known as Cornplanter.

Acknowledgments

As a farm boy growing up in the early 1930s and romping through the open fields and the woodlots of western Pennsylvania, and angling for trout in the mountain streams, I heard a lot about the Cornplanter Indians. And I learned that not far away, on the Allegheny River, there was still a community peopled by the descendants of the famous Seneca war-chief.

Later, because of a newly acquired passion for Indian artifacts, for countless hours I traipsed the plowed fields which included the village sites of the First Americans. These excursions brought me into the Cornplanter country of French Creek and the Allegheny, of Pine Creek and the Susquehanna.

As my interest in the First Americans grew ever more keen, I began now to read whatever I could find on these peoples, and especially the Senecas of western New York and northwestern Pennsylvania. At about the time of my retirement from teaching the poetry of Shakespeare and Chaucer and Hardy and Tennyson, which had nothing whatsoever to do with the culture and history of the Seneca people, I perceived a startling vacancy in the literature I was perusing. I resolved to do something about that.

Research provided lots of fascinating information on the life and times of Chief Cornplanter, but I found his story much fragmented, well scattered and often difficult to get at. I discovered that for this Seneca chieftain, perhaps the most influential of all American Indians during the late eighteenth century, including the American Revolution, and for a half-century beyond the end of the war, there had never been produced a real biography. Coming hard upon this discovery was my determination to put Cornplanter all together in one place. Accordingly, at the time of my retirement from teaching, in 1991, I took up the hatchet.

The consequence of some fifteen years of enjoyable, but much interrupted, research is *The Hatchet and the Plow*. It is not likely to be the definitive biography of Chief Cornplanter; it is meant as a contribution to the portrait that will finally emerge. It will clear up some of the historic confusion, and will resolve some of the persistent contradictions, as it strives to reach into the corners of the chief's very long and energetic life.

Naturally, I am much indebted to a great many people. From the literature that has gone before, I owe most to the sociologist Anthony Wallace, whose *Death and Rebirth of the Seneca*, which is so rich in description of Cornplanter Town, and so searching on the Iroquois culture, appeared in 1970. Barbara Graymont's account of the Iroquois in the Revolution (1972) has been most helpful for the war years. Nor could I have proceeded very far without the narrative account of Governor Blacksnake, who reports on Cornplanter's participation in the many councils and in the battles of the Revolution. Happily the most able historian Thomas Abler (in 1989) made this narrative, taken from the Draper manuscripts, not only accessible but intelligible. David Swatzler's *A Friend among the Senecas*, which appeared in the year 2000, accounts for the Quaker influence upon the Cornplanter Senecas and includes an edited version of the journal of Henry Simmons, which is most illuminating. An incalculable debt, too, is here acknowledged to a host of students and historians of the Iroquois nation. To mention but a few, there are Warren County's Merle Deardorff, the most prolific William Fenton, and, for the Indians of Pennsylvania, Chester Hale Sipe and Paul Wallace. And just as I laid my pen down, I heard from my Seneca friends that there would be appearing the first real biography very shortly. That turned out to be Thomas Abler's *Cornplanter* (Syracuse University Press). I trust *The Hatchet and the Plow* may prove a worthy companion piece.

Extremely helpful to the research have been the following: The Warren County Historical Society with its Cornplanter Files, a rich repository of documents illuminating the chief's long life; Philip Zorich, responsible for the Pennsylvania Room and the Special Collections of the Stapleton Library at the Indiana University of Pennsylvania; Daniel Shively, Reference Librarian at the Stapleton Library; the good people at the Warren County Historical Society (Abigail Skinner, David Olney, and Jim Chapman); Jack Ericson, who after twenty years is retired from the Reed Library at the State University of New York at Fredonia, where he was Curator of Special Collections. (Ericson is currently the family historian for the Cornplanter Descendants Association, and produces a most informative Cornplanter newsletter.) Mr. Robert Alexander, historian for the First Reformed Church of Albany, has been very helpful, and so, too, have been a number of people at the Allegany

Indian Reservation in Salamanca, New York, among whom are Pam Bowen, the Allegany Reservation Librarian, who is a great, great, great, great granddaughter of Cornplanter; Joshua George Chauncey Johnny-John, a Tonawanda Seneca of the Turtle Clan; and Ms. Sue Grey, of Public Relations and Marketing. For graphics and formatting the book owes much to Tom Betts, whose ancestor, a bombardier in Thomas Proctor's artillery, directed some cannon balls Cornplanter's way during the battle of Newtown.

Quotations from the Quaker Journal of Henry Simmons derive from David Swatzler's edited text and are reproduced here with the kind permission of David Swatzler and Stackpole Books. Quotations from Governor Blacksnake's Revolutionary War Memoirs are from the Layman Draper Manuscripts via Thomas Abler's *Chainbreaker* and are reproduced here with the gracious permission of the Wisconsin Historical Society and the University of Nebraska Press.

Order Of Events

Birth of Kayahsotha	1720-25
Birth of Johannes Abeel	April 8 (?), 1722
Birth of Cornplanter's mother	1724
Birth of Mary Jemison	1743
Birth of Gaiantwaka (Cornplanter)	1750-52
Birth of *Dahgr-ya-doh* (Blacksnake)	1753
Devil's Hole	Sept. 14, 1763
Treaty of Fort Stanwix	Oct. 24, 1768-Nov. 5, 1768
Death of Sir William Johnson	July 11, 1774
Councils at Pittsburgh	1774-1777
Council at Albany	April 26, 1776
Council at German Flats	Aug. 6, 1776
Council at Oswego	July 13-20, 1777
Siege of Fort Stanwix	Aug. 3-22, 1777
Battle of Oriskany	Aug. 6, 1777
Battle of Cobleskill	May 30, 1778
Harding Massacre	June 30, 1778
Battle of Wyoming	July 3, 1778
Thomas Hartley Expedition	Sept. 21-Oct. 5, 1778
Skirmish at Wyalusing	Sept. 29, 1778
Raid on Cherry Valley	Nov. 11, 1778
Fall of Fort Freeland	July 29, 1779
Sullivan Campaign	July 31-Sept. 14, 1779
Colonel Brodhead Expedition	Aug. 11-Sept. 14, 1779
Battle of Newtown	Aug. 29, 1779
Torture of Thomas Boyd and Michael Parker	September 13, 1779
Raid on Canajoharie	Aug. 2, 1780
Raid on Schoharie Valley	Oct. 16, 1780

Order Of Events

2nd Treaty of Fort Stanwix	Oct. 3-22, 1784
Cornplanter in New York City	April 25-May 5, 1786
Treaty of Fort Harmar	Dec. 13, 1788-Jan. 9, 1789
Cornplanter Grant	March 24, 1789
Inauguration of President Washington	April. 30, 1789
Pine Creek (Pa.) murders	June 27, 1790
Cornplanter trip to Philadelphia	October 1, 1790
Defeat of General Josiah Harmar by Little Turtle	October 20-22, 1790
Thomas Proctor's mission to the Indians	March 11-June 8, 1791
Defeat of General Arthur St. Clair by Little Turtle	Nov. 4, 1791
Death of Major General Richard Butler	Nov. 4, 1791
Meeting with Washington (in Philadelphia)	March 13-April 23, 1792
Council at Au Glaize	Sept. 30-October 9, 1792
John Adlum at Cornplanter Town	July 28-Aug. 5, Aug. 23-30, 1794
Battle of Fallen Timbers	Aug. 20, 1794
Treaty of Canandaigua	Oct. 14 -Nov. 11, 1794
Suicide of Big Tree	Jan. 23, 1795
Treaty of Greenville	Aug. 3, 1795
Death of General Anthony Wayne	Dec. 15, 1796
Cornplanter's farewell to President Washington	February, 1797
Treaty of Big Tree	Aug. 15-Sept. 15, 1797
Death of Cornplanter	Feb. 18, 1836
Cornplanter Monument Dedicated	Jan. 25, 1866
Cornplanter Senecas transplanted	1965

The Dark Hills

Dark hills at evening in the west,
Where sunset hovers like a sound
Of golden horns that sang to rest
Old bones of warriors under ground,
Far now from all the bannered ways
Where flash the legions of the sun,
You fade—as if the last of days
Were fading, and all wars were done.

~ Edwin Arlington Robinson

Prologue

How long he had sat thus, with his knees drawn up tightly under his chin, he did not know. What he did remember was waking with a start, just at first light, and stealing out of the bark house. And making the easy trek to the nearby banks of the river, and then picking his way down along the shore, through the river birch and sallows, and up a long and gradual slope away from the water—to this ledge, finally, his favorite spot, his sanctuary, a slender finger of rock which reached far out into the air and over the stream. He liked from this loft to savor the valley that lay straight ahead and below him, downriver.

On his left now the stars of the night began to fade and gradually to disappear; to his right a rosy glow advanced steadily. There was not a breath of wind. No leaf stirred. A heavy mist hung over the stream, but he could hear, even from this great height, the incessant commotion of the water amid the boulders below.

The Great Spirit spoke to him from the river. From its eddies, and from its quiet pools, and from its waterfalls, Nauwenneyu whispered to him of many things: of hazelnuts and huckleberries, of the delicate arbutus and violets of the forest floor, of the warning splash of the beaver's tail and of the drumming of the grouse, of awesome flocks of pigeons, of melting snows and falling leaves.

This was his special place. "My river," he always declared. To this outcropping in perplexity he came; in weariness he sought out the ledge. Here Nauwenneyu would speak to him.

Although he had barely reached his tenth year, he had adopted this vantage point a long time ago, and countless were the times he had perched here, just like this, to sit and stare. Generous views of the river were afforded by many other such spots also, and he knew them well, but this was his favorite. From here it seemed all right for him to claim the scene. "My river," he would whisper to himself.

Although his skin was uncommonly light for an Indian, his eyes were those of an Indian. For they were dark, intensely dark, even black, and at the same time strangely luminous. They were deep, absorbing eyes, and a great melancholy abided in them. No hint of laughter dwelt there.

Now the lad stirred slightly. From out of the mists which had collected over the waters, confused images swirled out at him, images of burning villages, of bound prisoners in long columns, of cruel tortures, of long council tables and strange papers, of a great tree swept away in a flood of churning water, of blood in the river—and a broken sword. He had seen them all before.

The boy stood up. Erect, he would seem to any observer much more than a lad of ten. There was something—what was it?—there was *something* about him.

He gazed once more upon the river, before turning upstream and toward the village. He heard now the familiar voices of the dawning: the stirring gobble of the wild turkey, which came from far across the river; the *whip-poor-whi-i-ill* of the spectral nightjar, which even now was lifting up from the path not far ahead of him; and the harsh croak of the black raven passing overhead. Far below three vultures circled lazily, floating on the mists.

There was a chill in the air. As he stepped out along the river path, the boy felt the chill in the air.

I

GANAWAUGUS AND THE STINKING WATER

When the youthful Dutch trader John Abeel first appeared at the Seneca Indian village known as Ganawaugus, he was doubtless not astonished by what he saw. For Ganawaugus was a typical Iroquois community, one of the many Seneca villages (which at that time accommodated perhaps 4000 Indians) to be found in the region that now is composed of New York, Ontario, and Pennsylvania. He would have perceived a town of 20-25 cabins, rude houses of pole and bark construction. These would be single-family dwellings, as the longhouse had all but disappeared; and there would be no stockade. Likely he could make out a council house, a somewhat larger structure, near the center of the village. Surrounding the cabins cleared fields reached for some distance, and, if it were summer, the "three sisters," maize and beans and squash, together with pumpkins perhaps, and tobacco, would catch his eye. Against the darkness of the forest stood peach trees and apple trees. Wandering in the fields straggled pigs and cows of various shades and sizes. Mangy, mongrel dogs rudely announced his appearance.

He probably had heard much about the one distinctive feature of the village, its hot springs, boiling pools of water—called "stinking water" by the Indians. And he doubtless discovered at these mineral springs on that day numbers of Indians bathing in the sulphur waters, for news of the healing effects of the springs of Ganawaugus had traveled far and wide.

Ganawaugus was a popular place in those days, a kind of meeting place and rest-stop, not only because of the springs so venerated by the medicine men, but also because the village lay on the Great Trail that reached from the Hudson to Niagara. Wandering tribesmen and trappers and fur traders traveled this trail. It was the trail that reached from Albany into the fur country. And the wealth for which Albany was famous came from the commerce that was enjoyed with the Indians all along it. It was a toll road, and for transporting goods John Abeel would pay a fee to the Senecas, who presided over it.[1]

On one of his spring visits to the village, the young trader must have been arrested by the stunning beauty of a Seneca woman whom he discovered there. Doubtless it was not long before the white man and the full-blooded Seneca were "married." We may presume a tribal ceremony and a formal union, but there is in fact no record at all of the event. It is not known how long the bride lived with her Dutch trader "husband," or whether she did at all, but in any case they were apparently not together as man and wife for very long. It is not known whether the mother and father were even living together, or where, at the time of the birth of the child Gaiantwaka. It is probable that the Seneca woman was back in her native village of Ganawaugus in time to give birth to their child. It is not known just when John Abeel abandoned little Gaiantwaka, but it was doubtless early, perhaps *very* early.

And just when was the child born? In the accounts of the long life that the Seneca Indian chief known as Cornplanter lived there appear many confusions and contradictions. One of the most baffling of these has always concerned his date of birth. Over the years by historians and researchers it has been recorded for a date as early as 1719 (!) and as late as 1753. Although we shall never know for certain the exact date at which Gaiantwaka arrived in this world, we are able now to establish a very close approximation.

We have a little to work with. We can identify Cornplanter's mother easily enough. No problem here. She was a full-blooded Seneca, of the Wolf Clan (though at least one historian has her in the Turtle clan) and nobility (almost certainly the daughter of a sachem), living in Ganawaugus, on the Genesee River at what is the present-day site of Avon, New York. Her name may have been Dey-og-oh-kah-heh.[2] (In much of the Cornplanter literature she is named Aliquipiso.) We know that at the time she met the young Johannes Abeel she was already the mother, by a full-blooded Seneca, of at least one child. This child became the celebrated visionary Handsome Lake, and his birth date is customarily given as 1735, which makes for a real problem, as the Cornplanter story that will be credited here would have the mother at age eleven in 1735. Doubtless the date for the birth of Handsome Lake needs to be revised upwards.

Do we know the identity of the child's father? Yes, we do. We know, first, that the infant's father was white, that the child was born a half-breed. All impressions of Gaiantwaka registered throughout his lifetime are agreed on the marked lightness of his skin. We know that the father did not live with the child's mother, not for any appreciable time, and that before long he had taken a second wife. Arthur Parker in 1927, when he was director of the Municipal Museum in Rochester, reported a most interesting remembrance from an interviewer's experience. Chief Cornplanter is speaking of his father, whom he has just captured: "I knew him but he did not know me till I told him who I was, and wanted him to stay with me, and have all the land he wanted. He never lived with my mother, but for a while they lived not far apart. I saw him often until I was twelve or thirteen years old and knew him when he did not know me, but when I told him who I was he seemed surprised. I wanted him to stay but he did not like to stay, so I let him go back to the white man, and that was the last time I ever saw my father. My mother was dead [1780]; she died on the Muskingum River." [3]

There can be no doubt about the identity of the father. We have, first, the name that Gaiantwaka was known by all his life long. That is John O'Bail, or O'Beel, or Abeel. By the British military and by colonists alike the warrior was known as Captain O'Bail. While it is true that the whites regularly addressed Indian men as "John" or as "Captain," the O'Bail, in all of its many spellings, is clearly a corruption of Abeel. And we know from his own testimony that the young Gaiantwaka paid a visit to his father, a man by the name of Johannes (John) Abeel who was living on a farm south and west of Albany at the time. Gaiantwaka was at this time just married, or just about to be, and he himself tells us about the visit. In a passage of a letter he dictated to an interpreter and dispatched to Governor Joseph Hiester of Pennsylvania in 1822, when he was seventy or seventy-two years old, we have this report: "I grew up to be a young man, and married me a wife, and I had no kettle or gun. I then knew where my father lived, and went to see him, and found he was a white man, and spoke the English language. He gave me victuals while I was at his house, but when I started to return home, he gave me no provision to eat on the way. He gave me neither kettle or gun." [4]

Is it not remarkable that the young Indian Gaiantwaka (Gyantwahia) at this time seems to want confirmation of what he has surely understood for a long time, that his father is a white man? We do not know precisely in what year this meeting occurred, but Gaiantwaka is apparently a very young man, because as yet he has no rifle, and because these words are preceded by remarks on his childhood, which we shall look at in a moment. In any case, it would seem that this is the first the Indian lad has seen his father in a long time. Except for one dramatic moment, to be described later, it was the last time he would cast eyes on Johannes Abeel.

For these two occasions only do we have any record of the relationship between son and father. But they are enough to help us to limit the time in which his birth could have occurred.

Now, let us proceed to what we know of John Abeel. We do not know a lot, but we know enough to throw some light upon the birth of the child. John Abeel is properly regarded a most important figure in American history, if for no other reason than that he was responsible for the birth of an infant who was to become one of the most prominent and influential figures in Indian-white relations during the critical years of the late eighteenth century. From Mr. Robert Alexander, who at the time of this writing was the historian for the First Reformed Church of Albany, "the oldest pulpit in America," we have a helpful letter. It is dated June 24, 1998, and includes the following most interesting information. It turns out that the Johannes Abeel, with whom we are concerned, was something of a black sheep in a most prominent family of Albany and colonial New York. From Mr. Alexander's letter we learn that Cornplanter's father was the grandson of Johannes Abeel (1677-1711), who served as the second Mayor of Albany (1694-95 and again 1709-10), and was a prosperous merchant. His wife was Catalyna Schuler, a member of a most prestigious Albany family. Their eldest son was born Dec. 16, 1696, and named Christoffel. He married Margarita Bries (sometimes Breese) on September 23, 1720. Their eldest son, Johannes, was baptized on April 8, 1722. While the church records do not provide a record of the child's birth, it must have been, insists Alexander, at some time between the September 23, 1720, marriage of his parents and the 1722 baptismal date, "both of which are unequivocal." Historians of the Abeel family regularly assign a birth date for Johannes of 1722, and sometimes even suggest April 8. It is the opinion of Alexander, and we are not differing with it here, that John Abeel "could scarcely have fathered a son prior to 1740."

We know that as a young man John Abeel was an Indian trader, one of those ubiquitous figures, so distinctive and conspicuous along the frontiers from the time the first settlements began to appear. Those of his ilk were the chief go-betweens in the early days of the Indian-white contacts, and thus played a not inconsiderable role in the relationship. But of course John Abeel was no ordinary trader. He was a member of one of the most prominent and prestigious families of colonial New York. And as the black sheep of the family, he had his name in the family records given the adornment of "lunatic."

Unfortunately, we know nothing about the actual birth of Gaiantwaka. Doubtless, it occurred, like most Indian births, in the privacy of the forest, perhaps with a midwife in attendance. But the Heavens did not gape at that time, no rumblings of the earth were felt, lightning did not flash. No unusual night sounds echoed from the forest. Nature, who could foresee the future and "knew" that an exceptional being had come into her world, simply chose not to announce the event. In the village of Ganawaugus no one made any note of the time of arrival, and no baptism occurred, and, so far as we know, no notch was made upon any sapling.

Because of his warrior record chiefly, which we shall follow, the popular view today is that Gaiantwaka entered the world at some time between 1750 and 1752. It is worth noting that, according to the Abeel Family Birth Report, Gaiantwaka's mother, was born "about" 1724 at "Conewagus on the Genesee River, N. Y." This, if true, would put her age in 1751, when the child was most likely conceived, at twenty-seven.

Sadly, we know nothing, either, of Gaiantwaka's infancy. We do not know whether his father attended on him, or how often. We know, to put it plainly, nothing. Unhappily, too, we know nothing of the boy's childhood. Although he was light-skinned and had no father whom he could point to, we can presume his growing up to have been like that of any other male Seneca youngster; but there is no record of any event of his childhood, or of his adolescence to which we can attach a date. All we have is this frequently printed excerpt from the letter he dispatched in 1822 to the governor of Pennsylvania, Joseph Hiester: "When I was a child, I played with the butterfly, the grasshopper, and the frogs; and as I grew up, I began to pay some attention and play with the Indian boys in the neighborhood; and they took notice of my skin being a different color from theirs, and spoke about it. I inquired of my mother the cause, and she told me that my father was a resident in Albany. I still ate my victuals out of a bark dish. I grew up to be a young man, and married me a wife . . . ." [5]

Notice that he did not as a child think of himself as an Indian, for he says, "I . . . began to play with the Indian boys." And note that the boy, at whatever age this is, apparently has *no* impression of his father.

So we are without anything definite. Yet we *know* that Cornplanter did not live the 100 years that he has regularly been credited with. How does it happen that we continue to see in reference works the birthdate 1732 or 1736? There are two explanations. First, Cornplanter is himself responsible for the mistaken notion. The chief enjoyed a well-deserved reputation for boasting. Like many (most?) of the Iroquois warriors (Blacksnake and Hiokatoo come to mind) he gloried in the numbers of the enemy slain. "While I was in the use of arms," he would explain, "I killed seven persons and took three and saved their lives." [6] To his captured father at Canajoharie, when Cornplanter was thirty years old, he declared "Many prisoners have I tortured to death!" There is no evidence that he ever personally tortured any prisoner. He liked, as we are wont to say, to "pull the long bow." He not only boasted of his exploits, he embellished them. He would start with an actual occurrence and dress it up for effect. There is no question that he did this. In the case of his age, he liked to think, and certainly wanted others to think, that he was born close to the year in which George Washington was born. He was very fond of Washington and took great pride in the relationship he enjoyed with the "Father of the thirteen fires." He liked to say, when asked about his age, that "I was born about the same time as Washington." [7] In 1831, Thomas (John?) Struthers, Esq., of Warren County, visited Cornplanter at his house in Jennesadaga. On this occasion, to Struthers's blunt "How old are you?" the chief replied simply, "One hundred years." And during a later meeting, in the summer of 1834, as Struthers remembers, Cornplanter declared he was "more than one hundred years of age."

It is even possible, of course, that he really believed that. In his middle years, when his age might first have become a matter of interest, he perhaps just made a guess at it. In any case, he *definitely* gave out the impression that he was born not long after 1732.

On top of this, we have his appearance. He simply "looked" old. By the time Cornplanter had arrived at his late middle years, his body had taken such a beating from the elements and from combat that he generally appeared to be much older than he really was.

In the summer of 1816 the Reverend Timothy Alden,[8] who founded Alleghany College (as it was then spelled) in Meadville, Pennsylvania, in the course of a missionary tour of the upper Allegheny, had occasion to spend some time at the village presided over by Cornplanter. In a letter to the Reverend Joseph McKean of Harvard University, which he wrote upon his return to Meadville, he described the "venerable chieftain" at some length. In his account, there appears the observation that "He appears to be about sixty-eight years of age." If Alden has made an accurate judgment here, then we have Cornplanter being born in the year 1748. But W. J. McKnight, in reporting all of this, is quick to "correct" Alden: "Mr. Alden was mistaken as to Cornplanter's age. He was born about 1732, and in 1816 was eighty-four years old." McKnight has him dying at age 104.[9] But if the child was born in 1732, then he was conceived in 1731, when his father was nine years old! And when his mother was seven years old! As we shall see, Alden is definitely closer to the truth.

Included in McKnight's *Pioneer History of Jefferson County, Pennsylvania* is a description of Cornplanter as he appeared to a correspondent to the *Democratic Arch*, a newspaper of Venango County, Pa. It is most interesting for the way in which the famous warrior's age is calculated. Here, composed some time after the death of Cornplanter, is a portion of the writer's recollection:

> *I once saw the aged and venerable chief, and had an interesting interview with him about a year and a half before his death. I thought of many things when seated near him, beneath the wide-spreading shade of an old sycamore, on the banks of the Allegheny,—many things to ask him, the scenes of the Revolution, the generals that fought its battles and conquered the Indians, his tribe, the Six Nations, and himself. He was constitutionally sedate, was never observed to smile, much less to indulge in the luxury of a laugh. When I saw him he estimated his age to be over one hundred; I think one hundred and three was about his reckoning of it. This would make him near one hundred and five years old at the time of his decease. His person was stooped, and his stature was far short of what it once had been, not being over five feet six inches at the time I speak of. Mr. John Struthers, of Ohio, told me, some years since, that he had seen him near fifty years ago,*

and at that period he was at his height,—viz., six feet one inch. Time and hardship had made dreadful impressions upon that ancient form. The chest was sunken and his shoulders were drawn forward, making the upper part of his body resemble a trough. His limbs had lost size and become crooked. His feet (for he had taken off his moccasins) were deformed and haggard by injury. I would say that most of the fingers on one hand were useless; the sinews had been severed by the blow of a tomahawk or scalping-knife. How I longed to ask him what scene of blood and strife had thus stamped the enduring evidence of its existence upon his person! But to have done so would, in all probability, have put an end to all further conversation on any subject. The information desired would certainly not have been received, and I had to forego my curiosity. He had but one eye, and even the socket of the lost organ was hid by the overhanging brow resting upon the high cheek-bone. His remaining eye was of the brightest and blackest hue. Never have I seen one, in young or old, that equalled it in brilliancy. Perhaps it had borrowed lustre from the eternal darkness that rested on its neighboring orbit. His ears had been dressed in the Indian mode, all but the outside ring had been cut away. On the one ear this ring had been torn asunder near the top, and hung down his neck like a useless rag. He had a full head of hair, white as the driven snow, which covered a head of ample dimensions and admirable shape. His face was not swarthy, but this may be accounted for from the fact, also, that he was but half Indian. He told me he had been at Franklin more than eighty years before the period of our conversation . . . . As he stood before me—the ancient chief in ruins—how forcibly was I struck with the truth of that beautiful figure of the old aboriginal chieftain, who, in describing himself, said he was "like an aged hemlock, dead at the top, and whose branches alone were green." After more than one hundred years of most varied life,—of strife, of danger, of peace,—he

> *at last slumbers in deep repose on the banks of his own beloved Allegheny.*[10]

What a beautiful portrait! One could produce a most impressive painting from the details provided here of the aged warrior.

But perhaps the coup de grace was delivered to all of this confusion as long ago as 1956, when Merle Deardorff, the highly respected scholar of Pennsylvania Indians, published, together with observations about life in Cornplanter Town, some portions of the journal kept by the chief's friend John Philips. Philips had been a Quaker missionary among the Indians and was bitterly opposed to alcohol. For the time he was among the Senecas living along the Allegheny, he confided his observations to a diary. The passage which interests us is one in which he is taking careful note of a dinner in Cornplanter Town: ". . . had a Comfortable oppertunity of setting together with our friends [Half Town, thought to be Cornplanter's brother, and others]—just before dinner Cornplanter arrived—Looked like an old sage with some Long hairs of beard upon his chin—was honored to Eat Dinner with a King for once—Looking at my head he Enquired my age—I told Taylor [a fellow missionary and the interpreter] to inform him what it was, and that I had a wish to come and see the Indians in their houses before I got too old to travel—he informed Jacob [Taylor] it was a very good wish and all good, that he himself was now got old and could not expect to Travel much more &c—upon asking his age, he said he was born about the Time the Corn was a foot high 7 years before General Johnson took Fort Niagara."[11] Deardorff, noting that Fort Niagara capitulated to the British on July 25, 1759, concludes, that "of all the dates assigned for Cornplanter's birth (usually on what is claimed to be his own authority), this is the most likely."

Moreover, the date for the birth of Cornplanter's first child, son Henry, is known. That is 1774. A 1752 birth date for Cornplanter would have him twenty-two years old at the time of the birth of his first child. No problem there. As Cornplanter does not achieve any kind of prominence before the 1777 council at Oswego, a 1752 date for his birth seems not only reasonable but quite probable. Certainly there is no evidence anywhere to rule out that date. If 1752 seems right to Merle Deardorff, who was a keen student of the Pennsylvania Indians, it certainly should sit well with historians generally.

Of course we shall never know just *exactly* how old the venerable warrior was at the time of his death. If indeed he was not born until 1752, when his mother was twenty-eight years old, and his father, Johannes Abeel, thirty, then we have for the life of the Seneca Chief Cornplanter not one hundred years after all, or 104, but something like a mere eighty-four.[12]

At the time he came upon the Seneca village of Ganawaugus the trader Abeel was traveling a well-worn trail, the Indian highway that connected Albany with Niagara. With his goods he always traveled by canoe or by packhorse. On his way to Niagara he was doubtless this day walking behind a packhorse laden with the customary trading articles. Trading with the Indians was a rather simple operation. The Indians had only one thing, besides the land of course, that the white traders really wanted—furs. And while the white man had lots of items that greatly appealed to the Indians—jewelry, knives, and hatchets and metal tools, fabrics of extravagant colors, beads, blankets, and, when permitted by the colonial authorities, the firewater —what the Indian really desired, what he passionately craved, was the rifle. For guns, for flints and powder and lead, he would give up almost anything. Rifles for pelts—that was at the center of trading on the frontier.[13]

Few of the early fur traders on the frontiers of New York and Pennsylvania ever bent over backwards to be fair to the Indians. Moreover, they operated without much concern for the regulations governing firearms and rum. There is evidence enough that Johannes Abeel was, like his fellows, to put it politely, an unscrupulous trader.

But the rifle, by the time Gaiantwaka came into the world, was a big item in the trading. The rifle had revolutionized for the Indian his two chief activities, his hunting and his warfare. The rifle was far, far superior, every Indian understood, to the bow and arrow, both for accuracy and for range. He therefore never missed an opportunity to acquire one, no matter what its condition.

Those who would understand war on the frontier have got to appreciate the role of the rifle. How abruptly and dramatically it transformed the life of the Iroquois, as well as that of all the other Indian tribes along the frontiers in the Northeast, can hardly be exaggerated.

The explosive powder, that we now call gunpowder, had been around for a long, long time; it was as old as the hills almost, dating as it did from 11th-century China. But the rifle, a machine that could utilize the projecting power of gunpowder, was a rather recent development. And it was not until historical times that the rifle as we know it today actually appeared. And strangely, for the history of firearms takes us back to ancient Asia, to medieval Europe, and particularly to Spain, it was the American gunsmiths that produced the finely finished rifle. Because powder was being exported from France to the American colonies in great quantities through the 16th century, and because the wilderness made the rifle an essential for all, the gunsmiths, by the time John Abeel found himself in the trading business, had developed a marvelous weapon.

Gunsmiths had emigrated from Germany, Switzerland, and Austria to the New World, coming chiefly into the land by way of the Port of Philadelphia. A great number of them found their way to the Lancaster-York area of southeast Pennsylvania. These were the finest gunsmiths in the world. From their shops came the Deckhard rifle, the Henry rifle, and the Hawken rifle. These guns became famous as the "Kentucky long rifle." The Deckhard rifle, remarkable for its precision and for its range, was typical of the guns being produced. It was generally about three and one-half feet long, and weighed about seven pounds.[14]

As early as 1750, close to the time of Cornplanter's birth, the Iroquois were almost completely armed with rifles, and we know that the Chickasaws, who became expert marksmen, had been hunting with the rifle as early as 1736.[15] Most Indians preferred the flintlock to the percussion rifle, for it required less of them. And certainly the Kentucky rifle was more accurate than the musket. It required a little more time to load, but its advantages were many: It delivered a smaller ball, needed less powder, and could be held more steady. It was ever so much more accurate; in the hands of a skilled marksman it was deadly at 100 yards and still dangerous at four times that distance.

The Indian had three means by which to secure his rifle. He could kill a white settler, or a hostile Indian, for it; or he could steal it from a careless or sleeping owner; or he could trade for it. Remarkable stories of exchanges have come down. A gun may have been purchased by an Indian from a trader, like John Abeel, with a stack of furs as high as the gun was long. How much this rifle was costing the Indian has been calculated by one interested accountant. Noting that beaver was the chief fur of the trading, and that some 200 pelts would be required for a stack three and one-half feet high, and that a beaver skin went in those days for about six shillings, he figured the cost to the Indian at 1200 shillings. The gun, in many cases not a high-quality piece, likely was actually worth 20 shillings.[16] And in fact, more often than not, the Indian was receiving a fourth-rate firearm.

Abeel, a gunsmith of sorts himself, could regularly present to the Indian villages a number of these weapons. But he could not carry many, and doubtless, like all the traders who had long distances to negotiate, simply took orders. He would exhibit samples of his wares, and schedule a meeting for later, at a specifically designated spot and time, not necessarily close to the village. For the Indian this might mean a long journey with a heavy load of furs. To purchase one rifle with raw beaver pelts he would need to deliver about 300 pounds. For such trading trips he depended upon companions, often pressing the Indian women into service. Most of this trading took place on the waterways, on such rivers as the Susquehanna and the Mohawk.[17]

Of course the rifle did not replace the tomahawk or the war club or the scalping knife. And certainly the bow and arrow did not completely disappear. Where stealth and quiet were required the bow had its advantages. The bow could also deliver flaming arrows to buildings and grain fields, when the Indian desired a fire. Besides, a skilled Indian could launch as many as twelve arrows in the time it took an expert rifleman to fire once and reload. But the rifle was the thing. And the Indian eventually became so attached that he was virtually inseparable from it. He would place on its stock some distinctive signature, a mark of adornment or identification; and he rarely left it from his sight. For the fifty years following the birth of the Seneca Cornplanter, nothing was more precious to the Indian than his rifle.

John Abeel traded rifles for furs; he repaired rifles for furs. Like all of the traveling traders in New York at this time, he was constantly abroad in the Indian country. He had abandoned the high social life of Albany, where his family was distinguished, for a life on the frontier. He had come on many days, and on one momentous day, to Ganawaugus, because the village was on the Great Trail that led from Albany to Niagara. He was during the years of his twenties a lithe and very confident young man. He became popular very early among the Indians for his abilities in educating them in the rifles that Senecas were only now getting used to. He had little to fear from warriors who saw in him a steady source of guns and powder and bullets.

But Abeel, though he loved the forest life and hunting and the fur trade, and was considered a lunatic for it, in a short while gave all of that up for the farmer's life. We know that he settled in the little town of Minden, in what is now New York's Montgomery County, in 1748. On September 22, 1759, having acquired several hundred acres of farmland and having built a stone house, he married Mary Knouts, who was of a prominent German family.[18]

As we know, Abeel saw his son Gaiantwaka rarely, and perhaps only once, after he married Mary Knouts, when the boy would have been nine or ten years of age. Johannes Abeel lived seventy-eight years, fifty-five on the frontier as trader and farmer, very close most of the time to the war activity of the Senecas. How often in all of that time did he hear about the exploits of his famous son?

II

GAIANTWAKA

There is no confusion to be found in the reports of Gaiantwaka's boyhood years—for there are no accounts. It may be presumed, though he clearly early recognized that he was "different" from his fellows, that he thought himself an Indian; it may be presumed, then, that he led a life typical of that enjoyed by the Seneca males of his generation.

That would mean a very active life in the village and in the forest: taking part in war games, and learning especially about the art of the ambush; and participating in athletic games, like bandy wicket; practicing the bow and arrow, and the musket; searching for flint and quartz and jasper, from which to fashion spearpoints; hunting and tracking of game, not only in the winter, when the snows made trails easy to follow, but in the other seasons as well, when turkey scratchings under the beeches and the faint imprints of the hooves of elk and deer presented a challenge. And certainly he would indulge in the trapping and skinning of mink, marten, muskrat, otter, and beaver, and in the collecting of the maple sap. How he must have enjoyed the taking of fish from the river with weighted nets or spears. That he was exceptional in the skills revered by the Indians may be inferred by a declaration made to the Quaker missionary Henry Simmons on February 3, 1799, when Cornplanter was inspired to reflect on the Great Spirit. To his journal Simmons confided: "Cornplanter informed me that when he was a young man, he was a great hunter. He said his good luck was due to the fact that he often thought of the Great Spirit, who made the wild beasts and all things." Simmons assured Cornplanter, who at that time was roughly fifty years old and Head Man of Cornplanter Town, that "that was the only way to receive a blessing, by thinking of, and returning thanks to the Great Spirit." [1]

Senecas were given a "baby name" at the time of their birth. When the youngster reached adulthood or warrior age, perhaps as early as age twelve, this baby name was replaced by another. We do not know by what name the lad was known by his people during these early years. One of his descendants, Edward Cornplanter,[2] has suggested that it might have been simply *Dja-a-nih* (the Seneca equivalent for the white man's "Johnny"). In any case, the name that eventually was bestowed upon him was Kaiiontwakon (Gaiantwaka, or Gyantwahia), which means *The one who plants*, or *By what one plants*. The sense of *corn* is not found in the Indian name, so the name *Cornplanter* is a rather free translation of the Indian Gaiantwaka.[3] There are some fanciful notions about how "planter" became Cornplanter. The historian Arthur Parker repeats one of them:

> *Gaiantwaka, the great chief, once went to Philadelphia. "How do your people procure food?" asked a white man, a Quaker.*
>
> *"We are hunters," answered the chief.*
>
> *"Have you not observed our great fields of corn and grain?" asked the white man, "and did you know that we never have famines as you do? Why do your people not cultivate gardens of size and till large fields of grain?"*
>
> *"My people used to do so," said the chief, "and not many years ago when they dwelt in the valley of the Genesee. Now I think that I will encourage this practice again."*
>
> *This conversation so impressed the chief that when he returned he spoke of the matter before the councils and exhorted people in private to plant more and hunt less.*
>
> *Because of this he received the name of "The Planter," but the whites called him "Cornplanter."*[4]

So we shall have to assume that the boy's growing up, even though he was light-skinned, and had no father he could point to, was "normal," while at the same time noting that his warrior skills and his leadership qualities must have been extraordinary. By a time very early in his manhood he had reached a position of prominence, not only among the Senecas but among the Six Nations of the Iroquois. Although his mother, as she belonged to the noble families and therefore had the right to designate any one of her sons to sachem (a civil chief of the highest rank), could have given him status, she did not. She singled out a younger son (by an Indian father) for the title. So Cornplanter (though it did not hurt him that his uncle was the celebrated Kayahsotha) came into prominence as a war-chief largely on his own prowess and achievement.

Since there is no actual mention of Gaiantwaka or Cornplanter much before 1775, and we have little to go on for his first twenty years or so, it is natural to wonder and then to speculate. In what battles did he so much distinguish himself? Early historians, crediting Cornplanter with the truth and a faultless memory, have him engaged in the battle which saw the defeat and death of General Braddock (1755) on the Monongahela near Little Meadows. Cornplanter is reported to have insisted to two different investigators, late in his life, that he was one of the many Indians who ambushed Braddock, and that it was there he first got to know George Washington, and that he was at the time seventeen years old.[5] This would make his father, John Abeel, fifteen or sixteen years old at the time of his son's conception, and his mother two years younger. Given what we know, all of this is *extremely* unlikely. It is possible that Cornplanter (supposing his birth to be in 1745) could have been in on the defeat of Braddock in 1755 at the age of ten, but that seems highly unlikely too. In any case, no one among recent historians credits this claim at all.

It is just barely possible that Cornplanter as a very young man (He could not have been more than thirteen.) was in on the taking of Fort Venango (site of present-day Franklin, Pa.) and Fort Le Bouef (site of present-day Waterford, Pa.) and Fort Presque Isle (Erie, Pa.), all in June of 1763. We "know" from Cornplanter's old-age recollections, cited earlier, that he had been in Franklin "more than eighty years before." These forts were all assaulted in the matter of a few days, and all were destroyed, some historians are convinced, by the same band of Senecas, most likely led by Cornplanter's uncle, the celebrated Kayahsotha (Guyasuta).[6]

And then there is the massacre that occurred on the Niagara River. Was Cornplanter as a youth involved in the ambush at Devil's Hole, which occurred on September 14, 1763? Certainly that is very possible. Likely, he would have been thirteen years old, and at least eleven. We know that Handsome Lake, Cornplanter's half-brother, was a member of the Seneca war party. Of course Handsome Lake (although his generally accepted birth date is very questionable) was a good bit older than Cornplanter, probably as much as six years.

We need here to bring in the story of Mary Jemison. She is the central figure of one of the best-known tales of the bloody frontier, and one of the most important figures in the history of Cornplanter. She was almost an exact contemporary of the famous chief, having been born a few years earlier and dying just three years earlier. Besides, she was for more than twenty years a very close neighbor on the Genesee, and had ample opportunity to observe Cornplanter and to take reports on his activities. On top of all this, Mary Jemison's second husband, the war chief Hiokatoo, was a frequent companion of Cornplanter, both in organized battles and in raids.

Mary Jemison

She was born aboard ship, as her parents made their way to the New World, in 1743. She was fifteen years old when on April 5, 1758, at the family home in the Marsh Creek settlement near South Mountain in the Gettysburg, Pa., region she was captured by a raiding party of French soldiers and Shawnee warriors. On the forced march west the Indians murdered all they had taken prisoner, including Mary's mother, except for Mary herself and a neighbor boy. At Pittsburgh, Mary was turned over to two Seneca women, who conducted her to the Seneca villages. Mary, whose Indian name was Dehgewanus, adjusted to the Indian ways and went on then to live among the Senecas for the rest of her long life, marrying two Seneca husbands, and dying on a reservation September 19, 1833, at age 90. There has been erected a memorial statue on the Council Grounds in Letchworth State Park in Livingston County, New York, at the present site of her grave.

She had been married to her first husband, a very noble Seneca Indian named Sheninjee, for some four years, and had given birth to two children, when the family elected to move to Genishau, a village on the Genesee river, very near to Ganawaugus. She was not educated formally at all and is generally considered illiterate, though she could speak English. But she is a rich source of impressions, both of the Seneca way of life and the war activities of her husband and his fellow warriors, because late in her life, when she was eighty years old, she dictated her illuminating recollections to James Seaver. Seaver has made the narrative into a very readable and fascinating story, telling it in the first person.

We have Mary Jemison's account of the Devil's Hole horrors. At least one historian supposes that Mary is confused and that she is describing another battle that had taken place earlier, in November, 1759, on the Niagara.[7] But this is because he has Mary Jemison coming to her new home at Genishau in 1759, when in fact she came, at the age of twenty, in 1763, and just in time for Devil's Hole.

"When we arrived at Genishau," she recollects, "the Indians were making active preparations to join the French." And she reports that the next day "they marched off . . . painted and accoutred in all the habiliments of Indian warfare." By some accounts there were 500 Senecas, under the leadership of Chief Gahnasqua. They were bent on the destruction of a portion of the British forces which was known to be moving supplies to Fort Sclusser (or Schlosser). Mary describes, many years after the event, how the Indians ambushed the procession, surrounding the whole, and driving over the bank and into a place in the Niagara River called Devil's Hole all of the soldiers, "together with their horses, carriages, artillery, and every thing pertaining to the army." Only one soldier escaped, according to Mary; and the Indians returned to their villages, with two prisoners for celebration.

The day after the return of the warriors to Genishau "was set apart as a day of feasting and frolicing, at the expense of the lives of their two unfortunate prisoners, on whom they purposed to glut their revenge, and satisfy their love for retaliation upon their enemies."[8]

Another account, this by a Jesse Ware, and included in the 1949 edition of Seaver's *Life of Mary Jemison* as an appendix to Mary's narration, reports that the savages numbered "thousands" and that there were three survivors of the 300 troops and an advance guard of twelve men. But the truth seems to be that the Senecas numbered "only" about 500, and that the British suffered "only" five officers and sixty-seven men killed.[9]

It is time now to bring on stage another principal in the drama that was Cornplanter's life. This is Cornplanter's nephew, the Seneca warrior chief known throughout the Revolution, by colonials and British alike, as "The Nephew" and later as Governor Blacksnake. His baby name was *Dahgr,ya,Doh* ("Boys Betting"),[10] but he was known to the Indians later as "Chainbreaker" or "Awl Breaker." He was a nephew also of Cornplanter's half-brother the "prophet" Handsome Lake, and a grand nephew of the celebrated Kayahsotha (Guyasuta).

As with Cornplanter, we cannot be certain of Blacksnake's birthdate, but the year1753 is certainly very close. Blacksnake said that he was two years old in 1755, when William Johnson defeated the French on Lake George; and he noted that he was twenty-two at the time of the battle of Bunker Hill,[11] in which case he is his uncle's junior by just a little. He was born at Kendaia, a very small village of perhaps twenty log cabins on the east side of Seneca Lake, renowned for its very extensive orchards; but very early in his youth his family moved to the village of Ganawaugus, probably because, as is thought, his mother was a half-sister to Cornplanter, and a half-sister, too, to Cornplanter's half-brother Handsome Lake. It is known for certain that Blacksnake's mother and the mother of the influential Seneca warrior-orator Red Jacket were sisters.[12]

Lyman Draper, who purchased the Benjamin Williams text of Blacksnake's narrative, remembered Blacksnake at age sixty-five: "spare, slim, about 6 feet in height—with a mild eye and intelligent countenance."[13]

He was given the nickname "Governor Blacksnake" when he was well along in years, but we don't know by whom. At one place he declares that Major Henry O'Bail, Cornplanter's oldest son, gave it to him while he was serving as an ensign in the American Indian forces at Buffalo during the War of 1812. But in another place he claimed that

Washington himself baptized him in 1791, while the Seneca delegation was in Philadelphia.[14] And indeed he might have—to acknowledge the growing reputation of the chief. The name seems not to have been popular until about 1800, when he would have been forty-seven years old and a veteran of many campaigns. He lived long enough to participate in the War of 1812. In fact he did not pass from this life until 1859, dying near Quaker Bridge on the day after Christmas, probably at the age of 106!

Throughout the Revolution he was in the company of Chief Cornplanter, serving for the most part as a runner or as a messenger, but fighting zealously as a warrior too. He was very fond of Chief Cornplanter and affectionately addressed him as "Uncle." He was very happy to be known by the British as "The Nephew."

About 1840, when Blacksnake was probably eighty-seven years old, Dr. Lyman C. Draper commissioned a poorly educated Indian named Benjamin Williams, who was Blacksnake's neighbor, to record and translate the chief's memoirs. The versions produced by Williams, and there are two, are next to impossible to read, and Draper himself, ten years later, when Blacksnake was now ninety-seven years old (!), tried to bring order to the document. It has recently appeared in an edited form, together with very helpful introductions and explanations, by Thomas S. Abler.[15] Happily Abler's very illuminating commentary closely accompanies the text, for the narrative much of the time is very difficult, next to impossible, to decipher. Many repetitions occur, for example the bloody battles of Oriskany and the description of the guards at Washington's quarters; dates are terribly confused; people are out of place; and details ascribed to one event actually belong to another. But it is invaluable as a record of the Revolution by a Seneca who was there.

Of the Devil's Hole massacre Blacksnake too has an account; but at this time (1763) he was scarcely old enough for such bloody work and seems not to have been actually present. He reports that Old Smoke was one of the principals, and recollected that he "never heard of any Indians being killed in that affair." [16] Blacksnake has his details most certainly from returning warriors, perhaps from his young uncle Cornplanter himself. Graphically he describes to Lyman Draper the Seneca ambush of the convoy of pack horses and wagons. Here is Draper's impression of Blacksnake's report: "One English officer on horseback got off—his horse jumping over one corner of the Devil's Hole. Understood that 3 were saved by falling into the tops of standing trees beneath: Took a few prisoners—thinks about 30, but does not know whether any of these were wounded or not: thinks those who were wounded & fell helpless on the battle-ground, were killed after the affair was over: The (30) prisoners were taken to Genesee, & kept until Sir Wm. Johnson sent word to have them given up, when they were sent to their friends. The prisoners were kept sometime [some time], when the breach was made up with Sir Wm. Johnson, & they surrendered."[17] Note that Mary Jemison's "two" prisoners have here become thirty. Apparently two were isolated for execution in her village, and the remainder returned. Anthropologist Anthony Wallace, who called it "a bloody piece of work," reports that five British officers and sixty-seven men were killed.[18]

In an interview recorded in the Lyman Draper manuscripts Cornplanter's son Charles said it was his impression always that there were three Indian leaders directing the massacre, and that only one Seneca was killed.

Of great interest is the story told by the historian Francis Parkman: "One of the actors in the tragedy, a Seneca warrior, named Blacksnake [not likely], was living a few years since at a very advanced age. He described the scene with great animation to a friend of the writer, and, as he related how the English were forced over the precipice, his small eyes glittered like those of the serpent whose name he bore."[19]

Did the neophyte warrior soon to be known as Captain O'Bail and later as Cornplanter participate in this massacre? We can hardly imagine that he would miss out on this war party, as it was assembled on his own ground. Perhaps here he began to build the warrior's reputation that eventually won him leadership among the Senecas. We can imagine the boy, probably eleven years old at this time, secreted in the bushes and bursting forth to terrify the horses.

Almost definitely the Seneca who was shortly to become Mary Jemison's second husband was a member of that war party. This is the ferocious and incredibly cruel warrior named Hiokatoo. He was an impressively large figure and had been in many battles by this time; at Braddock's defeat, as reported by Mary Jemison, he is supposed to have tortured two white prisoners, "burning them slowly to death in a fire of his own kindling."

III

"NONE OF OUR BUSINESS"

About the life the Seneca war-chief Cornplanter led during the decade 1764-1774 there is not much to report, as noted above, because not much is known. Certainly during these years, when he would be fourteen to twenty-four years old, he was not a prominent figure. He was active, and constantly in the company of the influential Senecas, like his uncle Kayahsotha and the venerable Old Smoke, but he had not yet risen to that eminence which would distinguish him during the next two decades.

This was a period characterized, as far as the Iroquois were concerned, by unsettled conditions and a great many councils. It was closed out with the devastating defeat of the Shawnees by an army of Virginians at Point Pleasant in October of 1774, a battle which put an end to Lord Dunmore's War and is regarded by many historians as the first battle of the American Revolution.

One of the most important events of the period was the agreement reached in 1768 between the Six Nations of the Iroquois and Sir William Johnson, who represented the British. Johnson, who had captured Niagara in a successful siege of the French fort, and who, with General Jeffrey Amherst, had taken Montreal, had just been appointed by the Crown to the post of General Superintendent of Indian Affairs North of the Ohio. The treaty sessions were held at Fort Stanwix (now Rome, New York), on the Mohawk River in central New York.[1] The site was a most strategic location, as from here the principal route from the Hudson River to Lake Ontario could be controlled. At this time it was a colonial outpost, hardly more than a way station, but it had been a lively French trading center before it was rebuilt by the English General John Stanwix in this year of 1768.[2] Johnson in September had sent out invitations to the chiefs and sachems of each of the members of the Iroquois Federation. He invited also the Delawares and the Shawnee, but he made it clear to these Indians that they were not to participate; they were welcome to observe the proceedings. It was the hope of Johnson and the Crown (1) to establish a new boundary line between Indian lands and those open to white settlement, and (2) in this way to avoid organized hostility, especially from the Six Nations.

Johnson arrived at the fort, which was in such disrepair that it could hardly be considered a fort, on September 20. He discovered some Indians already in camp, and the Delawares arrived on the 29th. By early October more that 800 Indians had assembled. They continued to appear steadily, and by October 22 they numbered probably 2200. By the time the council was convened, October 24, there were more than 3000, according to some estimates, camped out along the banks of the Mohawk River.

It is not known whether the young Seneca warrior Gaiantwaka was present at this council. He could have been, as he was probably eighteen years of age at this time, but at the head of the Seneca delegation were Guastrax and Odongot.

The weather went steadily downhill, turning very cold and rainy; but the sessions were amiable, without much heat. Everybody seemed to want the same thing, except of course the Delawares, who were not permitted to protest. Johnson was a skilled negotiator, with lots of experience in the art of diplomacy, and he knew the value of courtesy and the importance of providing comfort and attending to the delegates' welfare. He supplied ample clothing to stave off the cold and the rain. He was of course genuinely sympathetic to the interests of the Indians, and was especially sensitive to the concerns of the Mohawks.

But most important was his understanding of the Indian. Johnson was almost an Indian himself. Irish-born, he had been in the colonies since 1738, living among the Mohawks in the Mohawk Valley. By 1770, when he was fifty-five years of age, there would be very few white men, if any, who knew and understood the Iroquois Indians better than did Sir William Johnson. He had learned the language of the Mohawks and could speak to them in their own tongue; he made it a habit to dress as they did, even to the wearing of moccasins. And the Indians thought of him as an advocate; they could see that he was working earnestly to see that their lands were preserved. He had kept most of the Iroquois out of Pontiac's uprising. Among his many wives was the extraordinary Mohawk Molly Brant, by whom he had eight children.[3] And Molly's

Sir William Johnson

soon-to-be-famous younger brother, Joseph (Thayendanegea), very early became Johnson's protégé.

Here in the fall of 1768 he encouraged the principals to speak from the heart. He steered the negotiations straight down the course he had defined from the beginning. When it seemed plain that the discussions were nearing an end, after one long week, he addressed the Delawares and Shawnee who were present (probably very few of the latter), and spoke kindly to them directly, reassuring them that they must not mistake the bargaining for anything less than what was good for them, and urging them to remain peaceful with their neighbors in the South, the Cherokee.

The agreement that was reached at the end of that week was very little short of incredible. A new boundary line was fixed, and defined very precisely.[4] The Crown gave up a little land in western New York State, to accommodate the easternmost members of the League, but moved the boundary line way to the west as it moved south through Pennsylvania and Virginia and what is now Kentucky. The amazing thing is that the Six Nations had only a very doubtful, if any, claim to these lands they were so cavalierly ceding to the Crown. Even Johnson was extremely skeptical. These lands were the domain of the Shawnee, and the Delaware, and the Cherokee. The Iroquois had had once some claim to the lands in northeastern Pennsylvania that were a part of the bargain, but, in fact even these lands had been sold by the Six Nations fourteen years earlier—to the Susquehanna Company—lands that had been occupied now for many years by settlers from both Pennsylvania and Connecticut.[5]

The new boundary line ran from where "Canada Creek . . . empties into the Wood Creek at the west of the Carrying Place beyond Fort Stanwix" through the Delaware town of Kittanning, and along the Ohio River south and west through Pennsylvania and Virginia into the Kentucky territory, and to the place where the Cherokee River (also Hogahee, and now the Tennessee) flows into the Ohio, at present-day Paducah.[6]

And just what did the Iroquois Indians receive for this land that they did not own but were trading away? Well, Johnson, in return for this new boundary line, provided the Six Nations a little more than 10,460 pounds sterling, and the Pennsylvania Commissioners paid out 10,000 dollars for those lands that the colony gained.[7]

Naturally, the Ohio Valley Indians, notably the Shawnee, the Delaware, and the Cherokee, were embittered by the treaty. These Indians, who could no way see the Iroquois claims as legitimate, got none of the money. They felt cheated and betrayed by the Six Nations. The rift created here would only deepen as the years passed. And it would never heal.

The treaty was signed by one representative from each of the five original members of the Six Nations. Guastrax (Caustrax),[8] who was known as High Hill, signed for the Senecas, fixing his mark ∩.[9] The date was November 5, 1768. As before noted, it is not known whether the young Gaiantwaka made the trip from Ganawaugus to Fort Stanwix. If indeed he was present for the negotiations, he got a lesson in treaty talk that would stand him in good stead for the years to come.

But now the Iroquois Indians, with their hunting and village territory established, could look to a new problem, anything to occasion the council fire. More than the warpath, more than hunting, they loved the council fire. They loved to talk, and they loved to listen to talk. They longed to hear the announcement of a council date, for this meant a chance to dress up, to don their most elegant costumes. And women, as well as men, would make the trip. At times almost the whole of the village would be off to the council, often many, many miles away. Rarely did they require much persuasion to attend a council.

As a rebellion on the part of the colonists seemed ever more certain to occur, both the colonists and the King's men began to joust for the favor of the Indians. In the early going it seemed as though both the British authorities and the unhappy colonists would be satisfied to see the Iroquois on the sidelines. But by the time of the war's beginning, after Lexington and Concord, the Crown became increasingly aggressive, and began to woo the Six Nations with an ardor that would be difficult to match.

In the months leading up to the American Revolution, and during the first two years of the war (1775-1777), a number of conferences, some called by the British, some by the rebels, were convened. Sessions were joined all over New York and Pennsylvania, at Oswego, at Albany, at Fort Pitt, at Niagara, at Ganawaugus, and at German Flats, with the climactic council occurring at Oswego in 1777.

It has been noted many times, and most properly, that three passions governed the life of the male Indian: the warpath, the hunt, and the council fire. The council they made into a spectator sport. Thousands, women and children as well as warriors, might assemble to hear orations (often in a tongue that was very strange to them). These hordes of Indians had been summoned by runners trotting among the villages, and all would travel incredibly long distances to camp at the council grounds, and perhaps to stay for weeks.

Blacksnake, whose family had moved from Kendaia west to Cornplanter's village of Ganawaugus on the Genesee, when he was but a boy, has left an account of a council that was held in Pittsburgh, probably in the fall and early winter of 1774-75. It is most interesting for what it reveals of the trips that were made by the Indians in attending these various councils, for they would travel long distances, sometimes in impossible weather and through formidable territory, over many, many days, even weeks, even months, camping out, hunting game as they needed to, and even constructing bark canoes to facilitate their travel. The account is also quite interesting for what it suggests about the emergence of "uncle cornplanter" as a leader among the powerful Senecas. Governor Blacksnake, at the time of his recollection almost ninety years old, remembered how in April Cornplanter and Sagoyewatha (later Red Jacket) were invited to the council on difficulties between Great Britain and America, and how after assembling at Avone (Ganawaugus) they took a "westerly course" along Lake Erie and then down French Creek ("several days travel"). He remembered how they stopped for perhaps a week among the white settlers to hunt deer and build canoes, and how they then floated to Pittsburgh, where they met the Commissioner, who urged a neutral course for the Indians.[10]

The commissioner's speech was made in the morning. Sagoyewatha, who was only twenty-five years old at the time, had been appointed by Cornplanter, who was himself probably only twenty-five, to answer for the Indians. It was in fact at this conference, and because of Cornplanter, who had chosen Sagoyewatha to make the reply, that the Seneca who was soon to be known as Red Jacket, and as a great orator, got his start. In the afternoon Sagoyewatha did make the Indians' response, and by all accounts acquitted himself well. After his speech was followed by some polite exchange, the young Seneca concluded his remarks, noting that while all the delegates are of the mind "that you favor," we shall have to go home to persuade our people, and then we shall send you an answer.

The commissioner concluded the council by reminding the Indians, for the umpty-umpth time, that "this is a family quarrel between us and old England, you Indians are not concerned in it. We don't wish you to take up the hatchet with the King's troops; we desire you to remain at home, and not join either side, but keep the hatchet buried deep, in the name and behalf of all our people."

Then the commissioner invited the Indians on a tour of the garrison at Fort Pitt. As Blacksnake recalls, "So we all went with him, there was only a few Regular warriors [soldiers] in garrison and a few pieces of cannons and Balls for them." The Indians were grateful for the offer of provisions, and got what they wanted from the commissary, all they could carry. "Returned to our camp at the mouth of monangahella, and the Next morning we made preparation to Start home about at noon we got Ready to Start, some of our Bark canoes we away [discarded]—3 canoes we Kept for to Keep with our provisions in as we came up the River [the Allegheny] and Some of us came on foot and Some pushing up our canoes up stream, we came on about 10 miles that Day, and we kept agoing Every Day and came Back the same away [way] we went and we got home in the month of June [1775?] at avone on Genesee River." [11]

Sir William Johnson had died in July of 1774. His son-in-law, Guy Johnson, who was thirty-four years old, and had been a deputy superintendent for twelve years, was promptly named his successor as Superintendent of Indian Affairs.[12] Guy Johnson had presided over the Grand Council held at Onondaga through the month of October, 1774, at which the Iroquois League confirmed its continuing loyalty to the British. In July of 1775, after Lexington and Concord, Johnson, whose headquarters were at Niagara, had arranged for a meeting between the British and some of the Iroquois at Oswego, on the south shore of Lake Ontario. The young warrior Cornplanter *may* have been among the assembly of Senecas Johnson passed through on his way to the meetings, and he *may* have participated in the council, but Blacksnake who was himself not present, had the impression that "few or no Senecas attended."[13] The Mohawks were the principal figures among the Indians. According to their chief, Abraham, Johnson was even then still urging neutrality for the Six Nations. He desired that they "sit still and maintain peace."[14]

About one month later, in a council at Albany, representatives of all of the Six Nations were present. These sachems declared to the American Commissioners that they were definitely committed to neutrality,[15] even while the Mohawks were preparing to assist the British in resisting the rebel invasion of Canada. Cornplanter was not present at this conference. In fact, very few Senecas appeared, none from the westernmost villages.

Although Blacksnake's account of these various councils is at times definitely confused, there was convened at some time in the fall of 1775 at Pittsburgh a conference that was very different, in that the Six Nations, while represented, did not participate. The American Commissioners desired to placate the Ohio Valley Indians, that is, the Delawares and the Shawnee especially, and the farther west Indians, notably the Wyandot and the Ottawa. What they wanted was a pledge of neutrality. Among the Senecas present was Kayahsotha, generally thought to be brother to Cornplanter's mother, who with his family had left Ganawaugus for the Ohio River region years ago, and had by this time achieved great prominence, winning much renown for his role in Pontiac's uprising. Kayahsotha was considered an Allegheny Seneca, or a Mingo.[16] He was *extremely* active in council sessions during these years. At this particular session he played a leading role. He advocated neutrality, and in fact, though he did not have authority to speak for the western nations, he pretty much *promised* neutrality.

His remarks infuriated a Delaware chief known as White Eyes, who stood up to declare, somewhat defiantly, that the Delawares were in no way bound by this promise. The council, however, went the way of Kayahsotha, who was assuring the Commissioners that they would remain neutral. And Kayahsotha insisted that he would use his influence with the Six Nations. The young Cornplanter and his nephew Blacksnake were present, though not active. It is very likely that Cornplanter's half-brother, the older Handsome Lake was present also.[17]

That same fall, October 19-21, another council was held in Pittsburgh. This was a relatively short meeting. It was attended by Kightoi and Kenightie, who represented the Six Nations; and by Tetepuska, Winganum, and Joseph Pepy for the Delawares; and by Allanawissica and Wewelatimiha for the Shawnee. Kayahsotha was here also. The object of the council was to arrange for the return of the Negro prisoners and horses, which had been taken by the Shawnee, and "which remain among the Indians." Kayahsotha, who was recognized as "a Six Nations Chief," together with Captain Pipe of the Delawares, was appointed to travel to the Shawnee towns, to see to their return.[18]

In July of the succeeding summer still another council was held on the very serious subject of neutrality. Kayahsotha had persuaded the Shawnee Chief The Shade and the Muncy Chief Pemetamah to council with him and the Delaware Chief Captain Pipe. The Seneca was once again at the center of the action. And once more, he spoke as a champion of peace. Speaking now for the Six Nations, and as a Keeper of the Door to the West, he once more assured the Commissioners of the Iroquois neutrality. He declared, with his characteristic vehemence, that no army "would be permitted to pass through the territory of the Six Nations." Neutrality would not mean permission. Addressing the Indians as much as the Commissioners, he noted his authority: "I am appointed," he said, "to take care of this country, that is of the nations on the other side of the Ohio, and I desire you will not think of an expedition against Detroit, for I will repeat, we will not suffer either the English or the Americans to march an army through our country." [19]

This council was held in Pittsburgh on July 6, 1776. Just a few days later Simon Girty showed up in Pittsburgh with a company of Iroquois. They were bringing a report of the council held at Niagara, which had reaffirmed the policy of the Six Nations, which declared neutrality in the dispute between the colonials and the Crown.

At a Pittsburgh council, Sept. 30, with Big Knife (Big Knife was originally the Indian appellation for the people of Virginia, and Onas was the Indian term for the Governor of Pennsylvania.) the Mingoes marched to the Council House with their flag. They saluted a little before they entered by firing their guns, and were answered the same by the garrison

Pittsburgh hosted a number of councils during this period, but sessions on the matter of neutrality for the Indians were being convened everywhere.[20] Blacksnake, who, in recollecting the years 1774-1777, described how councils were arranged, with runners dispatched to the Indian villages to announce the date and subject and place, often, as noted, confuses dates, and even sites. But it is known, thanks to Blacksnake, that his uncle Cornplanter now in his mid-twenties and known to the British as Captain O'Bail was present for a number of them; in some he was a participant. When he did participate he regularly advocated neutrality. His reputation steadily soared.

One of the most important of all these conferences to which the Indians were constantly scurrying was the one scheduled for German

Flats in the Mohawk Valley in the summer of 1776, as George Washington was preparing the defense of New York City. The Indians had been summoned by Major General Philip Schuyler,[21] appointed by the Congress as Superintendent of Indian Affairs for the Northern Department. Schuyler, an energetic figure in the patriot cause, had, because of illness, to give up his command of the Canada invasion forces, which he had organized, but he was in good health again by this time.

He suffered two disappointments right off. First, the Indians were late to appear. Schuyler had hoped to get the congress underway on July 16, but it was more than two weeks beyond that date that the Senecas showed up. Finally, on August 6, he was able to convene the council. But his second disappointment appeared in the demon rum. His report of the proceedings included the observation that "The consumption of provision and Rum is incredible. It equals that of an army of three thousand Men; altho' the Indians here are not above twelve hundred, including Men, Women, and Children."[22]

Schuyler of course was determined to keep the Six Nations neutral, and he made that plain at the outset. With all the force of his strong personality he delivered a powerfully persuasive speech. He opened the council with a welcome, couched in the most friendly of terms. He explained the rebels' grievances, and noted that this was a family quarrel and not any of their concern. He reminded the Indians of the words spoken by the Mohawk sachem Abraham (Tyahanesera), who had declared that it was the determination of the Six Nations "Not to take any part, but as it is a Family Quarrel to sit still and see you fight it out."

He reviewed the history of the earlier councils, all of which had concluded in avowed neutrality. He praised the Indians for their good qualities, and expressed admiration for their honesty. He closed out his speech in a fervent appeal: To "our brothers" he declared, "We have done our Duty we have spoke plainly—we request you will do the same.—We shall become open Enemies or warm and inviolable Friends.—We wish for your Friendship not out of Fear but out of Love, And that a good Understanding may prevail Between the white Inhabitants of this great Island and the Six Nations until the Sun shall Grow dim with age.—And it will be your Fault if we do not part as good Friends with the Six Nations, and remain so hereafter, as Your Ancestors and ours were in the Time of Quedor, when they fought side by side against the common Enemy."

Then he reminded them that in the time since the Albany conference the colonies had "not said one thing and done another, as our Enemies have." And then he held aloft and presented *The Large Belt*, which "confirms our words."[23]

Blacksnake, some seventy years later, dictated his recollections of this event to his transcriber, his neighbor Benjamin Williams. But the aged chief has the council located at Albany. There are three possible explanations for his confusion. First, there was occurring such a steady succession of councils during these years, it would be difficult for any mind to keep them straight; second, Blacksnake at the time of his narration was nearly ninety years old, and the event he is recollecting had occurred almost seventy years ago. It would be a most remarkable feat of memory to get sites and dates and the names of the principal figures even roughly right, let alone exactly right. Third, Benjamin Williams may have confused matters some in his transcription. In any case, if indeed Blacksnake is here remembering what actually happened on August 6, 1776, at German Flats, the council is most important for what it discloses of the Seneca chief Cornplanter. By this time, Cornplanter, now probably twenty-six years old, has risen to great prominence among the Senecas, indeed among the Indians of the Six Nations. He is now not only a war-chief, but apparently *the* war-chief. He heads up the Seneca delegation to German Flats, on the south side of the Mohawk River. He speaks for all of the chiefs present, all of the Six Nations. Of course, Blacksnake's obvious adulation of his uncle may here as elsewhere exaggerate by a little the role of Cornplanter.

Blacksnake's account, though garbled, and confused with the Albany conference, is vivid. He remembered how at the convening one of the officials asked for the head man of the Seneca Nation: "Cornplanter Said I am he . . . very well said the officer how many Different Indians Nations are you here, Six Said the Cornplanter . . . officer . . . told the chiefs to . . . get orders on Some provision . . . for each Nation . . . uncle cornplanter gave me the order on the part of the Senecas . . . . [All] got our provisions Enouth that Night and we all went to the adge [edge] of the woods for to Built our tents So we could be by ourselves all the other tribes Done the same, there all we laid Down by fireside comfortable that Night . . . the Next morning after Blackvest [breakfast] . . . one of the officer . . . called upon us to come on the ground."

After the speech by General Schuyler, the members of the Six Nations retired to discuss and consider what it was they had heard, and, according to Blacksnake, were quick to agree unanimously to heed the advice that was given, which of course was to "stay out of it." And Blacksnake reports that "we Retire with good feeling for our pillow through Night." Next morning, after breakfast, when all were assembled, the commissioner asked whether the chiefs were ready to make answer. It was Cornplanter who replied. He declared that the chiefs were ready.

The speech of reply for all the Six Nations was delivered by the Seneca chief Sagoyewatha (Otetiania), who would later, because of the brilliant red jacket gifted him by the British, be known as Red Jacket. His speech was not in the oratorical vein that would characterize his later elocution, but even here there were signs that he had the gifts. He could wax poetic, and his capacious memory made possible all sorts of meaningful allusions.

For the Indians assembled at German Flats in August of 1776, he answered General Schuyler and the American Commissioners. After lamenting that the covenant chain had got perhaps a little rusted and needed to be mended, he declared that the chiefs were agreed that the Six Nations "has nothing to Do with your father children quarrels." We are therefore, he said, taking your advice. We shall stand neutral and will "keep hands Down for Peace with all Sides."

Blacksnake's account of the Senecas' trip home is most interesting, for it was leisurely and included a quite happy visit (hunting and dancing) with the Onondagas, whose villages they were passing through. [24]

Through these many council sessions, a close observer might have perceived a steady weakening of the Indians' neutrality position. Certainly by the end of the fateful year of 1776 neutrality would seem to be impossible for the Iroquois. In September of that year, not long after the close of the German Flats council, "a grand but secret council" was convened at Fort Niagara. This council was attended by Cornplanter. Present also were Old Smoke, who, like Cornplanter, was still strong for staying "out of it," and Farmer's Brother. Representatives of the Cayuga, the Onondaga, and the Mohawk were also in attendance. In spite of the Seneca position, the Iroquois chiefs at this session expressed a determination to serve the Crown in the dispute. But they did not at this time take up the hatchet.[25]

More councils would be needed.

IV

THE BORDER WARS

During the forty-year period following the beginning of the French and Indian War in 1754, fear and panic gripped the frontier settlements. In the years immediately preceding the Revolution, all through the Revolution, and even for years after the close of the War, bands of Indians continued to swoop down on unprotected cabins to ravage and kill, to burn crops and buildings, to scalp and to tomahawk, and to take captives. These raids, taken together, are generally called the Border Wars. For historians the Border Wars begin after Braddock's defeat with the massacre at Penn's Creek in 1755. By June of 1778 they had so much increased in frequency and violence that pioneer families in central Pennsylvania were fleeing in droves to the forts, and even back east, in what has been called "The Great Runaway."[1] The raids, with their frightful atrocities, do not end with the success of the Sullivan Expedition in 1779; they do not end with the surrender of Cornwallis at Yorktown on October 19, 1781; they do not end with the Treaty of Paris of September 3, 1783. The War of the Revolution may have been closed out, the border wars continue. The violence along the frontier does not end until 1795, with the Treaty of Greenville. For forty years it was an anxious life that the pioneer families led.

Of course what was happening in New York and Pennsylvania was occurring with pretty much the same kind of frequency in those regions that were to become Ohio and Kentucky and Tennessee. But we shall confine our account of the border wars to Pennsylvania and New York, to that region frequented by the Senecas and by their most active war-chief, Cornplanter.

The costly and tragic defeat of General Edward Braddock near Fort Duquesne in 1755 made very plain to the colonists that the native Indians were a force to be acknowledged. Finally the provincial government of Pennsylvania took action. The first thing that it did was to encourage and to supervise and to sponsor a chain of forts. Very few forts at this time were available to the pioneers and none at all west of the Alleghenies. These forts were not constructed willy-nilly but were built at strategic locations, accessible to the settlements, chiefly as refuges for imperiled frontier families. One chain of forts was erected along a 200-mile corridor between Easton, in Northampton County, Pa., and the present Fulton County near the Maryland state line.[2]

The forts were of two kinds. There were, first, those forts that were considered "official" and were constantly garrisoned. Then there were those "private" forts which were thrown up, sometimes hastily, for the protection of settlers who had come under attack, and for the housing of supplies.

Between 1756 and 1763 more than 200 forts and blockhouses were built in what was then considered the "western" country. Among these were Fort Bedford (1756), Fort Pitt (1759), and Fort Burd, at present-day Brownsville, Pa. (1759). After the War of the Revolution heated up, about 1777, of course a great many military bastions were constructed—Fort McIntosh at the mouth of the Beaver River in western Pennsylvania, and Fort Armstrong at Kittanning on the Allegheny River north of Pittsburgh, for example.[3]

These forts were not so awesome as to much discourage the Indian raids, but they did inspire in the pioneer families *some* sense of security, and of course did provide real refuge.

Cornplanter's Seneca Indians regularly traveled the rivers, the Susquehanna, the Mohawk, Pine Creek, the Allegheny, the Juniata, the Monongahela, and the Ohio. Besides, there were the war paths, well worn Indian trails, roads almost, which ran through the river valleys. The Shamokin Path, starting at present-day Sunbury, where the two branches of the Susquehanna come together, continued up the west branch of the river, passing the mouth of Warrior Run, and proceeding through a gap in the Muncy hills to the present site of Muncy. Wyoming Path left Muncy to run up Glade Run, then over to Fishing Creek, near present Millville, crossed the creek and passed through Huntingdon Valley and Nescopeck Gap, up the river to Wyoming. And there were the Wyalusing Path and the Great Sheshequin Path, and many others.[4] The regions tied together by the rivers and by these trails in central and western Pennsylvania and southern New York State had for hundreds of years been the favorite hunting grounds of the Senecas.

The defeat of Braddock seemed in 1755 to turn the Indians loose in an almost unrelenting war upon the frontier settlements. As one embittered historian put it, "The Indians, true to their character, struck wherever an opportunity presented—neither sex nor age was spared—the vindictive savage knew *no* pity."[5]

The massacre at Penn's Creek, which occurred on October 15, 1755, was chilling in its effect upon the pioneer families. A body of Delawares, arriving from the West Branch of the Susquehanna, barbarously killed and scalped, or carried into captivity, all but one (who miraculously escaped) of the people of the settlement.[6]

The settlers who came upon the scene described it thus: "We found but thirteen [dead], who were men and elderly women. The children we suppose to be carried away, prisoners. The house where we suppose they finished their murders, we found burnt up; the man of it, named Jacob King, a Swisser, lying just by it. He lay on his back, barbarously burnt, and two tomahawks sticking in his forehead; one of these marked newly W. D. . . . . The terror of which, has driven away almost all the back inhabitants, except the subscribers, with a few more, who are willing to stay and defend the land; but as we are not at all able to defend it for the want of guns and ammunition, and few in numbers, so that without assistance, we must flee and leave the country to the mercy of the enemy."[7]

After several other "barbarous murders" in the region of Shamokin, the Governor of the Province of Pennsylvania, Robert H. Morris, issued a Proclamation. The date was April 29, 1756: "For every male Indian enemy above twelve years old who shall be taken prisoner and delivered at any fort garrisoned by the troops . . . the sum of one hundred and fifty Spanish dollars or pieces of eight; for the scalp of every male Indian enemy above the age of twelve years, produced as evidence of their being killed, the sum of one hundred and thirty pieces of eight; for every female Indian taken prisoner and brought in as aforesaid, and for every male Indian prisoner under the age of twelve years taken and brought in as aforesaid, one hundred and thirty pieces of eight; for the scalp of every Indian woman, produced as evidence of their being killed, the sum of fifty pieces of eight. . . ."[8]

The bounty hunting had begun. And Pennsylvania officials were recognizing the age of twelve as the age at which one becomes a warrior.

It cannot be supposed that this proclamation had much effect upon the raiding Indians. No letup in their activity could be perceived. The abduction of Mary Jemison, and the murder of her family, which occurred on April 5, 1758, we have already noted. Sadly, that sort of thing was not an uncommon event. Of course, these atrocities, in the 1750s and '60s, are not the work of Senecas so much as of Shawnees and Delawares, as well as members of other tribes, sometimes in the company of the French, as with Mary Jemison. These were terrorizing the settlements. In fact, one of the most blood-curdling atrocities of the entire period, the grisly murder of Schoolmaster Enoch Brown and ten of his eleven pupils, not far south of Carlisle, was the work of the Delawares.

In the eastern region of Pennsylvania, the Indians, having suffered many atrocities and fiercely provoked, on October 8 of 1763, conducted massacre-raids on a number of homes in the Allen Town section of Northampton County.[9] A detailed account of the murders was sent by urgent messenger to Governor James Hamilton in Philadelphia. This letter was printed by Benjamin Franklin and published in the *Pennsylvania Gazette* on October 13.[10]

It was already time for another Proclamation. On July 7, 1764, Pennsylvania repeated its bounty offer, even for the scalps of children, "for the better carrying on of offensive operations against our Indian enemies." In its language the proclamation was almost identical to the pronouncement of 1756. One striking difference may be perceived. The cut-off age between child and warrior has here, in the second proclamation, been adjusted downwards to ten years old!

It is of course difficult to gauge the effect of the bounty offers, but there is some reason to believe that so-called "secret expeditions," operating often at night, on the part of the settlers, were having some effect. Certainly in central Pennsylvania fewer and fewer of the Indian incursions, as they were called, were occurring. Settlers were returning to their properties and tilling the fields and new settlers were coming forward. Conditions had almost become quiet.

Isolated incidents of course continued to occur, like the grisly murders carried out by Stump the Indian killer, in January of 1768.[11] And the year 1777 saw a steady stream of outrages.

We are now arrived, of course, at the War of the Revolution. By the time the Senecas commit to the King, Cornplanter is twenty-five, maybe twenty-seven, years old. He is a veteran warrior. He is not only pre-eminent among the Senecas, he is, with Old Smoke and Kayahsotha, foremost among all warriors of the Six Nations, always of course excepting Joseph Brant. The Iroquois, most of whom have sided with the British, are now occupied in actual military engagements, fighting in forces that include British Regulars and Rangers. But still they find time for raids on the frontier settlements.

Perhaps foremost among these is the bloody massacre of the Benjamins carried out by unidentified Indians at what is known now as the Buckley Farm, on the Loyalsock. This is too horrible to describe, and we shall not attempt it.

Atrocities occurred also on Pine Creek, Lycoming Creek, Bald Eagle Creek, Youngwoman's Creek, and on the West Branch of the Susquehanna.[12] These unspeakable murders were carried out by Indians and by whites. They were avenged by whites and by Indians.

The reports that came into the settlements, often much confused and garbled, regularly made mention of "big savages." We know that at this time the Seneca and the Munsee tribes were out in considerable force, and we know that they were extremely active on Pine Creek and Lycoming Creek, both of which are most of the time navigable by canoes almost north to the New York border. Was Cornplanter one of these "big" braves? He is now, in 1777, a mature man, a hardened warrior looked to for leadership, and certainly not the stay-at-home sort. As a matter of fact, the Seneca Indian Chief known as Cornplanter seems through the years 1775-1779 to be in on every battle, every raid, every skirmish. He is here, there, and everywhere. He is a wraith, albeit one of substance and size. He stood probably six feet one, tall for an Indian. But he was rarely identified positively, and the report that is made is generally of "Cornplanter Indians," rather than of Cornplanter himself. We can be almost certain that Mary Jemison's second husband, Hiokatoo, whose ferocity can hardly be exaggerated, and who sometimes traveled with Cornplanter, was a party to many of these raids. And he *was* a big man, six feet four and more.

Mary Jemison provides quite a portrait of her second husband: "Hiokatoo was an old man when I first saw him; but he was by no means enervated. During the term of nearly fifty years that I lived with him, I received, according to Indian customs, all the kindness and attention that was my due as his wife,—Although war was his trade from his youth till old age and decrepitude stopt his career, he uniformly treated me with tenderness and never offered an insult."

She notes that she has often "heard him repeat the history of his life . . . and when he came to that part which related to his actions, his bravery and his valor in war; when he spoke of the ambush, the combat, the spoiling of his enemies and the sacrifice of his victims, his nerves seemed strung with youthful ardor, the warmth of the able warrior seemed to animate his frame, and to produce the heated gestures which he had practiced in middle age. He was a man of tender feelings to his friends, ready and willing to assist them in distress, yet, as a warrior, his cruelties to his enemies perhaps were unparalleled, and will not admit a word of palliation."

She notes next that Hiokatoo was a cousin to the celebrated chief Farmer's Brother (their mothers being sisters), and that it was because of the influence of Farmer's Brother that she became the wife of Hiokatoo. Then she continues the portrait: "In early life, Hiokatoo showed some signs of thirst for blood, by attending only to the art of war, in the use of the tomahawk and scalping knife; and in practising cruelties upon every thing that chanced to fall into his hands, which was susceptible of pain. In that way he learned to use his implements of war effectually, and at the same time blunted all those fine feelings and tender sympathies that are naturally excited, by hearing or seeing, a fellow being in distress. He could inflict the most excruciating tortures upon his enemies, and prided himself upon his fortitude, in having performed the most barbarous ceremonies and tortures, without the least degree of pity or remorse." [13]

In no area of the struggling colonies were Indian depredations more numerous and more devastating and barbarous than in Northumberland County of Pennsylvania. Northumberland County, in the central portion of the state, and including the confluence of the two branches of the Susquehanna River, and at one time the important Indian town of Shamokin, was one of the eleven counties that composed the Commonwealth during the Revolution. Throughout the rebellion this region was constantly harassed by hostile savages. "No part of the Pennsylvania frontier," declares the historian Frederic Godcharles, "suffered more from their incursions." [14]

Eighty of these "incursions," as historians are wont to call them, have been described with names and dates by John Carter for the *Northumberland County Historical Proceedings*. These eighty are for the six-year period 1777-1782, for which he has reliable information.

These raids, Carter reports, claimed 446 lives, resulted in countless injuries, and led to the capture of an additional 140 persons.[15]

Perhaps a recital of two of these atrocities will be sufficient to suggest the tenor of the rest which were occurring along the frontier during these years. Here is one, which takes us to Williamsport on June 10, 1778: "A party of seventeen persons, seven men, two women, and eight children, had started from Lycoming Creek in a four-horse wagon to go to Fort Muncy. On reaching a spot of ground within the present limits of Williamsport, they were attacked by a party of Indians estimated at about twenty in number. Both women, Mrs. Peter Smith and Mrs. William King, were stabbed or tomahawked and scalped, as were Michael Campbell, Snodgrass and Hammond. Four children, including a little girl and a small boy, were killed and scalped. Another boy escaped and gave the alarm at Lycoming. It is believed that two other children were led into captivity. Peter Smith and his little daughter managed to reach Fort Muncy. The other three men, Michael Smith, William King, and David Chambers, also escaped."

We have this impression of the massacre from John Meginness: "This was indeed a bloody day—the savages glutted themselves with murder and plunder, and returned in triumph. A gloomy pall seemed suspended over the infant settlement, and weeping and wailing was heard on every hand. Children were murdered before their parents' eyes; husbands were compelled to witness the horrid death of their wives—and in turn children were compelled to gaze upon the mangled bodies of their parents. Neither age, sex, or condition was spared. The wails of helpless infants; the imploring cries of defenceless women, failed to awaken a chord of pity in the adamantine bosom of the tawny savage—he laughed their pitiful appeals to scorn, and with a fiendish grin of pleasure, plied the knife, and tore the reeking scalp from their heads." [16]

The chronicler, writing seventy-eight years after the event, raises a question: "How many of the present inhabitants of the beautiful town of Williamsport are aware that on the 10th day of June, 1778, such a fearful and bloody tragedy was enacted upon the site of that town, and the cry of helpless innocence mingled with the whoop of the savage, awoke the echoes of the forest, and ascended to the azure realms of heaven?"

Here is another of Carter's reports: "In the autumn of 1778, Mrs. McKnight and Mrs. Durham, with small children in their arms, left Fort Freeland for Northumberland. One mile below the mouth of Warrior

Run, they were unexpectedly fired upon by a party of Indians. Mrs. Durham's child was shot in her arms and Mrs. Durham was scalped and left for dead. However, she was rescued by Peter and Elias Williams, taken to Dr. Plunket in Sunbury and most remarkably survived for fifty years. Her grave may still be seen in the Warrior Run cemetery."

Another account provides more detail. It explains that the two women were on horseback, each with a child in her arms, "the husbands making the journey afoot." When they were fired upon, "Mrs. McKnight's horse suddenly wheeled about and galloped back to the fort. As the horse turned, her child slipped from her arms, but she held it in by the foot, and held it in this position until the frightened animal brought them safely to the stockade." [17]

This was in the time just a few months before the Cornplanter-led assault on Fort Freeland, about which more anon.

A very sad story, one that Cornplanter is sometimes identified with, must be recited here. We give the account as reported by Chester Hale Sipe in his *Indian Chiefs of Pennsylvania,* although Sipe has it from Meginness' *History of the West Branch Valley.* The date is August 8, 1778; the place is a site very near to Williamsport in Lycoming County: "A Corporal and four men, belonging to Colonel [Thomas] Hartley's regiment, and three militiamen, were ordered about two miles above Loyalsock . . . to protect fourteen reapers and cradlers, who went to assist Peter Smith, the unfortunate man that had his wife and four children murdered about a month previous, to cut his crop. Smith's farm was on Turkey Run, not far from Williamsport, on the opposite side of the river."

"Captain" of the party was James Brady of the famous Brady Indian-fighter family. When they reached the field they posted sentinels and protected the harvesters through the day, Friday. "A strict watch was kept all night, but nothing unusual occurred. In the morning they all went to work; the cradlers, four in number, by themselves, near the house; the reapers in another part of the field." All except young Brady, placed their guns round a tree. Thinking this was the wrong thing to do, he stood his rifle some distance from the rest.

"The morning proved to be very foggy, and about an hour after sunrise, the sentinels and reapers were surprised by a number of Indians, under cover of the fog, quietly approaching them. The sentinels fired and ran towards the reapers, when they all ran, with the exception of young Brady. He made towards his rifle, pursued by three Indians, and when within a few yards of it, was fired upon by a white man with a pistol, probably a tory." Happily, Brady at that moment fell over a sheaf of grain, and was not hit. When he rose, however, now close to his rifle, he was wounded. But he had reached his gun, and with it promptly dispatched two warriors.

Now they enclosed him in great numbers, "but being a stout active man, he struggled with them for some time. At length one of them struck a tomahawk into his head, when he fell, and was wounded with a spear in the hands of another. He was so stunned with the blow of the tomahawk that he remained powerless, but strange as it may seem, retained his senses. They ruthlessly tore the scalp from his head as he lay in apparent death; and it was a glorious trophy for them, for he had long and remarkably red hair."

But Brady was not dead. He was conscious enough to know that "a little Indian" was summoned and made to strike a tomahawk into his head "in four separate places." Here the Indians, fearing an attack apparently, fled. And Brady, still alive, managed to creep from the fields some distance to the cabin of an old man named Jerome Vaness, who did the cooking for the reapers. He had been hiding, but now insisted on caring for Brady. Though Brady urged him to fly to the fort, the worthy man "positively refused to leave him alone, but stayed and endeavored to dress his frightful wounds. Brady requested to be assisted down [to] the river, where he drank large quantities of water, when he still insisted on the old man leaving him and trying to save himself; but he would not do it. He then directed his faithful old friend to load the gun that was in the cabin, which was done, and put into his hands, when he lay down and appeared to sleep."

When the fort learned of the affair a company was dispatched to the scene, and when Brady heard them, and supposed it was the Indians returning, he "jumped to his feet and cocked his gun. But it was friends. They made a bier and placed him on it, and brought him away. He requested to be taken to Sunbury to his mother. His request was granted, and a party started with him, amongst whom was Robert Covenhoven. He became very feverish by the way, and drank large quantities of water, and became partly delirious. It was late at night when they arrived at Sunbury, and [they] did not intend to arouse his mother; but it seemed she had a presentiment of something that was to happen, and being awake to alarms, met them at the river and assisted to convey her wounded son to the house. He presented a frightful spectacle, and the meeting of mother and son is described to have been heart-rending. Her heart was wrung with the keenest anguish, and her lamentations were terrible to be heard."

For five days the young captain lingered, delirious for four. On the fifth day, his mind now clear, he described vividly his whole experience. He reported that the Indians "were of the Seneca tribe, and amongst them were two chiefs; one of whom was a very large man, and from the description was supposed to be Cornplanter; the other he personally knew to be the celebrated chief Bald Eagle, who had his nest near where Milesburg [on Bald Eagle Creek], Centre County, now stands."

That evening the young captain was taken in death, "deeply regretted by all who knew him; for he was a noble and promising young man. Vengeance, 'not loud but deep,' was breathed against the Bald Eagle, but he laughed it to scorn, till that fatal day at Brady's Bend on the Allegheny." [18]

Was Cornplanter indeed one of the two chiefs of this war party? He *could* have been present, as the date is exactly one month beyond the massacre at Wyoming, and there is no record of Cornplanter anywhere else for this date of August. But it is extremely unlikely that Cornplanter was a member of this war party. He was of course tall, but he was not really noteworthy for stature and body size. And the account of the awful death of Brady does not in its details smack of Cornplanter. And at no time ever, so far as is known, did Cornplanter speak of this episode; nor did Blacksnake. If indeed the "large" Indian was a Seneca, there is very good reason to suppose that Mary Jemison's fierce warrior husband, the cruel Hiokatoo, is the leading figure in the drama. He, after all, had a reputation for this kind of torture; as before noted, he liked to employ children to shoot arrows at bound victims. And, as he was 3-4 inches more than six feet tall he would be *most* impressive in size. Because of his reputation as war-chief of the Senecas, and because indeed he *seemed* to be here, there, and everywhere, Cornplanter doubtless got the credit for a good many incidents that he had nothing to do with at all. All along the frontier the settlers were hearing of the "Cornplanter Indians."

In any case, before the year was out the murder of young James Brady was avenged. Captain Samuel Brady,[19] the older brother of James, who had also lost his father to Indians, vowed "eternal vengeance" on the warriors. He had not long to wait. His chance came in the succeeding June on the Allegheny. Here in a skirmish with Indians who while coming down the Allegheny were intercepted by Brady's company of rangers, Bald Eagle was shot and killed, by Brady himself, so the story goes. But this Bald Eagle was a Delaware.[20]

The raids upon the frontier settlements did not cease abruptly of course as the end of the war drew near. As late as 1781, according to one historian, there were sixty-four war parties, comprising a total of 2945 warriors, active on the frontiers of Pennsylvania, Ohio, and New York. Most of these war parties were small, like the one headed up by the powerful Sayenqueraghta (Old Smoke), of Wyoming and Oriskany fame, which numbered thirty-six warriors, including perhaps Cornplanter, as it operated in the region of Fort Pitt, and assumed a much larger force with which to threaten Wheeling. And atrocities continued to be perpetrated by the whites, like that at Standing Stone, where Shawnee women and children were massacred. Such brutal attacks prompted Old Smoke to declare angrily that the Americans (meaning the rebellious colonists) "gave us great Reason to be revenged on them for their Cruelties to us and our Friends, and if we had the means of publishing to the world the many Acts of Treachery and Cruelty committed by them on our women and children . . . ."[21]

V

IROQUOIS TAKE UP THE HATCHET

We back up now to note how the Indians of the Six Nations, and particularly the Senecas, were drawn into the conflict between the King and the rebellious colonists. And to ascertain the role that the Senecas and their chiefs, including Cornplanter, played in the long and bloody struggle.

As tensions between the Rebels and the British increased dramatically in the early seventies, and the French began to pass beyond the Indians' interest or concern, overtures to the Indians, on the part of both parties, Rebels and Loyalists, were renewed. The American colonists seemed not so much interested in securing Indian allies, feeling apparently that they would be more trouble than they were worth, but the British eventually saw the value of their support and began aggressively to woo them. They were particularly eager to secure the friendship of the Six Nations, and especially that of the Senecas, who were not only the most populous of the six, but also enjoyed the reputation of being the most warlike and fierce. Besides, located as they were, at the western end of the "longhouse," as the Federation was called, they presided over the gateway to the interior and exercised an influence over the tribes to the west. The Senecas were known as the Keepers of the Western Door.

Consequently, as noted above, we have for the period 1770-1777 a steady succession of councils to which the Indians were invited, conducted by both the British and the Americans. The Senecas found themselves scurrying from their homes in the Allegheny region and the Valley of the Genesee back and forth to Fort Pitt, to Albany, to Oswego, and to German Flats in the Mohawk Valley. Most influential in all of the jousting for Indian favor were the Mohawk Chief Joseph Brant, his brother-in-law Sir William Johnson, who for a long time had been serving the Crown as Commissioner of Indian Affairs, and who was to die July 11, 1774, and the Tory John Butler.

John Butler had been born in the colonies, in New London, Connecticut, but he had decided when the trouble broke out to cast his lot with the British. He was a Loyalist, a Tory. At the time the courtship of the Iroquois began, he was forty-two years old, and already very close to the Indians, particularly to Brant and the easternmost tribes of the Six Nations, as he had moved from New England into the Mohawk Valley. As he negotiated with the Indians and sought vigorously to win an alliance with them, he organized the Loyalist troop soon to be known as Butler's Rangers.[1] With Butler out front and very aggressive, the British curried the favor of the Iroquois and urged them to take up the hatchet.

Cornplanter, as we have seen, probably was present at the 1775 fall conference called by the American Commissioners for Fort Pitt. In fact, this date appears to be the first date with which we can in much confidence associate Cornplanter. Cornplanter's nephew Blacksnake was at this time living near Cornplanter in Ganawaugus, which, because he is recollecting seventy years later, he regularly in his narrative refers to as "Avon." He describes how the runners came to the village to announce the conference and to explain that its purpose was to educate the Indians on the differences that had arisen between the colonists and the Crown. As noted above, he describes in great detail their travel to Pittsburgh;[2] and he indicates that as "head chiefs," and with "considerable influence amongst all other tribes," both his uncle Cornplanter and cousin Red Jacket played major roles. Thomas Abler, the editor of the Blacksnake narration, regards that impression as exaggerated. But he does acknowledge that Cornplanter, Blacksnake's senior by just a little, was at this time "a rapidly rising young man," and had influence, "but not to the extent that he could be ranked higher than other chiefs."[3]

Those who would know Cornplanter need to feel grateful for his nephew Blacksnake. We would know ever so much less than we do about the Seneca war-chief (and, for that matter, about the battles fought in the Revolution) if Blacksnake had not provided his recollections of the time, and particularly of the engagements, so many of which he participated in at the side of his uncle.

The American Commissioners continued to urge a neutral course for the Senecas. "You Indians are not concerned in it. We desire you to remain at home." They insisted that "you have nothing to do with our father-children quarrels." Blacksnake's account of the Fort Pitt council notes that Cornplanter, having declared himself "head man"of the Seneca Nation responded with an appeal for unanimity, a message that would become a constant with him in the council years ahead.[3] But apparently very little of consequence happened, and the council dissolved in the familiar way, "some wine to Drink for Better friendship & Exsess &c."[5]

In these early councils, and most particularly at German Flats in the Mohawk Valley, Cornplanter regularly pledged to the American Commissioners that the Senecas would remain neutral. For quite some time he and his uncle Kayahsotha, who thought very much alike on the matter and even inclined a little toward the rebels, were able to keep their Indians on the sidelines.

Was Cornplanter present at the congress called by the American commissioners for Albany in August of that year? Again the Americans did not here try to persuade the Indians into an alliance. They merely urged them to "stay out of it." Additional councils were held at Onondaga, in September, and at Fort Pitt later that fall. The year 1776, as the war heated up, saw numerous meetings at Fort Niagara and one at Onondaga. A big conference, called by the Americans, convened at Albany on April 26. There were no Senecas in attendance at this conference; all of the other Six Nations were represented. But the Seneca nation was represented at the conference with Americans held at Onondaga in June, and we know that Old Smoke was there[5] and that the chief was dispatched to Fort Niagara to recover some Seneca warriors who were serving with the British. Blacksnake recalls a conference that was held at Ganawaugus, Cornplanter's home village. According to him, this council took place in the summer of 1776, but, as Abler points out, inasmuch as it included "a heated exchange" between the Seneca chief Red Jacket and the Mohawk chief Joseph Brant, it could not have occurred during that summer. Brant was in England, hobnobbing with King George all of that summer.[7]

During the winter of 1776-77, the British worked most aggressively, with promises and gifts and arguments, to persuade the Iroquois to the Crown. Before the year was out they would have reason to be pleased.

The council that was convened at German Flats in the Mohawk Valley was held in August; and in September of 1776, at a Niagara council attended by Cornplanter, Red Jacket, Old Smoke, Farmer's Brother,[8] and Handsome Lake, four of the Six Nations confirmed their allegiance to the British, and when an appeal to the absent Tuscaroras and Oneidas fell on deaf ears, it was plain that the Confederacy had been "split irrevocably." [9]

The Iroquois commitment to the British cause, delayed for so long, became official in July of 1777. In June the British had determined on a strategy by which the war could surely be brought to a conclusion. The plan, put together by Lord George Germain and General John Burgoyne, was designed to split the colonies. It called for the coordination of three armies in a massive campaign. Burgoyne was to advance south from Canada, following a route along Lake Champlain to Albany, where he was to unite with Sir William Howe, coming up the Hudson River from New York City and with General Barry St. Leger, moving from west to east along the Mohawk River.

Far away, in Niagara, Major John Butler was making plans as well. His orders were to prepare for an expedition against the rebel settlers. He had been urged to round up as many allies from among the Indian tribes as he possibly could. Accordingly, he promptly invited the warriors of the Six Nations, with their families, as well as members of tribes to the west, to an assembly. He was particularly eager to win over the Iroquois, who numbered at this time about 10,000, of whom 4600 were well trained and much experienced in the business of war.[10] As it happened, the promise of presents from the King was sufficient to secure a good turnout. His announced object, according to one historian, was the rescue of the Loyalist families "left behind to the untender mercies of the Rebels." [11] The specific targets, as the British commissioner later made perfectly plain in his persuasions, would be the fur-trading post known as Fort Stanwix at Rome, and Wyoming.[12]

At this time the Iroquois of the Six Nations were not committed formally to the British, even though numerous warriors, particularly the Mohawks, had been participating in battles in the service of the King. The Senecas were definitely still on the fence, and a worry to the British. Consequently, in order to cement an alliance with the Six Nations, and most especially the Senecas, the British convened a council. But even before the council proceedings could be opened and before Butler could get his expedition underway, Indian activity was occurring in the region of Fort Stanwix. One episode of the war activity at this time involved the young Seneca chief Cornplanter. It occurred on the third day of July, 1777. We have the story from the narrative penned by Lt. Colonel Marinus Willett, who had been directed in June to join the garrison at Fort Stanwix, the site of the very important 1768 treaty signed by the Iroquois and by Sir William Johnson. The fort was under the command of Colonel Peter Gansevoort, who was, properly, expecting to be besieged by the British and Iroquois forces under General Barry St. Leger. Gansevoort and Willett, who was second in command, with the soldiers of the 3rd New York Regiment, had completely restored the historic fort, which they had discovered in useless ruins.

An ever swelling number of Indians, toward the end of June and during the first two days of July, were observed by Gansevoort and his officers. "The number of Indians increases" was the word sent out with Gansevoort's runners.

A portion of Colonel Willett's narrative, written in the third person, follows: "Another tragic incident occurred at nearly the same time. About noon, on the 3d day of July [1777], the day being perfectly clear, Colonel Willett was startled from his *siesta* by the report of musketry. Hastening to the parapet of the glacis, he saw a little girl running with a basket in her hand, while the blood was trickling down her bosom. On investigating the facts, it appeared that the girl, with two others, was picking berries, not two hundred yards from the fort, when they were fired upon by a party of Indians, and two of the number killed. Happily, she who only was left to tell the tale, was but slightly wounded. One of the girls killed was the daughter of an invalid, who had served many years in the British artillery. He was entitled to a situation in the Chelsea Hospital [the Royal Hospital for veteran soldiers built by Christopher Wren (1682-92), in West London], but had preferred rather to remain in the cultivation of a small piece of ground at Fort Stanwix, than again to cross the ocean."[13]

The eminent historian William Leete Stone in his *Life of Brant* insists that Cornplanter by his own confession was the murderer. When, years after the "incident," Cornplanter's recollection for Joseph Brant took the form of boasting, the chief found himself in big trouble, with the enraged hotel manager, who overheard the narration.[14] It was not the most glorious moment in the warrior life of the Seneca Chief.

It is worth noting that this conduct on the part of Cornplanter is nothing short of incredible, if in fact it took place *before* the Seneca commitment to the British at the council of Oswego. It does not seem possible that the Cornplanter here who ruthlessly murdered two children near a rebel fort is the same Cornplanter who ten days later would so vehemently urge his people to neutrality. The incident provides great support to the argument of those historians who feel that the Oswego conference was in fact held in the spring rather than in July.

However, most historians still opt for July as the date of the council that the British had been urging, and most feel that it was finally scheduled for the Oswego fort and trading post on the southeastern shore of Lake Ontario, at Irondequois Bay.[15] This bay was a popular route for the Indians traveling by canoe. For many years they had depended upon the bay and the Irondequoit Creek which flows into it for their passage. In this way they could get round the extremely high falls of the Genesee River as the stream flowed into the lake (at present-day Rochester).[16] In the long life of Cornplanter, this week, July 13-20, 1777, would prove to be perhaps his most critical moment; certainly for the League of the Iroquois it would prove to be most fateful.

Blacksnake described for Lyman Draper how the Genesee Valley Senecas constructed canoes in the valley below the falls of their river, and how they paddled the flotilla to the conference. According to him, some 2000 (!) Senecas, including women and the leaders Old Smoke (now in his seventies), Kayahsotha, Cornplanter, and Handsome Lake, had made their way to the council site.

Butler (who could speak the Mohawk tongue), in his desire to persuade the Indians to his cause, naturally was lavish in the distribution of gifts, especially rum. It was merrymaking and "getting to know you" that characterized the early going. Graymont explains that "after they had been mellowed for two or three days, the Indians were directed to . . . council." [17] Here Butler professed the King's friendship and promised a successful end to the campaign. The Senecas, at first, were not impressed. The old warrior Sayenqueraghta (*Gi-en-gwah-toh,* He-who-goes-in-the-Smoke, or Old Smoke) and the young warrior known to the British as Captain O'Beal were the two chiefs in command of the Iroquois forces. Old Smoke was at this time almost exactly three times as old as O'Beal, who, according to Graymont, was but twenty-five.[18] The old chief, born into the Turtle Clan, had fashioned a big reputation as a Seneca war-captain. He was still a powerful man, heavily built, and nearly as tall as Cornplanter himself. They made quite a pair. They expressed, in energetic language, their opposition to the alliance and to the campaign being proposed.

Also a member of the Seneca delegation was the celebrated Kayahsotha, the older brother of Cornplanter's mother.[19] Kayahsotha arrived at Oswego trailing quite a reputation. He had been born at Ganawaugus on the Genesee at some time between 1720 and 1725. When he was just a boy, his family moved south to the Allegheny River, in the region near present-day

Meadville. When he was in his early thirties, and now a highly skilled hunter and warrior, he enjoyed an acquaintance with a rather impressive tall young man, destined to become rather important to Kayahsotha's future. His name was George Washington. Kayahsotha was one of the three Indians who in 1753 accompanied Washington from Logstown to Fort Le Boeuf, when Washington was delivering Virginia Governor Robert Dinwiddie's famous "get out" message to the French. Washington knew Kayahsotha at that time only as The Hunter.

During the French and Indian Wars, Kayahsotha sided with the French and fought energetically in a number of engagements, including the defeat of General Edward Braddock on the Monongahela. He is thought by some to be one of the warrior-chiefs leading the modest resistance to General John Forbes' 1758 expedition against Fort Duquesne. In August of 1763 he was a principal figure, though not the leader, as was first thought, in the Indian ambush of Colonel Henry Bouquet in the bloody battle of Edge Hill (Bushy Run).

At the end of the war when the British assumed control of all the French territory east of the Mississippi, the Ottawa warrior-chief Pontiac led an uprising to protest the new trading laws the British had installed. Kayahsotha was one of the few Senecas (though he was considered a transplant, a Mingo) to join in the rebellion. In fact, Kayahsotha, as Pontiac's lieutenant, assumed the leadership of the Senecas operating in the Allegheny River-Lake Erie region. Although one can not be absolutely sure, it was almost certainly Cornplanter's uncle who commanded the war party which butchered the garrison at Fort Venango, on June 16, 1763.[20] The fort was located on French Creek, just at the point where it flows into the Allegheny, and in Cornplanter's future was replaced by Fort Franklin.

Just how cunning and duplicitous—and how terribly cruel—Kayahsotha's Senecas could be is apparent in all reports we have of the Fort's destruction. Although no soldier of the garrison survived, and only one woman, to tell the story, at a time long afterwards, an Indian "who was present" described the scene for Sir William Johnson. He explained just how it was that the warriors were able to do it. They "gained entrance under pretense of friendship, they closed the gates, fell upon the garrison, and butchered them all except the commanding officer, Lieutenant [Francis] Gordon, whom they forced to write, from their dictation, a statement of the grievances which had driven them to arms, and [whom they] then tortured over a slow fire for several nights till he expired. This done, they burned the place to the ground, and departed." [21]

A second account comes from a letter written to the Reverend S. J. M. Eaton by Mrs. M. A. Irvine, of Erie, Pennsylvania. As she wrote this letter on January 20, 1876, she was at the time ninety-two years old. Her recollection is vivid: "I must now tell you all I know about the old forts. The French fort [Machault, at Venango, now Franklin] was nearly obliterated, and where the pickets stood was grown up with blackberry bushes and grape vines. Both forts were near the Allegheny River; the British fort a little farther up. There was a little stream running between them, which supplied the British garrison with water. They had an underground passage to it in order to be protected against the Indians, in the same way. The Indians in playing football, would roll their ball inside the enclosure, as if by accident, and were allowed to go in and get it. Having done so several times, at last, when the garrison was off its guard, they rushed in in a body and killed every soul except one woman, whom they carried to Canada. A sister of mine saw this woman afterwards at Fort Erie, and she then told of the massacre."[22]

Still another account, quite consistent, is included in the narrative of Blacksnake, who could hardly have been present himself. When he was of an age very close to that of Mrs. Irvine, from stories which as a small boy he would have heard, he remembered it this way: "Forty Senecas under Hod-own-da-o-go,—Gi-yo-so-do [Guyasuta (Kayahsotha)]—& Goh-no-dunk, started on an expedition against the Cherokees: Encamped at the mouth of French Creek, & there concluded they would first attack the English fort there. They easily gained admittance under the guise of friendship, with their tomahawks & knives concealed, relying upon these to effect their purpose. Then suddenly & unexpectedly fell upon the unsuspecting inmates & killed 30 persons, some below & others in the Chambers. One prisoner only was taken—a woman, who was carried to Cattaraugus, where she lived some time & finally went to Canada … . This party then continued on their expedition against the Cherokees." [23] Fort Le Boeuf, which had been constructed in 1753 at present-day Waterford, Pennsylvania, was captured in the same manner two days later; and shortly thereafter Fort Presque Isle, which had been built in 1753 by the French on the southeast shore of Lake Erie (and burned and rebuilt by the French in 1759), fell, after a two days' siege, in the same way, to duplicity and lies. It has sometimes been presumed that it was the same body of Seneca (Mingo) Indians, headed by Kayahsotha, that was responsible for the destruction of this line of forts, but it is now thought that that was not the case, that Kayahsotha, even though the assaults were similar, did not figure in the fall of these latter two forts. (Blacksnake has Kayahsotha's warriors continuing their expedition against the Cherokees; and accounts of the Venango massacre refer to "several nights" of torture.) Apparently in the ravage of the fort at Presque Isle whatever Senecas were involved had the assistance of some Ottawas, some Ojibways, and some Wyandots, the war party numbering some 250 in all.[24]

On October 28 of 1770 Chief Kayahsotha once again met George Washington, whom he had not seen in seventeen years. Washington's party came upon the chief's hunting party about three miles down the Ohio from where Guyan Run (or Shade River) flows into the river, in present-day Meigs County, Ohio. Washington, remembering the chief as The Hunter, greeted him most warmly, and was promptly rewarded for his friendship with the invitation to him and his party to share in a woods bison the chief had just killed and to make use of his camp site. The two parties camped at different sites for the night, but in the morning the chief showed up with his warriors, and they all consulted (in what Washington, impatient to get going, found tedious talk) until 9:00 in the morning. Kayahsotha urged Washington to make the colony of Virginia aware that the Indians were of a friendly disposition and were eager to open up trade with the settlers. "This," confided Washington to his journal, "I promised to do."[25]

This meeting occurred long before the outbreak of the Revolution, and though Kayahsotha and Washington were never to meet again, they came very close, as the chief continued active in council sessions and throughout the war and into the problems with the Ohio Indians. Kayahsotha was not only present at the peace conference held the next year by Colonel Henri Bouquet with the Shawnee and other Indians, but most instrumental in working out the agreement.

Certainly Cornplanter's uncle was the principal Indian chief in the Ohio Valley region during these turbulent years. It would hardly be too much to observe of him that by the time of the conference at Oswego he was the most renowned of all the eastern Indians. Now, in his mid-fifties, he stood up with the even older Old Smoke and with his nephew Cornplanter for neutrality: "It is none of our business."

Most of the Senecas had little reason to feel close to the British. Certainly Kayahsotha was not warming up to them, and neither was his nephew. But, now that the colonies had rebelled against the king and a real war had broken out, all of the Six Nations and all of the Indians of the East had to consider with which party were their fortunes better placed.

Joseph Brant

And though the Onondagas and the Tuscaroras and the Oneidas were clearly still on the fence, most of the Iroquois population at this time were inclined favorably toward the British. While they debated among themselves, Butler persisted with his persuasions. Councils continued, and so did the gifting. Now the Indians were presented the most elaborate of gifts: clothing, guns, knives, hatchets, and kettles. Besides, they were promised handsome bounties for every scalp, every prisoner.[26]

Through it all Cornplanter had urged a neutral course ("It is none of our business."). And the Mohawk Joseph Brant was adamant for the British.[27] The Indians, having repaired to private council of their own, now debated. The exchange which ensued was fierce. Pitted against the powerful Mohawk leader Joseph Brant were Kayahsotha, Old Smoke, Cornplanter, and Red Jacket. Cornplanter saw the revolution as a "family quarrel," too complex for the Indians and nothing to them. It grew very plain to Brant that the Senecas were strongly united behind their leaders, but he *had* to have the Senecas in camp. Blacksnake, accounting for the affair almost seventy-five years later, as if it had occurred yesterday, remembers the words delivered by the principals. After Brant had spoken hard for war, Cornplanter, subtly making the point that the Americans had not solicited the aid of the Iroquois, addressed the Indians. Here is his speech as Blacksnake remembered it, in a "translation" of the garbled English of The Nephew's interpreter, Ben Williams: ". . . warriors, you must all mark and listen to what we have to say. War is death, and fighting is a hard business. . . . Here is America, which says to us not to lift our hands against either party, just because they got into difficulty. It is nothing to us. And America also says let him fight it out for his liberty in his rebellion against his own Brother. In fact, we of the Indian nations from several different parts of this continent do not know what it is all about. We are apt to make a mistake. I therefore implore you to wait a little, until we have heard more of the consultation between the two parties . . . ."

At this point, Joseph Brant, clearly in great anger, sprang to his feet, and told the young Cornplanter to "shut up." Blacksnake, possibly unhappy with Brant's condescending tone, remembers the drama. He recalls that Brant addressed the young Cornplanter as "nephew," and simply told him to hold his tongue. He declared Cornplanter "a very coward man," and insisted it was not worth their time to "take notice of what you have said," for you have showed your colors. Cornplanter, according to Blacksnake, said not a word until "next day after." [28]

Brant had played his trump card. It is a rare Seneca, a rare Iroquois, indeed a very rare Indian, who can stomach the term. In the consternation which followed, the Indians met in mini-councils. Neutrality was still popular, but it was not worth the stigma of cowardice. When the vote was taken, a large majority of the warriors, and, more importantly, the women, were for war, for war on the side of the British. It was a dramatic moment in the life of Cornplanter, and in the life of the Senecas and for the future of the Six Nations. The young warrior Dahgayadoh remembered till his dying day how his uncle Cornplanter rose soberly to his feet to pronounce the verdict for all: "[Let] Every Brave man Show himself Now hereafter for we will find an many Dangerous times During the actions of the war, for we will See a many Brave man amongsth american Soldiers which we Shall meet, with their Sharp adge Stools [edged swords], I therefore Say you must Stand like good Soldier against your own white Brother Because just as soon as he fined you out that are against him he than will Show you his wit no mercy on you on us, I therefore Say Stand to your Post where is time come Before you But a gard [agreed] yours be."

Mary Jemison's account of the deliberations is essentially the same as Blacksnake's. She remarks on the persuasive powers of the British speakers, who declared that the king's rum "was as plenty as the water in lake Ontario: that his men were as numerous as the sands upon the lake shore:—and that the Indians, if they would assist in the war, and persevere in their friendship to the King, till it was closed, should never want for money or goods." [29]

The die was cast. Brant next day reported the good news to the British commissioners. Mary Jemison, who throughout the Revolution would many times entertain in her home on the Genesee both the Mohawk Chief Joseph Brant and the Tory leader John Butler, remembers with what excited and undisguised delight they both received the verdict: " … as soon as the treaty was finished, the Commissioners, whose names Blacksnake could not remember, made a present to each Indian of a suit of clothes, a brass kettle, a gun and tomahawk, a scalping knife, a quantity of powder and lead, a piece of gold, and promised a bounty on every scalp that should be brought in . . . . Many of the kettles which the Indians received at that time are now [1823] in use on the Genesee Flats." [30]

Although Blacksnake reports that "not many of the Oneidas and Tuscaroras were in attendance," and even though the Onondagas would not actively support the king until their village was burned by the patriots two years later, apparently all six nations of the Federation accepted the war belt, Old Smoke and Kayahsotha representing the Senecas.[31]

And nothing more was done that day. And all retired to dinner and to "Drink Rum and sugar, and we done so that afternoon our head men was a little to much Rum." And then the Indians declared that "we . . . shall go to take wyoming," and America may surrender all at once. What had begun a week ago in rum now ended in rum, and in a naive and over-confident resolution. From this time until the end of the Revolution the Iroquois (excepting the Tuscaroras and the Oneidas) would stand with the British and the Tories. Old Smoke, though he was now some seventy years along the trail, was remembering well enough his warrior days, the glory and the fame that had been and continued to be his. He would take up the hatchet again. Cornplanter, still a young warrior, would play a major role as war-chief of the Senecas.

At just about the time the Indians decided for the warpath, Butler was notified that General St. Leger was planning a surprise attack on Fort Stanwix and that he needed 150 warriors. After dispatching the requested warriors, Butler set out for Oswego, arriving July 25.[32]

The fort that had been targeted by St. Leger had been in its beginning a colonial outpost near the site of present-day Rome. It was strategically located for war operations and advantageously located for fur trading, because it was but a short distance from its site on the Mohawk to Lake Oneida, which is connected to Lake Ontario by the Oswego River. It had been a trading center, and for the French a fortified post before it fell to the British and was then neglected. It was rebuilt, in 1758, by General John Stanwix; and, as we have seen, it was the site of the treaty in 1768 that was agreed to by Sir William Johnson and the Iroquois. Again it fell into disuse, but early in the Revolution, by order of General Washington, it was restored and garrisoned. It was, in 1777, an inviting target and a plum to be picked in the Burgoyne campaign.

In that summer it was under the command of twenty-eight-year-old Colonel Peter Gansevoort of Albany, who had fought under General Richard Montgomery in the failed invasion of Quebec, and had had the command at Fort George. Gansevoort had succeeded Colonel Samuel

Elmore in May. The departing Elmore had some sage advice for his successor: "Be friendly to the Indians." [33]

St. Leger, with a force of 1400, half of whom were Indians, arrived at the Fort on August 2. The British General was beginning to like less and less what he was seeing. He could perceive at once, from its structure and its ordnance, that the fort would not be easy to take. What he did not know, or he may have been even further dismayed, was that only a few days previous to his arrival the garrison had received a build-up of 200 fresh fighting men. Nevertheless, on the afternoon of August 3, he invited the fort to surrender, receiving, as expected, merely laughter. Indeed, Colonel Gansevoort refused even to listen to the suggestion, and, as Ensign Colbrath proudly recalled, rejected the invitation "with disdain."

Tory John Butler, at the head of a force of 200 Senecas, arrived on August 4.

Nicholas Herkimer

Meanwhile General Nicholas Herkimer, astride his white horse, with Colonel Ebenezer Cox, was marching with reinforcements for the fort, and in fact by August 5 was nearby. He was able to get word through to Gansevoort, but did not know that the British had been alerted to his presence by the ever-vigilant Mary Brant. The British at once prepared an ambush. The spot selected, apparently by the Mohawk chief Joseph Brant, was a mere five miles from the fort, near the Oneida village of Oriska, in the hollows drained by the Oriskany Creek. Here the British Royal Greens, under Sir John Johnson, the Tory Rangers, in the command of John Butler, some four hundred (!) Indians, including the Mohawks, under Brant, and the Senecas, under their chiefs Old Smoke, Cornplanter, and Kayahsotha waited. Kayahsotha was doubtless remembering the horrors of the Battle of Bushy Run, fought *exactly* fourteen years ago to the day.

The ambush, so carefully planned, was executed to perfection, except that the impatient Indians broke cover a little early. What occurred was a slaughter. Herkimer's advancing forces, which included a few Oneida Indians, all in some disarray, were trapped, as planned, in a narrow, marshy ravine. The fighting was largely hand-to-hand. It was bayonet and sword, scalping knife and hatchet. So fierce was the fighting, and so awful the surprise, that many of Herkimer's troops panicked and fled. And so did a number of the ambushing Indians, including Red Jacket, who simply went home, and thus began to earn a reputation for cowardice that he would build on steadily. One historian has described the scene as "a horror to behold." [34] And Blacksnake, who with knife and tomahawk killed so many that he could not keep count, in his recollections conveys this horror vividly:

> *. . . we have met the Enemey at the Place appointed Near a Small creek, where had the Six thousand men, that they [have] 3 cannon and we have none, But tomahawks and a few guns amongst us, But agreed to firght with Tomehawk Skulling [scalping] Knife as we approach to a firghting we had preparate to make one fire and Run amongst them we So, while we Doing of it, feels no more to Kill the Beast, and killed most all, the americans army, only a few whiteman Escape from us there I have seen many norrow places and close to hand to be Kill by the Speare in the End of*

> *muskett [bayonet], that I had to Denfended mysilfe By my hands and Exsivetive [excessive] act, During all the afternoon, But take tomehawk and knifes and Swords to cut Down men with it, there I have Seen the most Dead Bodies all it over that I never Did see, and never will again I thought at that time the Blood Shed a Stream Running Down on the Decending ground During the afternoon, and yet some living crying for help, But have no mercy on to be spared for them But as to the Distress of the Senecas only 30 kill at that time, and I have took prisoners at that time, and Some others took prisoners too, But they was Kill By Clubing & Running through a certain Distance [the gauntlet] and they were not one Escape they ware all put to Death by that way clubing them, and we never undertake to Barrying them, So many of them, we only Covered up with Brushes, &c after we Rested a little . . . .*[35]

Many good men and officers were lost, including Colonel Ebenezer Cox, and Herkimer himself. The general, who had been wounded in the knee by a musket ball which killed his horse, with great courage directed his men to the last, from the base of a beech tree, to which he had been carried. Happily he was provided some relief from a sudden and violent thunderstorm, and the late afternoon arrival of a sortie under Gansevoort's second-in-command, Lt. Colonel Marinus Willett, also a veteran of the Quebec disaster. Willett, who had been dispatched from the fort to provide whatever aid he could, was able to damage the British effort considerably, and Herkimer was able to rally his men somewhat. At about four o'clock in the afternoon the bloody business mercifully came to a close. As the few survivors of Herkimer's militia withdrew from the field, they carried their wounded with them. The Seneca war-chief Sayenqueraghta proposed a pursuit, a mop-up operation, and the Mohawk Joseph Brant was all for it. And, presumably, so were Cornplanter and Blacksnake and Kayahsotha and most of the Indians who had remained throughout the battle. Happily for the Americans, St. Leger rejected the proposal, apparently, as has been duly noted, for reasons practical rather than of mercy.

One of the wounded being carried off was, of course, the militia commander, General Herkimer, who was taken to his own home near the Mohawk River. But his wound was terribly serious. Eleven days from the time the battle ended the brave officer died from complications occurring from the necessary amputation of his leg.

In the battle of Oriskany, the Seneca Indians lost thirty-five[36] warriors; and Blacksnake noted for Lyman Draper that two Seneca chiefs were slain in the fighting: Hasquesahah (Axe Carrier) and Dahwahdeho (Fish Lapper). He remembered that another Seneca chief, Hah-no-gwus (Grease-Skimmer), had received a severe sword cut across the face, and another cut on the back of his head, but was confident that he had recovered.[37] Blacksnake also recalled that four rebel officers remained in the hands of the Indians after the battle had ended. These, he reports, were forced to run the gauntlet and were killed.[38]

It had been a very violent and a very costly battle. Thomas Abler, who regularly has high praise for the Senecas, calls it "the bloodiest fight of the Revolution."[39] Because the British regulars were held back from the fighting, there may be just a touch of bitterness in how Mary Jemison remembers it all: "Previous to the battle at Fort Stanwix, the British sent for the Indians to come and see them whip the rebels; and, at the same time stated that they did not wish to have them fight, but wanted to have them just sit down, smoke their pipes, and look on. Our Indians went, to a man; but contrary to their expectation, instead of smoking and looking on, they were obliged to fight for their lives, and in the end of the battle were completely beaten, with a great loss in killed and wounded. Our Indians alone had thirty-six killed, and a great number wounded. Our town exhibited a scene of real sorrow and distress, when our warriors returned and recounted their misfortunes, and stated the real loss they had sustained in the engagement. The mourning was excessive, and was expressed by the most doleful yells, shrieks, and howlings, and by inimitable gesticulations."[40]

One can presume that in the village of Ganawaugus the scene was much the same.

This battle, memorialized by the Oriskany Battlefield Monument, erected in 1883 near Rome, New York, produced a carnage that, sadly, turned out to be but the first of many for the war years 1777-1783.

Even with their heavy losses, the British and their Indian allies could look upon the bloody battle of Oriskany as a victory.[41] Perhaps as many as five hundred men perished at the hands of the Indians and the British, and probably no more than150 of the 800 men under Herkimer's command escaped without some serious injury. Four captured officers,

Oriskany Monument

as Blacksnake noted, were required to run the gauntlet and were killed. And Colonel Ebenezer Cox was a casualty. Herkimer was prevented from supplying relief to the beleagured fort. But, if the prelude at Oriskany can be considered a victory for the forces of Barry St. Leger, the siege of Fort Stanwix, which was the object of the expedition, has to be counted a miserable failure.

After the bloody business in the ravine, General St. Leger, with very modest artillery, surrounded the fort, which was garrisoned by 700-750 men, and on the evening of the 8th, sent one of his officers, at first thought to be the Tory John Butler himself, but now known to be Captain Gilbert Tice, "under a flag of truce" to the stockade. He was blindfolded, and when admitted delivered the written ultimatum to surrender. Not surprisingly, the fort's commander, no less stubborn and courageous than he had been five days ago, stoutly refused. Colonel Gansevoort drew himself up to his full six-feet-three, and declared in a carefully measured tone: "Sir, in answer to your letter of today's date I have only to say that it is my determined resolution with the forces under my command to defend this fort at every hazard to the last extremity in behalf of the United American States who have placed me here to defend it against all their enemies." [42]

Peter Gansevoort

As it happened, the assault launched by Herkimer, together with the most effective sortie led by Colonel Willett, had bought Gansevoort the necessary time. The siege of Fort Stanwix, begun on August 3, ended on August 22 in a standoff. St. Leger, with the information that a large force under General Benedict Arnold was on its way to relieve the garrison, considered withdrawing. He did not have to study for long. As the impression of danger grew stronger, panic began to seize the encampment, and Indians and soldiers alike began to flee. St. Leger was powerless to stop the flight. He afterwards blamed it on the Indians, who apparently were indeed the first to abandon the ground, though some analysts of the siege are not so quick to blame the warriors. In any case, the Siege of Fort Stanwix, while including a deadly slaughter, terribly costly to the Americans, was in the end an embarrassing failure for the British. General St. Leger, in one of the most understated observations of the entire Revolution, dolefully allowed of the fort that "we were not masters of its speedy subjection." Perhaps others could see in the failed siege an intimation of what lay at the end for the Burgoyne campaign.

And the Senecas, the Mohawks, the Cayugas, and the Onondagas, under the leadership of their spirited war-chiefs Old Smoke, Cornplanter, and Joseph Brant were now in the war for good.

Meanwhile, Howe, inexplicably, had not reached Albany. Burgoyne had taken Fort Ticonderoga (July 6) with very little trouble, but had found his march southward extremely difficult because of the Green Mountain Boys. At Saratoga, which he reached on October 17, he was stopped abruptly. In a defeat that many historians of the Revolution consider, though it was early, to be the decisive battle of the War, the forces of General Burgoyne were soundly routed by the Rebels under Benedict Arnold, Horatio Gates, and Daniel Morgan. In a concerted, all-out effort, now called the Saratoga Campaign, the British, hoping to put an end to the war in one way, may very well have ended it in another.

Among the devastating war-time raids on the frontier settlements, and now thought of as a warm-up for the blood bath that was to occur at Wyoming, was the battle of Cobleskill. On May 30, 1778, the tiny settlement in the Schoharie Valley was approached by a large war party of Senecas and Mohawks. The settlement was defended by patriot forces numbering 30-50 men under the command of Captains Parker and Christian Brown. The colonials were lured into a cunning ambush prepared by Joseph Brant. Under the impression that they were driving off a very small party of Indians, they were led into the trap.

Twenty-two of the defenders were killed, six were wounded, and two were captured. And the Indians destroyed twenty buildings of the settlement. Whether Cornplanter was a party to this raid, the only major engagement involving Indians between Oriskany and Wyoming, we do not know. Blacksnake's narrative is confused at this point, and he may himself not have been involved.[43] Joseph Brant, whose Mohawks made up much of the war party, seems to have had the command. In any case, the raid on Cobleskill was but a prelude to a greater horror.

VI

WYOMING

The Susquehanna River is one of the principal waterways of the Indian country now known as Pennsylvania. The West Branch of the wandering river flows east from its source at Cherry Tree some 150 miles to Williamsport, then abruptly turns south. The North (or East) Branch flows west a little on its way out of New York State, then south and east to meet its sister at Northumberland before striking out for the Chesapeake. One of the names given by the Indians to the North Branch is M'chewamisipu, "the river on which lie extensive clear flats."

These broad, clear flats, fertile and lush, are beautiful, spread out as they are on either side of the broad river. Perhaps the most beautiful of all is the valley known as Wyoming. No one has looked upon it but what he or she has sought in vain to account for the rapture of the scene. A noble effort was delivered in 1786 by Colonel Timothy Pickering, who was soon to be named Postmaster General of the United States and would later become Secretary of War and Secretary of State in President Washington's cabinet. When for the first time he came into a view of the valley he declared it "the most beautiful tract of land my eyes ever beheld!" He insisted that industrious farmers could make the whole a garden.[1] Some years later Reverend Edmund D. Griffin of Columbia University reported: "A scene more lovely than imagination ever painted presented itself to my sight—so beautiful, so exquisitely beautiful . . . ."[2] So it has been for thousands of years, and so is it still.

It is no wonder that those who come to Wyoming long to remain, no wonder that they become so possessive. It should surprise no one to learn that the valley and its embracing forests were for centuries the favored hunting grounds of the First Americans, and were to become the envy of the white settlers.

And it is no wonder either that a garden spot like this would invite violence—for it is a fatal beauty that is presented by the Valley of Wyoming. What happened at Wyoming during the latter years of the eighteenth century does not accord well at all with the quiet repose of the land along the beautiful river.

The story that concerns us here begins a long time ago with the rival claims of two of the colonies, Pennsylvania and Connecticut, for the land that had always belonged to the Indians. We have a foreshadowing of things to come in the first Indian massacre in the Valley of Wyoming. In the space of an hour, on the fifteenth of October, 1763, a Connecticut settlement was completely wiped out by a marauding band of Delawares. The discovery that was made by a company of Pennsylvania Rangers has been graphically described. It comes to us as an extract from a letter dated at Paxtamy, Lancaster County, October 23, 1763, and printed in *The Pennsylvania Gazette,* Number 1818, for October 27, 1763: "Our party under Captain Clayton is returned from Wyoming, where they met no Indians, but found the New Englanders, who had been killed and scalped a day or two before they got there. They buried the Dead, nine Men and one Woman, who had been most cruelly butchered; the Woman was roasted, and had two hinges in her hands, supposed to have been put in red hot; and several of the Men had Awls thrust into their Eyes, and Spears, Arrows, Pitchforks &c., sticking in their Bodies. They burned what houses the Indians left, and destroyed a Quantity of Indian Corn. The Enemy's tracks were up the River towards Wighalousing." [3]

Charles Miner, in his *History of Wyoming,* reflects on the tragedy: "The season had been favorable; their various crops on those fertile plains had proved abundant, and they were looking forward with hope to a scene of prosperity and happiness; but suddenly, without the least warning, on the 15th of October, a large party of savages raised the war-whoop, and attacked them with fury. Unprepared for resistance, about twenty men [later reports say thirty] fell and were scalped; the residue, men, women, and children, fled, in wild disorder, to the mountains. Language can not describe the sufferings of the fugitives as they traversed the wilderness, destitute of food or clothing, on their way to their former homes." [4]

In spite of atrocities like this, families from both Connecticut and Pennsylvania vied for the Wyoming Valley land, and not until 1799 (!) did the dispute (called the Pennamite Wars) come to an end, the Connecticut settlers giving up their claim.

Through much of this time, of course, a bigger war was in progress. The King of England continued to regard the colonies as just that—colonies. He was determined to put down the insurrection which had broken out. Connecticut and Pennsylvania, like the other eleven, were still the subjects of the crown. And a large population of the colonists remained loyal to George III. As it happened, the moment of truth for the valley of Wyoming was not an event of the Pennamite Wars, but an event of the Revolution.

The horrors of the Battle of Wyoming have fascinated historians for 220 years, and many are the accounts. Not all are accurate; in fact, none can be accurate. Some, especially those which appeared early, were composed out of such feeling and out of such confusion that they cannot be trusted in their details. Nevertheless, it would be difficult to exaggerate by much the terror of that day and night. The most faithful account, even the most restrained report, would chill the blood. If ever the term *massacre* was apt, it was most fitting for Wyoming on July 3 of 1778.

For the Connecticut settlers uneasy were the days of the early summer. Though hard at work, in the fields and on their buildings, everybody lived in fear and apprehension. One chronicler reports that "a sinister terror and suspicion," the kind that "so cruelly attends civil wars, religious wars, and witchmanias," now enveloped the valley. He describes the climate: "Sounds on the roads at night, heard through barred doors and windows, the hooded light in the field, were not friends or neighbors, but a man who lived in a lonely house in bitter loyalty to what cause no one knew. The little knot of men going north in the moonlight was a militia patrol going up the Susquehanna, or secret agents slipping out toward Niagara. There was something fearful in every footfall. The lone valley, pictured by so many as an Arcadia, was in reality a caldron in the hills boiling with greed and violence and fear." [5]

Blacksnake names in his autobiographical narrative the most celebrated of the 464 warriors who were accompanying Major John Butler and his 110 Rangers in their approach to the settlement: Sagwarithra, a Tuscarora sachem; Gahkoondenoiya of the Onondagas; Fish Carrier, a Cayuga; the Senecas Little Beard, Hiokatoo, Jeskaka (Little Billy), Honeyeus (Farmer's Brother), Dah-gon-wa-sha (Twenty Canoes), Donnegoesha (Jack Berry), Gahgeote (Half Town), Cornplanter, Ganiodaio (Handsome Lake), and Red Jacket, who was at the time still a very young man, about the same age as Cornplanter. Cornplanter, it needs to be noted, is at this time not only a celebrated warrior, but a chief, and not only a chief, but one of the two war-chiefs named by the Senecas (their traditional right in the league) to command the Iroquois.[6]

Wyoming, in those days called Westmoreland, was an attractive target. It was quite helplessly exposed, situated as it was some sixty miles from the white settlements east and south.[7] Butler's party apparently came downriver to Bowman's Creek, then across the mountain to Fort Wintermoot, arriving on the last day of June, 1778. On the way they came upon the Jenkins, Harding, and Gardner families. What chroniclers now call "the Harding massacre" abruptly occurred. Eight men of these families, ignorant of any hostile presence, had proceeded out that morning to work the fields. The Indians fell upon them, killing four, and taking three prisoner. John Harding, just a snip of a boy, escaped by secreting himself amid leafy willow boughs which overhung the water.[8] "Remember the Hardings!" was afterwards to become a rallying cry for the defenders at Wyoming.

The war party, and especially the Indians, were somewhat unsettled when they discovered before them now a number of occupied forts, manned, Butler was informed, by some 800 soldiers. While curbing the Indian enthusiasm for plundering, Butler made overtures to the forts and urged surrender. On July 1, both Wintermoot's Fort, under the command of Lt. Elisha Scovell, and Jenkins' Fort capitulated. Forty Fort (or Fort Forty), so named for the forty pioneers who had built it, and located right on the banks of the river, defied the ultimatum.

Graymont, via Blacksnake, reports that "Cornplanter with ten warriors [apparently including Blacksnake] crawled up a hill overlooking Forty Fort and counted the American militiamen within, watching them as they went through their various military exercises."[9] In describing this reconnoitering expedition, Blacksnake feels obliged to note that the timid Red Jacket discreetly remained "behind the main body of Indians."[10]

The defenders, under the command of Colonel Zebulon Butler and Colonel Nathan Dennison, fearing a long and perhaps fatal siege, resolved to meet the enemy in the field. When they marched out from the fort, at two o'clock in the afternoon, "they must have presented to the Indians a most gratifying sight." What followed has been vividly described by historian Graymont. Her account has the Rangers and Indians resorting to the Indians' favorite deception:

> *Butler ordered the two captured forts set afire, to give the impression of retreat, then had his force lie prostrate on the ground in the woods to await the approach of the Americans. When within 200 yards of the forest the*

> *Americans fired their first volley. The Indians and the Rangers lay quiet. At 100 yards, the Americans having fired three volleys, Sayenqueraghta, from his perch on horseback, gave the signal and the Indians opened fire, followed by a burst from the Rangers. The distance was so close and the fire so accurate that the Americans suffered greatly. The Indians closed in around the flanks and the American left wing attempted to fall back to a more advantageous position. The move was mistaken by the rest of the militiamen for a retreat, and the result was a rout. Many threw away their guns in their flight, while the Indians pursued relentlessly, giving no quarter. A few of the militiamen were fortunate enough to reach Forty Fort. Others were forced into the river where they were tomahawked. A number were able to swim to safety. Others were cut down while they fled from the field of battle. The shooting had lasted only a half hour before the militia fled in all directions. It was a pathetic remnant that made its way back to the fort.*[11]

From an earlier historian we have a similar picture of the frantic flight: "Men hid under the bushes in the water; some swam down the river with bullets striking around them, others crawled under rocks and in hollow logs, some ran as long as their legs would carry them. They went across the mountains, down the valley, anywhere to escape. They were desperately frightened, as well they might be, for all who did not speedily put themselves out of reach of the Indians' spears, tomahawks, and scalping knives, were murdered without mercy. The individual tragedies on the river and island were as fearful as those on the plain, while those taken prisoner had to face and suffer a fiendish death." [12]

Blacksnake in his narrative describes the fighting as it concerned him. Again he cannot remember how many he killed in the bloody business. He does appreciate that he was very lucky to have survived it. And Cornplanter's experience was doubtless the same, for the Indian warrior-chiefs, as was customary, were not supervising from the sidelines but constantly in the midst of the violence. Here is Blacksnake:

> *But as for mysilfe what I Done During the actions of this Battle—as I Start when all the Rest Start from*

> *But I Did not see of the Rest of them for some time after I got into the amongs the in the village, first man I came to him I fire it at him and kill em But in the Next one I just took the Butt end of my gun over head Down he went mind him no more about it Exspected him Dead, But in the third one I took him the same a way thought I may take his Skull as I Drawed my knife to his head and lookin back and saw this the sam man that I butt him over, just come to me, and Drawed his gun and appointed to me and was so Near to Sprong at him and he fire the gun at me But just as he fire there was the Indian behind him I give the war whoop just touch my clothes with his Ball never Draw no Blood out of me, I had me knife in hand I just Drawed upon his throat and cut it Down he go the second time I says to mysilfe now I guest Stayed Down and off again for another one, I run I saw a cobble [couple of] Indian wound it, and they are at able to go on I Run on farther and tell to other Indian to go Back and take care the Indian and Did so, I went to other Stret there was some more for me to Do I just than took my tomehawk and Strok one and to another and so on Don't minde anything about criing woman and children and men some just Diing some fighting and all Shap there was not many gun fired that fight, and Did not last great while another I Did not know how many I kill, only I kill some many and I have gon By very norrow places to be Kill mysilfe . . . .* [13]

Still the worst was to come. As evening settled over the bloody ground, the Indians, completely out of the control of Butler and his officers, and, whether inspired or simply unrestrained by their own chiefs, entered into an orgy of cruelty and torture that violates every sense of the humane. Fierce assaults were made upon the individual homes scattered throughout the valley and frightful atrocities perpetrated. And then the savage celebration, about which so much has been written. One historian, while noting the horror, declares he will not turn the picture with its face to the wall. "It is indelibly engraven on the minds of the civilized world and will remain." [14]

Near Tioga Point, not far from the battle scene, reposed Catherine's Town, the village of Queen Esther. It was a substantial village of some seventy houses. From her home here came the fiend of the night, to avenge, history infers, the death of her only son, who had been slain just the day before the battle. Queen Esther is the central figure of Wyoming's most awful moment. At the spot where an enormous boulder emerged from the ground she presided, and herself carried out the executions. The scene has been described a thousand times, and doubtless in many cases exaggeration occurs, but, as has been wisely noted, no account could ever "convey to our mind an adequate conception of what occurred." [15]

To the rock were brought the prisoners captured from the river and the swamp, some who had given up their persons to the promise that they would not be harmed. There were at least twelve, perhaps as many as sixteen. Here is one of the many descriptions we have of Queen Esther at the rock:

> *A fire was built on the level plain. The prisoners brought within the center, where they could witness the delight and feel the hatred of their tormentors. They knew how to get up a dramatic scene of the most fearful and spectacular character. The one at Wyoming was complete in every particular. The Indian was dressed for the occasion. The scalps were gloated over. They struck up their awful music and performed their grotesque dance. They shouted, whooped and grinned, the scene becoming a wild carnival that filled the hearts of the savages with delight. They knew that on the morrow they could turn themselves loose and plunder and burn without restraint. They came to the valley for revenge and plunder, and their day had come. They were wild men and this was their reward. Let us pass over the fate of the victims that suffered and were left mutilated and lifeless when the orgie was over. Queen Esther had presided and the death maul had done its work. The men who escaped at that time give us a good description that leaves little for the imagination.* [16]

In another version we have the prisoners placed in a circle with an Indian behind each, and Queen Esther going round the circle and braining each one with a tomahawk, except for one or two who somehow broke away and escaped. [17] And William Leete Stone, who, together with Blacksnake, takes exception to the presence of Queen Esther, in his *History of Wyoming* has the prisoners in two separate rings, sixteen in one, and nine in another. He has the prisoners murdered by the women. In any version the descriptions of the murders are so blood curdling that some historians are inclined to regard the whole episode as a myth. Too awful to have happened.[18] But Colonel John Franklin, writing in 1828 for the Towanda *Republican*, declares that a large number of soldiers surrendered on the battlefield and that these were afterwards most inhumanely murdered.[19]

Colonel Zebulon Butler with his wife at some time in the night fled the fort. Terms to govern in the case of all remaining forts were agreed to, on July 4, by Colonel Dennison (name spelled variously) and Major John Butler.[20]

For the battle of Wyoming and the cruelties that followed we have great confusion in the reports, both for the numbers involved, and for the count of casualties. Benson Lossing, in his *Pictorial Field-Book of the Revolution*, reports that the red and white men who came down the Susquehanna in canoes under Butler and camped, July 2, upriver from Fort Jenkins, numbered 1100. Richard Cartwright, who was with the expedition, suggests a number half of that. According to his tally, the force was composed of 574, and 110 were Rangers.[21] But as late as 1968, one researcher was accepting Lossing's figures, noting that at the time of its assault Major John Butler's force numbered "four hundred British and Tories and seven hundred Indians, mostly Senecas." [22] As for casualties, Butler's account does not accord with that of Dennison. We do know that the Indians killed and scalped *at least* 227 persons. We know this, because, as promised by the British, the Indians received ten dollars for each scalp, the records showing the delivery of 227.[23] John Mohawk, a Seneca, in an encyclopedic account prepared in 1996, notes that "more than 300 Americans were killed in this action (and fewer than ten Indians and Rangers) while eight forts and a thousand (!) dwellings were destroyed." [24]

Many who try to assess the carnage that was wrought, who try to explain to themselves how such horrors could be perpetrated by human beings upon each other, remind us that the Indian is conditioned throughout his life to such cruelty and torture. It is what he expects when captured. It is what he practices when the day is his. Benjamin Gilbert, who was taken from his farm on the Pennsylvania frontier and held captive, declared that the Indians "from infancy are taught a hardness of heart which deprives them of the common feelings of humanity." [25] Others insist that the Indians so much revere courage that they mistake uncommon acts of cruelty for it. But these explanations do little to ease the pain or assuage the feelings of abhorrence common to every heart. We look for something more, some thing or some one to blame for the unholy slaughter. Whom *are* we to blame? Surely history will indict, first of all, the commander of the Tory forces, Major John Butler, not only because he is ultimately responsible for the behavior of his troops, but because he actually admitted to an incapacity to control the Indians, and may even have been unable to hold back the ever-present rum.[26] What of the other officers, and the Rangers themselves? What of the Indian chiefs? For many years it was supposed that the Mohawk Joseph Brant was responsible for these horrors, but exhaustive investigation has "acquitted him of any participation at Wyoming." And in fact, there may have been involved no Mohawks at all. According to the celebrated chief Captain Pollard, who was quite young at this time but active in the battle, the leader of the Indians was Sayenqueraghta.[27] He and the lesser Seneca war-chiefs, including Cornplanter, should be considered responsible. Most probably we shall never know just how earnestly the Indian chiefs worked to restrain their warriors. At the moment we know only that whatever their effort it was in vain.

Some years after the Revolution had come to an end, and the colonists of the young nation had had time to bring some order to their recollections, there began to appear in the newspapers of the Wyoming region a number of letters and editorials urging the fitness of a monument erected to the memory of all who were lost here. Today a beautiful memorial remembers for the world forever what happened on that day and night. Today, within the limits of the borough of Wyoming, and between the site of the battlefield and Forty Fort there stands an impressive monument, sixty-two and one-half feet high, and presenting an impressive tablet, on which are recorded the 157 names of the defenders who perished here. Ceremonies occur here annually.

Queen Esther's rock remains also, at the southeast of the village. Much of the rock has been carried away by relic hunters, but it is now protected and can be viewed by the curious and the unbelieving.

VII

THE SULLIVAN CAMPAIGN

In the aftermath of the massacre, the Indians, and particularly the Iroquois, remained extremely active, all along the Pennsylvania frontier. History tends to fix on big events, naturally; often lost to posterity, therefore, are those incidents of war when casualties are few and consequences at first seem slight.

During the spring and summer leading up to the Wyoming disaster, and during the months immediately succeeding, atrocities occurred in an appallingly regular pattern. In fact, all of the years from this point on to a time long beyond the end of the Revolution were scarred by the same frequency of outrage.

Now the question for us is this: To what extent was the Seneca Chief Cornplanter involved in these border raids and outrages? Much of this Indian activity was the work of Delawares, and other Indian tribes were involved, but, clearly, the Senecas were conspicuous along the Pennsylvania-New York border, and many times the hostile Indians were identified as Senecas. It must be remarked also that while we have good records for Northumberland County they are by no means complete, and other counties of Pennsylvania, as well as many regions of New York which were within Cornplanter's purview, were reporting the same kind of outrage. Cornplanter is a Seneca chief. He is at this time (1777-1782), during the last years of the Revolution, still, remarkably, a very young warrior. He has the victory of Wyoming as a feather in his bonnet. He is at the head of the Iroquois alliance with the British. And with the defeat suffered by Burgoyne at Saratoga in October of 1777, the British were required to rely more and more upon the Iroquois, and most especially upon Cornplanter's warriors, the most powerful and fierce of them all.

The general anxiety and apprehension that these frequent atrocities occasioned among the settlers led in the fall of 1778 to organized reprisal. The Supreme Executive Council of Pennsylvania finally appreciated the necessity of providing a military defense of the frontier, and General Washington reluctantly recognized that the War of the Revolution would have to be fought on another front. The threat posed by the Indian allies of the King simply had to be acknowledged. And though Washington would have much preferred to fight Indians with Indians, he did not have the Indians to rely on; consequently he turned to the Continental Army, and made preparations to launch expeditions into the heart of the Indian country. But before the necessary soldiers could be assembled a great deal else occurred.

In September of 1778 Colonel Thomas Hartley's Pennsylvania regiment was called into action, together with a number of other troops of militia. One detachment of Hartley's regiment marched from New Jersey to Easton, uniting there with Colonel Kowatz. The remainder was ordered to march immediately from Philadelphia to Sunbury in Northumberland County, there to join with two companies lately formed in Wyoming.

Colonel Hartley was at this time thirty years old. He was a Pennsylvania-born practicing attorney and had been serving as a lieutenant colonel in Colonel William Irvine's Regiment of the Continental Army before his promotion to command of a regiment.[1] He had proved to be an able and resourceful military man, and was well suited for the assignment he was now accepting.

Hartley's Expedition, though modest when compared to that of Sullivan later, has to be counted a success. His forces, setting out from Fort Muncy on September 21, were able to negotiate the deep gorge of Lycoming Creek and make their way to Tioga. They were following what is known as the Sheshequin Path, a very rugged and formidable trail, and at this time made even more difficult by heavy rains. Hartley later reported that "The Difficulties in Crossing the Alps . . . could not have been greater than those our men experienced." [2] But his soldiers saw no sign of Indians until five days into the campaign. On this day Hartley's advance guard stumbled into a small party of warriors, who were so much surprised that they fled, although not in time to save "a very important . . . Chief," who was slain and scalped.[3] As the Indians were in full flight, Hartley might have assaulted the Indian village of Chemung, which he was approaching, but on learning of the great numbers of warriors quartered there he settled for the burning of Tioga and Catherine's Town.

Somewhat fatigued and almost completely without provisions, the company now started down the North (or East) branch of the Susquehanna, with many of the troops in captured canoes. Two skirmishes with ambushing Indians, whose numbers Hartley estimated at two hundred, cost the expedition four soldiers killed and twice that many more seriously wounded. The most considerable engagement was the second of these skirmishes, that fought at Wyalusing (Browntown Mountain),[4] on what is today called Indian Hill.[5]

If Governor Blacksnake's memoirs can be trusted, Chief Cornplanter, Red Jacket, Old Smoke, Blacksnake himself, "and all the . . . leading men [of the Six Nations, excepting Brant]" were in the midst of the battle. Blacksnake recalls how the Iroquois had heard from a runner that the Hartley Expedition was coming "to destroy the Delaware Nation of the Susquihannah." He describes how he and Cornplanter and the others prepared on short notice to provide help, and how in five days they had arrived in the region, only to find that with their 1400 (probably 200!) warriors they would be contending with Hartley's 3000 (200!) well armed men. But the Iroquois resolved to fight "till all Killed." He describes how the warriors, having chosen favorable ground received the enemy fire at "about 9 oclock A.M." and how until two o'clock in the afternoon the battle raged, with the Indians going at the enemy with "no mercy," but with tomahawks, knives, and swords, hardly ever firing guns. So fierce was the fighting that he thought he was sure to die.[6]

Blacksnake is clearly a good bit confused in his account of Wyalusing, for much of his description smacks of the battle of Oriskany, and certainly his tally for the battle, both in the numbers engaged and in the numbers slain, is absurd. He reported 2000 Americans killed, the rest in flight. And the losses to the Six Nations but five killed and a great many wounded. In fact, as noted above, Hartley lost four killed and ten wounded; the Indians ten dead. The "battle" could hardly be counted much more than a very sharp skirmish.[7]

Hartley, having dispatched a contingent of his force to support Colonel Zebulon Butler, who on August 4 had returned to Wyoming with 112 men, proceeded on downriver to Sunbury, where the two branches of the Susquehanna come together.

Although he never did catch up with Walter Butler and his Royal Greens, for they had just fled the region, he had set fire to Queen Esther's town and to other towns he came upon, including one, unfortunately, which was completely innocent. And not only did he burn the Indian villages in the region of Tioga, he confiscated a great deal of the plunder stolen by the Indians from Wyoming.[8] Hartley's expedition was meant to be punitive, and it certainly made a statement. For the short term it might be allowed that the campaign accomplished two things: It angered the Indians, not surprisingly, inflamed their naturally vengeful disposition, and inspired a fierce attack on the helpless village of Cherry Valley. Secondly, and ironically, the campaign, because of its military tactics and general deportment, and the damage that was done, practically insured the success of the Sullivan Expedition. Meanwhile . . . .

Cherry Valley is a sleepy village. It reposes fifty miles northwest of the city of Albany, the birthplace of Cornplanter's father, close to the source of the North Branch of the Susquehanna River and just a stone's throw from Otsego Lake. It was settled at just about the time that the Seneca Cornplanter came into this world. As the principal settlement south of the Mohawk, and located on a direct line between the Mohawk Castles and the Indian post at Oghkwaga, it was an obvious target, exposed and vulnerable. It was ill prepared, on November 11, 1778, for the Seneca Chief Cornplanter, the Mohawk Chief Joseph Brant, a horde of vengeful Indians, and British forces under the ruthless Walter Butler.[9]

As early as November 6, the officer in charge at Cherry Valley, Colonel Ichabod Alden, had received intelligence of the resolve of Butler and his Indian allies to attack. His response to this information was, tragically, to do nothing.

Butler's force was composed chiefly of Indians, most of them Senecas. Besides some 320 Indians, the party boasted 150 Rangers and fifty additional men from the British 8th Regiment.

From Blacksnake we have the names of the leading warriors, many of them fresh from the fighting at Wyoming: Cornplanter, Half Town, Little Beard, Little Billy, Farmer's Brother, Jack Berry, Twenty Canoes, Wundungohteh, Hiadeoni, Conneuesut, Souetdo, Hohnogwus, and Onongadaka.[10] Because Old Smoke was not present, Chief Cornplanter would seem to be at the head of the Senecas. Some thirty Mohawks were present, under the command of Joseph Brant, who had not been a party to the fighting at Wyoming. A very few Cayugas, Onondagas, and Delawares were in the company. The Tuscaroras who had been at Wyoming and were still under the leadership of Sagwarithra completed the war party.[11]

A Seneca warrior who was not a member of the company when it arrived at Cherry Valley was Red Jacket. According to his cousin Blacksnake, the young man, together with three companions, had vacated the enterprise while Butler was encamped somewhere between Chemung and Tioga. These deserters complained of "illness," but apparently they simply did not have the stomach for what was in store. Cornplanter would later reproach Red Jacket for cowardice (and so would Brant), and the warrior, though he became a great statesman and an inspiring orator, had to wait for the War of 1812 to lessen the blackness of that mark against him.

We do not know positively which of the Indian chiefs had assumed command. As noted above, it was most likely Cornplanter. The Seneca chief had been second in command at Wyoming, and had been impressive to the Indians. Now, in the absence of Old Smoke, it would seem the mantle would fall to him. Brant already enjoyed a big reputation among the Iroquois, but there were only thirty Mohawks on this expedition and probably 200-250 Senecas. Besides, we have the report of a white deserter. Some time after the battle he indicated to the Americans that the Seneca chief Cadaraqua and Brant were the Indian leaders. Since it appears that there was no "Cadaraqua" among the Iroquois chiefs, surely he was identifying Cornplanter.[12]

As Butler's forces, some 520 strong, drew ever nearer to the village, the chiefs Brant and Cornplanter, at the head of an advance party of some forty warriors, took four prisoners, whom they promptly presented to Butler. One of these, Adam Hunter, had Loyalist sympathies, and he provided for Butler the vital information concerning the size and the defense capacity of the garrison.[13] Butler, in a council with the Indian chiefs and his officers, disclosed his plans to assault the homes and the fort that very night. The Indians were in a mood to applaud the plan, and declared that they would observe "the same humanity towards women, children, and noncombatants as they had at Wyoming." [14]

The plan, however, had to be aborted and action postponed, for a relentless rain fell steadily through the night. But at first light the assault began, first with an attack on the house of Robert Wells, in which, Butler knew (presumably from Adam Hunter) that the commander of the fort, Alden, and his officers had their quarters. Little Beard's party of Senecas was in the van and overwhelmed the building. While desperately trying to escape to the fort, Alden was cut down by a tomahawk and scalped. Other officers and soldiers were slain, and a few were taken prisoner.[15]

The members of the Wells family were next. Little Beard turned his warriors loose on them. What the Indians did not appreciate sufficiently at this time was that the Wells family had enjoyed a close friendship with the Mohawk Chief Joseph Brant. They would later suffer the wrath of the distraught chief.

The massacre, for it was that, took its toll of at least forty-eight people, sixteen rebel soldiers and thirty-two civilians. Reportedly, both British and Indian commanders made earnest efforts to restrain the Indians, apparently determined in this way to show that they were not guilty of the atrocities of which they had been accused at Wyoming. But there was no holding them back Some students of the time regard Cherry Valley as a more horrible massacre than that which had occurred at Wyoming, or anywhere else so far in the Revolution, for here the rumors that women and children had been butchered turned out to be more than just rumors.[16]

The credit for all of this Mary Jemison preferred to bestow upon her husband. Her narrative reads: "In an expedition that went out against Cherry Valley and the neighboring settlements, Captain David, a Mohawk Indian, was first, and Hiokatoo the second in command. The force consisted of several hundred Indians, who were determined on mischief, and the destruction of the whites. A continued series of wantonness and barbarity characterized their career, for they plundered and burnt every thing that came in their way, and killed a number of persons, among whom were several infants, whom Hiokatoo butchered or dashed upon the stones with his own hands." [17]

As spring came on and hostilities intensified, Washington began steadily more and more to appreciate the need to address the "Indian problem." He had always felt that for the kind of fighting that characterized the frontier, Indians were needed to fight Indians. But now, even though of course he had no Indians (except for a handful of Delawares, and a few friendlies whom he could use as scouts and guides and runners), he was determined to carry the war to the Indian country. He was beginning to realize how damaging to the cause of the Revolution was the alliance between the British and the Iroquois.

And the year 1778 had simply proved to be too much for the American colonials. It was time to punish the Indians for Wyoming and Cherry Valley and for massacres like that occurring at Lycoming Creek on June 10. The Commander-in-Chief was compelled now to avenge these atrocities and to make the settlements along the frontier "safe."

In March of 1779 he began to search among his generals for the man to handle the Indian problem. After consulting with General Edward Hand, Colonel Zebulon Butler (who had had command at Wyoming), and the surveyor and one-time captive of the Indians, Lieutenant John Jenkins, Washington seemed to fix on Horatio Gates. As noted by Washington's biographer John Fitzpatrick, this was a remarkable choice, inasmuch as Gates was already known to Washington as vain and ambitious, and the kind of general who directs the battle from his tent. But he must have sensed, or hoped, that Gates would not accept the commission, for he worded his "appointment" letter in such a way as to make plain what would be required and what would be expected; and then he was careful to include in the dispatch to the general another letter addressed to Major General John Sullivan. This letter he directed Gates to forward to Sullivan if he did not himself care for the command.[18] And it worked. The general promptly responded: "Last night I had the honor of your Excellency's letter. The man who undertakes the Indian service, should enjoy youth and strength, requisites I do not possess. It therefore grieves me that your Excellency should offer me the only command to which I am entirely unequal. In obedience to your command I have forwarded your letter to General Sullivan." [19]

John Sullivan

But even Sullivan had his misgivings. First, he was not all that excited about the prospect of burning Indian villages through the summer; and, second, he was not confident that there was value to it. But after turning it over in his mind for a week he finally agreed at least to meet with Washington (at Middle Brook) to discuss the enterprise.

As Washington explained it to Sullivan, the campaign was not for show. It was to be punitive, of course; it was to put the Indians "in their place." But he was hoping that the villages and fields of the Indians could be so completely destroyed as to render their aid to the British negligible. To disable the British war machine—that was the primary mission. The expedition would be two-pronged in its organization, for Brigadier General James Clinton, father of one Colonial governor and brother to another, would lead a force along the Mohawk west while Sullivan was marching from the south up the Susquehanna. Or it might be called three-pronged, for Colonel Daniel Brodhead would at the same time command a force which would operate in the West, moving up the Allegheny north from Pittsburgh and into the Seneca country. If all went as planned, these three forces would come together at some convenient point, "advance against the stronghold of the enemy [the villages in the region of the finger lakes] in such force as could not possibly be resisted and then overrun the whole Iroquois country west of the Oneida villages."[20]

The plan called for a junction of Clinton's forces with Sullivan's wherever Sullivan would suggest. Brodhead's had become almost a separate operation. On the first day of May the columns set out, but Sullivan did not arrive at Wyoming until the middle of June, and was not assembled well enough to leave before the last day of July. Meanwhile the Indians and Tories had learned of the mission and had determined on assaults of their own.

Three days before the forces of General Sullivan were able to launch the Expedition from Wyoming, the tiny fort of Freeland, perched on Warrior's Run on the Susquehanna's West Branch, was savagely attacked by Captain John McDonnell[21] in command of a force of fifty Rangers and some British Regulars. Leading the major portion of the entire force, at the head of 120 Senecas and Cayugas, was Chief Cornplanter.[22] Blacksnake told Draper that among the Seneca participants, besides the Chief Cornplanter, were Jack Berry, Hiokatoo, Handsome Lake, Farmer's Brother, and Little Beard.[23]

Warrior's Run enters the West Branch of the Susquehanna four miles upstream from present-day Milton, Pa. The fort was located about two and a half miles still farther up the Susquehanna, but quite close to the small stream. The fort was garrisoned by twenty-one soldiers and sheltered fifty women and children. A number of reports, cited in the *Pennsylvania Archives* and in the *Colonial Records*, account, although with much confusion, for the destruction of the fort, which was rapid and complete.

There had been plenty of warning. Ominous neighborhood incidents were being reported with a steadily increasing frequency and Indians were being sighted everywhere in the region throughout the spring and early summer of this year, 1779. Fort Freeland itself had had its troubles. On April 26 it had suffered a fierce assault, called a "massacre" in eyewitness accounts, from unidentified Indians. On the day following, April 27, Colonel Samuel Hunter, writing from his post at Fort Augusta, dispatched a letter to "His Excellency, Joseph Reed, Esqr., President of the Supreme Executive Council," then in session in Philadelphia: "Yesterday, there was another party of Indians, about thirty or forty, kill'd and took seven of our Militia, that was stationed at a little Fort near Muncy Hill, call'd Fort Freeland; there was two or three of the inhabitants taken prisoner; among the latter is James McKnight, Esqr., one of our Assemblymen; the same day a party of thirteen of the inhabitants that went to hunt their Horses, about four or five miles from Fort Muncy was fired upon by a large party of Indians, and all taken or killed Except one man. Captain Walker of the Continental troops, who commands at that post, turned out with thirty-four men to the place he heard the fireing, and found four men kill'd and scalped, and supposes they Captured the Remainder." [24]

On the same day this massacre was reported to the Council by the surveyor William Maclay: "The whole Force of the six Nations seems to be poured down upon Us. How long we will be able to bear up under such complicated and Severe attacks, God only knows." [25]

In the summer of 1779 Fort Freeland, though but a small fort, as garrisoned forts go, was because of its position as one of two forts (Boone was the other) above Fort Augusta on the West Branch of the Susquehanna, and the most advanced, considered a "strong strategic post." By July conditions had worsened dramatically. As the Indian activity stepped up, the removal of supporting troops from the region became a matter of great distress to Colonel Hunter, commander of the

Fort at Augusta. In alarm he directed a dispatch to Colonel Matthew Smith on July 23. He recited a most distressing calendar of events for July.

But Colonel Hunter's letter had not yet been delivered when the trouble came. On July 29, the British Regulars and Rangers under Captain John McDonnell and a horde of Senecas and Cayugas under Cornplanter, and including Handsome Lake, Jack Berry, Farmer's Brother, and Little Beard, assaulted the tiny fort. The stockade contained a great number of women and children, but was defended by only twenty-one men.[26] In one account the attackers number 200 British and 300 Indians; in another the numbers are 100 and 200.[27] Still another provides figures of 100 British Regulars and 300 Indians.[28] No matter whose figures one goes with, it was clearly a mis-match. The fort was garrisoned by brave men, and they fought stubbornly against the terrible odds, but they were few, and before long their ammunition was expended. In the space of three hours it was all over, "its defenders either victims of the tomahawk or prisoners of war, the women and children objects of charity in the stronger fortification at Fort Augusta." [29]

Once the fort had capitulated the Indians took possession. Here is Mary Jemison's account: "The women and children were sent under an escort to the next fort below [Boone], and the men and boys were taken off by a party of British to the general Indian encampment. As soon as . . . the firing had ceased, Hiokatoo with the help of a few Indians tomahawked every wounded American while earnestly begging with uplifted hands for quarters." [30]

There are scores of eye-witness reports and a great many historical accounts. In one it is noted that the Indian women who were with the war party went wild, became "mischievous and destructive." When admitted to the surrendered fort, "they ripped open the feather beds, emptying the contents in a heap and burning them, while they danced about with fiendish glee." Whatever they could not carry away they destroyed. After the fort had been plundered, they rode off on the side saddles they had stolen, "in mockery of the women." [31]

The warriors and Captain McDonnell's men meanwhile had assembled on Warrior's Run and were celebrating by feasting. What they did not know is that when the siege was begun the firing could be heard at Fort Boone, which was just four miles to the south. In charge of the garrison there was Captain Hawkins Boone, a cousin of the famous

Daniel Boone. At the head of a relief party of thirty-two "as brave men as ever fired a gun" he set out for Fort Freeland.[32]

According to one account, Boone and his men found the Indians at their feast and carrying on in great glee on the opposite bank of the run and at once fired a volley into them, killing about thirty. The forces of Captain McDonnell and Cornplanter, however, surrounded the small party, and dispatched almost half, including Boone himself.[33]

Mary Jemison's version of this phase of the battle is a little different, and gives more prominence to Hiokatoo: "The massacre was just finished when Capts. Dougherty and Boon arrived with a reinforcement to assist the garrison. On their arriving in sight of the fort they saw that it had surrendered, and that an Indian was holding the flag. This so much inflamed Capt. Dougherty that he left his command, stept forward and shot the Indian at the first fire. Another took the flag, and had no sooner got it erected than Dougherty dropt him as he had the first. A third presumed to hold it, who was also shot down by Dougherty. Hiokatoo, exasperated at the sight of such bravery, sallied out with a party of his Indians, and killed Capts. Dougherty, Boon, and fourteen men, at the first fire. The remainder of the two companies escaped by taking to flight, and soon arrived at the fort which they had left but a few hours before."[34]

The fall of Fort Freeland excited consternation in central Pennsylvania, and settlers as far away as Williamsport and Lock Haven and the Great Island in the Susquehanna began to evacuate their homes and join the great runaway. Dispatches describing the destruction of the fort went out in a steady stream to General Sullivan, to the President of Pennsylvania, and to Pennsylvania's Executive Council.

Certainly it would be difficult to exaggerate when attempting to assess the significance of the collapse of this frontier fort. We have first of all the terrible toll that was taken in human lives. One tally shows 108 settlers killed or led away as prisoners, "not alone by the Indians in their savage and cruel treachery, but as well by the organized militia of Great Britain." Besides, there is the toll taken of the attackers, numbering perhaps as many more. The collapse of the fort had the effect of cutting off support for the rear of Sullivan's army; it also increased the pressure on magazines and stores in the neighboring forts. For these reasons the assault on Fort Freeland on July 29, 1779, "marks this as a definite battle of the Revolution."[35]

With Wyoming and Cherry Valley fresh in his mind, the surveyor William Maclay was inspired by what had happened at Freeland to revitalize the suggestion made twenty-four years ago by Benjamin Franklin that these Indians should be hunted down by dogs.[36]

Cornplanter and McDonnell had marched from the vicinity of Wyalusing, in present-day Bradford County. After the surrender of the fort, the war party plundered freely, and burned much of the country between Muncy Hill, north of Freeland, and Northumberland, downriver from the fort. According to one report, the expedition, following the taking of the fort, "burnt thirty miles of a close-settled country, which inhabitants had abandoned." [37] The war party killed sixteen men and took thirty others back to Niagara as prisoners. Records contained in the *Pennsylvania Archives* append this note: "As usual, women and children were left unharmed." [38] The Indian forces involved here would soon repair to the north country to resist as best they could the army of General Sullivan.

It was the first real battle of the Sullivan campaign, and, slight though it seemed to be, and though it was in the rear of Sullivan and did not actually involve his force, it was to be the only engagement that the Butlers and Old Smoke, and Joseph Brant, and Cornplanter, who would head up the resistance throughout, could possibly feel good about.

Finally the Expedition of General Sullivan lumbered into motion. It was very, very slow to get underway. The General had marshaled his forces at Easton. He arrived there in the first week of May, and in short order had assembled three brigades (3500 soldiers) under the veteran and battle hardened Generals William Maxwell, Edward Hand and Enoch Poor. Colonel Thomas Proctor's artillery arrived on May 20. But not for almost a month more was Sullivan provisioned and ready to go. *Finally*, at 5:00 in the morning of June 18, the General broke camp at Easton and began the trek to Wyoming. The most ambitious anti-Indian campaign of the Revolutionary War had been launched.

With some very rugged, but beautiful country to negotiate, the army on its march from Easton to Wyoming proceeded in an order which had General Maxwell's brigade in the van, followed by Proctor's regiment of artillery, then Poor's brigade, and last the baggage train, General Hand having been dispatched to round up additional provisions. Very alert to this movement were the Indians who would head up the resistance, such as it would be—the Mohawk Joseph Brant, the Senecas Cornplanter, Old Smoke, and Blacksnake, the war-chief Fish Carrier of the Cayugas, and Sagwarithra of the Tuscaroras.

For three days the soldiers fought their way through very dense stands of pine, poplar, oak and chestnut, as well as some very dense mountain laurel. The fourth day was rougher still, for, following a very narrow Indian trail, they were led into the Great Swamp and trees that were so lush and reached so high that no sunlight penetrated the forest. The constant gloom had inspired the name "Shades of Death" for notation on their maps. Somehow on this fourth day the troops made twenty miles, but by the time they were setting up tents they were so exhausted that Sullivan named the place Camp Fatigue. And because they had marched so far, and because some of the supply wagons did not reach the encampment until midnight the General proclaimed a day of rest. One of the sentinels who were posted at the camp reported the sighting of a bear and a wolf, but no scout returned any report of Indians.

When, after five days, at last the army reached Wyoming, all were afforded from "a fine eminence" a most thrilling view of the settlement on the river. "There it is," exclaimed an officer, and those who knew about Wyoming were moved to remark, "So this is where it happened."

What they were remembering the Reverend William Rogers, the army's young chaplain, was turning over slowly in his own mind: "At the battle . . . about two hundred and twenty were massacred within the space of an hour and a half, more than one hundred of whom were married men; their widows afterwards had all their property taken from them and several of them with their children were made prisoners. It is said that Queen Esther, of the Six Nations, who was with the enemy, scalped and tomahawked with her own hands in cold blood eight or ten persons. The Indian women in general were guilty of the greatest barbarities. Since this dreadful stroke they have visited the settlement several times, each time killing, or rather torturing to death [those they found], more or less. Many of their bones continue yet unburied where the main action happened." [39]

Sullivan was much disappointed to discover that the additional stores and provisions he required were *still* not here in Wyoming. He was most impatient to get moving, but he would have to wait. And he feared that he might have to wait a very long time. All he could do during this last week of June was to stock in the boats the equipment that they had and ready his soldiers for the expedition up the Susquehanna. On the 29th some of the much needed supplies that he had been awaiting, upwards of thirty fully loaded boats, arrived from Sunbury downriver.

While provisions continued to arrive, some of the officers (General Maxwell, Colonels Proctor, Butler, and Israel Shreve), with a number of other gentlemen, were given a tour of the region. They visited the remains of Forty Fort, discovering skulls and bones on the field of battle, now twelve months old. Particularly gruesome was the "place of skulls" near Wintermoote's Fort (up the river four miles from Forty Fort), where Colonel Zebulon Butler's routed soldiers were horribly butchered. They came to a grave where seventy-five skeletons were buried; and farther on they discovered a plot where the grass was distinctly different from the grass everywhere else. Here, it was explained to them, "fourteen wretched creatures, who having surrendered upon being promised mercy, were nevertheless made to sit down in a ring, and after the savages had worked themselves up to the extreme of fury in their usual manner, by dancing, singing, halloaing, etc., they proceeded deliberately to tomahawk the poor fellows one after another." [40]

For these barbarities which they were hearing about, and for which there was ample evidence, Reverend Rogers blamed King George. "Good God!" said he, "Who, after such repeated instances of cruelty, can ever be totally reconciled to that government which divesting itself of the feelings of humanity, has influenced the savage tribe to kill and wretchedly torture to death, persons of each sex and of every age—the prattling infant, the blooming maid and persons of venerable years, have alike fallen victims to its vindictive rage." [41]

On the 9th of July, more boats, fifty of them, loaded with supplies, arrived from Sunbury. These boats were guarded by the Eleventh Pennsylvania Regiment, under the command of Lt. Colonel Adam Hubley. Once the boats were unloaded they whipped back out into the river and headed downstream to secure even more provisions. And when on Saturday the 24th, General Hand at last showed up with 112 loaded boats, General Sullivan sent word throughout the army, "Get ready to march!"

It had required more than a month for Sullivan to acquire all that he needed, including 1200 pack horses and more than 700 cattle! It was not until the last day of July that the Expedition was completely assembled and equipped and pronounced ready.

As the immense army moved out from Wyoming, it moved in two parts, one on the river and one on the shores. The artillery, together with "the ammunition, the salted provisions, flour, liquors, and heavy baggage," was consigned to a flotilla of boats. These boats, of all shapes and sizes, some of them newly built, numbered 214.[42] They were manned by 450 enlisted boatmen, together with 250 soldiers and Proctor's artillery.

At precisely 1:00 in the afternoon of this last day of July, after nearly three months of preparing and waiting, the expedition got underway. Most of the soldiers were enjoying their first-ever view of the beautiful Susquehanna Valley.

This was the country over which Cornplanter and Little Beard and Blacksnake and Red Jacket had been roaming ever since their early childhood. This was the country in which their ancestors had been hunting game for hundreds, perhaps thousands, of years. And what a spectacle it was. The region through which the army was passing, with the deep forests on either side, and the lush riverbanks, seemed awesome to all. But these soldiers were not poets.[43]

The best way to appreciate just exactly what happened during the months of the Sullivan Campaign, from July 31, 1779, and into October, is to march with the soldiers who formed the various companies. You can experience the campaign almost as if you were participating. Happily, you can actually do this. We have the journal accounts of twenty-seven officers who served with Sullivan. They provide *vivid*, day-by-day (almost hour-by-hour) impressions of the marches and of the battles, of the burning of the Indian villages, the destruction of the fields of corn and squash and cucumbers, of peach trees and other fruits. Of course there will occur for the reader a great deal of repetition, for the writers are observing the same thing, but in these diaries the campaign will come alive for the sensitive reader.

What strikes one as he or she pores through these pages is the awe by which the officers are overcome. They revel in the beauty of the forests, the white pine and the spruce, and in the sparkle of the mountain streams. They are impressed by the size of the Indian villages, and even more so by the vast fields of corn (some extending to 200 acres) with the stalks reaching to seventeen feet! Lieutenant William Barton declares early in the march that this is "the best part of the country I have seen since I left Wyoming." He speaks of the rich and fertile flats, of the lush mountains which embrace them. And Lt. Colonel Adam Hubley sets down an impression of the valley of the Chemung. He has his view from a mountain height: "The summit was gained with the greatest difficulty; on the top of the mountain the lands, which are level and extensive, are exceedingly rich with large timber, chiefly oak, interspersed with underwood and excellent grass. The prospect from this mountain is most beautiful; we had a view of the country of at least twenty miles round; the fine, extensive plains, interspersed with streams of water, made the prospect pleasing and elegant from this mountain."[44]

It rains nearly every day. Sometimes the rains are heavy; sometimes the days are simply dismally damp, shrouded in fog. The officers describe in their diaries the picking of huckleberries, the sighting of rattlesnakes and blacksnakes, fishing parties, corn roasts, the execution of deserters and traitors, the monotonous hours of sentinel duty. They have news that Spain is declaring war against Great Britain.

Proctor's artillery had plenty to do. Besides the normal work of the artillery in "softening up" the hostile forces which may be making a stand, or lurking in ambush, the cannon crews had General Sullivan's program to follow. This program called for announcing to Cornplanter and Brant and to Butler's Rangers just exactly where the army was—morning and evening. Through the booming of the cannon, the location of the army was precisely established for all who might be interested. Apparently it was Sullivan's intent, first, to let the Indians know that this army was on the march, that it was moving so many miles a day, and that its march was unrelenting. This army is coming on! Second, it seemed to suit General Sullivan to avoid actual battles. His mission was to lay waste the corn and to destroy the habitation, livestock and fruit trees; to do all he could to make life for the Indian difficult if not impossible. If Cornplanter and Brant chose to make a stand, so be it. If they preferred simply to withdraw and leave the army to its work, well, maybe all the better. He would make it easy for them. Besides that, Sullivan seemed to understand that the sound of cannon, which the Indians called "thunder trees," was an unsettling disturbance to them. Anyway, he had the cannon sounded, morning and evening.

The army moves four to sixteen miles a day. There are occasional glimpses of Indians and sometimes actual skirmishes, but the enemy stays about two days ahead of Sullivan.

On the thirteenth day out, in the region of Tioga (present-day Athens, Pa.) the forces come upon the first of the Indian settlements, and the work of devastation commences. About a week later Sullivan's main force is joined by the troops of General James Clinton and his huge flotilla of boats.[45]

Clinton's arrival, on Sunday, August 22, at 10 a.m., is noted in almost every journal account of the expedition. He had brought his five regiments (1800-2000 men) down the Susquehanna from Lake Otsego, which he had left on August 9. The union took place within a mile of Tioga,[46] that narrow wedge of land that lies between the Chemung River and the North Branch of the Susquehanna, just before the streams come together.

James Clinton

Now the army, with Clinton's regiments, boasts probably 5,000 men.[47] Sullivan has laid waste the village of Chemung, which had been abandoned by the Indians; Clinton has destroyed a settlement of the Onondagas. Butler and the Indians under Cornplanter, Old Smoke, and Brant, have yet to make a stand. On August 26, the expedition moves up the river toward the Indian village of Newtown. The campaign is about to heat up.

For at Newtown (present-day Elmira), Butler's Rangers and the warriors of Cornplanter and Brant have resolved to make a fight. Their force, it was discovered from captured men, was now 700 strong ("500 savages, and 200 Tories, with about 20 British troops, commanded by a Seneca chief [Old Smoke or Cornplanter, presumably], the 2 Butlers, Brandt, & McDonald [McDonnell]").[48] The battle, joined on Sunday, August 29, was to be the closest thing to a real engagement experienced during the whole expedition. It was also to be one of the most important battles of the war for Cornplanter and the Seneca Indians.

With the strong impression that a stand was going to be made by the Indians on the next day, the Sullivan army made camp near the ruins of Chemung. The customary patrols were sent out, and were not long in reporting evidence to confirm the feeling. Major Jeremiah Fogg recalled for his journal that the patrol led by Captain Jason Wait perceived smoke from a number of fires that evening; and that six miles up the trail (north) fortifications were recognizable.[49]

As one historian put it, "As morning dawned on the 29 August, every soldier in Sullivan's army expected he would find himself in a fight before the end of the day." [50]

It was Sullivan's hope that the artillery could produce enough of a barrage to keep the Indians pinned down and buy enough time for General Poor to outflank them. So he had Proctor's guns deployed about 300 yards away and "directly in front of a long breastwork," which was manned by the warriors of Cornplanter and Old Smoke; and then he dispatched the flanking force of infantry to the left of the ambuscade to cut off any retreat. At just about three o'clock in the afternoon, he ordered the cannon to fire.

General John S. Clark, who years later carefully studied the scene and researched the conduct of the battle, reports that the conflict was "short, sharp, and decisive," that "the war whoop soon gave place to the retreat halloo." His account continues: "Poor with the remainder of his brigade, followed by the two regiments on the right of Clinton, had pushed rapidly for the defile. In the meantime Hand had advanced in front, and the left flanking division under Col. Ogden had worked its way along the river on the enemy's flank, when, the enemy, admirably commanded, and wisely discreet, sounded the signal for retreat just in time to escape." [51]

Later that afternoon Butler and Cornplanter and the Indian chiefs attempted to arrest the panic, but to no avail. According to one British account, "In this action Col. Butler and all his people was surrounded, and very near being taken prisoners. On the same day a few miles from this he attempted again to stop them, but in vain." [52]

Casualties were light on both sides. Colonel Butler "lost four rangers killed, two taken prisoner and seven wounded." And Clark reports that "Twelve Indians were found dead on the field, the number of wounded unknown. The enemy were pursued for two or three miles above Newtown by the light troops, where . . . they made another stand, which appears to be confirmed by the report [of the British] above quoted, but no details are given, and the matter is not alluded to in Gen. Sullivan's official report. The loss in killed according to the Indian official account, found four days after, near Catharine's town, showed: Sept. 3d.—This day found a tree marked 1779, Thandagana, the English of which is Brant, 12 men marked on it with arrows pierced through them, signifying the number they had lost in the action of the 29th ultimo. A small tree was twisted round like a rope and bent down [to signify] that if we drove and distressed them, yet we would not conquer them." [53]

Casualty figures for the action vary some in the many reports of the battle. But on the day following the battle, General Sullivan in his report produced the official figures. For his troops he had the total loss at three killed and thirty-nine wounded.

Colonel John Butler, who had been in charge of the Indian defense at Newtown, had afterwards great praise for Sullivan's artillery. He attributed the general consternation of the Indians to the effect of Proctor's six-pounders. He noted that the Americans had "six pieces of Cannon & Cohorns," which began "discharging shells, round & grape shot, Iron Spikes &c. Incessantly which soon obliged us to leave . . . ." He describes the flight: "The shells bursting beyond us, made the Indians imagine the Enemy had got their Artillery all round us, & so startled & confounded them that [a] great part of them run off." In fact, Butler notes, they panicked and were pell-mell in their flight: "Many of the Indians made no halt, but proceeded immediately to their respective Villages . . . ." [54] No wonder General Sullivan had the cannon fired morning and night, all through the expedition.

But the great irony here is that Sullivan did not want the Indians to flee. In a way, the artillery was too effective, perhaps too zealous. While it was actually the element that won the battle, Proctor's artillery could be blamed for the failure of the army to achieve the kind of victory that was desired.

Lt. Obadiah Gore notes that at three o'clock p. m. "we began a cannonade upon the breast-work, and in about six minutes [!] they began to run and quit their works, which our advance party took possession of immediately." That it was a panicky exit which ensued, just as Butler had described, Gore's description confirms: "The right flank of the enemy, in their flight, fell in with General Poor's brigade, who gave them a warm reception, which put them in such precipitation, as to leave packs, blankets, guns, powder and even an officer's commission etc. We found 9 dead and took 2 prisoners, and have reason to think that considerable other execution was done, as there was great quantities of blood found in their paths." [55]

It has been suggested that General Sullivan at Newtown ordered the artillery fire a little too early, for Poor had not yet out-flanked the Indians, and they were able to retire, albeit in confusion. But Sullivan had given Poor, he thought, plenty of time; and of course, besides that, he could hardly have expected the Indians to flee so early in the cannonading. Explained the general: "Fear had given them too great speed to be overtaken."

Lt. Robert Parker remembered that "a pleasing piece of Music ensued." Most amusing is his version of the effect: "But the Indians I believe did not admire the sound so much, nor could they be prevailed upon to listen to its music, although we made use of all the eloquence we were masters of for that purpose, but they were deaf to our entreaties and turned their backs upon us in token of their detestation for us." [56]

Of the battle of Newtown, Blacksnake, Cornplanter's companion here as ever, and a participant in the action, many years later reported, in artful understatement, that "the Indians did not manage well." [57] In fact, he seemed in his recollections to be most impressed by a shameful collateral episode, for it was during the Battle of Newtown, Blacksnake discloses, that Red Jacket suffered still one more costly blow to his already much sullied reputation as a warrior. As the story goes, Red Jacket, having slaughtered a cow in the field, showed up among his fellow Senecas with the bloody tomahawk held aloft. He was suggesting that he had slain an enemy soldier. According to Blacksnake, he was promptly exposed for a coward and had to suffer the shame, being known as "the cow killer," for the rest of his life.[58]

On the next day after Newtown there were no Indians to be seen anywhere. So almost the entire army was employed in cutting down the corn of the neighborhood, several hundred acres. General Sullivan was quick to commend the army for its performance in yesterday's action, and thanked the soldiers for their fine execution of the battle plan. As darkness began to fall that day, Sullivan determined on a shipment down the river. And by eleven o'clock the soldiers, a little weary from the wasting of the cornfields, had dismantled the wagons and carts and loaded them into the boats, together with two howitzers and two of the three-pounders. Then the wounded as well, and everything superfluous, were placed in the care of Captain McClure, whose job it was to get the flotilla downriver to the garrison at Tioga.

Newtown, although not a major battle as measured by casualties, definitely dealt a devastating blow to the Butlers and to their Indian allies. The engagement pretty much marked an end to any organized resistance to Sullivan. More importantly, it contributed to the feeling of resignation and sense of futility which was steadily coming over Cornplanter, by now the most influential of the Seneca braves. One day it would totally consume him.

Red Jacket was the most discouraged. According to William Leete Stone, after the battle of Newtown, Red Jacket got into the "habit of holding private councils with the young warriors and some of the more timid sachems," all in an effort to persuade them to sue for peace—peace at any cost! On at least one occasion, Stone notes, a runner carrying this overture for peace was sent clear into General Sullivan's camp.[59] Joseph Brant somehow got wind of these machinations; and naturally the Mohawk chief, who had labeled Red Jacket "an arrant coward" and thoroughly despised him, did all he could to suppress the impression that the Indians were throwing in the towel.

The Expedition now moved forward with great confidence and high morale, "much animated with this day's success." Intent now on the villages located on both sides of the finger lake called Seneca, the army arrived at Catherine's Town on the first day of September. The town had taken its name from Catharine Montour, the wife of a noted Seneca chief, Telenemut (Thomas Hudson), and sister of the "fiend of Wyoming," Queen Esther. This village had earlier (in the autumn of 1778) been wiped out by Colonel Thomas Hartley. It was promptly destroyed again.

As the army moved up the eastern shore of the beautiful lake it came to Kendaia (Appletown), Blacksnake's birthplace, a small village about a half mile from the lake and on both banks of a small stream. After erasing this community the army moved on along the shores of Seneca Lake, coming on September 7 to the capital of the Seneca nation, the home of the chief sachem. It was composed of nearly sixty solidly built houses and stood on both sides of Kanadaseaga Creek. Called Kanadaseaga (the grand village), it reposed about a mile and a half to the east of the site of present-day Geneva.[60]

Cornplanter had persuaded the Indians to make a stand on the beaches of the lake at this castle, but as a detachment of Sullivan's forces approached, the warriors grew skittish. Cornplanter tried to rally them. Leaping in front of the infamous Red Jacket, he insisted that the warrior stand and fight. When Red Jacket indicated that he certainly did not mean to do so, the enraged chief "turned to the young wife of the recreant warrior" and exclaimed in great heat, "Leave that man—he is a coward!" [61]

No battle occurred here. It required Sullivan only two days to put an end to the chief city of the Senecas.

Next to be destroyed were the villages of Canandaigua, Hanneyaye, Kanaghsaws (Great Tree's town), and Gathtsegwarohare.[62] But while the army was still in the region of Kanaghsaws, delayed because of the necessity to build a bridge over a large sunken place, so that the troops might cross the swamp, the Indians, under the leadership of Old Smoke, Cornplanter, Brant, Sagwarithra, Little Beard, Fish Carrier, and Blacksnake, prepared an ambush.[63] Only because Lieutenant Thomas Boyd and Michael Parker, who had been sent out on a scout with twenty-six men, stumbled into this ambush, was the plan of the Indians frustrated. Nine soldiers of Boyd's party escaped, but others, including Lt. Thaosagwat, whose brother was fighting on the side of the British, were killed, scalped, and mutilated. The captured Boyd and Parker, having been questioned by Butler, were dispatched under the guard of Butler's Rangers to the village of Little Beard.[64] On the next day, Tuesday, September 14, the men of Sullivan's army came upon the most grisly sight of the entire expedition. How it all happened is a gripping, chilling story.

Almost every journal that was kept by the soldiers on this expedition provides an image of this scene, or at least some reference to it, and while there may be noted some inconsistency in details, it is a gruesome picture in every account.

And though all accounts of the torture and murder of Boyd and Parker are awful in their description, many discreetly omit the most blood-curdling details. From the journal of Lt. Erkuries Beatty, who one day would be present at the surrender of Lord Cornwallis, emerges one of the fuller, eye-witness accounts of the terrifying scene, as the soldiers discovered it. Sullivan's forces are arriving at Genesee Castle, Little Beard's town.

He describes the crossing of a branch of the Genesee at about noon, and their coming upon "a very beautiful flat of great extent growing up with wild Grass higher in some places than our heads." The army crosses the Genesee and after three miles through the wood the soldiers come upon Genesee Town, "which is the largest we have yet seen." Beatty counted seventy houses, "very compact and well built." As they entered the town, "we found the body of Lt. Boyd and another Rifle Man [Parker] in a most terrible mangled condition." Both had been stripped naked "and their heads Cut off and the flesh of Lt. Boyds head was intirely taken off and his eyes punched out. The other mans head was not there." Both had been stabbed, Beatty supposes, "in 40 Diferent places in the Body with a spear and great gashes cut in their flesh with knifes, and Lt. Boyds Privates was nearly cut off & hanging down, his finger and Toe nails was bruised . . . and the Dogs had eat part of their Shoulders away likewise a knife was sticking in Lt. Boyds body. They was imediately buried with the honour of war." [65]

Mary Jemison, who had been living now among the Senecas for almost twenty years, most of the time in Little Beard's town, and was at the time of the Sullivan expedition thirty-five years old,[66] provides an even more horrifying account. She tells how Boyd and Parker were captured and were brought to Little Beard's Town, "where they were soon after put to death in the most shocking and cruel manner." Jemison in describing such scenes, particularly when her ruthless husband Hiokatoo is the agent of the cruelty, rarely registers much feeling. Here she seems moved to pity:

> *Little Beard in this, as in all other scenes of cruelty that happened at his town, was master of ceremonies, and principal actor. Poor Boyd was stripped of his clothing, and then tied to a sapling, where the Indians menaced his life by throwing their tomahawks at the tree, directly over his head, brandishing their scalping knives around him in the most frightful manner, and accompanying their ceremonies with terrific shouts of joy. Having punished him sufficiently in this way, they made a small opening in his abdomen, took out an intestine, which they tied to the sapling, and then*

> *unbound him from the tree, and drove him round it till he had drawn out the whole of his intestines. He was then beheaded, his head was stuck upon a pole, and his body left on the ground unburied. Thus ended the life of poor William [Thomas] Boyd, who, it was said, had every appearance of being an active and enterprizing officer, of the first talents. The other prisoner was (if I remember distinctly) only beheaded and left near Boyd.*[67]

Joseph Brant of course was not present at this torture death, and probably, because he had promised to spare Boyd, he would not have permitted it. Colonel John Butler was present and did not interfere. It is difficult to know whether the presence of Chief Cornplanter would have made a difference, but, apparently, he was not involved. Blacksnake, who clearly enjoys drama, does not mention this event in his narrative account of the Sullivan Expedition. Cornplanter, surely well aware that his home village of Ganawaugus, the westernmost Seneca town, was probably next on Sullivan's list, may very well have been engaged in its interest. Or it may be that at this time both Cornplanter and Blacksnake were on their way to assist the imperiled Chief Redeye on the Allegheny River.

Boyd, who was born in Washingtonville, in Pennsylvania's Northumberland County, had first marched into the wilderness in General Richard Montgomery's failed invasion of Quebec. A sergeant then, he served under Benedict Arnold, in Captain Matthew Smith's Pennsylvania Company of Riflers, and survived the torturous march through Maine to Quebec. He was still only twenty-two years old when he was murdered at Genesee Castle. He has been described as a soldier "of fine physique, engaging manners, brave almost to recklessness, he was endowed with the qualities which would command attention, without the cool judgment of firmness which would fit him for a leader." [68]

Michael Parker had been a corporal in the First Pennsylvania Regiment, from which he was promoted to sergeant in Michael Simpson's company.[69]

Sceptics are many ("too horrible to be true"), but the story is preserved by the locals. And to this day one may stand next to the tree (the "sapling") to which Boyd was bound. It is a huge tree now, a white oak, and is said to be 235 years old. Called "the torture tree," it is designated by an historical marker at the old site of Little Beard's Town.

Doubtless the sight of this scene of torture and mutilation and murder impelled the soldiers of General Sullivan to a greater zeal as they went about their business. It required the army only until the middle of the afternoon of the next day to destroy totally the enormous town of Little Beard, called Genishau (Genesee Castle).[70] At the end of the day, where there had been many houses (Lt. Beatty had counted seventy, Sullivan's official report gave the figure as 128, and Lt. Thomas Blake had tallied 180!) and a very, very expansive field of corn, there remained nothing.

In fact, enough was done at Genesee Castle to bring General Sullivan to satisfaction. The devastation accomplished here, though Little Beard's Town was not the last on the Indian trail of villages, seemed to register a note of finality. As the long day drew to a close, the weary army marched away, some four miles. It had not reached the village of Cornplanter's birth, which lay just a few miles beyond the town of Little Beard, and some smaller villages had escaped its attention altogether, but it seemed enough. The soldiers had been burning cornfields and firing villages for six long weeks, all of August and well into September. Next day, September 16, they set out on the return trip. Jabez Campfield would be back home in Easton early in October.

The expedition traveled, by water and along the river shores, by the same route it had followed into the Indian country. It reached the ruins of Catherine's Town in one week, and arrived back at Wyoming just two weeks after that, on Thursday, October 7, to a big celebration, which included the firing of cannon for every toast. On Saturday the 9th, at 6:00 a.m., the soldiers set out on the last leg of this summer-long campaign, the trek to Easton.

Meanwhile Colonel Daniel Brodhead had not been idle. His assignment had been to drive a stake into the heart of the Seneca country, which lay up the Allegheny River to the north of Pittsburgh. Brodhead was a Pennsylvanian. Though he had been born in Albany, his father had emigrated to Dansbury (now East Stroudsburg, Pa.). He had commanded a detachment of militia in the Battle of Long Island, and he had endured the winter at Valley Forge. An older man than Sullivan, by fifteen years, he would after the War serve the Commonwealth for eleven years as Surveyor General. In the Surveyor General's office at Harrisburg, a half century after his death, were discovered the letters he wrote during the time of the Sullivan Campaign. They date from early in 1779 to the end of 1780 and provide important details not only of the conduct of the War but also of the relationships among the Indians, in particular those of the Six Nations with the Delawares and the "western tribes."

In the time some months before Sullivan set out from Easton for Wyoming, Brodhead, Head of the Western Department, was complaining about the hostility and the depredations of the Indians in the region around Fort Pitt, his headquarters. In April he writes: ". . . the Indians at present are daily Committing Murders in Westmoreland to such a degree that . . . I have ordered ranging parties to cover them [inhabitants] and drive out the Indians." He suggests that the Delawares, though not so numerous, may be persuaded to fight against the Six Nations, but appreciates the need to pay them in goods and trinkets.[98]

On August 11, at just the time Sullivan was reaching Tioga-Chemung, Brodhead, with 605 Rank and File left Pittsburgh for Mahoning, fifteen miles upriver from Kittanning. Small garrisons of regular troops were left at Forts McIntosh, Crawford, and Armstrong, as well as at Fort Pitt. To Washington he reports from Pittsburgh five weeks later, September 14, the results of the mission. He explains that one engagement with a party of canoes on the Allegheny came to nothing, and that very little resistance did he encounter on the whole course of the expedition. Actually, there were no Seneca warriors at home to oppose the Brodhead expedition, for almost all had gone east and north to join Cornplanter and Old Smoke and those Indians of the Six Nations who were offering resistance to the Sullivan forces. Colonel Brodhead found that towns had been deserted long ago, or that they were promptly abandoned on the approach of his forces. The upper-river Seneca villages, numbering eight, he destroyed, together with the fields of corn, totaling at least 500 acres. The Colonel declared to Washington that "I never saw finer Corn, altho' it was planted much thicker than is common with our Farmers." [72]

Brodhead got as far north as Yahrungwago, some forty miles short of the Genesee, and thus very close to the expedition of Sullivan. He would have continued on to "Jenesseo" but for the want of shoes for his men. On his return he followed the old Venango Road and laid waste to Indian villages at Conewango (present-day Warren), Buchloons (Buckaloons, now Irvine, near present-day Youngsville), and Mahusquechikoken, upriver from where French Creek empties into the Allegheny.

The Brodhead expedition began on August 11, almost two weeks after Sullivan set out from Wyoming, and ended on September 14. In all, Brodhead burned eleven Seneca villages (165 houses) on the Allegheny and on French Creek.[73]

The one engagement with the Indians in canoes on the Allegheny, which "came to nothing," occurred just after Brodhead had returned to the Allegheny River, having struck out overland for a little distance, seven days into the mission. On the river, not far from where it receives Brokenstraw Creek, the soldiers perceived a party of warriors numbering (according to Brodhead) at least forty and perhaps fifty, headed downriver in canoes, apparently, so they supposed, to assault settlements in Westmoreland County. The Indians, in some accounts, made for the shore to attack the Brodhead forces, but were met rudely. Before they could escape, some by canoes, and the chief by swimming the river, they lost five warriors.

Allegheny River at Redbank

This episode is described by Blacksnake in his narrative, although he was not present, and presumably has the story from Redeye, whom he afterwards came to help. The principal figure is Captain Redeye, an Allegheny Seneca, and there is much drama in his narrow escape. Here is Blacksnake's account:

> *Captain Redeyes and anothers Indians was with redeye about ten of them together following Down stream on the Allegenny River with Bark canoes and hunting furs, Redeyes and his comrates [comrades] was Down about five miles below Brokenstraw [in the region now called] warrent [Warren] county Pennsylvania they had been camp out on the Bank of the River, Captain Redeye took his Rifle and walk it Down on the Bank the River, about quarter of a mile from his camp there he saw a company of men of war, and count them, how many it was the company they was about 500 men in the company and they saw him and he Run Back to his camp, they fire it at him But not toucth him the Ball, But he Rum as fast as he could, then they put after him about 50 of them, But he Rather out Rum them—as soon as he got into their camp he told his comrate that the whites company are coming close to hand that they had Better Run soon as possible So they start it and Run for their lives, some Run up the River, and Redeye and 3 others went with him and got into their Bark canoe and put across the River But before Reaching Crossing, the company come upon them and fire it and this 3 Indians was Kill in the River while crossing and Redeye jump it out the canoe into water and Dove in the water as far as he could go under water but the company kept fire gun at him as far as they see him.*
>
> *But he . . . cross the River life as soon as he got out the water and Run to the first tree and got behind that—till water drin [drain] from him—and made out Escape from them—But the whites company kept pursued him up the River . . . .*

Blacksnake explains that Redeye made good his escape, and describes how he "kept going Day and Night" until he came to what later became the Cornplanter Tract, at Burnt House. Although there was no real village there at the time, there were a few Indian families living at the site. These Redeye warned away from the "Danger of their enemy that are coming up the River." [74] And just in time too, for Brodhead's troops shortly laid waste to the whole.

Cornplanter was in on this action very late. According to Blacksnake, Redeye had summoned himself and Uncle Cornplanter from Ganawaugus just as they were preparing to abandon their native village at the tail end of the Sullivan Expedition. Blacksnake describes how he had come with Uncle Cornplanter and Red Jacket to protect Redeye and those living in the region of Cold Spring and Burnt House. By the time they got there, they found Redeye and the others wandering around in the woods, for "the whites has ben there, and cut all the corn and throw [it in] the River, so that we could not have any." As the Brodhead forces had obviously departed downriver, Cornplanter, Redeye, Blacksnake and Red Jacket "persued them as far as warren Pennsylvania and see nothing of them." So "we returned again and called upon all the Indians and we went long up stream and over to Genesee River and down home at avone [Ganawaugus] about [the time] winter sit in." [75]

Brodhead in his report to Washington provides a description of the incident that closely approximates Blacksnake's recollection, which of course the warrior has second-hand. [76]

Brodhead may have regarded the incident as just that, an "incident," which "came to nothing." But for Redeye it was a very close call.[77] And of course for the Indians who were killed it was no mere "incident."

Colonel Brodhead claimed to have suffered no casualties on his expedition, but, as Thomas Abler points out, reports from the Senecas don't agree. Abler notes that one of Cornplanter's lieutenants, the Allegheny Seneca known as Half Town, who had actually been the leader of the Senecas at Allegheny before Cornplanter, withdrew from the resistance to Sullivan in order to hurry home, with forty warriors, to defend the Allegheny River villages. Although he was to reach the river too late to oppose Brodhead, he reportedly caught up with some stragglers (probably four) and dispatched them. And the figures for two other engagements that were reported bring the tally of losses for Brodhead to twenty-two.[78]

In October, Brodhead responded to a letter he has had from Sullivan, who in the last week in September had been at Catherine's Town on his way home. In reply to Sullivan's curiosity, the Colonel repeated the report he had made to Washington, which adds up to great success; and he was very quick to congratulate Sullivan for what he understood had been so far a big step toward "lasting tranquility on the frontier."

On the 18th of October, Brodhead himself received congratulations. Writing to express the gratitude of the nation, Washington extended his compliments: "The activity, perseverance and firmness which marked the conduct of Colonel Brodhead, and that of all the officers and men of every description in this expedition, do them great honor, and their services entitle them to the thanks and to this testimonial of the General's acknowledgment." [79]

To Pennsylvania's Governor Reed on November 12, after the conclusion of the Campaign, Brodhead reported: "This Frontier is in perfect tranquility at present and I learn from Sandusky that the Indians who were lately driven from their towns to the number of 2000 are at Niagara, and live upon the pittance they receive from the Command's Office there. They are afraid to hunt lest the Americans should not have returned home . . . ."

It is difficult to assess the effect of the Sullivan-Clinton-Brodhead campaign. Some historians insist that the campaign did little more than to exacerbate the Indians, that it was in fact a failure. More than a decade later, the Seneca Chief Cornplanter, in his council speech to Washington in Philadelphia, reminded the President of the legacy of the General's decision to invade the Indian country on the Susquehanna. The Seneca Chief called him "Town Destroyer," and noted that the term whenever heard caused his people "to turn pale." [80] To the very end of his long life, which was closed out in extreme bitterness, the venerable Iroquois chieftain inveighed against the inhumanities of the Sullivan Expedition.

But the campaign did more than simply anger the Indians. They clearly suffered an almost total devastation of villages and grain fields and vegetable plots and fruit trees. Before the Battle of Lexington/ Concord, the Indians of the Six Nations lived in thirty-some widely scattered villages. By the spring of 1780, most of them had been reduced to ashes, had simply disappeared. Sullivan alone claimed to have destroyed forty (!) villages, and thirty is the total, with towns named, in another report.[81] Only two of all the Indian villages known to the settlers survived this period undamaged.[82]

When the object of the campaign is brought to mind, "to put the Indians in their place," and to render the Indian aid to the British negligible, and to disable the British war machine, it would seem that the Expedition was a success. Certainly the common soldier who served throughout the campaign would have some sound impressions. Most seemed to feel that the army had done its job. One who served throughout the entire war declared that these six weeks had "ruined them [the Indians], and they never recovered from the blow." [83]

It had been expected by many, in high places and low (but not by those who knew Sullivan), that, because the whole campaign was in essence in retribution for the Wyoming massacre and other atrocities suffered by the settlers on the frontier, horrible acts of cruelty would occur. In fact, what is remarkable is that almost nothing of this kind was carried out by Sullivan's soldiers. Just the contrary.

Owing probably to the insistence of General Sullivan, who had himself been a prisoner of war, captured women and children were treated most kindly. For one aged woman, whom the Indians had left behind, and who expected to be murdered, the soldiers built a house and equipped it with an ample supply of food and blankets. Samuel McNeill reported that "We found some Cattle, such as Horses, Cows and Hogs, also found in one of the houses an old Squaw Scarce able to walk, Supposed to be about 100 years of age. Our Indians took great care of her During our Stay at that place, and by General Sullivan's order built a Bark Cabin near the waterside and gave her Bread, meat and Indian Corn sufficient to last her six weeks. I confess I think she was the greatest object of Pity I ever Saw." [84]

What McNeill is describing occurred at Catherine's Town, during the forward march upriver. On the return march, this same old woman "greeted the soldiers with a smile of gratitude." And General Sullivan ordered that from the troops' meager supplies (The soldiers had been on half-rations for some time.) there be left "a keg of pork and some biscuit &c for the old creature to subsist on." [85]

Besides the skinning of two dead Indians, so that soldiers could fashion boots, only two instances of barbarity occurred during the whole campaign; and one of these, the murder of a woman found on the army's return to Catherine's Town, is "generally believed" to have been the work of express riders from Tioga.[86] The other is definitely a black mark for the campaign.

For the most part, villages that the army came upon were found totally abandoned, but occasionally women or children would be left behind. According to a well documented account of an incident that occurred at Cayuga Lake on the forward march, Colonel Henry Dearborn discovered three Indian women and a badly crippled Indian lad. He ordered that one house in the village be allowed to stand, that these four might be accommodated. But, somehow, his orders were not followed. Two of the women were taken along as prisoners; and the remaining, apparently the oldest, together with the crippled boy, was locked in the house, which was then burned down.[87] While that inhumanity is a blemish for the campaign, it clearly was not characteristic of the behavior of the soldiers, and should not be taken as a reflection generally of the treatment accorded captives.

Unfortunately, it was rumored among the Senecas that many atrocities had occurred; such beliefs did little to improve relations between Indians and whites. As above noted, Cornplanter referred to the Sullivan "barbarities" to the end of his life.

In judging the success of the campaign, one should note that it did not do what it might have done, that is to unite the Indians generally, and to bring closer together the fragments of the Six Nations. Besides, it had the beneficial effect (from the Americans' point of view) of making the members of the Six Nations increasingly dependent upon the British. And certainly the feeble, token resistance put up by the British under the Butlers and by the Indians under their war-chiefs must have sounded to them all a note of futility. Yet neither Brodhead nor Sullivan reached Ganawaugus, the home village of Cornplanter and Blacksnake. And the Indians had not submitted. Hostilities all along the frontier continued, and in many areas, as in Northumberland County in Pennsylvania, actually seemed to increase in frequency. It is putting it all too simply, but it might be said, with respect to the Six Nations, that their back was broken, but not their spirit. Or to put it another way, the road to despair was merely paved, not traveled. Still, for the chiefs, like Cornplanter, it would soon be time, not to regroup in an attitude of force but to adjust to all that the inevitable loss of their lands would mean.

But not yet. The war was not over, not by a long shot. There were critical battles yet to be fought. Harrowing raids on the settlements continued. And Cornplanter and his fellow chiefs were in the thick of things.

VIII

THE MOHAWK VALLEY

One of the most dramatic moments in the long life of Chief Cornplanter, alluded to earlier, occurred some ten months after the close of the Sullivan campaign, in August of 1780. Some 400 Indians and Tories under Old Smoke, Cornplanter and Brant burned the Canajoharie District of the Mohawk Valley. Sagwarithra of the Tuscaroras and Fish Carrier of the Cayugas were also present, commanding small parties of braves fierce in their war-paint. The Senecas, however, made up the largest percentage. Among the warriors serving as Cornplanter's lieutenants were many of the familiar names: Handsome Lake, Red Jacket, Farmer's Brother, Little Beard, Jack Berry, Hiokatoo, and Blacksnake.

Canajoharie is on the Mohawk River, sixty miles northwest of Albany and twenty miles northeast of Cherry Valley. The area was settled primarily by Dutch and German immigrants in the early days of the eighteenth century. The region gets its name (an Indian expression meaning "washed pot") from a large pothole conspicuous in the striking Canajoharie Creek Gorge. In many ways the stream and the gorge remind one of the Genesee River. A 45-foot waterfall is a feature of the gorge and can be seen from Wintergreen Park. As with the beauties of Wyoming, these scenic delights in no way accord with the events of August, 2, 1780.

The fierce assault on the region was part of the Schoharie Valley Expedition, the major British campaign of the year 1780, which was led by Sir John Johnson himself.

The story that is told of Cornplanter has been variously narrated. Among the homes razed by fire was one in which was residing his father, the Dutch trader John Abeel, now almost sixty years old. By the Indians a great many settlers were captured, among them Abeel. But, according to Blacksnake, "At a council of leaders, it was agreed to let old O'Bail and most of the other prisoners go free—which was accordingly done, as a compliment to Cornplanter." [1] But there are two varying reports of what happened here. In one account Abeel was simply taken captive by the Indians, along with everybody else, and only later was by the Senecas recognized among the prisoners.[2] According to another, earlier version, Cornplanter knew in advance that the elder Abeel resided here, and "repairing with a detachment of his warriors to his father's house, he made the old man a prisoner, and marched him off." [3] In the first version, after the warriors explained to Cornplanter that one of the prisoners was his father, the chief "apologized profusely for burning his house." In the second, Cornplanter said nothing to him until the march of the captives had proceeded ten or twelve miles. In both versions he presented his father the choice between returning home with him to his Indian village or going back to his white family. The oft-quoted speech by Cornplanter, by which he identified himself and expressed the hope that his father would come to live with him, was included by Mary Jemison in her narrative:

> *My name is John O'Bail, commonly called Cornplanter. I am your son! You are my father! You are now my prisoner, and subject to the customs of Indian warfare. But you shall not be harmed: you need not fear. I am a warrior! Many are the scalps which I have taken! Many prisoners I have tortured to death! I am your son! I was anxious to see you, and greet you in friendship. I went to your cabin and took you by force. But your life shall be spared. Indians love their friends and their kindred, and treat them with kindness. If now you choose to follow the fortune of your yellow son, and to live with our people, I will cherish your old age with plenty of venison, and you shall live easy. But if it is your choice to return to your fields and live with your white children, I will send a party of my trusty young men to conduct you back in safety. I respect you, my father: you have been friendly to Indians, and they are your friends.* [4]

Both Mary Jemison and Blacksnake locate the scene at Canajoharie.[5]

This dramatic speech has been variously rendered, but the essence, as Stone has noted, is essentially the same in all versions. This would be the last time that father and son would see each other. The elder Abeel elected to return to his home among the whites, and, as promised, was provided an escort, which took him safely out of harm's way.

"Most" of the other prisoners were also released "as a compliment to Cornplanter." We have no impression of the fate of the others, except that Mary Jemison reports that some prisoners were brought back to Genesee and that among them were William Newkirk, a man by the name of Price and two Negroes.[6] Abraham Wemple, in writing to General Abraham Ten Broeck about this latest disaster, most woefully remarked: "Such a Scean as we beheld since we left the River, passing dead Bodies of Men & Children most cruelly murdered, is not possible to be described." [7]

But Cornplanter did not accompany the captives. Together with his nephew Blacksnake, whose report we have, and his half-brother Handsome Lake, in a party of some thirty Senecas he sallied forth to the southeast, toward the Susquehanna, to secure horses, which were badly needed. The success of their venture required the killing of an additional eight persons (two by Blacksnake), and the taking of two more prisoners. Graymont sees the action as quite "typical of the way Indian war parties would frequently become fragmented to suit the whims of a few warriors." [8]

That same autumn, in October, there occurred, east and south of Canajoharie, in the shadows of Albany, still another border incursion involving Cornplanter. This most ferocious assault on the region was, like Canajoharie, part of the massive Schoharie Valley expedition launched by Johnson. Historians regard it as "comparable in size and destructiveness" to the Sullivan Expedition of the year before. Johnson had assembled the army at Montreal, and, according to Anthony Wallace, picked up "Tory Rangers and Indians, converging from north, west, and south . . . to make up an army of 1500 men, well armed and even carrying mortars." Wallace describes how this "formidable force" moved first, almost entirely unopposed, down the Schoharie Creek to where it merged with the Mohawk River, and then proceeded up the Mohawk in a wave of destruction. In his account the savage horde was ruthlessly undiscriminating in its ravage of the region, burning "everything that they found along their route, including forts and barns, churches and gristmills, not to mention scores of houses." By October 16 it had reached the Schoharie Valley.[9]

Although the devastation was widespread, Fort Hunter itself was never assaulted, and Johnson's forces, having mauled a troop of rebels dispatched from Fort Davis and mortally wounding its commander, Colonel Brown, were finally compelled to withdraw. Militia forces assembled in Albany and Schenectady, and commanded by General Robert Van Rensselaer, proved much too formidable for the much fatigued Tories and Indians.[10] But in the course of the withdrawal, much fighting continued. It was reported that a large body of Iroquois warriors, headed up by the chiefs Cornplanter, Brant, and Blacksnake, "captured three officers and fifty-three men of other ranks who had marched out . . . to destroy Johnson's boats on Onondaga Lake." [11]

Comparisons to the Sullivan campaign of the summer before were inevitable. According to Anthony Wallace, this raid is best regarded as the culmination of three years of "incendiary incursions." He observed that it had an effect comparable to that of the Sullivan Campaign in that it "virtually wiped out all the white settlements in the Mohawk Valley west of the environs of Schenectady." [12] And other historians have noted that "the devastation wreaked by this campaign was tremendous. At least 150,000 bushels of grain were destroyed—nearly the same amount Sullivan claimed to have destroyed in the Indian country the year before. Two hundred houses were burned." So great was the damage that New York State Governor George Clinton lamented that Schenectady was "now the western frontier of New York." [13]

Blacksnake was prominent in the raid that was directed at the town of Schoharie. According to his memoirs, there were 265 Indians in the assault party that fell upon Tyron County (present-day Montgomery County) that October. He reports that the Indians were under the command of the familiar trio, Cornplanter, Old Smoke, and the Mohawk Brant. Among other Senecas he mentions Red Jacket and Handsome Lake. Farmer's Brother, Jack Berry, and Little Beard were also at the head of the warriors. And Sagwarithra was here again too, with a band of Tuscaroras; and Blacksnake remembers Hung Face and his Cayuga warriors. In this phase of the Johnson campaign the settlement of Schoharie was the specific object, but by the time the war party arrived, having experienced many hardships (and actually so hungry they had eaten Old Smoke's horse!), the members of the community, doubtless warned, had fled to safety. Although some prisoners were taken and the buildings burned to ashes, this chapter of the Schoharie Valley raid turned out to be a massacre that didn't happen. It was a relatively uneventful incident of the border wars, one of those rare stories for which we do not have gory details. Even so it is of great interest to us, for it brings the dour Cornplanter as close to laughter as we ever see him.

Graymont resorts to polished English for Blacksnake's account:

> *Cornplanter, Ganiodaio (Handsome Lake), and Blacksnake with five other Indians entered one house which the tenants had left with much precipitation. Breakfast was already on the table ready to serve. The eight hungry Senecas helped themselves to the first food they had had in two days, never even bothering to sit down while they hurriedly ate everything edible they could find . . . . As the army was leaving the ruined Schoharie region, several Indians filled some sacks with a white floury substance they had found in some barrels. Later at meal time they mixed their flour with water and put the dough over the fire to bake. Their bread, instead of cooking, fell apart. Some of their comrades examined the "flour" more closely and identified it as slaked lime. The would-be cooks were thereupon the butt of all jokes in the camp.*[14]

These raids upon the settlements all along the NewYork-Pennsylvania border in the wake of the Sullivan Expedition, devastating as they were, may be regarded as the last gasp of the Senecas and the Iroquois Federation. Roving bands of warriors continued raids and were involved in skirmish action through 1783, and even beyond the end of the war, but Cornplanter and Blacksnake did never again participate in any formal military action against the rebels.

Although the Sullivan campaign did not put an end to the Iroquois participation in the war, and although some continue to question the value of it, the expedition pretty much did in the Indian allies of the British. Even before the troops of Sullivan had returned to Easton and Morristown, in October of that summer, hordes of Indian refugees were descending on the British post of Fort Niagara, which stood to the west of the Iroquois country, on the southeastern shore of Lake Ontario, at the point where the Niagara River enters the lake.[15] Some 5000 destitute Indians, not only Senecas, but Cayugas and Onondagas as well, in flight from the villages Sullivan had burned, appeared at the gates of the fort that fall, some as early as late September. The British garrison, naturally, was not happy to see them, and felt helpless to provide for so many. The refugees were politely sent packing, and vanished in many directions. Still, by the end of November, some 2900 remained.[16]

Because Sullivan's army, after destroying Little Beard's Genesee Castle, had stopped short of Ganawaugus, the home village of Cornplanter and Blacksnake, the Cornplanter family was apparently not among those Senecas immediately looking for relief at Fort Niagara. Cornplanter was able to ride out the winter of 1779-80 at Niagara, and at Ganawaugus, and in fact had been made Head Man of the village in 1780. It was not until the war was virtually over, at some time in 1781, that he withdrew from the Genesee. According to Cornplanter's son Charles, who was interviewed for the Lyman Draper manuscripts, the Chief took his family first to the "refuge" of British Fort Niagara, where they lingered "about one year," and then, afterwards, south to the upper Allegheny River region of Pennsylvania. It may be assumed that he was following the course taken so many years ago by the family of his uncle Kayahsotha, to whom he had grown much closer during the war years. Kayahsotha had lived in many different places in the Allegheny River region, but at the time of Cornplanter's coming he was at Cattaraugus Creek. The Cornplanter family, as son Charles remembers (although he was but an infant at the time), lived for "about two years" near Franklin Fort before going on over to the region that was to become the Cornplanter Grant.

It was the end of the warrior life for Cornplanter. He had made a choice at the critical hour of the Revolution to cast his lot with the British; and he had fought earnestly and valiantly for what he thought was best for his people. It was time now, in the aftermath of the bloody war, to do what he could for his people on the diplomatic front.

IX

THE 1784 FORT STANWIX TREATY

The Treaty of Paris put an end to a long, very costly and very painful civil war. It established in the "New World" a new nation, free and independent. The Revolution was a most dramatic moment in the history of civilization. It announced to all of Europe, in fact to all of the Old World, the power, if not the right, of one people to displace another. The monarchs of Europe had been squabbling, for almost 500 years, for domain over a land that had been inhabited for 20,000 years by another race. The Treaty of Paris, which no Indian was invited to sign, in which the Indians as a people were not even recognized or acknowledged, formalized an attitude in which could be read dire forebodings for the continent's First Americans as a race.

The War of Revolution and the agreement which officially concluded it had required more than eight years. During this time the most powerful and best organized of all the Indian nations was virtually destroyed as an effective fighting force and fragmented beyond repair.

In 1783 the Seneca Chief Cornplanter stood for all of the Iroquois, for all of the Indians of the Northeast, and, if the truth were known, for all of the Indians of the continent, at a threshold. He did not then see it this way, of course, but the first phase of what was to be a long life for him had come to a close. Of course the warrior was not dead. The fires still burned. The Seneca Cornplanter would fight, as he always had, with courage and ferocity, against Indians or whites, against whoever might threaten his people and their land. But there was not required a mind nearly so sharp as that of Cornplanter to perceive the long-term effects of the Revolution for the future of the Indian. Even those Iroquois and the members of other tribes, like the Delaware, some of whom had fought at the side of the patriots, were no better off than the Indians who had been hostile to the victor in the War. The borders had moved, and, it seemed plain, would continue to move, westward.

No, the warrior was not dead. But he was now thirty-three years of age. He had hunted and trapped and traded in the bountiful and beautiful forests of his country for almost three decades; for much of that time he had fought tenaciously, against both soldiers and settlers, for the land of the Iroquois. He had fought at Oriskany, at Wyoming, at Cherry Valley, at Freeland, at Newtown, at Canajoharie, and all over the Schoharie Valley. He had ravaged the frontier in New York and Pennsylvania, participating in, and leading, destructive raids against the ever encroaching settlers. Because he was by reputation ruthless and unmerciful, he excited fear in the settlements. Even in regions in which he never traveled settlers would identify suddenly appearing Indians as "Cornplanter Indians." His reputation had actually inspired the birth of a whole tribe.

But, with all of that, he would have to view his years to this point as a failure, if indeed they had as their principal object the retention of the land of the Iroquois and the salvation of a way of life. He was prepared now to lay down the rifle and the sword and the war club, the hatchet and the scalping knife. He was ready to take up the pen, ready to work now with an eloquence, cultivated in the Iroquois tongue, equal to the courage of an Iroquois warrior, for agreements with the whites to which with honor he could affix his X.

It might be noted that the Seneca chief Cornplanter lived two lives, that of the warrior and that of a statesman leading his people steadily into the white man's way of life.

From a time shortly after the close of the Sullivan Campaign until his dying day, except for a brief respite when he was "removed from office," the Seneca war-chief and Head Man Cornplanter presided over the community of his people at Cornplanter Town on the upper Allegheny in northwestern Pennsylvania. Merle Deardorff, who is normally complimentary, was yet struck by a meaningful analogy: "He was in a way the Marshal Petain of his day, and for nearly fifty years his town of Jennesadaga on the Cornplanter Grant was his Vichy, so to speak."

These last years, from the time Cornplanter was in his late thirties until his death in 1836 were not uneventful. In fact, they were attended by a great deal of drama, the chief obliged to address one crisis after another.

First and always foremost were the never-ending squabbles (now with Pennsylvania and the new United States rather than the Crown) over the land. These required of Cornplanter a number of pilgrimages to councils in the East. Second, until the defeat of the Ohio Indians at Fallen Timbers in 1794, there was the very grave problem posed by the continuing hostility of the Miamis, the Shawnees and the other tribes of the West. Cornplanter, who by this time had acquired quite a reputation as a go-between, was being requested by the Washington administration (1) to serve as an intermediary in the dispute and pacify the Ohio Indians; and (2) to keep the Senecas "out of it."

Besides these large matters, there were the local problems of Cornplanter Town. The chief was earnestly and vigorously trying to promote education and modern agriculture and lumbering, and to this end was soliciting aid from the United States Government, the government of the Quaker State, and from his good friends the Quakers of Philadelphia and New Jersey. He had to win his people over to this new way of life; he had to make arrangements for the installation of schools and the construction of sawmills and gristmills.

As if this were not enough there was the ever-present, almost overwhelming problem of alcohol. His own half-brother had for a long time been a victim of the demon rum, and his people continued to trade in Pittsburgh for incredibly excessive quantities of whiskey.

Then there was the "death" and subsequent vision of his half-brother Handsome Lake to provide a challenge. There were differences with the "northern" Seneca Red Jacket, a power among the sachems, and a rival to Cornplanter for prestige and leadership in the Seneca Nation.

There were other tough problems: (1) The chief was personally involved in the disgraceful matter of "witch hunting." (2) His daughter's strange and serious illness occasioned quite a crisis. (3) Threats against his life continued to be rumored. (4) The War of 1812 (for the Indians a most controversial matter) posed a real dilemma for Cornplanter.

Following the Sullivan campaign, with the destruction of most of the Iroquois settlements, hundreds of western New York Senecas, as above noted, took refuge in the vicinity of Fort Niagara, to which many of the Iroquois had retired, hopeful of British accommodation. This was in 1779. Cornplanter was still on the warpath, much involved in the Mohawk Valley raids. For a short time only the chief with his family (Henry would be five years old and Charles one) stayed on at Ganawaugus, which had not been directly affected by the forces of Sullivan. As before noted, in 1780 Cornplanter was made Head Man of the village in which he had been born. He seems then to have taken his family to Fort Niagara, which was doing the best it could to accommodate Indian refugees from the Sullivan campaign. But he could not have been there long, and, probably in the year1782, after some time at Tonawanda, Cornplanter removed to the upper Allegheny River, to that region north of Pittsburgh and Franklin where his uncle Kayahsotha had lived for so long.[2] On this river and in this spot, as remote and as nearly a sanctuary as ever he could find, he would live for the remainder of his days.

The Cornplanter Indians, as they came to be known, were refugees from the Genesee region of New York and from scattered villages destroyed by the Sullivan campaign. Many had been Allegheny Indians and were merely coming home to the villages that had been wiped out by Brodhead. According to Pickering's census of the Six Nations, produced in November of 1792, the Indian population which could be identified with Cornplanter's settlement, had grown in one decade from next to nothing to 1800, mostly Senecas.[3] These Indians lived in eight villages on and near the river.

Cornplanter, in 1782, and for the next two decades, would be consumed by four preoccupations. There was, first, the bitterness inspired by the Fort Stanwix Treaty of 1768. That, together with the subsequent losses of land in agreements, continued to threaten the health of all the Iroquois, and that he needed to address.

Then there was the problem of the western Indians and the disputed territory of the Northwest. Increasingly, he felt from the Miamis and Wyandots, the Shawnee and the Delaware, a great pressure to assist them in their resistance to the American encroachment beyond the Ohio. Once again, Chief Cornplanter's warriors were being urged to take up the hatchet, by brother Indians who accused them of cowardice. The Shawnee appealed to the Seneca "to go to War to secure [us] a Bed to lie upon." [4]

Thirdly, atrocities and outrages continued to occur wherever whites and Indians came together, and not only on the frontier. To cite but a few that date from this period, there are the murders at Pine Creek, to be discussed later, there is the incident in which two of Cornplanter's relatives were killed, there was the assault on Cornplanter's party on its return from Fort Harmar; there was the assassin's attempt on the life of Joseph Brant in New York; the Brady's Beaver Blockhouse affair, in which a hunting party of nine Indians was attacked by twenty-seven white hunters; and then Big Tree was shot in the leg during the celebrated visit of Cornplanter's entourage to Philadelphia.[5] In many of these incidents fatalities occurred, and loss of property was a constant.

Then, in the fourth place, there was the difference that arose between Cornplanter's faction and that of Red Jacket. Cornplanter, together with Joseph Brant, in accepting the realities of the Treaty of Paris and the hard facts and intimations of all the post-war land agreements, was urging the Senecas into the white man's ways, into farming and lumbering and education. Red Jacket would have none of it. He insisted that the Indians' way of life could for a long time yet be preserved.

In Cornplanter's fifty-four years of life on the Allegheny River, these four problems absorbed him. But they absorbed him only because he did not shrink from his obligation to his people.

The Seneca Chief Cornplanter was a Pennsylvania Indian. It is true that his birth occurred in that region that is known now as New York. It is true that the first half of his long life was lived actively in the Finger Lakes section of that state. It is true that he served for many years as war chief for the Six Nations of Iroquois, a confederation that headquartered in the "longhouse" of central New York. It is true that both his father and his mother were born in the region now known as New York, and that they lived their entire lives there. It is true that Gaiantwaka's growing up took place on the Genesee River. But Cornplanter was a Pennsylvania Indian. He knew no distinction between Pennsylvania and New York and operated freely in the regions as if they were one. He became enamored of the country immediately north and east of Pittsburgh. It was Pennsylvania, not New York, nor the infant nation of the United States, that rewarded him for his services during the post-Revolution period with a tract of land. It was Pennsylvania that invited him to settle down in a land still wild enough to make his people happy. And to Pennsylvania he came. And in Pennsylvania he lived among his people for fifty-four years, for more than half of his long life. It was

Pennsylvania who after his death erected to his memory a monument, the first such honor to be accorded any Indian anywhere in the world.

Actually, the Indian Cornplanter belonged to the rivers. He belonged to the Genesee, and to Pine Creek, which enlarges the West Branch of the Susquehanna at present Jersey Shore in Pennsylvania, and to the Allegheny. All three of these rivers have their origins in Potter County, Pennsylvania. Two of these cut deep, awe-inspiring gorges; two drain the valleys of both New York and Pennsylvania. On all three did Cornplanter and his fellow Senecas paddle their bark canoes and their dugouts.

Of all the struggling colonies, historians of the American Colonial Period seem agreed, the one that William Penn would have called New Wales but actually took its name from his father, is the one that treated the native Indians most fairly. In Pennsylvania the Indian was regarded with respect and was genuinely accorded a dignity. That the relationship, in the beginning, was an amiable and friendly one can be credited to the Quakers (as well as to the responsive Indians), who sensed a kinship to the Indian way of life. Famous are the sessions enjoyed by the Indians and William Penn. That the relationship should in time break down should come as no surprise to those who understand the larger human nature, or to those who know how the Quaker influence steadily diminished. Before long, the people who were settling Penn's Woods were taking the same unscrupulous advantage of the Indian that seemed so natural to the members of the other colonies.

As we study the treaty relationship that came to characterize the dealings between whites and Indians through the latter part of the eighteenth century, and in which Chief Cornplanter was up front, it may be instructive to follow, albeit sketchily, the history of land agreements as they occurred in Pennsylvania.[6]

The lands to be known as the Province of Pennsylvania were granted to William Penn by royal charter from Charles II, the reigning King of Great Britain, on the fourth day of March, 1681. These lands, of course, were not the King's to give. He did not possess them through the act of purchase, nor by conquest, and certainly not by discovery. But Penn and his Quakers were delighted, and took all for granted. In fact,

Penn promptly sold large tracts of the new land to parties in London, Liverpool, and Bristol.[7]

As settlers came to the shores of this exciting new continent, they came, naturally, with the attitude that theirs was the land to settle. And they began to build homes, and to till the land, and to establish governments. By and by it was noticed that a people were already living on this land, that in the forests young men hunted, and trapped, that on the rivers bark canoes plied up and down, with and against the current. In the fields, it was perceived, young women, and old, worked with rude instruments to hoe the bean hills and the patches of corn. Those who thought much about it may have surmised that these people had been doing this kind of thing in these same fields and forests for many, many years, perhaps centuries. Some might even have allowed that these people enjoyed "squatters' rights" to the land. Some, doubtless, sensed that if they were displaced, no matter what the means, they might be made unhappy.

In any case, it seemed proper to honorable folk to make allowances for pre-possession. And so the colonists, arrived from a far-away continent on the other side of the Big Water, began to purchase the land from the natives. In most cases, these purchases were effected through a document resulting in a deed, sometimes regarded as a bill of sale, and sometimes accorded the dignity of the term *treaty*. In most cases the real buyer is identifiable; in many cases the real original owner is not, for just which Indian tribe actually holds the rights to the land? In any case, out of a methodical parade of dealings, characterized by great confusion and disputed interests, there proceeded, inexorably, over the next 200 years a very steady transfer of the land in Cornplanter's Pennsylvania—from total Indian ownership to zero Indian ownership.

To William Penn's everlasting credit, his instructions to William Markham, whom he dispatched as his first Deputy Governor to the province, were "to treat with the Indians, arrange a peace with them, and purchase their title to their lands." [8] Dutifully, Markham, after he arrived in the province in the summer of 1681, accomplished, with his commissioners, the purchase of a significant parcel of land from the Indians he discovered there. The deed was executed by the chiefs of the several tribes who seemed to possess the land, which was a large tract in the extreme east, in what is known now as Bucks County.

It is interesting to note the consideration which was remitted the Indians in exchange for this section of land:

> *Three hundred and fifty fathoms of wampum, twenty white blankets, twenty fathoms of strawd waters, sixty fathoms of Duffields, twenty kettles, whereof four are large, twenty guns, twenty coats, forty shirts, forty pairs of stockings, forty hoes, forty axes, two barrels of powder, two hundred bars of lead, two hundred knives, two hundred small glasses, twelve pairs of shoes, forty copper boxes, forty tobacco tongs, two small barrels of pipes, forty pairs of scissors, forty combs, twenty-four pounds of red lead, one hundred awls, two handfulls of needles, forty pounds of shot, ten bundles of beads, ten small saws, twelve drawing-knives, four anchers of tobacco, two anchers of rum, two anchers of cider, two anchers of beer, and three hundred guilders.* [9]

Note here the supplying of guns and powder, already for a long time illegal among the Dutch of New Amsterdam.

The next really noteworthy purchase from the Indians occurred on October 11, 1736, although many small tracts of land had been sold off by various Indian chiefs during the years preceding. The 1736 sale was accomplished only through a great deal of confused dispute involving resident chiefs. So much difficulty occurred with the transaction that the Iroquois League, who had conquered the descendants of the Leni Lenape tribes (Delawares) in this region and thus considered themselves to be proprietors of the land, was called in. The Five Nations chiefs reproached the Pennsylvania chiefs for selling the lands at all, and then insisted that having done so they should have made good on the bargain. Finally, the Iroquois approved the sale, which meant the acquisition by Pennsylvania from the Indians of all those lands which comprise the present counties of Adams, York, Lancaster, Chester, Delaware, Philadelphia, Montgomery, Berks, Lehigh, Northampton, Bucks, Cumberland, and parts of Franklin, Dauphin, and Lebanon.[10]

The next purchase of any size (1749) further disturbed the Iroquois, for it had come to their notice that white settlers were trespassing upon lands that had not yet been sold. So much concerned were the Six Nations that they called a council for Onondaga in order to select delegates to attend the agreement conference in Philadelphia. Another enormous tract of land, the area represented today by the counties of Schuylkill,

Carbon, Monroe, and parts of Dauphin, Northumberland, Columbia, Lucerne, Lackawanna, and Pike, was signed over by the Senecas and the other members of the Six Nations, together with delegates from the Shawnee, Delaware, and Shamokin tribes.[11]

The purchases made by agreements executed in 1753 and 1754, and then limited in a compromise deed executed on October 3, 1757, constituted the transfer of another vast tract of land (present-day counties of Bedford, Fulton, Blair, Huntingdon, Mifflin, Juniata, Perry, and parts of Centre, Union, and Cumberland).[12]

Two matters of note now occurred. The friendly Indians were now urging a boundary line at the Allegheny Mountain range, and mildly insisting that the government of Pennsylvania remove intruders who had already crossed that line; second, a treaty conference, by order of the King, was held in Albany out of deference to the lords of trade and planters, who had recommended that "all the provinces might be comprised in one general treaty to be made in his majesty's name, as the practice of each province making a separate treaty for itself, in its own name, was considered to be improper." [13] The Royal Proclamation of 1763, which governed all of the colonies, drew a line. It forbade settlement of the region west of the crest of the Appalachian range of mountains. Still settlers moved into and laid claim to lands that had never been ceded by the Indians. The Indians were helpless to prevent encroachments upon their territory.

Even George Washington, at the time thirty-six years old, was not above winking at the law. With his friend Captain William Crawford, who had been at his side in the campaign against Fort Duquesne a decade earlier, he endeavored now to secure the right to an expansive tract of land that lay west of the line drawn by the Proclamation. To Crawford the young Washington in 1768 confided: "I can never, never look on that proclamation in any other light (but this I say between ourselves) than as a temporary expedient to quiet the minds of the Indians and must fall of course in a few years . . . . Any person therefore who neglects the present opportunity of hunting out good lands and in some measure marking . . . them for their own (in order to keep others from settling them) will never regain it." He even suggested a "strategy" (Washington's term) by which the Pennsylvania law that limited the size of the parcel to be purchased could be circumvented, and cautioned: "The scheme [must be] snugly carried on by you under the pretense of hunting other game." [14]

But Washington was a piker, small potatoes, next to Benjamin Franklin. The enterprising Franklin was one of the chief promoters of the sprawling Vandalia Company, which for a long time had operated chiefly in the peltry business. Now, with the fur-trade hurting some, the company began to speculate in land. It looked to the Ohio, way west of present limits to land acquisition. It set its sights on one and a quarter million acres in the Ohio Valley. On the advice of Franklin, rarely modest in his ambitions, the company enlarged its aim to ten million acres! For these, it was proposing to pay the Crown 10,000 pounds.[15]

In 1768 important developments occurred. The recently appointed Superintendents of the Indians reached some historic agreements with the complaining tribes. Three treaties in that year were consummated: The Treaty of Fort Stanwix, which was with the Iroquois; the Treaty of Hard Labour, which was made with the Cherokee of South Carolina; and the Treaty of Pensacola, made with the Creek nation. Not surprisingly, these agreements still farther extended the frontier line, still rather vague, westward, beyond that designated by the Royal Proclamation.[16] But even these treaties, which declared unceded lands to be "off limits" still did little to slow the expansion, and Indian land continued to be gobbled up in an unconscionable manner. These treaties, like all treaties with the Indians which concerned Indian land, were, to employ Washington's term, a "temporary expedient."

The treaty sessions at Fort Stanwix, referred to above, were convened by Sir William Johnson on October 26, 1768, when Cornplanter was a very young man, of sixteen or eighteen. The conference had been called because of Indian complaints about the definition of and respect for the boundary lines established by the Royal Proclamation. The result was a confirmation of the policy implicit in the Proclamation and the establishment of a boundary more precisely defined, which meant an additional cession of lands from the Indians to the Crown. A large body of land, south of the Susquehanna and Ohio Rivers, was turned over and thus opened up to settlement. One disquieting effect of the Treaty was that long-active Indian villages were now within the territory owned by the white settlers.

And still the line crumbled. All along the frontier in the decade following the Royal Proclamation, and in the seven years following the Treaty of Fort Stanwix, violations regularly occurred. Some were official. We have, for example, the colony of Virginia. The Governor of Virginia, the Earl of Dunsmore, disdaining the line drawn by the Treaty of Fort Stanwix, now proceeded to sign over to war veterans portions of the crown land that lay in the domain of the Indian. This action inspired the wrath of the British ministry, which in 1774 ordered governors of the several colonies "to make no land grants except in areas already ceded by the Indians." The proclamation of the ministry was a proper action, certainly, and one that the Congress of the new nation would repeat a decade later.

However, the Boston Tea Party slowed the westward march. The Revolution now became the central concern. But of course the civil war was yet a conflict inspired by the right to the land. Would it be the King, or would it be a new nation, that would displace the Indians? The Iroquois (excepting the Oneidas and the Tuscaroras), concerned chiefly for their lands, cast their lot with the British. Possibly they understood, deep down, that they could not hope to gain either way. But there should be some reward for service.

Chief Cornplanter until War's end was a warrior and only on the fringes of the treaty making and the land disputes. After the War he became a central figure in the diplomatic wars, proving himself a keen politician and an astute diplomat—and losing the respect of his people. For the Indian lands continued to shrink.

What Cornplanter apparently understood very early was what the young Washington had understood even earlier: that the march of the colonials westward was an inexorable one, that it would continue one way or another. It would go forward with the Indians' will, or it would go forward against their will, but it *would* go forward. What the Indians generally had to learn is what Cornplanter had already learned, that a treaty in which land is ceded is a holding action only, a stop-gap measure that would buy for the Indian a little more time in which to carry on the life he knew and loved. What Cornplanter understood was the need, in consequence of this fact of life, to adjust to the whites and their life-style. In the long run it could mean dramatic changes for the Indian civilization. It was forward-looking and practical, but this stance in negotiations was not to sit well with the people of the aging war-chief. It seemed like selling the store.

Red Jacket, as an accomplished orator, and the main body of the Iroquois would cling to the war posture and generally oppose Cornplanter.

Chief Cornplanter was seven travel days from his new home on the Allegheny to the region of Rome, New York, which he had come to know exceedingly well during the three-weeks' siege of Fort Stanwix that he had been party to in August of 1777. He was to know the community and the fort even better. With the War behind them now, the Indians and the victorious colonists returned to the treaty method of settling the land problems, by agreeing to a conference to be held in the fall of 1784 at Fort Stanwix, the site of the treaty sixteen years earlier. Although some 2000 Indians had assembled for the first treaty of Stanwix, called by Sir William Johnson, probably only a few hundred[18] (and perhaps as few as forty from the Six Nations) could be counted at the 1784 sessions. Although they had been invited, the western, or Ohio Valley Indians, namely the Delawares the Miamis, the Shawnee and the Wyandots, showed up in only insignificant numbers. And of course both the new United States, operating now under the Articles of Confederation, and Pennsylvania's President Thomas Mifflin[19] produced an intimidating body of troops numbering perhaps 300.[20]

Before the main session got underway the three Commissioners of New York State, concerned about how the new government might handle New York interests, invited the Iroquois to a kind of pre-session. For this pre-session only four of the Six Nations were represented. Cornplanter and Kaweaweatinen appeared for the Senecas. This warm-up assembled on August 31 in Rome, and was formally convened with an opening address by Governor George Clinton. It closed five days later with a thank-you from Chief Cornplanter. Speaking for the four nations which were present, the Chief commended the New York commissioners for "the candor and civility of their speeches and their attentive treatment of the Indians."[21]

At the main session the United States was represented by its three Commissioners: General Oliver Wolcott, Richard Butler, and Arthur Lee, and all six of the Six Nations were represented. Joseph Brant, because of illness in his family, was not present. Notables present at the conference included the Marquis de LaFayette and James Madison, who was at that time serving in the Virginia legislature. When it finally convened, On October 3, four members of the Six Nations were present. Represented were the Senecas, the Mohawks, the Onondagas, and the Cayugas. Lafayette, who was impatient to address the Indians, and was also in a big hurry to depart, actually got the conference going. This French hero of the Revolution, who was at this time on a tour of the country, made quite a speech. He praised those who had "adhered to us" (the Oneidas and Tuscaroras) and then castigated those "who had been our enemies with freedom," noting that they were the losers in the war. It appeared to observers Samuel Atlee, William Maclay, and Francis Johnston that the speech had some positive effect upon at least the Mohawks, who seemed particularly "repentant."

Though convened on October 3, the conference did not open officially until October 12. General Wolcott addressed the session with welcoming remarks designed to set a tone that would encourage friendly exchange. For the Indians the response was delivered by Cornplanter, and it, too, was amiable; it caused no one to bristle. In the course of the discussions which followed it became apparent that the Indians were impatient with failures in communication, that they were finding it difficult to regard themselves as a defeated enemy and to think of this as a peace treaty. They were not happy with the declaration from the commissioners: "You are a subdued people. You have been overcome in a war which you entered into with us, not only without provocation, but in violation of most sacred obligations." It was also plain that, as they worked out their reaction, the Iroquois were not of one mind.

All were saddened when on October 17 the news arrived that death had taken one of Cornplanter's children. The session was interrupted for a very touching expression of sympathy in the Indian manner.

The agreement that was finally reached saw the Indians, in return for peace, and the promise of protection (The Oneidas and Tuscaroras, of course, had not warred against the Americans, and, indeed, could be thought of as allies.), making large concessions to the United States.

The terms of the treaty, as they were finally defined, were accepted by all parties on October 22, and the Treaty was signed. It was signed first by the three commissioners of the United States (Wolcott, Butler, and Lee) and then by twelve Indians (with the customary **X)** representing the Six Nations of the Iroquois. Signing for the Mohawks were Onogwendahonji and Touighnatogon; for the Onondagas were Oheadarighton and Kendarindgon; for the Senecas were Tayagonendagighti, Tehonwaeaghrigagi, and Kayenthoghke (Seneka Abeal), who was the last to sign. Among the thirteen witnesses who signed the document were the three commissioners from Pennsylvania, who would shortly hold their own conference with the Iroquois.

The agreement, composed of six articles, was short, plain, and simple. But it was a *big* document.

The three commissioners from Pennsylvania, Samuel Atlee, William McClay (Maclay), and Francis Johnston, were present not only as observers to the proceedings. Seizing upon the opportunity afforded a victor in battle, and continuing to take advantage of the pressure that the Indians had been feeling, they now promptly presented a proposal to buy. What they wanted for Pennsylvania was all of that section in the northwest corner of the present state, which the Indians presently held. They were prepared to offer $4000. The Indians consulted. Cornplanter spoke for them. He informed the commissioners that the members of the Six Nations dearly loved their land, this same land on which they had been hunting for so long. He declared that they could not bear to part with it, and that they would not. In short, he refused.

The commissioners put their heads together. They upped the ante to $5000. The Indians agreed. The deed was drawn up and signed the next day, October 23.

Cornplanter would one day be offered a chunk of this tract, but for today it was a bargain only for Pennsylvania.

It is rather staggering to note what these agreements meant for the Indians whose domain had once been Pennsylvania. These cessions meant the end, the complete end of the Indian lands in the Commonwealth.[22] The Senecas did, of course, continue to hold claim to "some 5 million acres in western New York State." And other members of the Six Nations, the Oneidas, the Tuscaroras, and the Cayugas, were not required to give up their substantial lands in New York.[23]

The reaction among the Indian members of the Six Nations, as well as tribes elsewhere, was uniformly hostile. Bad news travels fast. Before the delegates were returned a storm of resentment was unleashed. In consequence the sachems of the Confederation called a council for Buffalo Creek (present-day Buffalo). At this council they expressed their disappointment with the terms, and insisted that the agreement be considered null and void, inasmuch as it had been signed only under duress. They declared their refusal to ratify the treatment their delegates had signed. Many resolved to go to see Washington for themselves. But for now it was a done deed.[24] And, as always when great pain is caused, a scapegoat must be found, some one person on whom to vent the disappointment, manifested in grief or rage. Cornplanter was, though somewhat unjustly, the one singled out for the blame.

Thus did the Seneca warrior-chief Cornplanter embark on his career as statesman.

The *Pennsylvania Archives* contain an illuminating announcement from the Pennsylvania Commissioners pursuant to the State's purchase of lands via the treaty. A letter directed to John Dickinson, President of the Supreme Executive Council of Pennsylvania, by the Pennsylvania Commissioners Samuel J. Atlee, William Maclay, and Francis Johnston, who served as witnesses to the entire proceedings at Fort Stanwix in the fall of 1784, contains the following order: "We the subscribers, Commissioners appointed to purchase of the Indians the late unpurchased territory within the acknowledged limits of Pennsylvania do promise to deliver as soon as soon as conveniently may be, to Cap. Aaron Hill of the Mohawk Tribe, and to Captain O'Bale of the Seneca Tribe two good rifles of neat workmanship, one for each of them, the Rifles to be sent to the new store near Tioga, if it should not be convenient for the said Captain Aaron Hill or Captain O'Bale to come themselves, the Rifles to be delivered to the Bearer of this obligation. These Rifles to be given them in consideration of their services at the late purchase." The document is dated October 27, 1784, five days after Cornplanter signed the Stanwix treaty.[25]

Cornplanter was so often given rewards in return for "services" rendered at negotiations that many of his people wondered whether he was not being bribed and bought off at the expense of their land. As the Indian lands continued to erode at the treaty table, these suspicions deepened.

For the most part in the treaty-making discussions Cornplanter did indeed play a conciliatory role. He certainly was not adversarial toward the Americans in most negotiations. He was quick to voice dissatisfaction when a real injustice was obvious, and he seemed always devoted to his people and working for their best interest. But what seemed to him to be the best interest was often not in accord with the view of the Six Nations, or with the prevailing opinion of his fellow Senecas. And he made some real blunders. In 1787 he affixed his X to the Livingston lease that was later exposed as a sham; and in the next year he agreed to the purchase by Phelps and Gorham which deprived the Senecas of a great deal of their eastern land, including Ganawaugus, the Chief's birthplace and early home.

The Indians were constantly being swindled—by the governments of the several states, by the United States government, by unscrupulous individuals, and by greedy corporations. Notable among these shameful transactions was the deal pulled off by John Livingston, a New York state assemblyman. Livingston, who had formed a company known as the New York and Genesee Land Company, was the principal figure in the land deal that also involved Colonel John Butler and a group known as the Niagara Genesee Company. Among the individuals participating in the scheme was Samuel Street, of whom Cornplanter was promptly and properly suspicious. Understanding that it was simply illegal for private individuals or companies to buy land from the Indians, the Livingston combine hit upon the idea of leasing the land. Accordingly, in 1787, they swindled (and that is the proper term) Cornplanter and the other Iroquois chiefs by getting them to agree to a lease for most of the lands (some eight million acres) that the Senecas regarded as theirs. For this lease, which was to extend for 999 years (!), Livingston agreed to pay $20,000 and a yearly rental of $2,000. Fortunately for the Iroquois, and particularly the Senecas, the New York State legislature promptly nixed the deal as a fraud; but Cornplanter and the chiefs who had agreed to the lease were embarrassed.

April 1, 1788, proved to be an even more disastrous day for the Seneca nation. It was on this date that two speculators from the state of Massachusetts purchased from the state the "pre-emptive right" to some six million acres of land in western New York State. The purchase price was one million dollars. The land that was thus acquired by Oliver Phelps[26] and Nathaniel Gorham (who was actually President of the United States from June 6, 1786, until Feb.1, 1787) [27] was that vast territory west of Seneca Lake between Lake Ontario and the present-day Pennsylvania border, including Cornplanter's home village of Ganawaugus. Actually, Phelps and Gorham did not in this purchase acquire a clear title, as Indian rights to the land were still recognized. But the speculators wasted little time in pursuing those rights. They arranged for a congenial site, receiving on June 21, from the Seneca Chief Red Jacket, Heap-of-Dogs, and Little Billy, an invitation to a council at Buffalo Creek. During the treaty sessions which were held with the Senecas July 4-8 they were able to extinguish the Indian rights to a portion of the land, specifically that region, some two and a quarter million acres, which lay east of the Genesee River. For the title to this land, plus a tract of some 184 thousand acres west of the Genesee, called the Mill Yard Tract (on which Phelps and Gorham planned to build a sawmill and a gristmill), the speculators paid the Indians $5000, plus an annuity "forever" of $500. One can easily imagine the consternation of the Indians when they learned that for the sawmill and the gristmill one acre, rather than 184 thousand acres, would have sufficed. July 8 thus became the fateful day. It was a black day for the Seneca chief Cornplanter.

Never mind that within two years Phelps and Gorham defaulted on the purchase of the land west of the Genesee. The land promptly reverted to Massachusetts, which government within a year sold it to the financier Robert Morris, who sold it off in a number of transactions. Never mind all of that. The land was lost to the Indians. And Cornplanter would be lamenting the transaction for a long time to come.

For these actions, regarded, naturally enough, as betrayals, Chief Cornplanter received threats upon his life.[29] In his speech to Washington in 1790 he was moved to observe that the "great God, and not man, has preserved the cornplanter from the hands of his own nation."[30]

The agreements which followed that of Fort Stanwix in 1784 all followed the pattern that was there established. At Canandaigua in 1794 the Indians did indeed win back some land, but at Fort Harmar, in 1789, at the Treaty of Greenville, in 1795, and in 1797 at the Treaty known as Big Tree, the Indians agreed to shrinking boundaries and acknowledged the sovereignty of the United States in return for rather meaningless annuities and a guarantee of rather meaningless services.[31]

X

PHILADELPHIA AND NEW YORK CITY

In the year following the second council at Fort Stanwix, Joseph Brant invited the Senecas to join his Mohawks on the land grant provided them in Canada, and some, probably fewer than 100, in fact did so. Most Senecas, perhaps as many as several thousand, stayed on in New York, at Buffalo, at Cattaraugus, and in the Genesee region. But Cornplanter, in part surely because of his Uncle Kayahsotha, had opted for, and was already settled in, the upper Allegheny River region. Cornplanter had been living on the upper Allegheny River for about three years, from a time just before the end of the war.

As the Six Nations, and particularly the Senecas, continued in great disappointment with the Treaty of Paris, which acknowledged Indian rights not at all, and in great discontent over the agreements reached at Stanwix in the succeeding year, he felt obliged to head up a delegation to present the Indian case to the Continental Congress, which at this time (1786) was meeting in New York City, then the new nation's capital.[1] Accordingly, he assembled his family, and with "five associates" [2] set out south for Pittsburgh, picking up the Allegheny River at the mouth of French Creek, where the company fashioned canoes. In Pittsburgh the chief traded in his family for an interpreter who understood Seneca and Cayuga (probably Joseph Nicholson) and proceeded from there east to Philadelphia. In all, it would be a very long trip, totaling a good 500 miles each way, and requiring months to negotiate. It begins with a brief sojourn on the Allegheny in canoes, and it ends with a frightful carriage ride into New York City from Philadelphia.

Blacksnake, who of course made the trip, is probably counting himself as one of Cornplanter's "five associates." In describing the journey, he suffers some confusion, and brings in details that belong to a later pilgrimage made to Philadelphia. It is difficult to know on which trip just what occurred. But they were doubtless quite similar. He is quite observant, and he notes especially how much the Indian cavalcade tended to frighten people all along the way:

> *So we made the praperation to Start before Snow fall . . . and . . . . Several families Started with us So we went on the lake [Erie] shore as far as to . . . a small village or settlement what was called Erie and from that to South So got on the stream on franck [French] creek and what now [1850] [is] called midvill [Meadville] and so on Down to the mouth of the franck creek, there was But a few whites families live at the mouth and we made a stop with them for they are some acquaintance with the Indians and they are a good people and visited Each other among the Indians as will as among their own kind folk, while we was there and Building our Bark canoes for us to sailed Down the River with it we Soon got Ready to go Down and we stayed there over winter with the Several Indians families to be Neithbors Each other in camping for winter hunting and injoying that way and for our support throught the winter . . . .*

After learning in Pittsburgh from the interpreter[3] whom they were picking up about big trouble with the Ohio Indians, Blacksnake tells us about their lay-over and their setting out. Here in improved language, is his account: "Cornplanter told him what our business was, how we were on our way to Washington to treat for all the different tribes of Indians. The white man wishes us to wait for him five days, and we told him we'd be glad to do it; and in five days we were ready to start out together on foot on the road to Philadelphia. We found but few people along the way, and the families fled from their cabins when they saw us coming. The white man yelled for them to come back, saying that we were not going to hurt them. But they are afraid of Indians, supposing us a savage people, and most every family we came to ran and hid away from our sight. This for sixty-seven days of our journey."

Because the procession seemed to be frightening everybody along the way, the interpreter proposed that at the next house he would go forward and explain to the people that there was nothing to fear. Cornplanter suggested that he further arrange for their purchase of bread from the family, and allowed that Blacksnake, because he was "not a bad looking fellow," might accompany the interpreter. Turned out the next house they came to was vacant, and at the one after that the children were *still* frightened by Blacksnake. But the family provided bread and some meat, and refused to charge them, and even arranged for them to spend the night. After breakfast the next morning the group set out on a three-days' travel before arriving at a small village some thirty miles west of Philadelphia. Here they stopped at the home of a friend of General Richard Butler, and were most graciously received: ". . . the gentleman tell us through interpreter, that he wanted us to Stay with him about 8 or 10 Days at this house, for he is calculated to get clothes made for us white people clothes and Fashion and on his own Expence."

The delegation certainly enjoyed their time (almost two weeks) in the home of this gentleman. Certainly Chief Cornplanter and his fellow Senecas learned here that whites and Indians are not so different, that indeed they can live together and enjoy each other's company. Blacksnake is rhapsodic. He recalls that they stayed on here ten days. He describes how well cared for they were, with the gentleman insisting on new clothes for the whole party (so that they would not frighten people so much), and how they engaged in hunting deer and in taking part in the fox hunts.[4]

When they reached Philadelphia, the party was obliged to stay on in the city for another ten days before they could meet (hopefully) with Washington, in New York City. Although Blacksnake makes little mention of it (except to recall that sketches were made of him and of uncle Cornplanter), the six Indians were during their lay-over entertained royally by the Tammany Society. The birth of the Society had been inspired by the relationship between King Tammany, a Delaware Chief, and William Penn. Legend has it that Tammany was one of the Delaware Indians who provided a generous welcome to William Penn when he showed up in the new world on October 27, 1682. It is supposed that the name "Tammany" means "the affable." In any case the Indians' early relationship to Penn and the Quakers was definitely friendly. The Society that was organized was devoted to the principles of peace and sincerity, of justice and regard for others. Its members felt a special kinship to the native American Indian, and revered much that was distinctive in their living.

The reception accorded the Seneca chiefs by the Society has been noted by the eminent historian Merle Deardorff: "When the infant society of the Sons of St. Tammany had lionized him, escorting him from [their lodgings at] the Indian Queen Hotel to their [the Society's] Wigwam on the Schuylkill's banks, where, to the tune of thirteen cannon-salutes and huzzas from the two thousand assembled, Cornplanter and the senior Tammany sachem had exchanged courtesies and speeches. . ." [5]

According to newspaper accounts printed afterwards, Cornplanter's speech, as interpreted, was most impressive to the vast audience: "This great gathering of our brothers is to commemorate the memory of our great-grand-father. It is a day of pleasure [pointing to St. Tammany colors]. You know that your and our grandfathers loved one another and strongly recommended to their children to live in union and friendship with all their brethren and to bury the hatchet forever. I also wish [looking up to heaven] that we may all live as our great-grand-fathers lived, in peace and unity!"

And he continued in the same ingratiating tone, "The business I am come on is to have us all united as one man, and it may be my happiness to have it so. Let us keep fast the chain of friendship, and put the same around us. Then we shall have nothing to fear from the great kings on the other side of the waters. Brothers, if we can effect this to become brothers united as one man there is no people that shall think evil of us, that a frown from us will not intimidate. I heard it said that our great-grand-fathers are dead. They are not dead. They now look down upon us and know what we are doing."

The response of the Society's sachem was in the same vein and equally eloquent:

> *We meet as brothers, and it is to us a day of pleasure. We meet here every year to remember our great-grand-father Tammany, and three years ago we buried the hatchet in a great deep hole near that stump; we covered it with heavy stones because we wished it never to rise again. You will see great trees growing over it under which we wish our children to sit. We kindled a fire here, it is a bright fire, for our young men to sit by, and there are twelve other fires. But there is a greater fire than all of them. We are glad you are going to that great fire. You will find the road plain and bright. They will*

> *bind the chain of friendship round their bodies, and it cannot be broken, but by cutting them in two. We have nothing to fear. Our great men will dry the tears from your eyes. We are pleased that you came; to effect this God sent you. He loves peace and friendship. We love you because you are from the great-grand-father, and we shall never forget that you visited our wigwam.* [6]

Several weeks after this reception, at its annual meeting, a Miss Eliza Phile presented to Jonathan Bayard Smith, a sachem of the Society, a portrait of Cornplanter, certainly the sketch referred to by Blacksnake.[7] It was "taken from life," she said, to commemorate the visit. And on that occasion an affectionate toast was drunk to "Our Brother Iontonkque or the Corn Plant." And from the Society's thirteen sachems the second in rank was selected to wear a gorget which bore the name of Iontonkque, and thus marked him as a "patron saint of the society next below their eponym." [8]

At this annual meeting a number of toasts were solemnly made. Among them was this: "The Great Council Fire of the United States—May the [thirteen] fires glow in one blended blaze and illumine the Eagle in his flight to the stars . . . . Our great grand sachem George Washington, Esq. . . . . Our Brother Iontonkque or the Corn Plant—May we ever remember that he visited our wigwam and spoke a good talk from our great-grand-fathers . . . .The Friendly Indian Nations — our warriors and young men who fought, bled and gave good council for our nation." [9]

But the road from Philadelphia to New York City did not prove to be altogether "plain and bright," as the Tammany sachem had hoped. Some drama occurred on the trip from the Quaker City to the seat of government. Chief Cornplanter, who had seen his share of tomahawks and scalping knives and who had heard many a musket ball whizzing by, had somehow weathered the many battles without serious injury. He discovered here that the city streets are ever so much more dangerous. Blacksnake has the story:

> *So we went on Broad [board] the coach or carriages and went toward Newyork, while was Riding During the Day our coach which I was in & cornplanter and one of this two white man was in the same coach Capsize*

> *this white man was some hurd by falling against his face on the ground & Broke his specticles and hurd him on his eyes little & the cornplanter use to ware a pease of Shilver mildtle [medal] under his chin or on his Breast Rather that threw to his face and Stroke on his Brow on the left eye that was cut considerable gash at that time probable Same of you took Notice of him if you ever Seen him when he was life his Brow was lop Down Nearly covered over his eye, this was only some bad luck on a way of our Journey But Did not Great Deil handed about our carriages hurd it injured and our Determination is to get to Newyork this Day, So our Driver had to go and get other carriage to with therefore we Did not get to Newyork until Next morning after Blackvest [breakfast] than cross the River . . . .* [10]

At this point in the narrative, as dictated to Benjamin Williams by Blacksnake, there is described their reception by Washington and the ensuing exchange of speeches. As Washington was not in New York, but at home at Mount Vernon at this time, Blacksnake must be remembering the meeting with Washington that occurred on the pilgrimage to Philadelphia that the Indian delegation made four years later.

On this 1786 occasion, in New York, Cornplanter, who doubtless had hoped to meet with Washington, whom he much respected and felt would be sympathetic, would instead be addressing the Continental Congress. Serving as Acting President of the United States at this time, under the Articles of Confederation, which had been in force for five years now,[11] was David Ramsay of South Carolina.[12]

It was May 2 before Chief Cornplanter had a chance to speak. When he did he spoke with feeling. He made it as clear as he could to the Congress that the Indians whom he represented were much displeased with the Treaty of Paris, that they felt cheated. Three days later Ramsay, an ardent and very active patriot,[13] delivered the response for the Congress, noting, first, that England had surrendered the lands in question to the new United States, and, second, pledging the government's protection of the lands presently occupied by Indians. He expressed concern about the troublesome western Indians, and hoped that Cornplanter might be helpful in settling the differences.[14]

David Ramsay

Chief Cornplanter, who probably did not appreciate at this time just what he was getting into with this new problem, in return for the government's assurances of protection, promised to do what he could as Head of the Senecas, to pacify the western Indians. The council ended in fairly good spirits all around.

But it was not long before Cornplanter and his Senecas were participating in another big conference between the young government of the United States and the Indians. For the Allegheny Senecas, the site was a little more congenial, just down the river "a few miles."

XI

FORT HARMAR

Fort Harmar was built by Major Doughty in 1785 at Marietta, Ohio, at the mouth of the Muskingum and on the "beautiful river" known as the Ohio. It was named for General Josiah Harmar, who had served the patriot cause throughout the Revolution, and who would lead the ill-fated expedition in 1790 against the Shawnee and the Miamis in the valleys of the Scioto and Maumee Rivers.[1] The fort became the site for a council in December of 1788 and into January of 1789. The fort was just across the river from the settlement known as Marietta, which was at this time a community of some thirty New England families. Both Generals Josiah Harmar and Arthur St. Clair were living here at the time.[2]

The council was called by the Governor of the Northwest Territory, General Arthur St. Clair, for December 13, but some Indians began showing up as early as September 9! These Indians established a common temporary campground on a broad bottom along a small unnamed stream two miles north of the fort; a stream that was since being called Indian Camp Run."[3] As other Indians arrived, they proceeded to these campgrounds, and before long quite a sizable encampment had grown up. Cornplanter, at the head of some fifty Senecas, and a few sachems from others of the Six Nations, who had followed various routes to Fort Pitt, was escorted from there, according to some accounts, in boats manned "by General Richard Butler,[4] and two companies of regulars under Captains David Zeigler and James O'Hara." Eventually, except for Brant's Mohawks, all of the Six Nations were represented. Besides, the so-called western Indians had showed up, albeit in small numbers, the Wyandots, the Chippewas, the Delawares, the Potawatomies, the Ottawas, the Mingos, some 200 in all, counting women and children. As it was generally with these councils, many of these Indians had come great distances. And they had come in high spirits, their "colorful and decorative costumes"[5] reflecting their love of the council fire.

According to every report, the incoming Indians were welcomed most cordially by General Harmar, who revealed, however, some uneasiness in the proclamation he had posted. Noting that the council would require "several weeks," he ordered a peace period. He declared that none of the Indians already in camp, nor any of the others yet to come, was to be "molested in any way." [6]

As it turned out, General Harmar's fears were well founded. It was not long, on November 6, before the infamous Lewis Wetzel had murdered one of the Indian delegates. This was a warrior ranked as a subchief. He was known by the name Tegunteh, but was quite proud of the new name he had just recently assumed, George Washington. In the consternation which followed, Wetzel was arrested, confessed, in his typically arrogant fashion, and was jailed. And escaped.[7] Cornplanter's reaction to all of this is not known. But it was an unfortunate beginning to the conference.

According to one historian, the convention was a "fiasco." [8] The western tribes for whom the sessions were primarily called, dispatched only a few delegates, and of these hardly any could claim chief status. The Mohawks sent nobody. Cornplanter's delegation, however, was substantial, including as it did not only his Allegany Senecas, and a few from the Genesee region, but a number of sachems and warriors of the Six Nations as well. The influential Joseph Brant, by this time no friend to Cornplanter, was absent; and the Seneca chief wasted no time in ripping into the Mohawk chief. He delivered some pointed accusations and spoke in great heat. "Brothers," he said, "I now tell you that I take Brant & Set him down in his Chair at home and he shall not Stir out of his house, but will keep him there fast, he shall no more run about amongst the Nations disturbing them and causing trouble." [9]

Cornplanter and some other chiefs made plaintive appeals to St. Clair, stressing the need for the Indians to have land on which to hunt, and urging the commissioners to honor the Ohio River boundary line; but their entreaties went pretty much unheard. In the end, St. Clair did not give in to the Indians. He made it plain that while the United States preferred peace to war, it would have the land—one way or the other. The sessions ended with the promise of gifts and in some confusion, the Indians adjourning in great bewilderment.

The Allegany Senecas throughout the discussions supported the United States against the western Indians.[10] Anthony Wallace explains the transactions: ". . . one with the United States, which renewed the land cession made at Stanwix, and another with Pennsylvania, ceding to the state the Erie Triangle, but reserving to the Six Nations the Seneca-occupied lands east of the Conewango Creek and Chautauqua Lake (which Cornplanter and white officials alike mistakenly believed to be west of the line sold earlier)." [11]

Arthur St. Clair

With the Governor of the Northwest Territory, General Arthur St. Clair presiding, in what one historian describes as an "arrogant and imperious" manner, two treaties were consummated at Fort Harmar on January 9, 1789. One was with the Wyandots and the other western Indians; the other was with the Six Nations, which meant in this case the Senecas. Actually very little was accomplished, as "the transactions at Fort Harmar basically confirmed the cessions that had been made at the treaties of Fort Stanwix in 1784 and by the Wyandots and other western Indians at Fort McIntosh in January of the next year.[12] The Senecas did receive compensation, some $3,000 worth of goods (apparently intended for all the Iroquois), which were supplied to them before their leaving; [13] and a sum of $6000 dollars was provided to the other Indian tribes represented.[14] The Commissioners from Pennsylvania also seized the opportunity in the wake of the council to cement their acquisition of Pennsylvania's Erie Triangle, and even to enlarge it by some 200,000 acres. Chief Cornplanter was most helpful to the Commissioners in this arrangement.

Though St. Clair could have hoped for a greater attendance, and though the proceedings did drag on, and though he must have been aware that he was taking advantage of some confusion, he was much pleased by the conference. And, noting the abuse suffered by the absent Joseph Brant, he reported to Henry Knox that the Iroquois Confederacy "is broken." [15]

The Treaty with the Six Nations made at Fort Harmar, January 9, 1789, was Fort Stanwix all over again. It was composed of four main articles, and a separate one providing protection for whites from Indians and conversely was appended.

And so the "Old Line," as the boundary established in 1768 had come to be known, was reaffirmed, and the Indians, by such terms as "forever" and "perpetual" got the impression of permanence. And Pennsylvania at a cost of $2000 in goods secured the "Erie Triangle." Cornplanter was the prime mover in all of this. He obviously felt that whatever future his people could have would be with the new government. Twenty-two Indians, including Blacksnake, signed the document, most of them with an X only. Big Tree signed with the four names he was known by. Cornplanter signed as "Gyantwaia, or Cornplanter." Half Town, New Arrow (known also as Captain Strong), and Gyasota (Big Cross) of the Senecas also signed.

According to one contemporary account, the treaty sessions "terminated entirely to the satisfaction of all concerned." The occasion deserved to be marked by celebration. And so a most elegant entertainment was provided, and the report has the Indian chiefs behaving with the "greatest decorum" throughout. The dinner was topped off with generous offerings of wine, which prompted a toast from Chief Cornplanter. Raising his glass, he addressed the gathering in his Seneca tongue: "I thank the Great Spirit for this opportunity of smoking the pipe of friendship and love. May we plant our own vines, be the fathers of our own children, and maintain them." [16]

It is not too much to say that it was largely because of the influence of Chief Cornplanter that the Indians here at Fort Harmar gave up their claims to the much disputed Erie Triangle. Pennsylvania acknowledged his role, and it was definitely in part because of his cooperation at Fort Harmar that Cornplanter was shortly thereafter awarded officially the 1500 acres of land in the Allegheny region, completing the arrangement that General Richard Butler had urged. Cornplanter and his people also received some goods and some monies. And Cornplanter, in return for his generous service to the Ohio Land Company, was by officials of the company presented a grant. The Ohio Land Company had been organized just three years earlier, in 1786, and through their agents had contracted with the government of the United States the purchase of one and one-half million acres of land in the Northwest Territory for one million dollars in Loan Certificates. The Ohio Company Records include an account of the grant to Cornplanter of "one mile square."

The meeting of the directors and agents of the company, held at Campus Martius [Marietta] Ohio, Feb. 9, 1789, included the following proceedings:

> *Whereas, Gyantwachia, or the Cornplanter, a Chief of the Seneca nation, has, since the Treaty of Peace [Stanwix], made in the year 1784, between the United States and the Indian nations, in many instances, been of great service to the United States; and the friendship he has manifested to the proprietors of land purchased by the Ohio Company, has been of particular service to them; therefore, Resolved, That one mile square of the donation lands be granted to Gyantwachia, and his heirs forever, in such place as the committee appointed to examine proper places of settlement shall assign; and that the dates, conditions and limitations required of other settlers on such land, shall in this grant be dispensed with. And the said committee of five are directed to give him a deed accordingly.*[17]

Although there is much confusion over whatever happened to this deed (some arguing that Cornplanter never received it), it seems probable now that Cornplanter did in fact receive a deed, and that, as he later lamented, it was stolen, either while on his way home from Fort Harmar, or in the next year, while he was returning from his conferences with Governor Mifflin and President Washington in Philadelphia. In any case, although he even employed the Pittsburgh attorney Hugh Brackenridge to recover the property for him, there is no record at all of any selection of the "one mile square" plot of land.[18]

It was a rough trip home for Chief Cornplanter. In a speech made in October of the next year to Governor Thomas Mifflin and the Executive Council of Pennsylvania in Philadelphia, the Chief disclosed some of the events of his return trip. "When I was leaving Muskingum," he reported, "my own son [probably Henry, who would be fifteen years old] who remained a little while behind to warm himself at the fire was robbed of a rifle by one of the white men, who, I believe, to have been a Yankee." And it was downhill after that. Having separated from the interpreter Joseph Nicholson, who took some of Cornplanter's people with him, Cornplanter found himself still in charge of 170 persons of his own nation, "consisting of men, women and children, to conduct thro' the wilderness, through heaps of briars, and having lost our way, we, with great difficulty reached Wheelen [Wheeling]." After securing provisions (which put him into debt in the amount of $17), he led his party on toward Fort Pitt. Ten miles from Wheeling "my party were fired upon by three white people, and one of my people in the rear of my party received two shots thro' his blanket."

That should have been enough for this trip, but it was not all. To the Pennsylvania Council in Philadelphia he confessed another incident of their going home from Harmar:

> *It was a constant practice with me throughout the whole journey to take great care of my people, and not suffer them to commit any outrages or drink more than what their necessities required. During the whole of my journey only one accident happened, which was owing to the kindness of the people of the town of Catfish [in Washington County, south of Pittsburgh] in the Quaker State, who, while I was talking with the head man of the town, gave to my people more liquor than was proper, and some of them got drunk, which obliged me to continue there with my people all night, and in the night my people were robbed of three rifles and one shot gun; and though every endeavor was used by the head man of the town . . . to discover the perpetrators of the robbery, they could not be found; and on my people's complaining to me I told them it was their own fault by getting drunk.* [19]

Not all of the treaty sessions proved to be so eventful.

XII

THOMAS MIFFLIN AND GEORGE WASHINGTON

The year of 1790 was going to be a big year for the Seneca Chief Cornplanter.

All kinds of atrocities had continued to occur along the frontier during the seven years following the Treaty of Paris. Whole families were murdered by Indians from the Ohio country, and the now-peaceful Senecas were likewise murdered by white men. A great many members of Cornplanter's own family had been robbed, and a few had been killed. For a long time the chief had been reporting these crimes to the state authorities in Philadelphia. Time and time again he petitioned the Executive Council of Pennsylvania for protection and relief. *Finally*, on the 10th of May, 1790, the President of the Executive Council, Thomas Mifflin[1] dispatched a letter to eleven of the "Chief Counsellors and Warriors of the Six Nations of Indians." Chief Cornplanter, at this time living on the upper Allegheny River, was addressed as Kientwoughko, and was the first listed name. Among the others addressed were Dog Barker, Oldnews, Large Tree (Big Tree), Broken Tree, and Half Town. The letter read: "It gives us pain to hear from you that some bad people have plundered your camps and taken your property. Our laws do not permit one man to injure another. We are willing to give you an opportunity of laying before the government of Pennsylvania your grievances, and of explaining your wishes; and agreeably to your request, we hereby invite three of your chief counsellors and warriors, vizt.: Cornplanter, Half Town, and the New Arrow, to come to Philadelphia, on Wednesday the first day of September next, when the General Assembly will be in session. We have granted a commission to your particular friend, Joseph

Nicholson, to act as interpreter to your three Chiefs, and will give him directions to conduct them to this city." [2]

Thomas Mifflin

Apparently this invitation was not received by the chiefs until the seventh of July,[3] but when they had it they promptly made preparations to visit the state capital in Philadelphia. They secured a passport from Ensign John Jeffers, of the 1st U. S. Regiment, the commanding officer of Fort Franklin (at the confluence of French Creek and the Allegheny River), with whom Cornplanter was on very good terms: "My age, rank & situation in the world," noted the officer, "renders it rather improper for me to say anything on the subject I am about to relate, but I cannot but mention that the Bearer hereof, Cyentwokee [Cornplanter], the head Chief of the Senica Nation, is an undoubted friend to the United States. When Indians have stolen Horses & other things from the good people, I have known him with the greatest dignity to give orders for them to be returned, & never knew his orders to be disobeyed."

Well aware that the deputation might frighten people along the way, he continued his reassuring recommendation: "When the people of Cussawaga [now Meadville] were about to flee on account of unfavorable accounts about some of the Southern Indians, he [Cornplanter] sent a Speech to me, & said [that he] wished 'the people to keep their minds easy, & take care of their Cornfields, that the Six Nations were friends, that should the Southern Indians invade the Settlement he would gather his Warriors & help to drive them to the setting of the Sun.' In consequence of this the people rest intirely easy. On his arrival here, he told me that should I be invaded so that I could not get provision, that he & his warriors would clear the way—he said that at the Council at Muskingum [Fort Harmar], the great men asked him which side he would die on? He told them on the side of the Americans, he says he is of the same mind yet."

And Ensign Jeffers was not through: "Sundry other things might be said, but as he is now on his way to attend the Assembly at Philadelphia I will only recommend him to the particular attention of the good people of Pennsylvania between here and that place. They may depend upon it that they not only entertain a friend, but a consequential friend, for the Senica Nation is so much Governed by him that if he says *War*, it is *war,* & if he says peace it is peace—of Course he is a Man worthy of the greatest attention. The other Chiefs with him second him in every thing, & are Men worthy of great attention." And the letter was signed and directed to the "Good people between here & Philadelphia." [4] This letter doubtless stood the Indians in good stead, and Cornplanter was happy to present it to Thomas Mifflin when he did finally arrive in Philadelphia.

But before Cornplanter could assemble the chiefs and get his expedition on the road, he had a crisis to resolve. He had received some *very* painful news. The source of this news was a river valley that he knew well and had always loved. Pine Creek was one of the most beautiful streams of the Indian country. In its centuries-long passage through the mountains it had cut a breathtaking gorge known now as Pennsylvania's Grand Canyon. The stream, rising in northeast central present-day Potter County, five miles southwest of Ulysses, flows southeast past Galeton, then south through Pine Creek Gorge (the "Grand Canyon"), and then into the West Branch of the Susquehanna River between present-day Jersey Shore and Avis. Along the way it is enlarged by four tributaries, known as West Branch Pine Creek, Marsh Creek, Babb Creek, and Little Pine Creek (Blockhouse Creek). The Indian activity on its waters had for a long, long time been constant and heavy. Cornplanter had many, many times plied his canoe through its rapids and along its scenic shores.

On June 27, two friendly Seneca Indians who had come into the Pine Creek settlement, seventeen miles upstream from the confluence of Pine Creek and the West Branch of the Susquehanna, near present-day Jersey Shore, were brutally murdered by four settlers. According to one version there was no provocation. According to another, the Indians had become intoxicated in Stephenson's Tavern near the Walker farm operated by three brothers. The Walkers were not friendly to the Indians, for their father had been barbarously killed and scalped at Turtle Creek, near Pittsburgh. According to one account, "The old Indian threw himself down before the Walkers, and went through several performances, exhibiting the most horrid grimaces and contortions of the face, remarking to them, 'This is the way your father acted when I killed and scalped him.'" The Walkers (Benjamin, Joseph and Henry), assisted by a man by the name of Doyle, allegedly stole up the creek later that night a short distance to where the Indians were encamped and murdered them. The brothers then fled and disappeared completely. Doyle was imprisoned briefly, tried and acquitted. The Indians for miles around were incensed, the more so as the two victims were chiefs; and elaborate preparations were made to invade the settlement, and before long a large body of warriors had been assembled and were marching on the settlement. Cornplanter, who had been promptly notified of the murders and had been advised of the Indian response, had made no move to interfere; but, on learning that the authorities were determined to bring the murderers in for punishment, and that a reward had been offered, considered it best to call off the warriors. Accordingly, he dispatched one of his swift-footed runners with orders for the warriors to return to their homes. To what extent the authority of the Chief was yet recognized is quite apparent in all of this, for the Seneca warriors, though enraged, felt obliged to obey.[5]

But the murders remained a sore point with the Indians. And the settlers, fearing retribution, formally petitioned Lt. Bernard Hubley (with twenty-six signatures) for "thirty or forty men, with arms, ammunition, and provisions."

On the day that he received the request, July 12, from his militia post at Northumberland, some sixty-five miles southeast of the settlement, Lieutenant Hubley dispatched a reply, sending both the letter of petition and his answer to President of the Supreme Executive Council, Thomas Mifflin. To the apprehensive settlers, Hubley replied in the negative, and gave his reasons. The letter is addressed to "Robert Fleming, Esq., Colonel John Chatham, & other Inhabitants at and near Pine Creek, Northumberland Co." The letter is composed out of a genuine and helpless concern. Hubley, expressing his regrets, explained that he wanted the authority of the Executive Council, and that he very much feared that the appearance of troops would provoke violence.[6]

Letters continued to be exchanged between Mifflin's office and the uneasy settlement, and the affair was still very much alive as late as October, when Cornplanter, on his way to Philadelphia with his delegation of chiefs, met in council with Dr. John Wilkins, Jr., of Shippensburgh. Wilkins, in a letter dated October 14, reported to Mifflin: "I have just met at this place Cornplanter and the other Indian Chiefs . . . . Cornplanter says that when he was preparing to come down [to Philadelphia], agreeable to the invitation from Council, his Nation was excited to great tumult by the killing of the two Chiefs on Pine Creek, and he was obliged to stay to pacify them . . . . The subject of this visit of the Chiefs of the Sennaca Nation is of great Consequence to the people of the western country—they border on our frontier settlement to a great extent, and if they are disposed to war will tend greatly to the injury of our defenceless country—exclusive of the people that may be killed by them, the inhabitants will be expelled from their settlements and many reduced to beggary and misery . . . . I need not give you a Character of the Cornplanter, his friendship for the people of Pennsylvania, his pacific temper and integrity are sufficiently known."

Earlier, August 5, Thomas Mifflin and his Executive Council had received a letter from a man by the name of Freeman, Justice of the Peace in Portland, Maine. In this letter Freeman describes in great detail some suspicious strangers who had lately shown up in the community. He had read the notices put out by Pennsylvania for the apprehending of the Walker brothers, and he was "absolutely convinced" that these strangers were indeed the murderers. He reported that one was confined to jail at that very moment. Apparently nothing ever came of that, and nothing is today known further about the Walker brothers.

In September, as the affair continued hot and threatened to boil over, Ensign John Jeffers, still the commander at Fort Franklin, and always sympathetic to Cornplanter and the Senecas, wrote in disgust to Josiah Harmar,[8] who still in the Army would command the forces that would next month be overwhelmed by the Shawnee and Miami Indians in the valleys of the Scioto and Maumee Rivers. Declared Jeffers: "The people who committed the murder might be given up to the Indians and be by them burnt at the Stake—for I believe the Senecas before this, were at heart friendly." [9]

But it was all moot. You cannot burn at the stake, nor imprison, nor punish in any way murderers whom you cannot find. The Walker brothers were never brought to justice. And all credit to Cornplanter for keeping the situation cool.

But for a long, long time, the Pine Creek murders tormented the Chief. In his meeting with Mifflin and the Pennsylvania Council, and again in his session with President Washington, he would refer to the event, and hold it out as an instance of the treatment regularly accorded the Indians.

But that wasn't all. That summer Cornplanter was also obliged to meet with the restless Shawnees, a council that would have delayed his trip to Philadelphia, even without the Pine Creek episode.

But finally, Chief Cornplanter, armed with the passport furnished by Ensign Jeffers, was able to set out from the upper Allegheny with his delegation. Besides Half Town and Big Tree, he would have in his company James Hutchins, Seneca Billy, and John Deckart.

In a letter to Brigadier General Josiah Harmar, dated October 1, Fort Franklin, Ensign Jeffers provided an update: "The Cornplanter and his Councillors arrived at the garrison three days since on their way to Philadelphia. The Cornplanter told me to keep my mind easy, for he was determined on peace, he gave me a speach for the people at Cussawaga, he said they must keep their minds." [10]

It may be presumed that this trip to Philadelphia was roughly similar to that made to New York City via Philadelphia four years earlier and described by Blacksnake, who was not particularly invited in 1790 and probably did not accompany his uncle.

The trip was in response to President Mifflin's invitation, of course, and Cornplanter and his fellow chiefs were determined to lay before the Pennsylvania Council an account of their many grievances. They paused in Pittsburgh, to permit Cornplanter and Half Town to consult with the town's most distinguished citizen, the writer-attorney-newspaper man Hugh Henry Brackenridge.[11] Cornplanter and his fellow chiefs had been badgering Brackenridge for a long time, complaining about the cheating and fraudulent practices of the traders in Pittsburgh. Now, with an audience with the Council in Philadelphia, it looked as though they were getting some place. Brackenridge, who, naturally, was well aware of the nefarious practices carried on in the bargaining with Indians, was very glad to help. To His Excellency Gen'l Thomas Mifflin, on October 4, he addressed a letter of support:

> *Sir, two Chiefs, of the name of Cornplanter and Half Town, Conceiving themselves injured by Colonel John Gibson,*[12] *have been directed to apply to me, to obtain for them redress by law. I have recommended to them, now that they are going down [to Philadelphia] to present themselves before your Excellency, to make complaint to the Council, who will enquire into this affair, and call Mr. Gibson to an account, if he shall be seen to have defrauded them. It is so customary with Traders to Cheat Indians, that I think it not improbable that their Complaints are well founded. General Gibson acting as a Commissioner under your authority, will be properly amenable before you. It is a misdemeanour, which I conceive will support an indictment, if the fact is established. If so, the Councils can direct an inquiry at this place. For the course of six months I have been importuned by those Chiefs to give them advice in this matter, and the Common Opinion here is strong in their favour with regard to the injustice done them. I know well that such ground of dissatisfaction on the part of the savages is often the occasion of war, and certainly it behooves the government to take care of their officers, and oblige them to act honestly with them [the Indians].* [13]

Apparently the delegation stopped off also in Greensburg, some forty miles east of Fort Pitt, to visit some with a good friend of Big Tree. To His Excellency, Thomas Mifflin, Esq. of Philadelphia, Robert Galbraith of that community, on October 7, dispatched a letter which he hoped would arrive in the Quaker City before the Indian chiefs. If it did, he was confident it would surely help to insure a gracious welcome for the Seneca delegation: "Having met with the Cornplanter and his company on their way to Philad'a, I would take the liberty to inform your Excellency that I have been acquainted with Stif-knee [Big Tree], one of his company, the greatest part of this summer, as he has resided about twelve miles from Pittsburgh on the Allegheny River, near to where I now reside; and have known the said Stif-knee to watch the frontier on that quarter, and use every exertion in his power to prevent Horses being stolen or any injury done to the good people at that place, that he has been friendly and useful to the Americans in general, and is a man of a general good character. The Cornplanter's Zeal and Attachment to the American cause is so well known, that it would be unnecessary for me to say any thing on that subject." [14]

The delegation, delayed by the affair at Pine Creek and by the necessary council with the Shawnee, reached Philadelphia at the end of the third week of October. They were promptly welcomed, and on Saturday, October 23, were formally presented to President Mifflin and the members of the Executive Council. Cornplanter thanked the Council for the invitation, and made his apologies for arriving late: "*Brothers,* We were very happy when we received the answer to our letter sent to the Quaker State; we are happy to see you. We could not come at the time appointed, it was too soon afterwards. When we were coming we heard of the murder of two of our people. I was obliged to satisfy my people. After I had satisfied my people, I received a message from the Shawanese and other nations that I should not come till we had a Council with them. When the fire was kindled with the Shawanese they brought a Virginia scalp and insisted on our seizing the scalp, or they would treat us the same way as the Big Knife [the Virginians]; we told them the Council was for peace not for war, I sent to all the tribes to be at peace with the Thirteen Fires."

The Council was scheduled for October 25, but on the day before, which was a Monday, Cornplanter asked for a little more time in which to prepare: "*Brothers* I am much fatigued, I want to get a friend to write my speech, as no interpreter can do it as well as if it was wrote. I will be ready on Tuesday morning." [15]

Still not ready by Tuesday morning, Cornplanter dispatched a request to the Council for some additional time: "Having come to the City for the purpose of laying before You some Grievances which the Seneca nation, over which I preside, have to complain of; and which I fully intended to have laid before You to-morrow; but having luckily [fallen in] with a Mr. Phelps [the infamous Oliver Phelps of the Phelps & Gorham Purchase], between whom & my Nation, the difference in a great Measure subsists; and a long talk having taken place between him [and] me, in the presence of some of my Friends [the Quakers of Philadelphia], which has delayed the time, & made it impossible for me to do as I wished; I take the liberty of requesting that you will pardon & forgive my not complying with my Engagements; And that you will give me another Opportunity of talking with you." The letter was closed with an expression of "great Respect & Esteem, I am Your affectionate Son, Cornplanter," and signed with his mark.

The Council politely agreed to a postponement. In three more days, the chief felt himself as well prepared as ever he could be; and at the head of his delegation of six he marched into session with the Supreme Executive Council of Pennsylvania. The date was October 29, a Friday. With his interpreter Joseph Nicholson[16] rendering the Seneca tongue into palatable English, Cornplanter addressed President Mifflin and the Council. The Senecas are now the children of Father Pennsylvania. They need protection from evil people. They need care. Spoke the Chief: "I hope that you Fathers of the Quaker State will fix some person at Fort Pitt to take care of me and my people. I wish, and it is the wish of my people if agreeable to you, that my present interpreter, Joseph Nicholson may be the person."

Cornplanter then paraded a long litany of wrongs done his people by the Pennsylvania authorities, and by the settlers, including the most awful murder of his brother-in-law (about five years ago) and the murder, just last winter, of his nephew, who was treacherously slain by a white man because the young man had a fine riding horse, and was possessed of fine clothes and silver, and a rifle.

Toward the end of his remarks he noted, "I have heard that you have been pleased to present me a tract of land, but as yet I have seen no writings for the same; Well, Fathers, if it is true that you have given me this tract of land I can only thank you for the same, but I hope you will also give me tools and materials for working the same." And he appeals to the Fathers of the Quaker State for a grant of land for his interpreter, Joseph Nicholson, "six miles square at the site of the August 1779 skirmish with Brodhead's forces."

It is a very long speech, a most plaintive and deeply moving speech. And Cornplanter concludes with the hope "you will consider well all I have mentioned." [17] The address was signed by all who were with him, Half Town, Big Tree, James Hutchins, Seneca Billy, and John Deckart.

The response of the Council was prompt, for on the very next day appeared a letter of reply. It was addressed to Chief Cornplanter and to the Indians who had come with him to Philadelphia. It was presented to the Executive Board, read and adopted. The date was October 30, 1790.

Apparently that part of the delegation which Cornplanter had released was now ready to go home, for Colonel Thomas Proctor on November 1 notified President Mifflin that Captain Obeal had called upon him (It was only ten years ago that Proctor had ordered cannonballs launched at Cornplanter and his ambushed warriors!) to advise him that his people were ready to leave for Fort Pitt, "as soon as your pleasure and that of the Executive Council are made known to us." Cornplanter also politely reminded Proctor that the Indians had not yet received the coats they had been promised by Council.[18]

But nobody was going home, not yet, not for quite a while.

First they had to have the reply of Council, which, though quite prompt did not at that time address the grievances laid before them by Cornplanter. And it attended to only two of his requests. It was explained to Cornplanter and to the others that the Commonwealth of Pennsylvania would in December be changed in its government. The Supreme Executive Council, with its President, was being replaced by a Governor and a legislature. "When those events take place," the chiefs were told, "your speech, together with such further representation of a public nature, which you may think proper to make to us, shall be faithfully communicated to the new Government for their consideration and decision."

The two points on which the present administration of the Quaker State felt authorized to deal with were (1) the grant to Cornplanter (which had already been accomplished, without formal notice to the Chief), and (2) Cornplanter's request for permission to stay on in Philadelphia until such time as he could meet with President Washington.[19]

The Executive Council reported to Cornplanter that the grant of which he was speaking was a fait accompli, the General Assembly having approved the awarding of 1500 acres of land on March 24, 1789. "We would long ago have ordered the survey of the land for the Cornplanter, but being willing to gratify him in his choice of a tract, we instructed General Butler to consult with him on that subject, and have waited to this time for his determination. If he will inform us in what part of the unlocated lands of the State he wishes his survey to be made, we will order the Surveyor General to have the tract laid out without further delay."

On Cornplanter's request that he, together with Half Town and Nicholson, be permitted to remain in the city until the United States Congress convened, the Council "cheerfully" complied with his request. And certainly it was all right with Council for Cornplanter to send the other Indians home. Council went further: "In order to make the residence of the Cornplanter, Half Town and Mr. Nicholson in Philadelphia as convenient and agreeable as possible, Council will instruct their Secretary to provide suitable lodgings for them in a private family."

The council had a particular instruction for those chiefs and warriors who were returning to their homes: "We desire you to inform the Seneca Nation that the Government of Pennsylvania entertains sentiments of the most sincere friendship for them, and are anxious to prevent injuries being done by its citizens to their persons and property." The Council recognized that men disposed to evil exist in every society (bad things will happen), and they urged the chiefs to make certain that when violence occurs it is reported, so that "the offenders may be apprehended and brought to justice."

Cornplanter's reference to the unpunished Pine Creek murderers was duly noted. The Council declared it had done everything it could to have them apprehended, and, though successful only with Doyle, would continue the search for the Walker brothers. Doyle, Cornplanter was assured would be "capitally punished." Of course, Doyle, as noted, was acquitted.

But before the discharged chiefs and warriors could get underway for the return trip to Pittsburgh, Chief Big Tree, while taking in the sights of the Quaker City, somehow managed to get himself shot in the leg. Because of the wound and the attention it required, Cornplanter in another meeting with the Council requested that those Indians who were to go home be permitted to stay on. Council graciously honored the request.[20]

Apparently Cornplanter, when he set out for Philadelphia at the invitation of Thomas Mifflin had no expectation of meeting with President Washington; and it is thought that Washington was himself much surprised to find the Indian chiefs on a dark winter day on the doorstep of Congress, which was headquartered in the Philadelphia County Building, called Congress Hall.

But though he may have been startled, and though he had lots of urgent business to tackle, President Washington, who had returned to

Philadelphia on November 27, granted Cornplanter an audience for December 1. Actually, Philadelphia would not officially become the capital of the United States under the Constitution until December 6 of this year, but it had been moved from New York City during the summer.[21]

One wonders about this meeting between the two principals, which must have been their first. Surely it could not have been anything like a confrontation. Cornplanter had long been respectful of the Father of the Thirteen Fires, even though he would address him as Town Destroyer, and had long been inclined to trust him. And Washington was certainly very curious to know firsthand the Seneca chieftain, about whom he had been hearing steadily for some thirteen years now. It must have been a dramatic meeting, this between the Commander-in-Chief of the Continental Army, now President of the United States, and the Seneca Indian Chief Cornplanter. It was a coming together of the commanding general who had ordered the burning of the Seneca villages and the most influential Indian ally of the British, known as Captain O'Bail. The Seneca Indian chief is at this time thirty-eight, perhaps forty years old. Washington is almost fifty-nine. As Blacksnake does not supply any details of the actual meeting of the two, we can only imagine the moment. Actually it is not likely that Blacksnake even made this trip to Philadelphia. A meeting with Washington is described at this point in the chronology of his narrative, but that would seem to be a recollection of the later 1792 excursion to Philadelphia. Blacksnake mentions Red Jacket here. Chief Red Jacket was not in the 1790 delegation; he was a prominent figure in the 1792 Philadelphia council.

As this council might properly be regarded as a big event in American history, certainly a momentous scene in the history of Indian-White relations, and as it does much to enlarge our impression of one of the most important figures of the Revolution and the succeeding half-century, the reader is invited to the speeches. Happily, the exchange has been preserved in the American State Papers (Indian Affairs). The Indian remarks are signed by Half Town and Great Tree, as well as by Cornplanter, but it has always been assumed that Cornplanter was the chief orator, and perhaps the only one.

The writers of the *History of Venango County* were very high on Cornplanter's oratory: "In the impassioned utterances of Cornplanter . . . we find an impressive and effective style that excites our liveliest imagination, and in the annals of eloquence more fervid oratory is rarely found." They were high on the speaking of Red Jacket over the years, too, and acknowledged that he came finally to enjoy a greater reputation for oratorical skill than did Cornplanter. Still, they declared, "If one may judge . . . from the specimens of their eloquence that have come down to us, while we have much to admire in both, we rather conclude that Red Jacket's superiority must have been more in *manner* than in *matter*. The address delivered to General Washington, in Philadelphia, 1790, though in the names of Great Tree, Half Town and Cornplanter, was undoubtedly dictated by the latter, and to him is due the credit. It will bear comparison to any Indian speech on record. While not so declamatory as the ordinary Indian style, it is closely logical, and ranks as a rare specimen of impressive and effective oratory." [22]

Definitely Cornplanter must have been impressive to Washington at this time, in both manner and matter. In the customary council way his opening is almost plaintive; certainly it is respectful, while allowing the discontent and bitterness to seep through. Throughout the long speech, Cornplanter skillfully employs pointed rhetorical questions. It should be noted, also, that the chief, whenever he is referring to the Indian negotiators at the treaty councils, uses the third person, though he was himself primary. Of course, it must be remembered that all is rendered into English, most skillfully, by the interpreter Joseph Nicholson. And Chief Cornplanter is pausing periodically to allow Nicholson to translate for the most attentive Congress. To know Cornplanter, one must hear him speak:

> *Father: The voice of the Seneca nation speaks to you, the great councillor, in whose heart the wise men of all the Thirteen Fires have placed their wisdom. It may be very small in your ears, and we therefore entreat you to hearken with attention: for we are about to speak of things which are to us very great. When your army entered the country of the Six Nations, we called you the town destroyer; and to this day, when that name is heard, our women look behind them and turn pale, and our children cling close to the necks of their mothers. Our councillors and warriors are men, and cannot be afraid; but their hearts are grieved with the fears of our women and children, and desire it may be buried so deep as to be heard no more. Our warriors are men,*

> *and cannot be afraid, but their hearts are grieved with the fears of our women and children and desire that it [the pain inflicted by the Sullivan campaign] may be buried so deep as to be heard no more.*

After a meaningful pause, the Chief continued, "When you gave us peace, we called you father, because you promised to secure us in the possession of our lands. Do this, and, so long as the lands shall remain, that beloved name will live in the heart of every Seneca."

He never spoke at length anymore without referring to the injustices done at Stanwix and Fort Harmar. Here he asks, "What have we done to deserve such severe chastisement?"

At this point Cornplanter pauses dramatically, then resumes with an explanation of why the Seneca nation sided with the British against the rebel cause, acknowledges it was a mistake, and with a good bit of logic suggests that the rebellious thirteen fires should assume some of the blame for that mistake. "Is the blame all ours?"

Then the Chief notes for the assembled Congress the injustice of what has transpired so far with respect to the Indian lands, and declares that the Indians have been deceived and coerced into unconscionable agreements. He reviews in the familiar way the negotiations that have transpired since the war's end, at Fort Stanwix, etc.; and then the Treaty of Paris, by which the British ceded to the Americans the land that belonged to the Indians, becomes his subject.

Of the shyster John Livingston and the machinations of the Phelps and Gorham Purchase he, naturally, had nothing good to say. He regarded both deals as swindles, couched in arrogance and deceit, in keeping with the general attitude toward the Indians and their land.

Throughout Cornplanter is speaking from a capacious mind and a most reliable memory. He knows every detail, down to the last dollar. How desperate is the plight of the Senecas, how fervently they long for justice, the Seneca Chief, still impressive in his bearing (after two hours), now brings home to Washington and the Congress: "Father, You have said that we are in your hand, and that, by closing it, you could crush us to nothing. Are you determined to crush us? If you are, tell us so, that those of our nation who have become your children, and have determined to die so, may know what to do. In this case, one chief has said he would ask you to put him out of pain. Another, who will not think of dying by the hand of his father or of his brother, has said he will retire to the Chateaugay, eat of the fatal root, and sleep with his fathers, in peace. Before you determine on a measure unjust, look up to God, who made us as well as you. We hope he will not permit you to destroy the whole of our nation."

After another long pause, the Chief now resorts to history. In order to make his case, to strengthen the impression of injustice, he reviews for Washington the events affecting the Iroquois Confederation, and emerges with mention of the situation in the west. The President, already very much concerned about the restless agitation characterizing the so-called Ohio Indians, could not have missed the subtle reference, and he must have perceived a lightly veiled threat: "Father, *You* have compelled us to do that which has made us ashamed. We have nothing to answer to the children of the brothers of our fathers. When, last spring, they called upon us to go to war, to secure them a bed to lie upon, the Senecas entreated them to be quiet, till we have spoken to you. But, on our way down, we heard that your army [Harmar] had gone toward the country which those nations inhabit, and if they meet together, the best blood on both sides will stain the ground."

In a most poignant moment of the address, Cornplanter makes his first direct reference to himself, intimating that the Senecas tend to blame him for the loss of their land, and that they have become so desperate that almost anything is possible. Even the life of Cornplanter is not safe. And the Chief has no answer for his people:

> *When the sun goes down, he opens his heart before God, and earlier than that sun appears again upon the hills, he gives thanks for his protection during the night; for he feels that, among men, become desperate by their danger, it is God only that can preserve him. He loves peace, and all he had in store, he has given to those who have been robbed by your people, lest they should plunder the innocent to repay themselves. The whole season which others have employed in providing for their families, he has spent in his endeavors to preserve peace; and, at this moment, his wife and children are lying on the ground, and in want of food; his heart is in pain for them, but he perceives that the great God will try his firmness, in doing what is right.*

How does it happen, Cornplanter asks, that the King of England can turn over to you Americans lands which he does not possess? And, though we would very much like to discuss farming and learn from you about tilling the soil, how can we do so when we do not know whether we have ground to call our own? [23]

The Seneca Chief Cornplanter has spoken his piece. He has been on his feet for a very long time, to speak for all Indians everywhere, defining the great injustice and placing their plight in the hands of their Father. In closing he declares, "These to us are very great things. We know that you are very strong, and we have heard that you are wise, and we wait to hear your answer to what we have said, that we may know that you are just."

A document of the address was signed, at Philadelphia, on the first day of December, 1790, by Cornplanter, Half Town, and Great-Tree, all with their X mark. The signing was witnessed by the interpreter Joseph Nicholson, and by T'y. Matlack. But Cornplanter and the others would have a month to wait for the response from President Washington. Until that time they could cool their heels in the City of Brotherly Love, which time, because of Cornplanter's warm relationship with the Quakers, could hardly be an unhappy experience.

Washington had listened attentively, and it is clear that he took the address very seriously. He may have been aware of some confusion Cornplanter experienced in his speech, especially with regard to responsibility, and he most certainly appreciated the need for more information if he was to make a proper response. Accordingly, he asked his Secretary of War, Henry Knox, to brief his friend Governor George Clinton of New York in the hope that the Governor might advise him. When the President did finally respond, on December 29, he was armed not only with Governor Clinton's reply, but with Colonel Timothy Pickering's report on the Tioga Conference, which had been held with the so-called northern Seneca chiefs, who represented the Indians of the Genesee and Buffalo Creek regions of New York.[24]

Opening with a declaration of friendship, Washington in his response urged that "all the miseries of the late war should be forgotten, and buried forever." He acknowledged that the Six Nations in the matter of lands "have been led into some difficulties," but, he explained, these evils should not be laid at the door of the United States, and the "case is now entirely altered." Then he declared forcefully that "No State, nor person, can purchase your lands, unless at some public treaty, held under the authority of the United States. The General Government will never consent to your being defrauded, but it will protect you in all your just rights."

Drawing upon information supplied by Governor Clinton, he acknowledged that the Indians were cheated by John Livingston, and he declared the deal "null and void." He did not agree that the Indians had been defrauded by Oliver Phelps.

Declaring that you Indians absolutely have "the right to sell," as well as "the right of refusing to sell," your lands, he cautioned them to be very sure to determine who among them has the authority to deal.

The President insisted that the United States is ready to provide "every assistance" in enabling you to develop improved methods of farming. He assured Cornplanter, as had Pennsylvania's Executive Council, that the Pine Creek murderers would be brought to justice, "punished as they deserve."

Josiah Harmar

President Washington's big concern at the time of this council was of course the Ohio Indian problem. His General Josiah Harmar, whom he had dispatched to the Ohio country with an army of 1500, had been roundly defeated, just six weeks ago. Because of that he was not only willing to grant the Southern Senecas an audience here in Philadelphia, but actually eager to meet with them. He very much hoped to get on good terms with the influential chiefs. He could not afford to have them allied with the troublesome western Indians. "My desire is, that you would caution all the Senecas, and Six Nations, to prevent their rash young men from joining the Maumee Indians."

Washington extolled the "merits of the Cornplanter, and his friendship for the United States," which, he declared, are "well known to me." Finally, with a promise of gifts, for Cornplanter, and for the other chiefs, and for chiefs not here, he closed his remarks with an admonition: "Remember my words, Senecas! Continue to be strong in your friendship for the United States."

Cornplanter was now convinced that there would be no re-writing of the arrangement made at Fort Stanwix. Accordingly, that very evening he composed a letter to the governor of the Quaker State, to remind Mifflin (1) that an injustice had been done at Stanwix, that in fact the Indians had been cheated, and (2) to propose a way of providing the Indians *some* satisfaction. In the names of Half Town and Great Tree, chiefs of the Seneca Nation, he appealed for redress of the great wrong: "We desire you to pay us a reasonable price for it." [25]

Cornplanter's reply to the President's speech was delivered almost two weeks later, on January 10. In it the Chief dealt once more with the Stanwix Treaty, which he indignantly insisted was illegal and unjust. It was his opinion that the new United States government could and should do something about that. He expressed disappointment in Washington's estimate of the Phelps & Gorham Purchase. He referred again to the Pine Creek murders. In his closing he revealed how very willing were the Senecas to adopt the ways of the white man and to live peaceably with him. He spoke once more of the tilling of the land, and of education, actually the subjects which were perhaps closest to his heart at this time: "Father, you give us leave to speak our minds concerning the tilling of the ground. We ask you to teach us to plough and to grind corn; to assist us in building saw mills, and to supply us with broad axes, saws, augers, and other tools, so as that we may make our houses more comfortable and more durable; that you will send smiths among us, and, above all, that you will teach our children to read and write, and our women to spin and to weave."

This address, too, was signed by Cornplanter, Half Town, and Great Tree. Among the witnesses, besides the interpreter Joseph Nicholson, who was ill at the time, were the warriors John Deckart and Jem Hudson. The date was January 10, 1791.

Washington's reply came nine days later. Although he made response to each issue raised, he was just a little curt. It would seem that he was growing impatient. He pointed out to Cornplanter that the Treaty of Fort Stanwix might just as well be forgotten. Any injustice that occurred there had been erased, or at least accepted, by the very recent Treaty of Fort Harmar, which delivered compensation.

Washington insisted that "The lines fixed at Fort Stanwix and Fort Harmar must, therefore, remain established." But, he noted, "Half Town, and the others, who reside on the land you desire [to be] relinquished, have not been disturbed in their possession." Apparently expecting that New York and Pennsylvania could make some accommodation, perhaps in the form of a reservation, the President expressed the hope that if the Indians "continue to demean themselves peaceably, and to manifest their friendly dispositions to the people of the United States, . . . they will be suffered to remain where they are."

On the matter of the Indians' desire to learn the ways of the white man, Washington promised aid: "You may, when you return from this city to your own country, mention to your nation my desire to promote their prosperity, by teaching them the use of domestic animals, and the manner that the white people plough, and raise so much corn. And if, upon consideration, it would be agreeable to the nation at large to learn these valuable arts, I will find some means of teaching them, at such places within your country as shall be agreed upon."

That Washington has become just a little weary of tilling the same old ground is apparent in his close: "I have nothing more to add, but to refer you to my former speech, and to repeat my wishes for the happiness of the Seneca nation."

Cornplanter got the message. In two minutes he said goodbye to the council: "No Seneca ever goes from the fire of his friend, until he has said to him, 'I am going.' We therefore tell you that we are now setting out for our own country. Father, we thank you, from our hearts, that we now know there is a country we may call our own, and on which me may lie down in peace." He promised to go among the western nations "early in the spring." His very last words were these: "You have not asked any security for peace on our part, but we have agreed to send nine Seneca boys, to be under your care for education. Tell us at what time you will receive them, and they shall be sent at the time you shall appoint. This will assure you that we are, indeed, at peace with you, and determined to continue so. If you can teach them to become wise and good men, we will take care that our nation shall be willing to receive instruction from them."

This final speech Cornplanter signed on February 7. Once more Half Town and Big Tree, with their marks, also signed, all in the presence of Joseph Nicholson, T'y. Matlack, and Colonel Thomas Proctor, Washington's commander of the 4th Continental Regiment of Artillery during the war.

Washington had had enough. He asked Secretary of War Henry Knox to address a farewell to the Indians, and to present them instructions. On February 8, Knox did just that:

> *The President of the United States . . . assures you of his good wishes for your happiness, and that you may have a pleasant journey to your own country.*
>
> *The Governor of the Western Territory [General Arthur St. Clair] will appoint you an interpreter whenever one shall be necessary. The President of the United States does not choose to interfere on this point.*
>
> *The President of the United States thinks it will be the best mode of teaching you how to raise your corn, by sending one or two sober men to reside in your nation, with proper implements of husbandry. It will, therefore, be proper that you should, upon consultation, appoint a proper place for such persons to till the ground. They are not to claim the land on which they shall plough.*
>
> *The President of the United States, also, thinks it will be the best mode of teaching your children to read and write, to send a schoolmaster among you, and not for you to send your children among us. He will, therefore, look out for a proper person for this business.*
>
> *As soon as you shall learn any thing of the intentions of the Western Indians, you will inform the Governor of*

> *the Western territory thereof, or the officer commanding at Fort Washington, in order to be communicated to the President of the United States.* [26]

Even before the Indian chiefs left the city of Philadelphia, Thomas Mifflin, now the "Governor" of the Commonwealth, took action to redress the grievances the chiefs had laid before the Council. On January 29 he signed an Act of the General Assembly by which Big Tree was granted a patent to "a certain island in the Allegheny river," on which he already had his home. And three days later he approved an Act of the General Assembly by which there was granted "eight hundred dollars to Corn-Planter, Half Town and Big Tree, Seneca Chiefs, in trust for the Seneca Nation, and for other purposes therein mentioned." [27]

Cornplanter and his fellow chiefs had been in the City of Brotherly Love for fourteen weeks. It was time to go home. Little did they know what a trip this would be.

XIII

HOME AGAIN

Pittsburgh at this time was enjoying a well deserved reputation for villainy and ugly behavior. Colonel Daniel Brodhead, while he was Commander of the Western Department and responsible for Fort Pitt and a number of other forts, was constantly complaining. In a letter composed in the summer on which he set out on his Expedition up the Allegheny, dated June 27, 1779, he expressed his low opinion of the settlers (whites and Indians) of "this place." Even Fort Pitt was not sacred. Brodhead reported that "The inhabitants of this place are continually encroaching on what I conceive to be the rights of the Garrison and which was always considered as such when the Fort was occupied by the King of Britain's Troops. They have now the assurance [impudence?] to erect their fences within a few yards of the Bastion. I have mentioned the impropriety of their Conduct but without effect. The Block-houses, likewise, which are part of the strength of the place, are occupied and claimed by private persons to the injury of the service."

Not two weeks later the Colonel registered another complaint: "Whilst I am writing, I am tormented by at least a dozen drunken Indians, and I shall be obliged to remove my Quarters from hence on account of a cursed villainous set of inhabitants, who, in spite of every exertion continue to rob the soldiers, or cheat them and the Indians out of everything they are possessed of." [1]

But by the time of Cornplanter's arrival in Pittsburgh from Philadelphia it was a whole lot more than mere rowdiness and drunken brawling that had broken out. According to the *History of Warren County*, the Indians were "well loaded with good and substantial presents." These gifts had been sent on to Pittsburgh by wagons, and were there transferred to "a large bateau or keel boat." Unfortunately, not long after the Indians had commenced their voyage up the Allegheny River, "unprincipled white wretches from Pittsburgh attempted to steal—both boat and cargo." [2]

The Seneca chiefs with their gifts from Washington and the Quaker State came right into the middle of a bad situation. Cornplanter, well aware of conditions in the Pittsburgh area, still could hardly have expected what happened. Several Delawares had been killed by whites (reported to be Virginians) near Fort Pitt; in retaliation the surviving Indians murdered and scalped seventeen white settlers in their homes just upriver from Pittsburgh. The Westmoreland Militia, in searching for the offending Indians, came upon Cornplanter's boatload of supplies on the Allegheny, and, in a general anger at Indians, or out of confusion, promptly confiscated the goods and carried off to Fort Pitt the sachem New Arrow, who had been delivering the supplies to Cornplanter.

Colonel Thomas Proctor, who had been commissioned by Washington to go west to work for peace with the hostile Indians, had left Philadelphia on March 11, and had arrived at Cornplanter Town on April 6. He was astonished to find that Cornplanter and all of the men of the village had taken refuge at Fort Franklin. So he arranged for escort there and of course got the story from the officers at the garrison. He assured the much distressed Cornplanter that no harm would come to New Arrow. And eventually calm prevailed.

Some light is thrown upon the affair by a cascade of frantic communications. In response to a dispatch from Ensign John Jeffers at Fort Franklin, which he had received on April 8, Lieutenant Matthew Ernest, of the Federal Artillery at Fort Pitt, hurried off a letter to Henry Knox, the Secretary of War. The letter is most interesting, both for what it says about the Cornplanter incident on the river and for the mention of the threat to Fort Franklin:

> *Sir:—Mr. Jeffers informed me by Express, two days since, that he had just received good information of one thousand of the lower Indians [the Indians of the Ohio Valley (the Shawnee, the Delaware, the Miami, etc.)] being within thirty miles of him, and that their views were to destroy the Cussawaga [Meadville] settlement and the post at Venango [Fort Franklin]; that his garrison is reinforced by forty Seneka Indians and white men from Cussawaga, and that he had then but ten days' provisions on hand, the contractor's boat having been stopped on its passage to Fort Franklin by the militia of Westmoreland County, on account of their being*

friendly Indians on board who assisted in navigating her up the Allegheny. These Indians were a part of Cornplanter's party who had with them the presents they received from Congress and State of Pennsylvania, which was taken from them and exposed at public sale. The party that did this mischief was under the command of Major Guthrie, of Westmoreland. The Contractor's boat set out again from this place [Fort Pitt] and [is] expected to arrive at Fort Franklin the 14th or 15th at farthest. Mr. Jefffers' letter is dated the 5th, so that it is probable the supply may arrive seasonably. [3]

Two weeks later, on April 20, a copy of the Matthew Ernest letter was relayed by the Secretary of War to Governor Mifflin, both of whom were in Philadelphia: "Sir:—I have the honor to enclose to your Excellency, the copy of a letter from Lieutenant Ernest, at Fort Pitt. The affair of which he speaks is of a most atrocious nature. It may be expected that a more particular account will be received by the post of to-morrow, when I shall have the honor of communicating further with your Excellency on the subject." [4]

Had they done any calculating, when they returned to their homes on the upper Allegheny, Half Town and the others would have found that they had given up the better part of a year to their journey to see Presidents Mifflin and Washington. Just how good they felt about what may have been accomplished is not known. So many of their councils must have seemed exercises in futility. But one thing was accomplished for sure. The grant to Cornplanter had been made formal and official and fixed in its boundaries.

Way back on the 23rd of March, 1789, General Richard Butler, taking note of the fact that Cornplanter had been of great assistance to Pennsylvania in the negotiations that followed the end of the War of the Revolution, had dispatched a proposal to Thomas Mifflin:

I beg leave to mention to your Excellency & Council that Capt. Abeal, alias the Cornplanter, one of the principal Chiefs of the seneca Tribe of the six Nations, has been very useful in all the Treaties since 1784 inclusive, & particularly to the State of Penns'a, this he has demonstrated very fully, & his attachment at present to the State appears very great. This has induced me to suggest to your Excellency and Council whether it might not be good Policy in the state to fix this attachment by making it his interest to continue it. This from the Ideas he possesses of Civilization induces me to think if the state would be pleased to grant him a small tract of land within the late purchase [the Erie Triangle], it would be very grateful to him, & have that Effect. This may be done in a manner that would render him service without lessening his influence with his own people or Exposing him to jealousy. The quantity need not be large, perhaps one thousand or fifteen hundred acres. How far your Excellency & Council may concur in this opinion will rest with your Excellency & them. My wishes for the quiet & interest of the state as well as the merits of the man, has induced me to take the liberty to mention this matter and hope the notice will be my apology. [5]

Butler's suggestion found a ready home with Mifflin. The letter had to travel no distance, as all parties were in Philadelphia, and the very next day, March 24, 1789, by act of the General Assembly, 1500 acres were granted by the State of Pennsylvania to Chief Cornplanter.[6] Cornplanter clearly had had some notice of this grant, but he had seen nothing in writing by the time he met with Governor Mifflin in Philadelphia, some eighteen months after the action. And he had not of course made a selection of the land he preferred. Now, having been advised that the grant was official, soon after he returned home from Philadelphia he advised Governor Mifflin that he would prefer the land on which he had been living for many years now. This decision came as a surprise to Butler, who had supposed Cornplanter would elect the land near Lake Erie, some more desirable portion of what was called the Erie Triangle, which had been put forward.

In notifying the Governor of his choice, the Chief requested that a survey be made "as early as practicable." As the land on which the Cornplanter community had been living had no strings attached, was "open" land, the Chief's choice suited Mifflin all right. He promptly reported the decision to the newly organized Senate and House of Representatives of the Commonwealth: "Gentlemen: I have directed the Secretary to lay before you a Copy of a Letter from Cornplanter, in which that Chief requests that orders of survey may be issued for three tracts of Land, amounting in quantity to the 1500 acres which were granted to him by a resolution of the General Assembly of the 24th March, 1789, but differing in point of situation." And he was very happy to discover that nothing stood in the way of what Cornplanter preferred: "From the information, however, contained in a Letter from the officers of the Land Office, a copy of which will likewise be transmitted to you, I find that the proposed tracts are unappropriated; and as the resolution referred to describes Lands within the Tract of Country lately purchased from the United States, which Country has not yet been the subject of any Legislative provision, in respect to grants, and confirmations by Patent, permit me to suggest the propriety of complying with Cornplanter's request, and of authorizing the officers in the Land Office to grant the Warrants, direct the surveys and issue the Patent which may be necessary upon the occasion." [7] The communication to the Congress was signed and dated, Philadelphia, January 22, 1791.

The survey was eventually completed, as directed by Mifflin. On July 2, 1795, Cornplanter met Alexander McDowell, the District Surveyor at the Oil City tract. This property, always known as "the Gift," was promptly surveyed (303 acres, 87 perches). On Independence Day, McDowell proceeded to the Forest County tract, and there laid out the specified 613 acres, 142 perches. This area, later to be identified with present-day West Hickory, north of Tionesta, on the Allegheny, came to be known as the "Richland" tract. On July 9 the survey was done for "Donation Island" (53 acres, 67 perches). Three days later there was completed the survey of the area called first "Planter's Field" (660 acres, 45 perches). By and by, the Planter's Field tract, together with the two islands in the river, came to be known as the Cornplanter Grant. Patents for all but Richland, the Forest County tract, were made to Cornplanter on March 16, 1796. In fact, Cornplanter, just two days before the survey was done, had sold Richland to General John Wilkins, Jr.[8] Altogether Cornplanter had received over 1600 acres. Unfortunately, the Chief very early gave up his title to much more than half the total land included in the four tracts, selling off all but the Planter's Field area.[9]

The *History of Warren County* notes that "Cornplanter, with his two wives,[10] his children, and a following of many others of his band . . . became permanently established." Of course Cornplanter with his family and a number of the other dislocated Genesee Senecas had been living here in this village long before the surveying was done, in fact ever since about three years after it had been destroyed by Colonel Brodhead in 1779. This was the location known as "Burnt House," after the burning the village suffered even before the arrival of Brodhead's forces. The Indian name for "Burnt House," according to the Reverend Timothy Alden, the founder of Allegheny College in nearby Meadville, was *Jen-ne-sa-de-go* or *Tin-nes-hau-ta-go.* This portion of Cornplanter's grant was composed of 640 acres, located on the west bank of the Allegheny River, some sixteen miles upriver from present-day Warren, and about two miles downstream from Conewango Creek. With the two adjacent islands in the river included, the size of the grant retained was 750-780 acres.

After the land was surveyed[11] most of the Indians of the upper village (New Arrow's town) came down to the lower town, a distance of some eight or nine miles.

With the help of white men sent to assist him expressly for that purpose, Cornplanter commenced the construction of log houses, and, as the *History of Warren County* suggests, these Seneca Indians thus became "the first permanent residents in the county after the acquisition of its territory by Pennsylvania." [12]

And we know that as early as 1791 Cornplanter was determined that his Indians would learn how to cultivate the soil. He was determined that they should "learn the arts of civilized life" and that they should be educated to read and write. Naturally he turned to his good friends, the Quakers of Philadelphia. In this year, while he was still in Philadelphia to parley with Mifflin and with Washington, he dictated a letter to the friends of Onas:

> *Brothers, The Seneca Nation see, that the great Spirit intends they shall not continue to live by hunting, & they look around on every side, and inquire, who is it that shall teach them what is best for them to do. Your fathers have delt [dealt] fairly and honestly with our fathers, and they have charged us to remember it and we think it right to tell you, that we wish our Children to be taught the same principles by which your Fathers were guided in their Councils. Brothers, We have too little wisdom among us. We cannot teach our Children what we perceive their situation requires them to know,*

> *&. we therefore ask you to instruct some of them—We wish them to be instructed to read and to write, and such other things as you teach your own Children, and especially teach them to love peace.*
>
> *Brothers, We Desire of you to take under your care two Seneca boys and teach them as your own, & in order that they may be satisfied to remain with you & be easy in their minds that you will take with them the son of our interpreter and teach him also according to his desire.*
>
> *Brothers, You know that it is not in our power to pay you for the education of these three boys, and theirfore you must, if you do this thing look up to God for your reward.*
>
> *Brothers, you will consider of this request, & let us know what you determine to do—If your Hearts are inclined toward us, & you will afford our Nation this great advantage, I will send my son as one of the boys to receive your instruction and at the time which you shall appoint.* [13]

The letter is dated February 10, 1791. It is signed by Cornplanter with his X mark and witnessed by Joseph Nicholson, who of course provided the English. And, happily, the Quakers would before long come through for the Senecas in a big way.

But this was a bad time for the Cornplanter community. Even while it grew steadily into a solid Indian village or town, Indian depredations, which had occurred in an alarming frequency in the Pittsburgh region through the seven years which followed the Treaty of Paris, continued. The years 1790-91 particularly were marked by Indian raids, by violence and murder, and by reprisals too, of course. The government in Philadelphia was receiving a constant barrage of harrowing letters from the frontier, and repeated cries for protection. Typical was the report of William Findley to the Secretary of the Commonwealth. Dated April 29, 1791, his letter describes an attack on the house of James Kilpatrick, on Crooked Creek, not far from Kittanning on the Allegheny. Findley lamented that two men had been killed by the marauding Indians and that the villains had broken a child's leg. At about the same time a block house "opposite to Pittsburgh" was fiercely assaulted.[14]

A settler by the name of David Stewart, on May 8, in a letter directed to Governor Thomas Mifflin, provided another report of the Kilpatrick incident, but Stewart has three killed. (Another report, by Andrew Gregg and dated May 10, has three killed.) Stewart attributes the murders to the Senecas: "Our Settlements are in considerable fear and danger, and unless some Guards are stationed along the wilderness back of our Settlement, I am afraid they will give way particularly as the murders were committed by a Nation we expected were upon the most friendly terms with us. A Capt. McGuire who lives the most exposed, informs me that he has discovered traces of the Indians in several parts of the Country in which he lives, and as he informs me they are Senecas, we have too little right to expect anything from their placable disposition. Your Excellency, we trust, will take such measures as will be necessary to strengthen our Frontiers."[15] Major John Irwin of the Allegheny Militia, however, in a letter to Secretary of War Knox, exonerates the Cornplanter Senecas and declares the violence to be the work of the Beaver Valley Indians, whose relatives had been killed by Captain Samuel Brady.[16]

The long life of Chief Cornplanter was a rough one, no question. And it would be difficult to determine which period of his life was the most trying. But certainly the years 1791 to 1795 would be right up there. Through this period the United States was at war with the hostile western Indians of the Ohio River Valley. And Cornplanter had been "commissioned" by Washington to work for peace—which he did, zealously and religiously. But during these years he never traveled anywhere, and certainly not into the Shawnee country, except at great risk to his person and his companions. And even at home in Jennesadaga he was not safe.

During this anxious time, Fort Franklin, which was some eighty miles down the river from Cornplanter Town, remained ever the refuge for Indians and whites alike. Cornplanter and his people had been on good terms with the garrison for a long time, and regularly traded there and secured provisions. On their trips downriver to Pittsburgh they would stop at Venango and Cussawaga for rest or supplies, or just plain socializing. And as they were grateful for all the Fort provided, they were quick to offer aid of their own. Cornplanter constantly had his warriors on watch for any approach of the so-called Ohio Indians, who had become increasingly hostile and confident since their resounding victories over the forces of General Josiah Harmar (in October of 1790) and over General Arthur St. Clair a little over a year later. And of course these Indians of the Western Confederation had no use at all for the Senecas, who had betrayed them at the treaty conferences. In fact, they were brazenly contemptuous of the Iroquois "cowards."

So Cornplanter, always sensitive to any threat, was quick to warn the Fort of any danger. And not only that, but he was prompt also to offer his warriors in support of the garrison. And all this time he was trying to make good on his promise to George Washington. In councils at Buffalo Creek, in which he could meet with the "northern" Senecas," he took the stance of neutrality in the dispute. On very risky missions to the western Indians he urged peace and negotiation.

On the ninth day of May, 1791, Ensign Jeffers dispatched an urgent message to David Mead at Cussawaga: "Having received two speaches, one from GEN. KNOX and one from GOV. ST. CLAIR directed to the Senecas and the Six Nations and considering them important: You will therefor proceed immediately to the Cornplanter's town—gather the Chiefs and Warriors most contegious [convenient?]—read the speaches and deliver them up to the Chiefs. Should the Head Chiefs be at Catarogas [Cattaraugus] you had better proceed to that place. For your Service you will receive 1 dollar pr. Day till you return—You will employ ELIJAH MATTHEWS as interpreter whom I will pay—You shall be allowed all necessary expenses but in order not to run the public to needless expense. I expect you will lose no time in accomplishing this business."

Mead's answer was dated May 16: "Sir: Agreeable to your instruction of the 9th I proceded to the ONESADAGA [Onondaga] and SHINNESHANGOTHA TOWNS with several Messages to the Six Nations of Indians, viz:—One from the Secretary of War—One from the Commander in Chief of the Armies of the U.S. and one from yourself, together with a proclamation of the Governor of Pennsylvania—& after having Assembled the Chiefs and Warriors most convenient then and there dis [did] cause Mennuages [messages] in due order to be explained to them, who discovered great marks of their APPROBATION AND Instantly sent off runners to the Other Towns, when the Chiefs promised as soon as possible their answer should be forwarded to you."

And Mead closes out his letter to Jeffers in acute consciousness of the gravity of the situation: "In the meantime, the Chiefs informed me they had Information that a Body of Bad Indians about 400, were prepairing to strike your Garrison. After this information I thought it my duty to return as fast as possible though they pressed me hard to stay another Day that they will have time to make more friendly preparations in the Provision Way. When I returned them Many Thanks and Bid them Farewell and have this moment returned." [17]

By Christmastime of 1791, the pot was boiling. Still gloating over the awesome destruction of St. Clair's army, the Miami Chief Little Turtle (Michikinkna), and more particularly the Shawnee Blue Jacket (Weyapiersenwah), were poised to punish the white man's hirelings, the give-away Senecas. Threats against Cussawaga and the other frontier communities, and against the fort at Franklin were being heard in such numbers that they had to be credited. On December 26, a frantic John Jeffers (now a lieutenant) shot off a dispatch to Major John Irwin of the Allegheny Militia: "Sir:—I have this moment rec'd authentic account from the Cornplanter, that an attack on this Garrison will almost immediately take place, for the Indians from below [Ohio Valley Indians] declare that they are determined to reduce this place, shake the Cornplanter by the head & sweep the river from end to end."

Then in his letter he makes a request for a junior officer and thirty men, as well as his own men who have been left sick at Fort Pitt. These reinforcements he hopes to see "without loss of time." Moreover he desires provisions "to make five months' rations for seventy men." And he concludes by declaring that "this news is not fictitious nor this letter to be trifled with. I have written to the Minister of war, but his order will come too late." [18]

Throbbing with the same urgency was another communication prepared the same day by Colonel George McCully, of the Fort Franklin garrison. It was sent express to John Wilkins, Esq.: "By express this moment rec'd from the Cornplanter, he advises that the Women at this Garrison be immediately sent to Pittsburgh for safety." McCully added that according to the runner who had delivered Cornplanter's letter, "a Council of the Hostile Indians was then sitting at Buffaloe Creek and that Cornplanter was summoned to it; how far this information may be depended on, can only be judged of from our late disasters." [19]

During all of this time, the settlers were moving westward, and Governor Mifflin was intent on opening up the northwestern area of the

Commonwealth. In April of 1793 he got off a letter to General William Irvine, who had been serving the state as the agent to designate the free lands that had been promised to Continental Army soldiers, and had also been very busy in surveying village sites. The same letter went to Andrew Ellicott, the well known astronomer, who was at that time doing the surveying and planning for the city of Washington, D. C. In this letter Mifflin was proposing the laying out of a town at Presque Isle which had been recently authorized by the Pennsylvania Legislature. The Governor was also intent upon a road, for at this time there was no road north from Pittsburgh to Presque Isle. There was a fairly good road from Reading to Pittsburgh, but from there on there was only the Indian trail which the young George Washington had traveled forty years ago with his message for the French. It led overland from Fort Pitt to Venango and then along French Creek up to Lac Le Boeuf, and concluded in a long portage to Lake Erie.

Ellicott, feeling that his work in Washington was far enough along that he could leave it to his brothers and his assistants, was shortly on his way from Philadelphia. He arrived in Pittsburgh on May 30, and there met with his fellow surveying commissioners, which, besides General Irvine, now included General John Wilkins, Jr., and the soon-to-be famous Albert Gallatin. Gallatin, now thirty-two years old, had come west to Pittsburgh nine years before and was at this time living at his estate known as "Friendship Hill."

But for a whole year almost nothing was accomplished in the way of surveying, or in building the road. The Indians were extremely hostile, and naturally resisted every suggestion of surveying, which they properly regarded as a sign of impending white settlement. And the concern was not only for the so-called "western" Indians, but for the Senecas as well. Nobody could be sure just what their allegiances were going to be. Rumors were flying. A letter written by Ellicott from Fort Franklin to Captain Denny, in command of a detachment of soldiers, makes plain how apprehensive the commissioners were of big trouble: "Sir, From the best information which can be collected respecting the present disposition of the six nations there is reason to apprehend that owing to British influence they are meditating an attack on this place—On which account considering the weak state and great importance of this post to the United States and State of Pennsylvania it appears necessary for your detachment to remain at this place until the arrival of Capt Obeal who has been sent for by Ge. Wilkins and myself." It is a very serious situation. "It must be evident," declares Ellicott, "that if we should proceed to Lebeuf and the Indians [were] to obtain possession of this post that our retreat would be cut off and the inhabitants of Cussawago left to the mercy of the savages."[20]

Ellicott did well to express concern about Meadville. The settlers of Cussawaga, indeed of the entire region of Lake Conneaut, had been ever since the spring of 1791 fleeing from their homes over and over again to refuge at Fort Franklin. David Mead, the founder of the settlement, years afterwards recollected the terror of these years. In an address to a Circuit Court of the United States, he described the dangers the settlers lived amid: "In the month of April 1788 I moved from the County of Northumberland thro' the Wilderness to Cussawaga, now Meadville on French Creek, in Company with several Adventurers, and some hired Hands, to make a Settlement where we arrived in the month of May, and I have made it my place of Residence ever since except when compelled to abandon it to seek safety from Indian Hostilities. The year 1789 I erected a Saw Mill, the first known West of Allegheny River, and in 1790 I set a pair of Mill Stones running—connected with the Saw Mill which made very good meal."[21]

He notes that early in the spring of 1791, his settlement was "much alarmed" by fears that the hostile Western Indians, then embroiled in a war with the United States, might descend upon the village. But at the same time he declared that the community had "kept up a friendly intercourse with the Senecas on the Allegheny River."

He recalls that before long their apprehensions of danger had grown so great "that about the first of May, the entire Settlement broke up, and moved to Fort Franklin, at the mouth of French Creek, mostly on Rafts of Boards prepared for the purpose, escorted by 'Half Town' and other Chiefs and Indians of the Six Nations in Number I think between 20 & 30."

Mead for these times reported great numbers of atrocities by the Ohio Indians, including the murder of his own father, Darius Mead, who had been captured and then later killed at Shenango (just south of present-day Greenville, Pa.). Back and forth from the mills at Cussawaga to Fort Franklin the settlers moved, David Mead with his family sometimes spending unusually long periods of time at the fort.

In his recollections years later, he remembered that in 1792, "there was not one Person resident of the Country, North and West of the Rivers Ohio and Allegheny and Conewango Creek, within the State of Pennsylvania, except the remains of the Settlement that had been at my Mills, and these were then obtaining Shelter and protection at Fort Franklin [commanded then by Captain Cass]." [22]

The latter part of the summer of 1793, Mead recalls, was particularly trying: "We did not consider ourselves in safety & no person ventured to Reside out of the little Settlement at my Mills. In the latter part of the Summer we were very much alarmed in consequence of an Express being sent from Franklin to the Commanding Officer informing us of the failure of the Treat under Genl [Benjamin] Lincoln at Detroit & other reports, & of his being appraised [apprised] by Cornplanter, of the intention of the Western Indians to destroy the Settlements. In Consequence of this Intelligence move almost all of the People out looking at the Country fled, and the few Families that were with us moved away." [23]

What was happening now in western Pennsylvania could only remind the Governor in Philadelphia of the Great Runaway of central Pennsylvania in 1778.

But David Mead stuck it out. He was confident that "we could defend ourselves" effectively for some time against any body of Indians that might appear. And he was depending upon Cornplanter for warning. He reported in later years that he was certain "we should be informed in time, for Escape, or defence, of their approach by the Indians of Cornplanters Town." [24]

But Indian raids continued and many were the depredations and murders in the region of French Creek and Fort Franklin and all the way north to Presque Isle. Mead remembered that "During the years 1792, 1793, 1794, and for the greater part of 1795, I did not consider it prudent, for a single Family with Women and Children to attempt to Make a Settlement and Residence in the Woods . . . and it is a truth, that none did make any attempt West of French Creek during that Period, nor to any other place to remain Permanently until the Fall of 1795." [25]

Ellicott and the surveyors, while unable to do all they had hoped for in this time, had also stuck it out. Ellicott was at Fort Le Boeuf in June of 1794. Apparently he had heard of a complaint Cornplanter had lodged with the Indian Commissioner about the murder of one of his warriors. On the 25th, hoping to forestall a needless discussion of the matter, he dispatched a letter to General Israel Chapin to clear up Cornplanter's confusion: "Dear Sir: I shall have no objection to an interview with the Chiefs of the six nations and hearing their complaints if any—Capt

Obeal is mistaken about his warrior being lost below Venango—he is now at that place and has been constantly treated with respect by the white people—In a drunken frolic an Indian was killed by one Robinson at that Post and they in return have killed five for him . . . I shall be glad to see you, my old friend. I am with much esteem Your real Friend."[26]

Five days later, from Fort Le Boeuf, Ellicott, out of great concern for the defenses both at Le Boeuf and at Fort Franklin, put in the hands of a runner an urgent message to Governor Mifflin, to whom he has been reporting frequently: "Sir, In my last Letter . . . I mentioned that you might expect to hear from me both from Fort Franklin and Le Boeuf, but . . . no opportunity occurred of writing from the first. On my arrival there the place appeared to be in such a defenceless Situation that we . . . remained there some time and employed the troops in rendering it more tenable." He noted that "The Garrison at present consists of twenty-five men," and that "double that number would not be more than sufficient, considering the Importance of the safety of the Settlements on French Creek. At Fort Franklin Gen[l] [John] Wilkins, and myself wrote to the corn-planter to attend there that we might have an opportunity of explaining to him the nature of our business . . . .After repairing Fort Franklin we proceeded to this place [Le Boeuf], and are now beginning to strengthen the works here so as to render it a safe deposit for military and other Stores. I am your Real Friend."[27]

Tensions increased even more, with the stepped up activity of General Anthony Wayne, who had assembled an army and had for some months now been marching from Fort Pitt into the Ohio Indian country. Not only that, he was building forts.

During the late spring of 1794, Cornplanter from his home dispatched a letter (dated "Ginashdago, May 25") to the Commandant at Fort Franklin, Lieutenant John Polhemus. It concerns the murder of a man on French Creek (probably the same warrior of whom Ellicott would be writing about in June, as noted above), but chiefly it has to do with the continuing threat posed by the hostile Indians of the West. Just how dangerous were conditions for travelers, and just how confused were the efforts at council, and just how suspicious everyone was of everyone else is apparent from the letter. The air was charged with questions. Would the western Indians arrive in force? Would the British, as they seemed to be promising, ally themselves with the Iroquois, if indeed the Iroquois determined to support the western Indians? The strange and much garbled letter is, to say the least, confusing in itself. It apparently was not composed by Cornplanter's favorite interpreter. Chief Bears Oil, who occupies much of the letter, was, apparently a Conneaut Seneca, and very wary of the western Indians. Long, and terribly confusing, it is signed "John X O Bail." [28]

That the threatened assault on Fort Franklin did never occur can be credited to a number of conditions. In the first place, the Ohio Indians, though made a little arrogant by their recent successes, were astute enough to know that the army of the United States would be returning to the Valley sooner or later. They needed to brace for that. They also knew that to carry the war east could only worsen their slim chance to draw the line at "the beautiful river." It did not make a lot of sense to send a war party against Fort Franklin. In the third place, though they engaged in a good bit of bluster, they knew, deep down, that the Senecas were not to be fooled with. Besides, they could bury their pride, and likely would be happy to have the help of the Iroquois Nation, including that of the Senecas, in their resistance to the steady advance of the white settlers. There was still a chance that the Senecas could be won over. Even Cornplanter had conveyed hints of it.

And, as a matter of fact, in the time immediately before the battle of Fallen Timbers, there was everywhere such a great fear that Cornplanter was on the verge of allying the Senecas with the hostiles of the West that Fort Franklin was improved in its structure and bolstered by regular soldiers to the number of 100. All was not quiet on the western front.

XIV

WAR IN THE WEST

Chief Cornplanter had been living with his family on the headwaters of the Allegheny River since 1782, two years before the second Treaty of Fort Stanwix. Through all of the treaty-making he was rearing a family and caring for a community of Senecas.

In his early years, before the War of the Revolution, Washington, as above noted, was passionate about land, and even scorned the King's Proclamation, which forbade settlement beyond the Alleghenies. He acquired, through the services chiefly of his friends William Crawford and Colonel John Armstrong of Carlisle, a great deal of land, almost 60,000 acres eventually. He was operating under the conviction that the Indians' lands were certain to fall to somebody. Through these years of course he could have no idea that down the road a little way he would be compelled to respond to the Indians' claims to the lands west and north of the Ohio, and that one way or another, he would have to establish the government position on settlement. He would have to make his own proclamation on this subject at the highest level.

Washington, as President, now assumed a moral responsibility for these people he had thought of as "wolves." His earlier vision of colonial settlement ever westward was now enlarged to provide for the land's first inhabitants. As one historian has put it, the President "envisioned multiple sanctuaries under tribal control that would be by-passed by the surging wave of white settlers and whose occupants would gradually, over the course of the next century, become assimilated as full fledged American citizens." [1]

To make it plain that he actually wanted to and expected to see this happen, as well as to clarify what it was he intended for the Indians, Washington in 1790 issued a Proclamation (remarkably similar to that of King George twenty-seven years earlier). It was in the form of an Executive Order, and it forbade "private or state encroachments on all Indian lands guaranteed by treaty with the United States." [2] And, like the Proclamation of King George, there was never any chance that it would prove the least bit effective.

At the same time, although the young government, largely because of Cornplanter, was steadily improving relations with the eastern Indians, the continuing belligerence of the Indians in the Ohio Valley region offended the President. Although the use of force was distasteful to him, Washington made it clear to these tribes that he would resort to whatever means necessary to put an end to hostile activity.

The Indians were unmoved. They made it equally clear to the young government that force would indeed be necessary.

Of course President Washington, from the time he assumed office on April 30, 1789, was compelled, naturally with an infant government, to tackle a bewildering array of both foreign and domestic problems. But far from the least of these was this unceasing hostility of the Indians on the outer reaches of colonial settlement. When in the fall of 1791 he opened the session of Congress and assessed the "state of the nation," he did so with an intense consciousness of the depredations and aggressions that were continuing unabated. It may have been that the Indians were really not much more than a nuisance to him, "a bother that Providence would somehow dispose of," as some historians have insisted,[3] for something bordering upon contempt and impatience is revealed in his remarks to Cornplanter. To his friend he spoke sharply: "The United States requires only that these people should demean themselves peaceably. But they may be assured the United States are able, and will most certainly punish them severely for all their robberies and murders." [4]

But he simply had to take most seriously the Indian activity on the frontier. It is now estimated that in the period between the signing of the Treaty of Paris and the end of Washington's first year as President some fifteen hundred men, women, and children had been murdered or captured along the banks of the Ohio, the new frontier. Besides, more than two thousand horses had been run off by the Indians, and homes were burned and fields destroyed.[5]

A little more than one year after his inauguration, in the fall of 1790, Washington had dispatched Brigadier General Josiah Harmer, with a somewhat modest and makeshift military force of 1500 men, into the Indian country of the Ohio. Most of his army, which included some Federal troops, was composed of militia and backwoodsmen. The Ohio Indians, a confederation mostly of those tribes located in the Maumee Valley, north of the Ohio River, were led by the cunning and resourceful

Miami war-chief Little Turtle.[6] The result was a most embarrassing disaster. Chiefly because of the great strategic skills of Little Turtle, an ambush, which killed 183 Americans, put an abrupt and tragic end to that expedition. This devastating and total defeat of Harmar's army did little to assuage the fears of the settlers in the West. When the President turned to negotiation and diplomacy he experienced the same paucity of success. The mission of Thomas Proctor, a Revolutionary War artillery officer from Philadelphia, in whom Washington had great confidence, accomplished little to excite optimism for peace. The messages he carried from Philadelphia to the Miami and Wabash Indians near Lake Erie did not bury the hatchet.

But Proctor's relationship to Cornplanter and the influence he exercised among the Senecas generally paid off in huge dividends for a government concerned, especially after Harmar's disastrous defeat, about peace on the frontier. It was in large measure because of Proctor, and later the surveyor John Adlum, that the Iroquois did not align themselves with the Miami and the Shawnee and the Delaware and the western Indians.

Thomas Proctor was a native of Ireland.[7] When he first came to the colonies, he worked as a carpenter. With the Battle of Lexington and Concord and the outbreak of hostilities he formed a company of militia, accepted command with the rank of Captain, and was promptly promoted to Colonel and given command of the 4th Continental Artillery, which his Pennsylvania unit had become. He had to his credit the battles of Trenton and Princeton, the Brandywine and Germantown, the winter encampments at Valley Forge and Morristown, and the experience of the Sullivan campaign. (This was the Colonel Proctor, of course, who had directed the artillery fire in the routing of Cornplanter and Brant at Newtown.) Besides, a great deal of post-war administrative experience qualified him extremely well for the assignment made by the President.

Proctor set out for the Indian country from Philadelphia on March 11, 1791, armed with $600 from the Secretary of War and messages from the government to the several Indian nations inhabiting the waters near Lake Erie. His mission was a big one: "The establishment of peace and friendly intercourse between the said nations and the United States of America." [8] Specifically, he was to persuade the influential Cornplanter to work upon the Ohio Indians. Proctor kept a careful diary of his trip, which ended with his return to Philadelphia on June 8. Happily, we have this day-by-day record of the mission. The Secretary of War, Henry Knox, relayed it on June 25 to the Governor of Pennsylvania,

Thomas Mifflin, and it was later included in the *Pennsylvania Archives* as "Narrative of Colonel Thomas Proctor." It is most interesting to us for the light it sheds on Cornplanter's role in the delicate maneuvering between the western Indians, the Six Nations, and the United States; but at the same time we learn a lot about the Chief and his living on the Allegheny, and a lot, too, about his fellow chiefs, New Arrow, Red Jacket, Little Beard, the Black Chief, Stump Foot, Big Sky, Fish Carrier, Half Town, and Big Tree.

Chief Cornplanter was at this time living on the land delivered to him officially by the Commonwealth of Pennsylvania just a year ago. Two "Cornplanter Towns" reposed on the banks of the Allegheny River, the upper town and the lower town. Cornplanter lived in the lower, on the north (or west) side of the river. The village of twenty-eight houses and some 350 people was very near the mouth of the stream known as Cornplanter Run, some five miles up the river from the mouth of Kinzua Creek. The chief's very good friend New Arrow was sachem of the upper town. Proctor is headed for Cornplanter, who, he supposes, is just returned from meeting with President Washington in Philadelphia. His route is roughly that of the Sullivan Expedition, from Philadelphia to Tioga to Newtown to the Genesee River. At Painted Post (Cohocton), the company, having paused to dine and refresh the horses, was joined by a Mr. George Slocum, who had followed them from Wyoming, and desired to place himself "under our protection and assistance, until we should reach the Cornplanter's settlement on the headwaters of the Allegheny."

On March 31 Proctor finds himself in a settlement of Indians called the Squawkey tribe, a branch of the Seneca nation, in the Genesee River region. He here sends out runners, at a dollar a head, to the villages of Little Beard and Big Tree and to whatever other Indian chiefs are met with, urging a meeting at Squawkey Hill, which, confides Proctor to his reader, is a lovely site. From the high lands above the River it "commands a beautiful landscape of the great flats on the Genesee, being in width about four miles, and the length from Carahaderra about forty-seven miles towards Lake Ontario, where the said river empties into it; the soil exceedingly rich, the land as level as a bowling green, beautifully interspersed with groves of trees, some of three acres and not more than five."

With the arrival of an Indian interpreter, Mr. Horatio Jones, Proctor calls a council, thirty odd Indians having assembled. He has the message from the Secretary of War, which urges peace, to read to them. He prefaces that with remarks stressing the "candor and justice of the

United States" and of the "unexampled conduct of his excellency the President." He continues with an account of his recent interview with the Cornplanter and with those others who appeared as representatives of the Six Nations. He promised the restoration of their lands, which naturally they feared had been lost forever. He insisted that if they "should demean themselves as faithful friends to the United States" their lives would be made "comfortable." "Such a becoming deportment," he declared "would entail lasting happiness to their children's children."

This was to be Proctor's manner and message throughout his mission. He leaned heavily upon the name Washington, and properly so, for it rarely failed to inspire good feeling.

Chief Little Beard made the Indians' response to Proctor. Here he speaks highly of Washington, whose General Sullivan has destroyed his village: "Brothers of the Thirteen Fires, Hear what we have to say to you. The Lord has spared us this day to meet together, and for you to let us know what has been done at Philadelphia a few days ago, for our nation. You say our lands are secured for us, and that the grant given by the Great Chief General Washington, will last as long as the sun goes over us. That is the reason why we give you great thanks, our lands being secured to our children's children. And great reason we have for doing so."

But of course Little Beard desired more than a pretty promise: "Every one of us will wish well to the great Chief, Honanadaganius [General Washington], and our women and our children will thank him, and will look up to him as a strong sun for protecting of the right of their lands to them forever. And you will tell us that there is a great paper in the hands of O'Beal for us. Now we want you to shew with your finger how large the lands are given to us." [9]

After Proctor designated certain tracts in several of the states, including Massachusetts, New York, and Pennsylvania, Little Beard reported news of Cornplanter. He informed the council that their "great warrior, Captain O'Beel, or Gyantawanka . . . had arrived at Pittsburgh from Philadelphia, and sent out runners from thence to summon the chiefs and warriors of the Six Nations to Buffalo, where he desired that the great council fire might be kindled, and where he should lay before them all the business that had been done by him at Philadelphia, and the public papers and documents which he had received for the Six Nations from the President of the United States, the Secretary of War, and from the Governor of the State of Pennsylvania." Abruptly, of course, Colonel Proctor changed course, and determined to repair to

Buffalo instead of pressing on to the village of Cornplanter. This was on April 1. On the next day, Proctor embarked on the 100-mile journey to Buffalo, but, to fulfill a promise made to the chiefs, he turned aside into the sugar camps to visit with them there. To his astonishment he now learned that the Buffalo council had been delayed one moon. So again he changed plans, electing now to go for the Oil Springs, near which he knew Cornplanter resided. He insisted to the chiefs that he would do his all to bring Cornplanter to Buffalo.

By April 6 he had advanced close to Cornplanter's town. Here the party was met by two runners dispatched by Cornplanter to the Indians in the resident towns at the headwaters of the Allegheny. Proctor's group now got the horror story and the most distressing news about the arrival of Cornplanter in Pittsburgh from Philadelphia and the loss of their gifts and their chief New Arrow. Having had some trouble following the meanders of the Allegheny, but still hopeful of eventually catching up with Cornplanter, Washington's emissary now employed one of the runners to convey the party to O'Beel's town, called in the Indian language "Tenachshegouchtongee," or "the burnt house." At this time there were some 350 souls, not all Senecas, living in or near this village on the north side of the river.

Proctor was impressed by the community. He found it "pleasantly situated," and he counted twenty-eight "tolerably good houses or cabins." He was led to a very comfortable and "uncommonly clean," well-built house. The party was provided ample food in the way of boiled venison and dumplings. But when he expressed a desire to council with all of the chiefs, he was advised that all had gone down river to Fort Franklin, where Cornplanter and his warriors, "for the protection of their lives," had taken sanctuary. No one remained in town but three old men and the women and children. Proctor now requested a canoe and a guide, as he was impatient to meet with Cornplanter wherever he was to be found. A canoe was finally brought, from five miles distant, by two warriors, who then accompanied him, on April 8, to the garrison at French Creek. Promptly, with the Indians who had accompanied him to Philadelphia, Cornplanter appeared, all of them immensely happy to see Colonel Proctor and all at the same time most anxious for the safety of New Arrow, who had been returned to Pittsburgh in the garrison boat, but still lamenting the loss of all their goods.

Proctor, reassuringly, pledged the safety of New Arrow and urged a short council. Cornplanter summoned the chiefs of his party, eleven in all, and Proctor explained to them his mission. In a full council the next morning, with seventy-five warriors present, Proctor read the message of the Secretary of War, and the message of Governor St. Clair to the Wyandot and Delaware tribes, considered "friends of the United States"; then, on his own, Proctor ran past them a "last solemn warning" to those western Indians responsible for "wanton depredations and cruelties on the defenceless inhabitants resident near the Ohio."

The Indians now urged Proctor to withdraw that they might debate his message. After about an hour and a half, they requested his return to the council fire. Here Proctor found that they wanted to make two matters plain: (1) that the business would have to be determined in full council with the Six Nations; and (2) that Colonel Proctor had no choice but to accompany them to Buffalo. They had also appointed Cornplanter to speak for them, and he did so, at Fort Franklin on April 9, 1791. He graciously welcomed Proctor to "the Indian country," but he was still so absorbed over the misadventure at Pittsburgh, that the better part of his speech was taken up with a review of all that. He did note that they would shortly be attending the council at Buffalo Creek, and he promised to advise Proctor on who and how many would after that be visiting the Miamis.

From Fort Franklin, that very day, Proctor composed a letter for General St. Clair, in which he enclosed copies of the speeches made by Little Beard and Cornplanter. Shortly, all had the good news that New Arrow was being returned, and the bad news that the canoes had been plundered. Most of the Indians, on hearing of the fate of the canoes registered an undisguised disgust, but Cornplanter received the news "with that composure that he was usually wont to do."

About ten o'clock in the forenoon of Monday, on the 11th of April, the party set out by canoe for Buffalo. Cornplanter assumed the lead, and Proctor sidled up to him, hoping to stimulate him to a good pace. Cornplanter's wife and one daughter were among the company. On the 12th they arrived at the Munsee settlement that lay on their route. There several Indian women came forward with kettles full of boiled corn and bear's meat, and placed all before Chief Cornplanter, whom they had been expecting. The bill that was presented to Colonel Proctor for his share of the repast came to 22s., 6d. In addition he was expected to meet the expense of one gallon of whiskey that had been supplied Cornplanter and his people—15s.

A kind of council, at which Proctor, and Captain Snake, the principal Delaware, and Cornplanter spoke, was then convened and concluded in good spirit.

By the 15th, Proctor, because of illness, was required to leave Cornplanter's fleet of canoes and push on ahead to the lower town. Eight miles farther on he came to a large river, which he knew to be the Conewango, and which he felt doubled the size of the Allegheny at the juncture. Here it was, of course, that Pennsylvania had laid out the Grant for Cornplanter. He proceeded to the upper town, New Arrow's village, the chiefs informing him that not one would go with Proctor to Buffalo until New Arrow was returned. Cornplanter, with his party of chiefs, arrived from the lower town on the 19th, and ordered, by the sounding of their conch shell, all head-men into council. Not much happening in council, or in Proctor's hut afterwards, the Indians entered into dancing for the major part of the night, with lots of drumming and spirited songs.

On the 20th the chiefs received an express from Buffalo declaring the impatience of the Six Nations and urging the arrival of the sachems of the Senecas. Proctor was commissioned by Cornplanter to compose a reply. On the 21st Cornplanter having announced their readiness to proceed, all at noon on the 23rd finally set out, taking the route through the village of Cattaraugus, and traveling the sandy beach of Lake Erie, taking to the woods when big bluffs or rocks required.

The party arrived at Buffalo Creek on the 27th. Here at this time, in the principal village, which was Seneca, resided Farmer's Brother and Red Jacket. The Young King was attired in a military red and blue, and Proctor confided to his diary that it should surprise no one to find him much under the influence of the British.

The company had not been long in the village before they were invited to council. "Just as we approached the porch of the council house," writes Proctor, "they had a two pounder swivel gun, which they had loaded very high, having put into her an uncommon charge, which the acting gunner being sensible of, stood within the door, and fired it from the end of a long stick, which he passed between the logs, which being done, the explosion upset the gun and its fixture. This, they said, was done as a treat for our safe arrival through the dangers that we had encountered, and for which they were thankful to the Great Keeper."

The introductory speech was delivered by Red Jacket, and Cornplanter, having been singled out for flattery by Red Jacket, rose to return the compliment on the part of the newcomers. As it was too late for real business the council was held over until next day, the 28th, when it convened with 150 Indians present. At Cornplanter's request, Colonel Proctor then explained his mission and read a number of documents and letters and the deed from his Excellency the President, for the restoration of their lands in the Six Nations. When the council re-convened on the next day Colonel Proctor read, as he had so many times before, the Secretary of War's message to the Six Nations, and the warning to the Wyandots and the Miamis, and declared the greatness and the power of the United States. He concluded with an instance he considered proof of the good-will of the United States. He referred to the late negotiations carried on by the President with Cornplanter and others in Philadelphia.

When Proctor had concluded his remarks, Red Jacket rose to make response for the Six Nations. Addressing his "Brother from Pennsylvania," he made it plain that he understood Colonel Proctor to be proffering a request for assistance from the Six Nations in dealing with "the bad Indians." Then he made it clear that no such assistance would be forthcoming without consultation with the British (represented by Colonel Butler, who was at Niagara). Proctor, having noted that Red Jacket was constantly being prompted by Fish Carrier and by Young King, took it all to be a reflection of how much most of the chiefs of the Six Nations remained under the influence of the British.

But the assembly was required to wait almost a week for the arrival of Colonel Butler. During that time, Cornplanter called a meeting of the chiefs to advise them to do no harm to Colonel Proctor. To the council called by Butler for May 4 Proctor was not invited. "I pressed my friend O'Beel," he records in his diary, "to go forward with them by all means, lest the United States should not be represented." Proctor was, however, politely invited to dine with Butler, and was able to engage in a dialogue that turned out to be fruitful chiefly for education. On May 5th, when Butler took his leave, to be rowed across the lake to Fort Erie by six British soldiers, Colonel Proctor saw to it that "each and every public paper received by Cornplanter at Philadelphia, together with the message that I brought to the Six Nations," was in Butler's possession and to be delivered to the commanding officer of Niagara (Colonel Andrew Gordon), "as concluded upon by the council of the Six Nations."

Red Jacket and Cornplanter informed Proctor early in the morning of the 6th that there would be no council that day. The reason, they explained, was that this was "pigeon time." It was the season of the year when the pigeons are found nesting in great abundance, perhaps as many as a hundred nests in a single tree, and it is the time when they are fat. So all our men, women and children are gone from the towns. This is the passenger pigeon that Cornplanter and Red Jacket are speaking of. Once the birds were so numerous that they passed by in flocks numbering into the billions and extending hundreds of miles! It was not long after this time, however, that the bird was to be seen nowhere, harvested as it was into a tragic extinction by Indians and whites alike.

Cornplanter called a council for the 7th. He asked the chiefs to consider which lands should be selected for the accommodation of certain tribes and families. At this time, too, it was reported that hostile Indians, notably the Miamis, were preparing to assault garrisons and settlements on or near the Ohio. It was also reported that the Squawky Indians were now in great fear of the white people and about to leave their settlements for Buffalo. When Proctor insisted that such a report could not contain a particle of truth, Cornplanter accepted his advice to tell the Indians of those settlements not to stir from their property but to continue planting.

A little council and a lot of dancing characterized the next few days. Proctor was encouraged some by something said by Red Jacket, given to believe that just maybe some assistance might be forthcoming from the Senecas. Worship on May 10. On May 11 the great dance that followed the council matters was attended "with a very drunken entertainment, from the Young King to the meanest subject, Cornplanter and some of the elders of the women excepted."

As Colonel Proctor prepared to take his leave of the chiefs, he offered presents. To some, including the Young King, who had not behaved so well in the councils as the Colonel would have liked, he gave rum. "And, as I perceived that Captain O'Beel's modesty prevented his calling on me in that way, to him and Cuyaratta I was not less liberal." On the 21st, all of the chiefs repaired to the cabin of Colonel Proctor. As appointed ahead of time, the Young King made the farewell speech, "but not without the aid of Fish Carrier, whose physiognomy, when speaking, put me in remembrance of the old Roman senators, possessing so much keen gravity in his manner."

On the evening of the 24th he found himself at New Arrow's town, where he hoped to secure fresh horses for the journey to Pittsburgh, a distance of eighty miles. Here he took leave of his Indian interpreter, Joseph Smith, paying him for sixty-one days of service. That evening he was in Cornplanter's company again. While sitting between him and his friend New Arrow, Proctor intimated to Cornplanter that if he would "go and join General St. Clair with 35 or 40 of his warriors, as well equipped as he could make them, purely to counterbalance the force that Brant had taken with him to the unfriendly Indians," he would try to persuade the Secretary of War to procure him a commission that should yield to him and his people a handsome stipend. To this Cornplanter replied that the Senecas had just been struck a blow by the "bad Indians," who had taken two prisoners, a woman and a boy from Conyatt (Conneaut), and that if the hatchet should fall upon any of his people hereafter, he would then let Proctor know what he would do.

That evening Colonel Proctor set out for Pittsburgh from Cornplanter's Town. He had left the castle of the Six Nations on the 21st of May. He proceeded by way of Forts Franklin and Pitt and arrived in Philadelphia on June 8. He had not persuaded the Senecas, nor any of the Iroquois to assist the Americans in their troubles with the Miamis and the Shawnees and the western Indians. But he had succeeded in preserving their friendship, and he had discouraged any all-out alliance of the Iroquois with the hostiles. It was apparent to Proctor that the British were continuing to cultivate the breach that remained between most of the Six Nations and the Americans, and his report to the Secretary of War presented a clear picture of the situation. The important thing perhaps was that Colonel Thomas Proctor emerged from the Indian country still on very good terms with his friends Cornplanter and New Arrow.

During part of the time Cornplanter was entertaining Proctor, from mid-April until the middle of November, 1791, the village was receiving aid from Captain Waterman Baldwin, whom Washington had dispatched in response to the request for help that Cornplanter had made last December while in Philadelphia. Baldwin was a most impressive man. He was one of eight sons of Isaac Baldwin, one of the early settlers of the Chemung Valley, which was ravaged by the Sullivan forces in the summer of 1779. While he was serving the Continental Army, he was captured three times by the Indians. The third capture produced some high drama. The officer was condemned to the Indians' favorite torture-death. According to the story that is told and credited by the family, as he was about to be secured to the stake, he extended his hand to a number of the warriors and was reaching for that of Chief Cornplanter. The Chief was so impressed by the coolness and the courage here exhibited that he not only called off the burning but adopted Baldwin as his son. Baldwin was shortly thereafter released and permitted to proceed to Philadelphia.

Now, after twelve years he would meet his "father" again, this time under *very* different circumstances. In a letter (his first?) dispatched to The Honorable Henry Knox, Secretary of War, and dated Obeals Town, May 17, 1791, he describes his coming to Jennesadaga:

> *Sir, Col. Thomas Proctor capped [prevailed] upon me the 20th of March last to accompany him and Capt. Loudon into the Jenessee Country—knowing the Business that I had to perform I thought proper to hire an Indian, a young man to farm who lived with my parent[s]. I have also taken with me two good work horses believing there [their] horses generally are poor at this Season of the year, which on my arrival at Abeal's Town I found true. These Matters Having the appearance of forwarding the Business which your Excellency was pleased to lay upon me I hope will meet with your approbation; this is truly a poverty struck place—Eatables four pieces above what we can have Bread and Meat for in the Settlements. David Mead, Esq. just arrived at this place, brings the following Nuse [news] that on the 7th Inst. a party of Indians came to Cassewago [Cussawaga (Meadville)] and Took three Men from there plowing—one, Cornelius Van Horn, one of the three prisoners informs that the Indians took him Back into the woods and tied him fast to a tree, he having a small knife, cut himself loose.*[10]

More than a month earlier, on April 8, 1791, together with Colonel Thomas Proctor, Baldwin had met his old captor, friend and "father" Cornplanter at Fort Franklin. And then he accompanied Cornplanter to Jennesadaga as a teacher and an interpreter.

Cornplanter, even before he left Philadelphia in the winter of 1791, had written to the Quakers, asking them to receive for education three boys. He had in mind the son of his interpreter, Joseph Nicholson, and two village boys, one of whom was his own son Henry, at that time seventeen years old.

Cornplanter on June 2 received a message from the Quakers in Philadelphia in which they agreed to accept the children whom he had designated for schooling among them. In his response the Chief thanked them profusely, but reported that inasmuch "as General Washington has sent a schoolmaster amongst us, Mr. Baldwin . . . we mean to let him teach them a little first and then take your offer and will send them down." To this the Friends responded in September, in the care of Joseph Nicholas [Nicholson] reaffirming their willingness to take the boys "if and when they came." [11]

Although Baldwin, who served Washington regularly as emissary, was clearly at the village to deliver the promised aid as "teacher and farming instructor" (He had been commissioned by the government to "instruct the children in their letters and their elders in farming."), he was, according to some, probably only a spy. It was thought that he was in Jennesadaga only to audit the relationship of the Senecas to the western Indians, a very nervous business. And because he made many reports directly to the Secretary of War, this suspicion might be credited.[12] But by all accounts from those close to him during the Revolution, he seems to have been a man of impeccable character, great courage, and devotion to duty. His many letters, which are dispatched from Fort Franklin, from Cornplanter Town, and from Chemung, while reporting on the Indian activity, consistently, like the one quoted above, reflect a genuine concern for the Indians. Indeed many are full of self-laudatory accounts of his service to the Indians. And he did seem genuinely to desire appointment as Indian Agent for the Western Department. Most interesting in this regard are two letters addressed to General Knox in Philadelphia from Cornplanter. In both it is plain that Chief Cornplanter has a high regard for Baldwin and is grateful for his service. There is not a hint of suspicion. Both letters, though in Baldwin's hand, are signed by Cornplanter with his mark.

Here is the first, dated 1791:

> *Sir: It gives me the greatest pleasure that I have it in my power to inform you that all my people are Determined for peace and happy to be friends with so great and so good a nation—I am pleased to hear . . . The good success of Genll [Charles] Scott against the*

> *Southern Indians. They are a bad people and enemies to me as well as you—*
>
> *My indians are now employed in hunting & have had more than common good luck with our crops . . . come in much better than before have great advantage from Capt. Baldwin the man you were so kind and good to send us. He has learnt us to plow the ground and many other good things—he had such a tedious journey to go we advised him to go before the winters weary sleet. What ever your success may be against our enemies I am determined to keep the chain of friendship bright and good as I agreed when I had the honour to be in Philadelphia.*

And the letter closes with ". . . we have the honour to be Sir your dutiful children."

The second is short and undated and concerns Baldwin: "We wish him to be our agent for this Department [the Western Department, headquartered at Fort Pitt] as he is a going to move his family here in the Spring we have tried him We find we can put our trust in him to our father the chiefs [of] the United States."

As it turned out, Baldwin, because of his father's illness, was at Jennesadaga only a short time. He had come in April. He left that November.

But the presence of Waterman Baldwin was not the only reason why the Quakers did not follow up more ardently their willingness to accept the Indian boys for schooling. Because of the western Indians it was simply a very bad time.

For those who had been hopeful of pacifying the western Indians, the worst was yet to come. The young government, determined now to put the Indian in his place, assembled a new and more formidable army. This force was placed under the command of Major General Arthur St. Clair, a most distinguished and experienced veteran of the border wars, and dispatched to the Ohio Valley. On the 4th of November, 1791, St. Clair's forces arrived at Kekionga, on the Wabash. Because this army, like that of Harmar, also ran into Little Turtle, who continued to provide the leadership for the Miami Confederacy, the result was quite the opposite of what was expected in Philadelphia.

Washington had warned St. Clair to "beware of surprise," and to "be sure to build fortifications" at every encampment. But the General did not require fortifications of the travel-weary soldiers when they finally made camp November 3 on the Wabash River, near present-day Fort Recovery. And he fell asleep that night feeling quite secure. The attack came at daybreak, St. Clair's troops awakening in the bitter cold to find the encampment almost completely surrounded by a boundless sea of Indians, one thousand warriors made hideous by the garish war-paint, and fired to a battle frenzy by the inspiring Miami war-chief Little Turtle and the Shawnee Blue Jacket. What happened during the next three hours has many times been described as "the bloodiest battle ever fought against the Indians." It was a massacre. In the melee, St. Clair lost at least 700 soldiers, and perhaps as many as 900 (!), including almost all of the eighty-six officers, seventy-five per cent of his fighting force, killed or wounded.[13] Besides, there were slaughtered a great many of the soldiers' wives, who had accompanied the expedition; and many children were carried off. The General himself only barely escaped, finding refuge in Fort Jefferson, which lay to the south. The Indians lost 66 (!) warriors.

Little Turtle

One does not have to imagine Washington's reaction to the terrible news when it arrived in Philadelphia. His early biographer, Washington Irving, has recorded it. The President had the news earlier in the day and had sat on it through a dinner party, but after Mrs. Washington had retired and the guests had all left, about ten o'clock, Washington, left alone with his private secretary, Tobias Lear, erupted. Here is Irving's account:

> *The general walked slowly backward and forward for some moments in silence. As yet there had been no change in his manner. Taking a seat by the fire he told Mr. Lear to sit down; the latter had scarce time to notice that he was extremely agitated, when he broke out suddenly: "It's all over!—St. Clair's defeated! —routed! The officers nearly all killed, the men by wholesale; the rout complete; too shocking to think of, and a surprise into the bargain!" All this was uttered with great vehemence. Then pausing and rising from the sofa, he walked up and down the room in silence, violently agitated, but saying nothing. When near the door he stopped short; stood still for a few moments, when there was another terrible explosion of wrath.*
>
> *"Yes," exclaimed he, "**HERE**, on this very spot, I took leave of him; I wished him success and honor. 'You have your instructions from the Secretary of War,' said I. 'I had a strict eye to them, and will add but one word, **BEWARE OF SURPRISE!** You know how the Indians fight us. I repeat it, **BEWARE OF A SURPRISE.**' He went off with that, my last warning, thrown into his ears. And yet!! To suffer that army to be cut to pieces, hacked, butchered, tomahawked, by a surprise—the very thing I guarded him against—O God!" exclaimed he, throwing up his hands, and while his very frame shook with emotion, "He's worse than a murderer! How can he answer it to his country! The blood of the slain is upon him—the curse of widows and orphans—the curse of heaven!"* [14]

One of the most costly losses was that of Major General Richard Butler,[15] who was serving as St. Clair's second in command, and was a very good friend to Cornplanter. Butler, who had been a Commissioner at Fort Stanwix in 1784, when all of northwestern Pennsylvania was purchased from the Indians, had been in command of St. Clair's right wing during the battle. He fought most heroically, repeatedly leading spirited charges in the face of the fierce horde. Several times he suffered very serious wounds, but he continued gallantly to fight off the warriors, until finally tomahawked and scalped. More than three years later, Big Tree, a Seneca war chief, and long a very close friend to Butler, carried his grief still. To General Anthony Wayne at Legionville, and in the presence of Cornplanter and New Arrow, in the spring before the battle of Fallen Timbers, he had expressed his feeling: "I have lost a very dear friend—the friend of my Heart—*General Richard Butler,*—I loved him so much that when I heard of his Death I determined to eat a *root* that wou'd soon have made me follow & join him." This was in March. The following January, at three o'clock in the afternoon of the 23rd, he "put a period to his own existence." [16] Anthony Wallace, reporting that he "stabbed himself to death in Wayne's camp during the winter of 1793-94," explains, "Apparently he had felt publicly dishonored. He had been pro-American during the Revolution, had been an associate of Cornplanter's thereafter, had urged the western Indians to accept the American terms, and at the last was reported to have become melancholic and deranged." [17]

Richard Butler

Certainly this unthinkable, crushing defeat was a terrible blow to the young government. Disappointment and discouragement settled over Washington and General Knox and the Cabinet and the Congress. And, in fact, the Army of the United States, by this single battle, had been almost totally destroyed, reduced as it was to hardly more than 300 regular soldiers.

Dismayed by the costly and tragic failure of these two campaigns, Washington and his Cabinet yet kept trying. In the spring of 1792, they took three promising actions.

First, because of the terrible massacre of the troops of General Arthur St. Clair, and the heating up of the war with the Indians of the West, Washington felt increasingly determined to keep the Iroquois on the sidelines, and especially the Senecas, who were the westernmost tribe of the Confederation. Accordingly, he began more aggressively and formally to solicit the aid of the Six Nations (He knew, of course, that he had a good friend in the Seneca Chief Cornplanter.). The Secretary of War, Henry Knox, commissioned the Reverend Samuel Kirkland, a Massachusetts Commissioner, to urge negotiations with the Six Nations for this purpose; at the same time he dispatched the longtime friend of the Americans, Captain Hendrick Aupaumut, the brave old Mahican chief of the Stockbridge community, to the hostile tribes to urge a council which would include the chiefs of the Six Nations.[18]

Washington's council with the Six Nations was scheduled for the spring. The Senecas were most eager to attend, but not because of Washington's Ohio Indian problem. What they, and especially Cornplanter, wanted most to talk about was education for their young people and assistance for their farming.[19] The President was gratified to discover on his doorstep on March 15, quite a delegation, Chief Cornplanter and forty-eight other chiefs of the Six Nations (but not Joseph Brant).[20] Blacksnake was among them, and inasmuch as he could not have met Washington in New York City, and seems not to have been present at the 1790 council in Philadelphia, it must be this meeting with Washington that he was recollecting when he dictated to Benjamin Williams two strikingly similar accounts.

Blacksnake recalls how the Indians were invited to council with Washington, and how "we treveraled on the same old path" and that they totaled 199 [!] souls from the state of New York. He recalled how their landlord located Washington's house for them, how when they showed up there, the armed guard admitted them and Washington scheduled a meeting for 9:00 a.m at the court house. Armed with chits for provisions, they were off to the "provision Store and got all we could carried on our backs with flour & pork tea Chorklaw [chocolate] & sugar." And how at the court house next morning President Washington urged them all to sit together.[21]

When Washington at the meeting asked for an identification of the tribes and the head men, Cornplanter, according to Blacksnake, promptly rose to declare "I am the head and Redjackett and I chief warriors." [22] For Washington he recognized the Seneca Chiefs Governor Blacksnake, Captain Strong (New Arrow), and "Young," which name is struck out in the Draper manuscript,[23] but is probably a reference to the Young King. He noted that the head chiefs of the Six Nations and the "chiefs of other tribes" are here "with us," and then he launched into his address. His purpose was, of course, to air the grievances of the Six Nations, and, as always the number one subject for the table was the land.

Blacksnake's narration continues then with the chief noting that Washington then explained why he had called the Iroquois to this conference. He desired their assistance in making peace with the western Indians. Noting that he did not want to see any more blood shed, he urged the chiefs to do what they could to make peace. This, he declared was his sole subject for the conference.

After the speech by Washington, which was made on March 23, the Indians repaired to mini councils to mull it over. It was the next day, according to Blacksnake, that Cornplanter, speaking for the delegation, made answer. He rose to inform Washington the chiefs had come to a conclusion, that they would go where they were ordered to go, regardless of danger, and do the best for our abilities for peace and no more bloodshed. We wish to go (to meet with the western Indians) as soon as we can make ready, and we desire to be back again "as Soon as possible and bring the News from them and Shall be faithful." [24]

Washington was gratified, of course, to have this answer, and he said so when he addressed the delegation again on April 25. He promised an annuity of $1500 "for the use and benefit of the Five Nations," and declared, "Let it be spread among all your villages, and throughout your land, that the United States are desirous not only of a general peace with all the Indian tribes, but of being their friends and protectors." The Indians were promised also the appointment of an agent (It would be General Israel Chapin.[25]). Washington consoled the chiefs for the loss of two of their warriors who had died during this residence in Philadelphia.

He concluded his remarks with his sincere best wishes. "Having happily settled all your business, and being about to return to your own country, I wish you a pleasant journey, and that you may safely return to your families after so long a journey, and find them all in good health."

With Colonel Timothy Pickering's speech of April 30, in which it was urged that those of you who "propose to attend the great council of Western Indians soon to be held near the west end of Lake Erie" work hard for peace, the council was concluded.[26]

Before long, the fruits of Aupaumut's efforts began to appear. "For the first time in four years," he had got an assembly scheduled for the heads of the hostile tribes of the west, with the chiefs of the Six Nations to serve as intermediaries. Fort Washington (Cincinnati), and even Philadelphia, had been considered as a site for this critical conference, but both were rejected as uncongenial to the western Indians. This Grand Council would instead convene at Au Glaize, on the rapids of the Maumee River, some distance south of Detroit and well within the western Indians' country.[27] It was a site that very much suited the Miamis, the Shawnee, the Wyandots, and the Ottawa. Au Glaize (now the Auglaize River) is actually a tributary of the Maumee. The name comes from a Shawnee phrase meaning "fallen timbers." Approximately 100 miles long, the stream rises in southeast Alden County, ten miles southeast of present-day Lima, flows southwest to Wapakoneta, then generally north in a zigzag course to join the Maumee from the south at present-day Defiance. Most of this area in Cornplanter's time was inhabited by the Shawnee and by the Ottawa. The Shawanese Chief Blue Jacket lived in a village on the east side of the Auglaize, just about a mile from its mouth. And it was near the confluence of the Auglaize and the Maumee that the battle of Fallen Timbers would be fought.

In the middle of June the Iroquois assembled at Buffalo Creek, intent on attending, as they had promised in Philadelphia to do, the Au Glaize council with the hostile Indians. But the mid-summer sessions in Buffalo Creek produced no immediate resolve. "Owing to their frequent counselling, and dilatory manner of conducting business," it was not until three months later that the Iroquois set out for Au Glaize.[28] The delegation, although thought of only as intermediaries between the Americans and the hostile Indians, assembled in great force. Cornplanter would be attending with some trepidation, as he was not unaware of the not so subtly veiled threats that had been made against his life. Feeling had been building against the Seneca chief, whom the western Indians, and even some of his own people, were steadily more and more blaming for selling the store. Both Cornplanter's Uncle Kayahsotha and General Wayne had had intimations that the chief's life was in real danger.[29]

Early in September of that year (1792) the Indians launched their expedition. Blacksnake describes the early part of the Cornplanter delegation's trip from Pittsburgh to Au Glaize. On the Monongahela shores there were five boats ready for them, of size enough to hold "about 220 men." But it was several days before they had proceeded far enough down the Ohio to reach the Little Muskingum River. He reports that they went upon that river several miles before leaving their boat and camping out. After three days in camp, they traveled "something like 15 miles . . . before we come to the Indians Settlement Something like 8 families together into one place." He reports that their delegation was graciously received by the women, who invited them to supper "till their men Return from hunting." And, though they had fixed their tents, Blacksnake, fearing rain, stayed with a Shawnee family.[30]

Of interest is Blacksnake's personal disclosure in his narrative of his romance with an Indian maid, apparently a Shawnee. Blacksnake had early become enamored of the young woman, but had experienced great trouble in his courtship of her because of the differences in the language each was speaking. "I could not understand what She Says to me She appeared that She feels the Same my feeling in Relation to talking with me I wanted to know whither She is married or promiss or not But trouble we could not understand Each other what we talking about it, I feel Desirious to larnt Something about her, for She was the handsomes that I never See among my own people." Later in his narrative he returns to this subject, which was distracting him from the council business. After a dance one night, "when we got back to their tent where this young Squaw live I talk with old man about his Daughter By Signs asking him whither She is married or promiss for her husban Near I could Larnt that she is not married and Never was I said no more to him or her about it till uncle cornplanter I ask him advice concerning of my having lover to that young Squaw he Says to me that I had better let her a lone and Speak no more about it, &c I than said no more about . . . marriage I have felt sorrow."[31]

The British, in the person of Upper Canada's first Lieutenant Governor, John Graves Simcoe, who during the Revolution enjoyed a distinguished career,[32] were much interested in this conference. They continued in the hope that much of the territory which lay to the south of Detroit might one day be annexed to Canada. Naturally they favored hostility between the Americans and the western Indians. In a letter to Joseph Brant, dated September 4, Alexander McKee, the notorious British Indian agent,[33] referring to the peacemakers Knox had dispatched to the Maumee, assured the Mohawk Chief that nothing would come of the American peace proposals to the western Indians. "You must be perfectly sensible," he wrote, "that after two successful general engagements [Little Turtle's victories over Harmar and St. Clair], in which a great deal of blood has been spilt, the Indians will not quietly give up by negotiation what they have been contending for with their lives since the commencement of these troubles." [34]

Joseph Brant, who remained very close to the British, insisted that he was too ill to attend the conference. But he had some good news. He reported, first, that it was his opinion that the new generation of Senecas, the young warriors, "were ready to help their western friends." He even suggested, not without reason, that Cornplanter might be having second thoughts, that he might be coming back into the Iroquois fold, that he might soon move away from his home on the Allegheny.[35]

But the British were not represented at the conference. The most conspicuous white man present for the proceedings, if you can count him a white man, was the notorious Simon Girty, who had so far survived the bounty on his head. Colonel John Hardin and Captain Alexander Trueman, together with another emissary of peace, were murdered along the way. Hardin, who was a year younger than Cornplanter, had served with Daniel Morgan's Rifle Corps during the Revolution. He was in on the defeat of Burgoyne at Saratoga. After the war he moved from Virginia to Kentucky, where he farmed and fought the hostile Indians. He was well known to General Henry Knox, who thought he would be a good man to carry the President's peace message to the Shawnee. A portion of the letter that he carried read as follows: "To all the tribes south of the [Great] Lakes, east of the Mississippi and northwest of the Ohio—Brothers The President of the United States entertains the opinion, that the war which exists is founded in error and mistake on your part. That you believe that the United States wants to deprive you of your lands and drive you out of the country. Be assured that this is not so; on the contrary, that we should be greatly gratified with the opportunity of imparting to you all the blessings of civilized life, of teaching you to cultivate corn, to raise oxen, sheep and other domestic animals; to build comfortable houses; so as ever to dwell upon the land."

With a guide and an interpreter for each, both Hardin and Trueman departed Fort Washington in that spring, Colonel Hardin dispatching a note to his wife to assure her that though there were dangers he would be all right: "The Indians have killed several persons in the quarter lately and leave behind them war clubs, which denotes their intentions of war. But do not let this give you any uneasiness as I have not a doubt that I shall meet with good treatment, as the speech and the belt I shall take is from the President of the United States."

Hardin's party was met by a small party of Shawnee near Turtle Creek in present-day Shelby County. As the Indians appeared friendly, all turned in for the night together. In the hours just before morning, most members of Hardin's party, including the colonel himself, were brutally murdered.

In the same manner was Major Alexander Trueman murdered. Trueman, with a waiter and William Smalley, who served as guide and interpreter, had also departed from Fort Washington, but followed a different route into the Shawnee country. Only Smalley survived. His report speaks also of the apparent friendliness of the Indians and of the fatal failure of his company to recognize the ruse.

On Christmas Day, at Legionville, some time after the Council at Au Glaize, General Wayne heard from Chief Cornplanter and the sachem New Arrow an account of the council proceedings which included a note of consolation: "General Washington must not think hard of the loss of Colonel Harding [Hardin] and others, as we have since understood they were sent with messages of peace; unluckily for them and us, they had taken the bad road; if four spies, whom we left on that road, saw any of your people, they took them for enemies, and treated them as such; we know that your people would have done the same." [36]

Historian Isabel Kelsay notes that General Rufus Putnam and the Moravian Missionary Reverend John Heckewelder were able to make their way to the Wabash in time to persuade "some of the less belligerent Wabash Indians to come to Philadelphia to make peace." Secretary Knox, of course, was very happy to have this news. Tragically, a great many of these Indians perished to the dreaded smallpox before they ever reached the city.[37]

At this time, the Shawnee and the Miami and the other western tribes were growing steadily more nervous, as their runners reported the building of forts. Particularly unsettling was the report that General Wayne had constructed a new stockade, called St. Clair and located on the line including Fort Hamilton and Fort Jefferson.

But the council was convened. Originally scheduled for the rapids, it finally opened at the point where the Maumee and the Auglaize come together (present-day Defiance, Ohio). Kelsay accounts for the setting: "Here were two Shawnee villages, a Delaware village, some displaced Cherokees from the south, and the dwellings of some newly arrived Miamis who had fled their towns on the upper Maumee.[38] Another village of Delawares was situated a few miles away. From the Glaize, as the forks were often called, the Indians could watch General Wayne's movements."[39]

The conference itself, which had convened on the last day of September, turned out to be surely the largest Indian council of the times. Attending were the chiefs of all the tribes of the Northwest, representatives of the Seven Nations of Canada, sachems and chiefs of the twenty-seven nations "beyond Canada," and Cornplanter, Red Jacket, and New Arrow, and forty-six other Six Nations chiefs. And countless were the warriors. Indeed, the numbers were so staggering that Cornplanter observed, "There were so many nations we cannot tell the names of them."

The lines were drawn early. Red Jacket and of course Washington's Indian emissaries were for peace. The Shawanese chiefs, as well as the Delaware and the other principal tribes of the west, were for war. And the lines remained firm. The Senecas and other Iroquois made but little impression on the Ohio hostiles. The Shawnees, much emboldened by their recent successes, were particularly unreceptive. Haughtily, they reminded the delegates of the overwhelming defeats suffered by the forces of General Harmar and St. Clair. And their principal orator passionately declared, "The President well knows why the blood is so deep in our paths."[40] To all of this, Chief Red Jacket, who played an important role at the council, responded (speaking from his own experience about the effect of chance in matters of war) with the suggestion that the Indians in those battles had been lucky, that they should not count on continued success: "You were very fortunate that the great Spirit above was so kind as to assist you to throw the Americans twice on their back when they came against your villages, your women & children."[41]

Reflecting well the bitterness of the western Indians was the indignant accusation delivered by a Delaware chief: "I remember when we last met 4 years ago you [the Six Nations] told us, and all Nations agreed to it, that if any one of us were struck, we should consider it as if the whole of the Nations had received a Blow and that the whole should join in revenging it, think well of this Uncles of the 6 Nations." [42]

The western Indians, pretty much without exception, expressed only contempt for the Six Nations, who had given in to the United States. The Shawnees were particularly agitated and angry at the council, remembering as they did the deprivations they had steadily suffered.

Chief Red Jacket, who did most of the talking for the Senecas, and for the Six Nations generally (Joseph Brant arrived too late to participate.), did all he could to make good the promise Cornplanter had made to President Washington. He spoke for five (!) hours. Against the bitter and angry discontent he urged reason and cautious consideration. He suggested that pride goeth before a fall. He spoke for peace: "Now Brothers, we know that the Americans have held out their hands to offer you peace. Don't be too proud Spirited and reject it, the great Spirit should be angry with you, but let us go on in the best manner we can to make peace with them." [43] But even the eloquent Red Jacket could do little.[44] In short the negotiations met with no success for the would-be pacifiers, and, if anything, the difference between the Six Nations and the Ohio Indians, which had begun with the sell-out at the first treaty of Fort Stanwix, was only widened.

After arriving home from the conference, Chief Cornplanter and his good friend the sachem New Arrow (who had already dispatched a report to President Washington), in response to a request from General Wayne, who desired to know who were in attendance and what the conclusions were, prepared a "speech" for him. It was dated Chinuchshungutho, 8th Dec., 1792, and was translated by Nicholas Rosencrantz. It makes a good point (that "we were here first"), but it is somewhat ambiguous on the position taken by the Indians at the council, as it speaks of a willingness to make peace while all the while insisting on terms known to be impossible to Washington. It is clear from the address that the western Indians, and, it may be supposed, the Iroquois as well, are much under the influence of the Crown. And it is also clear that they desire another council, this time with the American heads of state, and of course on the Indians' ground. It concludes with Cornplanter's reminder to General Wayne that he and New Arrow, as well as the fifteen warriors "who neglected their hunting to accompany us," are due a "reward" for their services.[45]

Nicholas Rosencrantz signed the documents as interpreter and certified "upon oath," that the foregoing is a "true translation of that delivered *viva voce,* by the Cornplanter and New Arrow, to me, at Chinuchshunguthо, on the 8th instant." And Anthony Wayne signed it too, on Christmas Day, "Sworn before me, at Legionville, this 25th day of December, 1792."

Henry Knox had this document delivered to the President of the Senate on January 5. And on January 7, 1793, the document was read to that body, after Knox's prefatory note: "In obedience to the order of the President of the United States, I have the honor to submit to the Senate, a message of the Cornplanter and New arrow, to Major General Wayne, of the 8th ultimo. The subject of Indian affairs being under the consideration of Congress, the President has conceived it proper that they should be possessed of the message now submitted." [46]

As for Washington, he was simply not too sure just what to make of the report from the conference. The communication seemed to convey *some* willingness to reach a peaceful settlement, but at the same time the western Indians were clearly and definitely insisting that the Ohio River be recognized as the line, the western boundary for whites.[47] He would prepare for the worst.

Joseph Brant's biographer, Isabel Kelsay, explains that the decision of the western Indians, to hold fast to the Ohio River line, was in consequence of a number of notions (many of them mistaken) that the Indians nurtured: (1) the impression that General St. Clair had been ordered to build three forts in their country: at the head of the Maumee, at the Glaize, and at the point where the Maumee flows into Lake Erie; (2) the belief that the government of the United States meant to drive them across the Mississippi; (3) the conviction that Indians agreeing to peace would be assigned to demeaning labor; (4) their pride in the recent victories over Harmar and St. Clair; (5) their confidence that their "father," the British "would see that they received justice." [48] Cornplanter's delegation finally agreed to endorse this decision. And of course the British were delighted with the conclusion reached by the council. So what Washington received was an agreement for peace only under conditions which would assuage all of these fears.

With the failure of the Au Glaize Council to assure a peaceful settlement, and hostilities steadily becoming more heated, there occurred some scrambling for another council. The site was a problem. A letter from Secretary of War Henry Knox to the western Indians, dated February 28,

1793, is a part of the correspondence. It is addressed to the sachems, chiefs, and warriors of all the Ohio tribes and to the Headmen of any tribes in alliance with them. It expresses disappointment in the failure to get together, but pledges a meeting on "the first of June next." [49]

The council eventually got scheduled for April at the junction of the Miamis. The Lieutenant Governor of Upper Canada, John Graves Simcoe (although he was finding Brant difficult to deal with) remained hopeful of an alliance between the Iroquois and the western Indians. From Niagara on April 1, 1793, he addressed a letter to Alured Clarke,[50] Lieutenant Governor of Lower Canada. It reflects his great concern for Cornplanter's role: "I apprehend O'Beal, the Cornplanter, will be there [council of the Six Nations, scheduled for April 20]. In his speech to Captain Brant, he assures him that he will not falter from the general interests, and having consulted that chief upon a late message from Mr. Washington to invite the 6 Nations to Philadelphia, as I understand, he has not gone there, but agreed with him in opinion, that it was unnecessary. The Farmer's Brother is gone to Philadelphia, but Colonel [John] Butler assures me that he is firm to the Indian interest."

Governor Simcoe defined his object and his hopes: " . . . I cannot but entertain a strong belief that the Indians will universally persist in those rights; that they will declare them to be unalienable without common consent, and that in consequence of their resolutions, Great Britain will nearly obtain that intermediate boundary which his Majesty's Ministers have in their contemplation. This is the object I aim at, and in the present critical situation of affairs, I am persuaded in every point of view, it is most necessary to maintain his Majesty's interest with all the Indian nations." [51]

But Cornplanter did not attend the Six Nations council at Niagara, which was convened as a preliminary and preparatory conference for the larger council to be held with the western Indians on the Maumee. Simcoe shot off another letter to Major General Clarke: "O'Beal or the Cornplanter was to have been present, but by the drunkenness of the messengers, the answer of the Buffalo Creek Indians to his message appointing the time and place of the meeting was not forwarded to that Chieftain. It is understood that he is at present at Pittsburgh, but it seems rather to be believed, that to use his own expression, he will not falter from his promise of abiding by the result of the determination of the approaching meeting." [52]

But the Maumee conference, which was held in July, failed also to reach any kind of settlement for peace. Simcoe had predicted it. On June 14 he had directed to Clarke a most interesting appraisal of the situation:

> *It appears to me that there is little probability of effecting a Peace, and I am inclined to believe that the Commissioners do not expect it; that General Wayne does not expect it; and that the Mission of the Commissioners is in general contemplated by the People of the United States as necessary to adjust the ceremonial of the destruction and pre-determined extirpation of the Indian Americans. Your Excellency will no doubt observe, from the general tenor of the conversation & conduct of the United States, that an alliance with the Six Nations and turning them against the Western Indians, and ultimately Great Britain is their favorite object. It is therefore a fortunate circumstance in my Ideas that should even the present treaty totally fail, as I suspect it will, that all the Indians have combined in the request that Great Britain should furnish them with Provisions, and that the Superintendents, Captain Brandt, the Farmer's Brother, and O'Beal the Corn Planter, have separately observed, and no doubt will dilate on the Kindness of His majesty's Government in this respect, and on the independent footing which by these means the Indian Nations can meet the Commissioners: and I hope . . . whatever may be the events of the Treaty, will fully support His Majesty's influence and conciliate the Affections of the Indians so necessary to the safety of this Colony.* [53]

Cornplanter was not at this council apparently, nor at a later conference at Detroit. At both, the Wyandots, the Miamis and the Delawares repeated their demands that the line be drawn at the Ohio River. They wanted the white settlers who had already come into the region removed. When the American commissioners replied that that would be impossible, the western Indians made a suggestion: "We know that these settlers are poor . . . . Divide, therefore, this large sum of money, which you have offered to us, among these people." [54] It was the feeling of the Indians that the settlers might in this way be persuaded to vacate. That idea of course did not fly. And the results were similar at succeeding councils held in the fall of 1793 and the spring of 1794.[55] Peace was not emerging from the discussions.

And Cornplanter was participating very little. At some time in the summer succeeding the council at Au Glaize, according to Seneca legend, there occurred a blow to Cornplanter's desire to serve as intermediary in the dispute. The episode took place in the spring, while Cornplanter and "a few comrades more brave than wise" were on another peace mission into the Shawnee-Delaware country. Anthony Wallace tells the story. He explains that at the very time preparations were being made by Washington to launch a third invasion into the Ohio Indian country, the party of Senecas was embarked on a trip to the Indian villages on the Sandusky River. As they came into the encampments, "they were seized, held prisoner, and threatened with death." When, after a most anxious time, the Indian ambassadors were finally released, they were now offered food. Because they feared poison, "Cornplanter and a few others . . . refused to eat and fasted all the way home." And, according to the legend which has persisted among the Senecas until this day, a number of the Indians did in fact die on the homeward trip (presumably those who had eaten of the proffered victuals).[56]

If this story is true, and most likely it is, there is no need to wonder why Cornplanter from this time on declined to participate in a great many of the councils that had the Ohio Indian hostility as their subject. In fact, the wonder is that Cornplanter considered as much as he did the matter of Seneca aid to the western Indians. He must surely have appreciated (1) that even with the support of the Six Nations the Indian forces could not prevail. Even the Miami Chief Little Turtle, who was responsible for the overwhelming defeats of Generals Harmar and St. Clair, was far from confident. And (2) he must have understood that any gesture of Seneca aid on his part could only damage his situation on the Allegheny. He was, obviously, in a most vulnerable location. It did not make sense to risk everything in a war with the United States. He was surely agreeing with Red Jacket that the Indian victories over Harmar and St. Clair were provided by luck, luck that could not regularly be counted on.

While these councils were occurring, through the rest of this year and into early 1794, General Anthony Wayne was making mighty preparation for a showdown. And the Iroquois continued to function as intermediaries. And Chief Cornplanter was caught between a rock and a hard place. Although not much involved in formal councils any more, he was growing steadily more apprehensive about what was happening, as Joseph Brant had predicted. He was particularly distressed by the matter of Presque Isle.

During this anxious decade immediately following the Treaty of Paris and made tense by the continued presence of the British and the hostility of the Ohio Indians and their victories over Generals Harmar and St. Clair, Simcoe and other British officials worked tirelessly to promote friendly relations between the Mohawks and the Senecas. It was their hope, obviously, that the Ohio Indians would resist with force the Americans' claim to Presque Isle and the so-called Erie Triangle, and the territory beyond the Ohio. They even harbored the notion that the Ohio Indians might be successful in an all-out war, especially with the support of the Six Nations and with whatever aid the British might be able to supply. The British, in defiant violation of the terms of the Treaty of Paris, continued to hold the forts of Niagara and Detroit and continued to nurture hope of land south of Ontario. They were not shy about their interest, continuing, as they did, "to provision the Indian confederacy and supply it with ammunition." [57] It was Simcoe's hope that a united Six Nations supporting the Ohio Indians might be enough to persuade the United States to negotiate a peaceful settlement, one that would recognize the claims of the Indians to those lands west of the Ohio.

At this time, of course the most powerful figures in the Six Nations were the Mohawk Joseph Brant and the Senecas Cornplanter and Red Jacket. It was Simcoe's earnest desire to make them all one in this dispute. He had his work cut out for him. Brant and Cornplanter, though fighting shoulder to shoulder, were really friendly only off and on. Cornplanter and Red Jacket had clearly become rivals for leadership and had had their differences.

Joseph Brant and Cornplanter were in fact much alike in many ways. Both were extremely vain; both enjoyed authority and exploited it; both were passionately fond of attention. Both were extremely courageous, even fierce, war-chiefs, could fight like wildcats, and could inspire their warriors. Although it was not always clear who was in command of the Six Nations warriors in some of the engagements, the chiefs Cornplanter and Brant had fought side by side in many raids and battles, at Oriskany, at Cherry Valley, and in the Schoharie Valley. At this time both were hardened veterans of the Revolutionary War. Brant had served the British from the time of the Howe brothers' assault on Long Island and New York City in the fall of 1776. Cornplanter had come formally into the action in the summer of 1778, and had pretty much bowed out with the Johnson campaign into the Schoharie Valley in October of 1780. Both were dedicated to their people and would in earnest devotion champion their cause by whatever means they could; but both, after the end of the War of the Revolution were actively opposed to armed resistance. At this point the similarities give way to some pronounced differences.

Joseph Brant was seven to nine years older than Cornplanter. He was a sophisticate, well educated and comfortable in "polite society." He was well versed in the English language, having enjoyed two years of schooling in Connecticut. He was so good with the language that he would one day translate into Mohawk the Gospel of St. Mark and the Book of Common Prayer. He had visited in London for a long time during 1775-76, and had even enjoyed an audience with King George III, and had experienced happy associations with such luminaries as James Boswell, the famous biographer of Samuel Johnson. He had visited again in England some three years after the conclusion of the war.

Brant, though probably more Indian in blood than was Cornplanter, who was definitely a half-breed, was much more at home in the white culture than was the Seneca. Of course he was an Indian, a Mohawk tried and true. He is supposed to have remarked, "After every exertion to divest myself of prejudice, I am obliged to give my opinion in favor of my own people." [58]

Brant continued after the war his alliance with the British. And, in 1785, grateful for the vast expanse of land provided his people by the Crown, "led nearly half of the Six Nations population [including perhaps 100 Senecas, and most of the Cayugas] to new homes on the Grand River." [59]

Cornplanter had never made any real effort to learn the English language and always required an interpreter. He had never been as close to the British as was Joseph Brant, and, for as long as he could, had stood for neutrality in the dispute between the King and the colonies, insisting that "it is none of our business." He disdained Brant's invitation to join the Mohawks on the Grand River. His favors came chiefly from Pennsylvania.

Because of the concessions he made to the negotiating Commissioners over the years in the many treaty sessions, Cornplanter was not always so popular with his people as was Joseph Brant. But he was "Head Man" most of the time.

Red Jacket was just a little younger than Cornplanter and, as for Cornplanter, the circumstances of his birth are unknown, and not a whole lot is known of his early life. It is not known definitely where or when he was born, although Red Jacket himself was certain that he was born at Canoga (*Gah-noh-geh*, Oil on the water), in the region of Cayuga Lake. The date, it is regularly supposed, was 1756 or 1758, most probably the latter.[60] His mother was a Seneca of the Wolf Clan, by name *Ah-wey-ney-oh;* and his father, it is thought, was a Cayuga of the Turtle Clan. When he was just a youngster, possibly ten or twelve years old, he was given the name *Oti-ti-ani* (Always Ready), which turned out to be more apt for his public speaking than for his willingness to fight. At some time before Lexington and Concord his family moved to Ganawaugus on the Genesee, the home of Cornplanter, then a little over twenty years of age.

Red Jacket was clearly not the warrior that was Cornplanter or Joseph Brant. In fact, though he was present for some battles, he was in his youth and middle years not a willing warrior at all.[61] He was much of that time serving the British as a messenger, and for that service was rewarded with the very bright scarlet coat that inspired the name he would thereafter be known by.

His gifts were in public speaking. He became a most accomplished orator, and, not only for the Senecas but for all of the Six Nations. By 1780 he had assumed the role as council orator and had taken on a new name, *Sa-go-ye-wat-ha-whih* ("He Keeps Them Awake").[62] For forty years thereafter he was active in nearly every council that concerned the rights of the Indians. He was generally not so conciliatory or as accommodating as Cornplanter, but he would sign the Treaty of Big Tree in 1797, and, when he was seventy-six years old, he would affix his mark to the 1826 treaty made at Buffalo Creek.

In these councils he delivered many very stirring speeches. He could be plaintive, he could be logical. He could even be blunt, as when, in 1792, in Philadelphia, he rebuked the President of the United States, who was looking for help from the Senecas in quieting the western Indians: "The President has assured us that he is not the cause of hostilities. Brother, we wish you to point out to us . . . what you think is the real cause." [63]

He continued in his public speaking until the last hours of his life. At the age of eighty, having just met the newly inaugurated President Andrew Jackson, he paused in Albany on his way home to address an audience. In those remarks he somewhat indiscreetly compared Old Hickory most unfavorably to the nation's first president. During the administration of John Quincy Adams, together with Henry O'Bail and a third Seneca, he journeyed to Washington to protest land sales. It was during their stay in the capital city that Charles Bird King painted both Red Jacket and Henry O'Bail. Red Jacket lived out his life at Buffalo Creek. He died on January 20, 1830, and was interred at the Buffalo Creek Mission Cemetery, though he was not a Christian. Because his grave site was constantly being disturbed by relic hunters, with great ceremony his descendants and the Buffalo Historical Society consigned his remains to a new grave, in the city's Forest Lawn Cemetery, where a number of Seneca chiefs are buried. The date was October 9, 1884. A monument to Red Jacket, placed at the site by the Buffalo Historical Society, now overlooks the grave. It is a bronze likeness of the famous chief.[64]

Red Jacket after the Revolution was considered a "northern Seneca," as he made his home at Buffalo Creek, while Cornplanter was considered a "southern Seneca." And because of the force of their personalities real differences developed between the communities, and something of a rivalry. Because of Red Jacket's reputation as a timid soul in battle, it was ironic that in the late years he acquired a reputation for a much more militant stance than that assumed regularly by Cornplanter.

Among the dying words of the Seneca known popularly as Red Jacket are these: "Be sure that my grave be not made by a white man; let them not pursue me there!" [65] It is doubtful, though he bowed out in extreme bitterness, that Cornplanter could have spoken these words.

Cornplanter enjoyed a somewhat different relationship with the Mohawk Joseph Brant. In spite of some very real differences (notably in their feelings for the British), Brant and Cornplanter were all of the time experiencing the same anxieties, and had therefore a common concern. Cooperation was in the best interest of each party. Governor Simcoe, noting this, worked hard to bring the two closer together, "promising Cornplanter a pension," and suggesting to Brant that he might have, in return for help to the British, "a council house for the Mohawks and a gunboat on the Grand River." [66] In his sessions with Cornplanter, Simcoe was quick to point out to the Seneca chief that the land on the Grand River which was presented to the Indians had been granted by the

Crown not only to the Mohawks but to all members of the Six Nations.[67] He was trying to bring the Senecas closer to the other nations, to make the Six Nations a solid federation.

John Graves Simcoe

Even though President Washington had persuaded the Governor of Pennsylvania, Thomas Mifflin, to put an end to the state's activities at Presque Isle, tensions continued. With the threat of war looming ever larger, and General Anthony Wayne in preparation with his army, the Indians entered into two mid-summer councils, both at Buffalo Creek, one on June 18, and the other on the United States Independence Day. According to Isabel Kelsay, these councils were unabashedly combative. During the sessions, she reports, "Threats were made against the people of the United States. Cornplanter began to make veiled threats of his own to such Americans as he met; and Joseph [Brant] wrote a threatening letter to Israel Chapin, predicting that if the Americans 'go on striving to carry everything before them by force the consequences may be dreadful.'" [68] Simcoe could only have been delighted.

Most interesting is a communication (one of several) dispatched at this time by General John Gibson to Pennsylvania Governor Mifflin. Dated Pittsburgh, June 20, 1794, the letter, which contains communications come to Gibson, and refers to an incident in Jennesadaga, reveals just how very close not only the Senecas but indeed the entire Six Nations, were to a union with the western Indians:

> *Dear Sir: I had the honour of receiving yours per this day's post. In my last, I informed you that I had ordered 150 Militia for the protection of the Frontiers of Westmoreland, and have wrote to the difer[t] Brigade Inspectors to have their quotas complete. The Inclosed letters have since come to hand, and from their contents, and the information rec[d] by a man who left Corn planter's town about twelve day's [sic] ago, we have every reason to conclude that the Six Nations will be obliged to join the Western Indians. This man declares that an attempt had been made to take his life by an Indian, But that the Corn planter prevented it by telling the Indians the time was not yet come for them to strike, that the Indians at the town appeared very surly and Ill-natured, and that a person by the name of Jennings, who lives at the Cornplanter's town, informed him that he thought the Cornplanter must join the Western Indians.*[69]

The second of the important actions taken by Washington following the ignominious defeat of Arthur St. Clair was the appointment of a successor to the General. For this most important post Washington turned to one of his most distinguished officers of the Continental Army, General Anthony Wayne. In Wayne, President Washington had unbounded confidence, and, from his point of view, the General seemed yet quite a young man. Surely his name alone would mean much to the nation's hopes. He was a hero of the Revolution, one of the most zealous of the patriots. It was Wayne who, while representing Chester County in the Pennsylvania Assembly, agitated so vigorously against British indignities, who organized and commanded a regiment from Chester County, who assumed command of the 4th Pennsylvania Battalion in the Continental Army, who commanded at Fort Ticonderoga during the tough winter of 1776-77, who had fought gallantly at Brandywine, at Germantown, at Monmouth, who was responsible for one of the most famous achievements of the War (the capture of Stony Point on the Hudson by a night attack in July of 1779), who was active in the Yorktown campaign, and who had fought so successfully against the Indians in Georgia. Except for the tragedy suffered at Paoli, General Wayne had never disappointed his Commander-in-Chief. Surely Anthony Wayne could bring peace to the northwestern frontier.

On the 25th day of May, 1792, the new Commander of the United States Army, General Anthony Wayne, equipped with his instructions from President Washington, which included the admonition "that another defeat would be inexpressibly ruinous to the reputation of the government," set out for Pittsburgh.[70] By late fall he had organized his army (in spite of a steady stream of constant desertions), and had closely studied the Indian situation. From Pittsburgh he marched his army to the Miami territory downriver on the Ohio, establishing Headquarters at Legionville, and at Hobson's Choice, and intending first to open negotiations with the hostile tribes.

XV

JOHN ADLUM AT CORNPLANTER TOWN

During all of this time, in the early years of the last decade of the 18th century, Chief Cornplanter is living in Cornplanter Town on the headwaters of the Allegheny, north of Pittsburgh, on the land given him by the Pennsylvania Assembly in 1790. He is the Head Man of the Upper Allegheny Senecas. A fellow chief, a sachem, in the same community, and his erstwhile companion throughout the various councils and conferences during this period, is the highly regarded New Arrow (Kanassee, or Captain Strong).

Few white men ever got to know Chief Cornplanter as well as did the surveyor John Adlum, for he was among the upper Allegheny Senecas off and on for a number of years, both as surveyor and as Pennsylvania Commissioner. Like Thomas Proctor he regarded Cornplanter as a good friend, and respected him for his devotion to his people and for his capacity to weather adversity. And like Proctor, too, though he was here chiefly as a surveyor, he was coming to Cornplanter as an ambassador from Pennsylvania, with letters from the Secretary of War and the Governor of Pennsylvania.

Readers of his Memoirs[1] and of his letters emerge with four satisfactions. First, they acquire, from a surveyor's point of view, vivid impressions of the beautiful upper Allegheny region as it was 200 years ago. Second, they get to know really well the Chief Cornplanter, who is at this time middle-aged. Third, they are provided an accurate reading of the traditional Seneca way of life, which, while threatened, was continued here on Cornplanter's river. Finally, readers will applaud the tact and sympathetic understanding with which Adlum read and addressed the Indian situation.

Adlum was a Pennsylvanian, a native of York. He was fairly well educated, but was as a youngster most enthusiastic about hunting and

John Adlum

fishing and trapping. He was some nine years younger than Cornplanter, and had been a surveyor for some time before the year in which we meet him here, which is 1794. In fact, because of his surveying assignments, he had by this time come to know Chief Cornplanter quite well. His first meeting with the Chief had occurred five years ago during the time Adlum was helping to fix the northern boundary of Pennsylvania.

At the time of this first meeting with Chief Cornplanter, he was working some with the surveyor Samuel Maclay,[2] brother to the surveyor William Maclay, who had witnessed the entire proceedings at the treaty of Fort Stanwix and had been so horrified by Cornplanter's ravage of Fort Freeland.

Adlum was back in the northwest two years later to plot town sites, and again in the succeeding year to map the river routes and locate portages. After five years of surveying for the Quaker State, he was appointed Deputy Surveyor.[3] He is now on assignment for James Wilson and the Holland Land Company, surveying lands in this northwestern corner of Pennsylvania, which is well known to him, but is still dangerous Indian country. It is July. He has been in this region before, once as one of the surveyors who were drawing the line between Pennsylvania and New York, and also, in April of 1790, as a Pennsylvania commissioner. He tells us himself that he was not only well known to the Indians, but enjoyed considerable influence among them, for he has cut off from the old surveys "two great bodies of land in their favour." And he tells us that many times warriors would come with their families to his surveying camps, sometimes to stay a fortnight.

It was at this time, during the spring and summer of 1790, that John Adlum enjoyed his first meeting with the famous Chief Cornplanter. And before long, as is apparent from his memoirs, he would be on very good terms with Cornplanter and the upper Allegheny Senecas.[4] It was at this time, too, that the farmer-surveyor Samuel Maclay was in the region, on assignment to conduct a study of the streams in this northeastern section of the state, particularly the Allegheny, the West Branch of the Susquehanna, and its principal tributary, the Sinnemahoning, known to the Indians as Achsinni-mahoni ("stony lick").

On Tuesday, July 6, Maclay, though suffering from a raging toothache, intended to call on the Cornplanter, "where he lived." But his Indian guides discouraged it, declaring it was not manly "to call about Bus[i]ness at a Cabbin in the woods." As they had hold of the stern of the canoe, it was plain to Maclay that they would effectively object to any such meeting. Thus impressed, Maclay urged them to send for Cornplanter, that he would wait here for him. Their chief returned shortly to report that Cornplanter would be along. But night arrived without his appearance. Next day the chief did appear, about eight o'clock, and the two met in a comfortable spot. Maclay delivered the news that a road was being considered for the region, and all "appeared in good humor." Cornplanter then delivered a welcoming speech in which he said he was glad to see them and they might have anything they might catch in his country.

An "Oritor" then spoke for the women, thanking the party for the good news and expressing the hope that "as soon as the Good Road . . . was made, they would be able to purchase what things they wanted on Better terms." The congenial meeting ended just as it started to rain. Maclay's party then boarded their canoes and pushed down the river, "and took up our camp op[p]osite Capt'n Obeal's Town and had the honor of his company at supper."

John Adlum was apparently present for all of this, as on the next day, soon as the rain cleared, he went up to the State line to survey the Allegheny & to assist Maclay in "making a survey for the Cornplanter." That business kept the both of them employed until late afternoon, when they returned to camp "quite wet and fatigued." [5]

Now, nearly four years later, at the time Adlum is readying himself for his trip, General Wayne is making preparations for a crushing blow to the Indians along the Ohio, and President Washington is hoping that the Senecas, and the rest of the Iroquois nations, will remain quiet. Adlum is aware that the armies of Generals Harmar and St. Clair have suffered devastating defeats and that the situation is volatile. It is not a good time to travel through the Indian country.

On July 27, 1794, the surveyor wrote to his friend John Wallis: "To morrow morning I go up to the Cornplanters Town to inform him I intend going out to Survey some lands and to demand of him and the other Chiefs to furnish me with a guard while on business & I expect to be able from his answers to know how to proceed—there is about a dozen Indians going with me from this place [Fort Franklin] up to his Town and [I] expect to return in nine or ten days." He ventured the observation that "every thing wears an unpleasing Aspect here," but seemed confident that "all will yet be quiet for a fortnight." [6]

On the 28th, then, the surveying party, with Indian guides and two interpreters, set out against the current by canoe for Cornplanter's Town.

Half Town is the "Commodore." Adlum, who was expected of course, receives quite a reception:

> *We at length arrived at the town of Jenuchshadega where the Cornplanter resided—in front of which there was a long sheet of still and deep water*[7] *and before we arrived opposite the lower end of the town, my Comodore, gave me notice that I must now assume the command and go to the front—I accordingly took my place in the front, and ordered the other canoes to follow me two abreast, and parallel to each other, and about 20 yards apart and 30 yards distant in the rear of me so that we made a double line behind me of near one hundred yards—And I ordered the Canoes to move slowly up the Stream—the Cornplanter had collected most of the warriors from the two Towns (which were about nine miles apart), and they were formed in a single line the men about six feet apart and dressed in all their finery, and painted as if for war—with the down of Swans on their heads—They had a colours on the left of their line up the river they being on the left bank of it—I took it for granted that I was to pass the whole line to the colours, and immediately upon our arriving at the lower end of the Town, The Cornplanter gave the word of command & a loud Whoop, Whoop, Whoop, when they immediately commenced firing with ball, all of which passed between the young Indian in the head of my canoe & my self many of them within less than a yard of me—I was standing in my canoe with my hat off—I counted eighty odd as we passed, those that fired first reloaded and fired a shot over our heads, when the last had fired, I fired off my pistols which I carried in my belt & I requested my Comodore, Halftown, to direct the Indians that were with him to fire their rifles, all which was done before we landed—*[8]

After he had recovered from this astonishing welcome, Adlum was escorted to the council house, where the chiefs exclaimed how happy they were to see him, and the women received him graciously, declaring their hope that he was bringing good news, and that there would be no war. Adlum assured them all that there would be no war, unless the Indians were the aggressors. He was placed between the "two principal chiefs, the Cornplanter on my right, and the dark chief [The Black Chief, whom Proctor had met near Squawkie Hill] on my left," with his two interpreters ten feet in front. The council scene, with its lively discussion, is fascinating:

> *There was a fire in the centre of the house, and the Cornplanter took a large pipe ornamented with feathers, into which he put some tobacco mixed with the bark of a species of Viburnum, when he lit the pipe and took a few whiffs and handed it to me, and after I had taken a few whiffs I passed it to my left hand man, who also passed it round in the same way each taking some whiffs, and each as he passed it lit his own pipe, and commenced smoking, and then the large pipe was brought back, but I do not recollect how it was eventually disposed of—The house was quite crowded, with men and women, the latter shewed by their countenances great anxiety. As the house was full, a good many young men and boys got on the beams or joice [joists] that passed across the house—After the pipe was returned the Cornplanter, addressing himself to me, enquired what news I had; I handed him General Knox's letter and my commission from the Governor of Pennsa. recommending me to their good offices &c. He first broke the seal of the letter from General Knox, and returned it to me and requested me to read it, which I did, & When the interpreters had finished translating the first paragraph—The young indians on the beams above, saluted me with an univer[sal] roar, vulgarly called farting. I heard several of the elderly women exclaim Yaugh-ti-Yaughti which was as much as to say—shame, scandalous—I made a pause, ruminating within my self how I should act, and concluded to read another paragraph, and received another salute of the same kind—I felt a considerable degree of indignation, which I endeavoured to conceal—(we were all sitting).*

> *When I arose on my feet; and addressing myself to the chiefs, I told them that I was very sorry that the young men had spent all their ammunition in saluting me while I was on the water, and that by the stench I supposed they intended to drive me out of the house; That their ammunition must be very bad and fired out of very dirty guns—that if they wished to compliment me I would give them a cask of Powder, with which they might amuse themselves, until I had finished my business with the chiefs and I ordered them a quarter cask of powder (I had two with me) which they immediately got—*

Here Cornplanter arose to reprimand the young men, and so did another chief, and so, too did Mrs. Chit-ti-aw-dunk (Hummingbird, possibly Kayahsotha's sister, and therefore Cornplanter's aunt), at which the boys "descended from their roosts, and sneaked off." Adlum read on without further interruption, explained his business and left a map showing the lands he intended to survey. Next morning there occurred the familiar hassle over the Stanwix treaty and animated discussion of the Ohio Indians' hostility, and the prospect of war involving the British.[9]

And so on. The Indians loved to talk. Cornplanter loved to talk. There seemed never to be a hurry. Before Adlum took his leave, he cautioned the Senecas, before they determined on war, to recall the effects of the Revolution, and to note that the Americans were now double the strength they were then. He urged them "to determine wisely and act accordingly." He hoped that they would wait until the great battle between General Wayne's army and the western Indians was fought.

Adlum was then lodged in Cornplanter's house, which was so close to the Council House that his interpreters, had he permitted, could have made out what the Indians were saying through the rest of the session.

The Indians met again the next morning, and debated until noon, advising Adlum at that point that they would re-convene when (pointing) the sun reached that position in the heavens. About three o'clock a horn sounded the call to council, and Adlum was invited, with his interpreters, to accompany the two principal chiefs again. After the ritual of smoking was concluded, Cornplanter, through an interpreter, spoke for the Council.

He spoke of what had happened since the Revolution, reviewing ad nauseam what had happened at Stanwix, and noting that his people had been charged "with doing many things that we were not guilty of," and insisting that the white men were much more cruel than were the Indians and declaring that whenever he commanded a party of warriors he would not therefore permit a white man to go with him.

Here Cornplanter interjected that Adlum might go on with his survey, but only within the boundaries marked by the Indians on the map. He then proceeded to reproach the surveyor for threatening them with destruction if they opted for war. He recalled the defeats administered to the armies of Harmar and St. Clair, and noted that the Indians of the west were even more powerful than before.[10]

From these remarks it was very plain to Adlum that Cornplanter was yet on the fence and that he might yet ally the Senecas with the western Indians. He responded to the Chief first by casting doubt on whether the Indians had actually beat General Harmer and second by reminding Cornplanter that the Indians were ill equipped right now to expect success in a great battle. Then he proceeded to a review of his surveying business, and the council was finally adjourned. Adlum eventually returned to Fort Franklin on August 5.

Some confusion appears in the second part of Adlum's memoirs. It is not clear whether he made one or two additional trips to Cornplanter's country. He may himself be confused in his recollections. But three trips were possible in that summer, and one authority feels it was "very likely" that he made a third trip.[11] In any case, we do know that he had from Cornplanter, on August 17, an invitation to come to Buffalo Creek, "to hear General Washington's Answer." [12] We know that he accepted that; and his letters suggest that either a second or a third surveying expedition had him reaching Cornplanter's village on August 23, and returning to Fort Franklin on August 30. He could have made still another trip in September.

During the time Adlum was in Cornplanter's village, and that of New Arrow, the last half of August, some remarkable events occurred. First of all, the surveyor found the Senecas very much determined upon war and hoping to meet Washington's representative, Colonel Pickering, at Buffalo Creek. The women, and the old men, were invariably for peace, and Adlum exhorted them to "preserve peace if possible." The warriors he did not try to dissuade.

Old Half Town reported to him a wild dream of a hog, and Adlum pretended next day to have had a dream himself of a hog. When the horn sounded the call to council, he immediately attended with his interpreter. He found all the men seated and Cornplanter smoking. After a pause Cornplanter related not only Half Town's dream but that of Adlum and insisted that they be taken seriously. In the end all this required Adlum to purchase a hog for eight dollars, which taken together with the hog provided by Half Town, as insisted by the dream, would make a feast for the town. Late in the day, a man came to Adlum with a stick notched on three sides. Each notch, he explained, represented a man or a warrior who would be present at Adlum's feast—not counting nineteen strangers. Adlum calculated that there would be upwards of 200 warriors present. Next occurred an Eagle Dance, which had to be performed before sundown. This wild dance inspired the party to a great deal of bragging and unrestrained carrying-on. At well beyond sundown there took place during the council some rather chilling drama. Adlum for his memoirs recalls it vividly: "There was then some more pine splits put on the fire so as to give a good light, when the Cornplanter, came and struck the war post, he had a tomahawk in one hand and a pair of mocasins in the other,—He fixed his eyes sternly on me, and then again struck the post most violently three times, I felt some alarm, but could not believe he intended to do me any harm,—I rose on my feet, when he again struck the war post three times, keeping his eyes, fixed sternly upon me; I held my breath, and my teeth together to keep the blood in my face, and fixed my eyes on his, as sternly as I could—and seeing the mocasins, in his hand I could not conjecture what it meant, but I supposed they were intended for me."

After a long pause, Cornplanter in great heat, and with his eyes fixed intently upon the surveyor, reviewed Adlum's history among his people,[13] noting finally the great influence he enjoyed with the women and the young warriors, and declaring that "you are the most dangerous man we know of." But, though you are here and in our power, we have made promises, and "you and all your people shall be safe." But "**tomorrow you must depart from this place**."

After noting that "we are at peace now but in a few days it will be otherwise," he presented Adlum with the moccasins, "handsomely ornamented with porcupine quills of various colors." With one hand Adlum accepted the moccasins; with the other he seized the tomahawk from Cornplanter's hand and struck the post in return, declaring that it was with great grief he was finding them so determined on war and "certain destruction."

All then gave a great shout, "which ended the bragging and the dancing—And every man took a wooden spit which he had provided, and also took a portion of meat on it which was tied up with linden bark," and from the kettles they took soup "with a dumplin in a green corn husk and immediately disappeared," [13] without offering Adlum a morsel or a drop. "And in a few minutes I was standing by the war post alone—I went to the Cornplanters house where I lodged and found him and his family enjoying themselves on the meat dumplins and soup." [14]

Cornplanter suggested that Adlum doubtless found this a curious feast, and then proceeded to educate him on Seneca customs and etiquette. All in all, it was a most remarkable evening. And through it all John Adlum was nothing if not spunky. The whole proceeding was alive with dramatic irony, too, for even while they spoke about war, General Wayne was marching on the Miamis. The defeat of the Indians at Fallen Timbers would render moot the bluster of this occasion.

Adlum heard the council horn shortly after sunrise the next morning, and, having been invited, he discovered a number of young warriors assembled, including Little Crow, son-in-law of Cornplanter, and Blacksnake, Cornplanter's nephew. There were fifty-six warriors in all, every one painted and attired for war. The Cornplanter explained that he wanted to dispel any doubts that Adlum might entertain about their determination if they did not have their country returned to them. Adlum responded that whatever doubts he might have had had all vanished with the feast of the evening before. At that point Cornplanter addressed the assembled warriors, pausing politely from time to time to permit Adlum's interpreters to translate.

> *Brothers from the other side of the great Waters, and Brothers, who are a part of us—You are to go to such and such places [naming them]—There to kill Elk, Deer, and bears, which you will carefully dry and preserve, until you hear further from us—And if you meet any white people, tell them they had better go home, as times will soon be bad; but do not injure nor hurt any one until you hear from us. We are going to Buffaloe-Creek, Where a number of chiefs from all our tribes are*

> *to meet us, And the great woemen from our Towns will accompany us, and there we will meet the great woemen of our other Towns and tribes, There we will form the plan of our operations, and from thence you will receive our orders how to act, and what you are to do—We would give you orders at once: but our great woemen are opposed to our going to war; and we may in a great degree thank our friend [Adlum] for that: if thanks are due to him for preventing us from carrying our views into execution. But perhaps it is for the best, as the Great Spirit above directs all things, all we have to do is to submit patiently to what he wills—When we are all assembled chiefs, warriors, and the great Woemen, at Buffaloe the woemen may change their minds, and join us in our wishes, as it is the only chance we shall ever have of getting back a part of our Country—*[15]

Cornplanter then declared that Colonel Pickering would meet the Indians at Buffalo or not at all. At the close of his remarks, he turned directly to Adlum and spoke in a resolute voice: "You told us not to deceive ourselves, we *tell you the same, do not deceive yourself,* for if we do not get a[n]swer soon, **war will follow."** [16]

Adlum waited for a moment to respond, then declared that he was sure Pickering would not meet them in council at Buffalo, and then he spelled out the consequences should they determine on war. When he expressed the hope that the Indians, if indeed they did decide for war, would carry it on in a fashion different from their wont in previous wars (meaning that they would cease to put to death women and children), he provoked a violent reaction. Hardly had he spoken the words when every man present rose as one, all fixing their eyes on Adlum in fierce resentment. Cornplanter spoke for them all, asking whether Adlum meant to insult or to affront them. On this delicate and very sensitive matter the chief then spoke in a loud voice, with great emphasis and energy:

> *Who began that business . . . . If you do not know I will tell you. When the white people first came to this country and before that—as well as since we were so foolish as to make war on each other —And if we were*

successful we took the Woemen and children prisoners, whom we invariably adopted into our families, and they according to their age, were called, mother, Sister, brother, or child, and they were considered as related to the family —The men with few exceptions were put to death—But sometimes a woman who had lost a son had a right to chuse one, and sometimes a widow would claim a man for a husband and take them as such. When you first came to this Country our fathers have informed us . . . . it was not long before you increased in numbers . . . and power, Our fathers were then content to call you brothers, and they also gave you land to till, to raise corn & other things—But you still increased in numbers and power and you took possession of any part of our country that suited you, and when our fathers remonstrated—they were told, that they did not worship the true great spirit, and the country did not belong to them, and that it was meritorious to drive them (our fathers) from the face of the earth, and they were treated by the whites as if they were beasts and not men—Our fathers built houses, and fortified them, but the whites with their superior arms took those places where there was men, woemen and children, and did they ever spare one great or small—As I suppose your books do not tell these things, I will answer for you, **no.** *You in your books charge us with many things we never were guilty of—But if we were to or could write books we could tell you of things, that an indian never practiced and would be ashamed to be charged with. Whenever we treated with you at the end of a war, there was always an article that all prisoners on both sides should be delivered up,—Did you ever deliver up any? Did you ever deliver up one? I answer for you* **no.** *When at the end of the war of the revolution as you call it, we delivered up to you hundreds, hundreds & hundreds—whether your books tell you of this or not I do not know; But I know the fact, and the truth of my assertion—Does your books tell you of indians legs*

> *being skin[n]ed and tanned, and those skins being dressed and made razor strops of? [a reference to the Sullivan campaign] I know that all these things were done by the whites and I heard them boast of it. Does your books tell you, that an indian ever did such a thing—If they had done those things they would have been recorded in your books—And I know that there is a great many lies written in your books respecting us—We have thought of your suggestion before, and at Buffaloe we will decide how this war is to be carried on—And if my advice is taken, we will never again injure woemen and children, for it is mean, & contemptible, for a warrior to put to death those that do not, or cannot, fight. And it is of no use to take them prisoners, as they must be returned—at the end of the war—But we will give you men no quarters.*[17]

This is one of Cornplanter's most passionate speeches. Here he speaks for all Indians, in anger and indignation. His words strike out at injustice, but they reflect a stricken conscience, and their real target is war itself, which pits brother against brother. Remarkably, the address is directed at a single surveyor and his party. It should have been ringing in the council house at Buffalo or in the halls of Philadelphia.

Adlum was careful in his response, declaring only that he understood all that about no quarter, and that it works both ways. He insisted, after the meeting, that he did not need the escort which had been promised, that he could make his way safely back to Fort Franklin; but Cornplanter provided twelve warriors anyway. Then the surveyor went about among the houses thanking all for their generous hospitality and promising gifts of flour to any who could come with him to Franklin. He was also killing time, for he wished desperately to hear news of the battle that had been fought. He expected any hour to hear that General Wayne had defeated the western Indians. When at dark he was still in the village and obliged to return to Cornplanter's house to spend another night, the Chief expressed his vexation. When Adlum assured his friend that he would definitely be departing on the morrow, Cornplanter replied, petulantly, "*It is quite time.*" [18]

So the Senecas did not take up the hatchet against Wayne and for the western Indians. In very large measure the credit for this must be attributed to Colonel Thomas Proctor and to the surveyor John Adlum, and to the Indian women, with whom these two men enjoyed a remarkable influence. In smaller measure some credit goes to General Wayne himself, as we shall see.

XVI

FALLEN TIMBERS

Just how important Chief Cornplanter was to the hostilities in the Ohio River region is apparent from the letters which passed between General Wayne and the Secretary of War, Henry Knox. For the period July 27, 1792-August 8, 1793, in no fewer than thirty-four of these communications is Cornplanter a serious subject. In many he is *the* subject.

Knox is of course writing from the capital in Philadelphia. Wayne is communicating first from Pittsburgh and after that from Legionville and Hobson's Choice, as he worked his way ever closer to the Indian villages at what is today Cincinnati. The letters were requiring, generally, about one week to make the trip.

President Washington is a party to the correspondence, as he is kept well informed by Knox, who in many cases simply relays the letters which have come from Wayne.

As early as July 27, 1792, Wayne from Pittsburgh advised Knox that he was now urging Captain Cass to prevail upon Cornplanter to attend the hoped for Council, "for the purpose of using his influence with the Hostile Indians to listen to peace or if for War to give us timely information." [1]

In a letter to Knox some three weeks later he reported on Cornplanter's flag mission to Fort Franklin.

Most interesting is Wayne's report from Pittsburgh on September 14, as the relationships among the Indians begin to heat up: "The same day Ensign Sullivan [John Sullivan, Jr., soon to be Captain] arrived from Fort Franklin, which place he left two days later than Geyesutha [Kayahsotha] just before he set out. The Cornplanters interpreter came in from the Nation, with intelligence, that he with the New Arrow and other Indians of influence from that town, had gone to accompany about Five Hundred of the Senekas & Canada Indians to visit the Hostile Indians, and had set out from Buffalo Creek a few days since—he also mentioned that the first Messengers from the Five Nations were put to Death, by the Delawares—that the Senecas or second Messengers were saved, but had not returned, that the Cornplanter was very uneasy, & said if any of his people were killed, he would immediately go to War with the Hostile Indians, so much for Indian intelligence." [2]

Knox's response was penned one week later. The Secretary acknowledged receipt of Wayne's letter, and expressed the hope that the six nations "have gone forward to the hostile indians in the numbers mentioned by the Cornplanter's interpreter. If so most probably peace would be the effect—It is to be very much desired that the *first* messengers of the five nations should not have been put to death, whom I take to be Captain Hendricks [the Oneida Captain Hendrick] and his brother." [3]

On October 12, Knox wrote to Wayne: "I am glad to learn that the Cornplanter has gone forward to the hostile tribes—we may I am convinced depend upon his attachment and his veracity to make a faithful report. If upon his return you see him, pray request him and the New Arrow to repair here if consistent with his own view of the subject." [4]

One week later we find Wayne expressing to Knox his great anxiety: "I feel uneasy for the safe return of the Cornplanter as by the deposition of Wm May, & by direct intelligence from the Indians who were sent early to the hostile tribes, mentioned in the enclosed Copy of a letter from Capt Hughes, gives but too much ground to apprehend some premeditated mischief, intended him; both the Cornplanter & New Arrow were induced to undertake this business, at my request, with a promise of a Certain reward for procuring peace, or in case of war, to give me an exact account of the tribes & Number of Indians with whom we might have to Contend . . . ." [5]

But within the week his fears are assuaged and he writes with some relief to the Secretary: "I have now the honor to enclose a communication from the Cornplanter thro' four Huron Indians brought by them to Buffaloe Creek & by Connowaingo [present-day Warren, Pa.] to Fort Franklin, & by Geyesutha [Kayahsotha] to this place deliver'd viva voce by him to me this morning—Agreeably to his request I shall direct Mr. Rosencrantz to remain at the *Burnt towns,* & allow him a suitable compensation:—there is an other interpreter there who can neither read or write; notwithstanding this it may be prudent to retain him for the present." [6]

By this time General Wayne, as above noted, had had quite enough of Pittsburgh. Much disgusted by its brothels and by the rampant drunkenness, which he regarded as most unhealthy for his men, he determined to move the army out. On the first day of November he set out for a new campsite down the Ohio River. From the journal of one of Wayne's officers, Captain Thomas T. Underwood of Petersburg, Virginia, comes an account. He notes that Wayne, feeling that Pittsburgh. was too much of a distraction to his men, moved the army (now 1000 men) on November 1, 1793 "into bivouac 17 miles down the Ohio on a high bluff with a level plateau 60 feet above the river on the right [the north side, some eight miles above the mouth of Beaver Creek]." The General, remembering the observation of General Knox, that Wayne's army was "the Legion of the United States," called the new encampment Legionville. He was quite happy with it, and was confident that here he could safely ride out the winter.[7] General Wayne's encampment was precisely on the present site of Ambridge, in what would be now the western end of Fourteenth Street.[8]

During the first week of that November, General Wayne met with Chiefs Cornplanter and New Arrow. On November 7 he delivered a pessimistic view to Philadelphia: "Little prospect of Cornplanter's being able to effect a peace with the hostile Indians (who have been increasing in strength)."[9] Knox meanwhile had his own information and expressed himself to Wayne on November 9 in a more optimistic tone: "General Chapin residing at the Genesee who is now here [Philadelphia] informs me that he has heard through Indians, that the hostile tribes were in the beginning of October assembled at Au Glaise to the number of three thousand and upwards and that it was probable they would agree to a place of Treaty—That the Senekas and the Cornplanter were with them and that Captain Brant had gone forward."[10]

Wayne, having had this latest dispatch from Knox, refers on November 16 to the subject of Cornplanter's hoped-for visit to Philadelphia, a matter that for the next three months will receive constant attention: "Permit me now to inform you, that we have a report that the Cornplanter has returned from the Council of the Hostile Indians at Au Glaize—& that he is expected at Fort Franklin about this time in consequence of which I immediately dispatched Mr. Rosencrantz to meet & invite him with the New Arrow & Red Jacket to visit Philadelphia agreeably to your desire in a former letter. Enclosed is a Copy of my instructions to him upon that subject."[11]

At the very end of the month Wayne received a long letter from Knox. A portion of it is of considerable interest here: "I hope the Cornplanter may have arrived and brought you information of the determination of the hostile Indians intending a treaty. I think from some circumstances the Indians will consent to treat, but they will most probably make extravagant claims about a boundary. If a treaty should be agreed upon it is not probable it will take place until in the spring—" [12]

Now dug in for the winter at Legionville, seventeen miles downstream from Pittsburgh, Wayne keeps the Secretary informed on the activities of Cornplanter: "By a person who landed at Wheeling, we have information that Lieut. Prior with the Indian chiefs had arrived at Marietta & may be hourly expected at this place. I also expect the Cornplanter in the course of a few days; but have not as yet received any direct account of the terms upon which the hostile Indians have condescended to grant peace to the United States of America." Seven days later he reports regretfully: ". . .no account as yet from the Cornplanter." [13]

Knox replies, again fervently expressing the hope that the Cornplanter may find his way to Philadelphia: "I hope the Cornplanter may have complied with your invitation to visit you, and that you may prevail upon him to repair to this place. If any thing should prevent his coming to you I pray you to send him an invitation afresh, and urge him to come to this place. He is much wanted to inform of, and explain, facts contained in the communications of the six Nations transmitted you by the last Post—Persuade him to come here as soon as possible—as an inducement you may hold forth to him reasonable rewards—We have also sent for Red Jacket—" [14]

This most desirable visit of Cornplanter to Philadelphia seemed to be the chief occupation of President Washington, Secretary Knox, and Colonel Proctor from mid-November to the 23rd of February, as a great flurry of letters passed among them. The Chief was being "most urgently" invited to the capital, with Proctor to serve as escort; and he was responding not at all.

On the 16th of February, Wayne expressed his concern for the mission: "Mr.Rosencrantz has probably returned to the Cornplanters town—shou'd that Chief ultimately decline to come forward—will it be proper or Necessary for Colo Procter to go to him under present circumstances?" [15]

By this time the President was beginning to feel it less necessary for Cornplanter to come east. He apparently considered that the government had all the information that it really needed. In any case, it was much too late to expect Cornplanter to make the long journey. A note in the President's journal, which, though written in the first person, was kept by his secretaries, is set down for Saturday, February 23, 1793: ". . . too late to bring the Cornplanter here." [16] It was on this same day that Knox consulted with Washington on the matter. To Wayne he responded: "As the case for which the Cornplanter was wanted is now circumstanced, it is unnecessary for him to come here. It is probable that we have obtained from the Farmer's Brother, and the other chiefs all the information that could be obtained from the Cornplanter were he here. The expence therefore is not to be incurred and Colonel Procter is to be directed by you to return to this city—The President conceives that as Colonel Procter was sent expressly for this purpose he ought to have gone on to the Cornplanter's residence; But, that under the present circumstances, he is to return." [17]

For impressions of the Indian situation on the Ohio the President would have to be content with the dispatches from General Wayne. Anyway, it was fairly plain now, to the President and to his Cabinet, that the Indians were unshakably opposed to any expansion of the United States westward from their position. The domain of the Indians would have as its eastern limits the "beautiful river," the Ohio, period.

It is not easy to define exactly the feelings of President Washington for the Indians. His observations are not all that consistent. Are they a cruel and ruthless people who should be annihilated? Are they a nuisance merely, to be tolerated? Are they fellow human beings with a legitimate claim to the land which they occupy?

But at this time, in this moment of extreme crisis, with the immigrant nation on a collision course with the First Americans, history sees the President working genuinely and industriously for a peaceful settlement. On February 25, after he had determined that it was too late to make any more use of Cornplanter, he assembled his Cabinet to ask of them two questions pertaining to the trouble on the frontier. He wanted to know, in the first place, whether the Executive had the power to relinquish to the Indians any lands beyond the Ohio acquired by previous treaty. He wanted to know, in the second place, whether the commissioners should be instructed to effect such recessions if necessary to the achievement of peace. On both questions Alexander Hamilton, Henry Knox, and Edmund Randolph responded in the affirmative. Jefferson dissented on both.[18]

Meanwhile dispatches from General Wayne continued to arrive. On March 1 he reports "Nothing further from the Cornplanter." [19] Three days later he writes to Knox at length about the Cornplanter. Included is his supposition that Cornplanter may side with the Ohio Indians:

> *I . . . am very sorry that the President, shou'd be displeased at the detention of Colo Procter from proceeding to the Cornplanters town, the reasons for which I had the honor to communicate to you as early as the 24th of January last—they then appeared to me conclusive, & from your long silence upon that subject I had fondly flattered myself, that the measure had met with approbation?—however I shall be more circumspect in future; Shou'd the Cornplanter now come forward—it will have a strange appearance —& will probably give umbrage, to tell him (after all the ceremony & pains that has been taken, in order to prevail upon him to visit the seat of Government) 'Brother—your presence, is no longer necessary—you are not wanted—you may return home'—however it shall be done with the best grace, that I am capable of! But it's more than probable that I shall not be honored with his presence until I meet him in a hostile manner in the field [!], provided that the intelligence respecting the present disposition of those Indians with regards to the proposed boundary be true . . . .* [20]

On March 9 Secretary Knox, concerned about Cornplanter's image, endeavored to set right some mistaken notions. To Wayne he wote: "I am sorry to observe that sundry persons at Pittsburg have communicated the idea to this City as if the Cornplanter was disaffected to us. But the true state of the case is, that he by his former visits without authority from his Brethren at Buffaloe Creek excited their jealousy—and they sent him a string of Wampum tied in the middle signifying their prohibition of his coming to Philadelphia without leave—this he has not been able to obtain—It would be proper that this statement should circulate in order to prevent those opinions and apprehensions of the Cornplanter which might be propagated to his injury." [21]

On the 14th of March, Cornplanter led a delegation into the presence of General Wayne at Legionville. The General reported the next day to Secretary Knox:

> *I have now to announce the arrival of the Cornplanter, New arrow, S[t]iff knee (alias) Big tree & old Quiasutha [Kayahsotha], Chief of the Allegheny—with three young warriors under the Conduct of Mr. Rosencrantz, they came in time to dine with me yesterday—but we have not had any conversation, as yet except merely the common placid [place?] gratulations of meeting. I shall endeavour to send them home in good temper, if practicable—which will require some expenses & address. I will write you fully upon this subject—& other Matters, as soon as I can with decency get clear of my Red brothers.* [22]

Ten days later Knox relayed this letter to President Washington.

Washington and Knox were made uneasy by this latest communication. The Iroquois remained still a question mark in the dispute. The representatives of the Six Nations generate a nervousness when they appear. Of course for the western Indians (the Miami, the Shawnee, the Chippewa, the Ottawa, the Sac, the Wyandot, the Fox, and the Potawatami), there is no question. They have long ago written off the Iroquois, whom they regard as cowards, and by whom they feel betrayed. Their disgust is undisguised.

Two days after he had dictated this letter announcing the arrival of the chiefs, Wayne did get together with Cornplanter, New Arrow, Big Tree and Kayahsotha. He had in fact invited them to dinner and council at Legionville. He reported that he had learned nothing of which he had not already been aware. It remained plain that the Indian position (including that of the Iroquois) was that the Ohio River should forever separate the two races. Some say it was Kayahsotha, now sixty-eight years old, who flung out his braceleted arm and declared: "My heart and my mind is fixed on that river. May that water continue to run and remain the boundary between the White and Red People on its opposite shores."

But from the journal of Captain Underwood, who had been all winter continuing to record his impressions of all that was occurring at

Legionville, we have this account of the incident: "Gen. Wayne sent an invitation to Corn Planter and New Arrow, two chiefs of the Six Nations, to meet him at Legionville. They both arrived 19th March accompanied by Big Tree and old Chief Guyasutha [Kayahsotha]; during their talk with Gen. Wayne they insisted that the Ohio River should be the boundary between the White and the Red People. The day the Great Chief [surely Cornplanter] dined with Gen. Wayne he pointed to the Ohio River and said, 'My heart and Mind is fixed on that River and may that Water continue to run and remain the boundary of everlasting Peace between the White & Red People on its opposite Shores.'" [23]

If General Wayne at this time was capable of remembering short term, it was indeed Cornplanter who spoke thus, for we have the remark attributed to him just one day later in Wayne's March 22 letter to Knox. Of great interest here, too, is Wayne's complaint that these Iroquois are consuming so much of his time that he cannot attend to the military situation. What a delicate matter it was to handle the Six Nations is apparent. This letter does much to enlarge our understandings of both General Wayne and Chief Cornplanter. In it, Wayne, speaking of Cornplanter, writes: "And Yesterday Evening after all the business was over he gave a toast—prefaced in this manner 'My mind & heart is upon that river (Pointing to the Ohio) may that Water ever continue to run, & remain the boundary of a lasting peace between the Americans & the Indians on its opposite shores.' This is strong & plain language & proves . . . that his mind is fully made up upon the subject of a boundary line."

But Wayne is most impatient with the Indians. He has agreed to furnish them with horses and other necessaries, declaring that he shall "be happy to get clear of them at so cheap a rate, especially as they promise to continue friendly." He complains that "My time & Attention has been so much taken up with those people" that he hasn't been able to organize his garrisons or his scouts. He encloses certified copies of the speeches made at this meeting, those by New Arrow, Captain O. Bale, and one that he had not heard, by Big Tree.

It was shortly after the meeting with Wayne that Cornplanter set out on a peace mission to the western Indians. The Chief had been much distressed by accusations directed at his people by the settlers of the Pittsburgh region, charges of wrongdoing and serious crimes. He was so annoyed that he had a signed advertisement published: "My people having been charged with committing depredations on the frontier inhabitants near Pittsburgh, I hereby contradict the assertion, as it is certainly without foundation. I pledge myself to those inhabitants, that they may rest perfectly secure from any danger from the Senecas residing on the Alleghany waters, and that my people have been and still are, friendly to the United States." Now, at just the time he is preparing to journey west, at the real risk of his own life, to encourage peace between the United States and the western Indians, he receives the news of still another frightful atrocity. The report was of three Senecas "travelling through a settlement on the Genesee [who] stopped at a house to light their pipes." As it happened, the several white men within the house were not friendly toward Indians. As the first Indian to enter knelt to light his pipe, one of these men dealt him a fatal blow with an axe, and then attacked a second member of the party, seriously wounding him. As the wounded man fled the house, together with a boy who was unhurt, he was not pursued. A much distressed Cornplanter, when delivered the sad news, was heard to lament: "It is hard when I and my people are trying to make peace for the whites that we should be thus rewarded. I can govern my young men and warriors better than the Thirteen Fires can theirs." [24]

The distraught Chief, practicing a most remarkable restraint, did not embark on revenge, and, remarkably, simply proceeded on his mission. Of course he experienced absolutely no success with the western Indians. And Wayne continued on his two fronts. Which is the more important, he must have wondered, to prepare for the known enemy, or to keep the Six Nations happy? So far, the General was doing a good job of the latter. Cornplanter remained "friendly," and the Iroquois neutral.

On the 27th of April, Wayne described for Knox some of the maneuvering that he and the hostiles were constantly engaged in. He noted that the Indians "are an artful enemy," and that they (especially Cornplanter) rely on procrastination. He assures Secretary Knox that he means to be prepared for war.[25] In this letter there is recalled the promise made to Cornplanter by Wayne that no new posts or garrisons would be established in advance of the troops' present position. When, as it turned out, Wayne proceeded to open up roads, to lay up stores, to reinforce garrisons, and to graze cattle well downstream from Legionville, Cornplanter complained vigorously. The Chief acknowledged that no new fortifications had been established, but he pointed out that Wayne was acting in a manner quite contrary to the spirit of his promise. It was obvious, he insisted, that the forces were preparing for a forward move.[26]

Wayne apparently received some static from high places on this matter. In any case, he backed off. In a letter posted the 2nd of July from Hobson's Choice, near Fort Washington, he repeated to Knox his promise to Cornplanter: "There has not—nor will not—be any additional demonstrations of troops or stores at the head of the line other than what was, is, & will be indispensably necessary; preparatory to a forward move, & such the hostile Indians had a right to expect from my speech to the Cornplanter & New Arrow on the 20th of March; wherein I told them, that the best, & only means to insure a permanent peace, was to be well prepar'd for War but promised not to advance or establish any new posts in front of those we now possessed (unless compelled thereto by the Conduct of the Hostile Indians) until the result of the pending treaty was known, which speech has undoubtedly been communicated to them."[27]

Cornplanter was offended by a second event occurring at about this same time. Newly appointed as Commissioners, and now serving as envoys to a peace conference meeting in Niagara in April, were General Benjamin Lincoln, Timothy Pickering, and Beverley Randolph. These were probably not the best choices for such a delicate assignment. Simcoe, headquartered at Niagara, in fact baldly described Pickering as a "violent, low, philosophic, cunning New Englander." Certainly the trio behaved ineptly in Niagara, boasting that the United States was not really intent on peace out here, but were hoping only to divide the hostile Indians by securing an alliance with the Iroquois in order to oppose effectively the western Indians and the British. According to one historian, this "careless confession" had two unhappy effects. In the first place it held the Indians firm in their allegiance to Great Britain; in the second place, it alienated the most powerful friend the United States had among the Indians. Cornplanter, in fact, was so much annoyed by the manner of the commissioners that he refused to call upon them, even though they had escorted his son Henry all the way from Philadelphia to Niagara.[28]

The Chief did attend a council held at Buffalo Creek on June 18, the purpose of which was to address some perplexing boundary questions. It was during these sessions that the Chief made a most impassioned declaration. Speaking to the American commission as if it were in fact the President of the United States George Washington himself, he exploded: "Brother! You know our demands; we ask but for a small piece of land, and we trust, as you are a great man, you can easily grant our request."[29] And it was after this council that Cornplanter met with General Israel Chapin and persuaded the Indian Agent to accompany him to Presque Isle for the purpose of surveying military conditions.

Just how close was Cornplanter to bringing in the Senecas on the side of the Alliance? History does not provide a clear answer to this question. Certainly the Chief had his runners out; he had his ear to the ground. He *seemed* to be awaiting some hard evidence that an Alliance victory was probable. But he must have been well aware just how calamitous for *all* Indians would be a battle defeat of the western Indians. And at the same time, he was close enough to the army of General Wayne to appreciate that the odds were extremely heavy against the Alliance. Besides, he had suffered a great deal of personal abuse from the Ohio Indians, particularly from the Shawnee. Most important, though, was his larger view, that the loss of the Indian lands to the westward-moving white settlers was inevitable. Even an effective resistance here could be but a temporary slowing of the tide. And had he not made a sincere promise to General Washington to work for peace on the frontier?

Still, the failure of the Alliance to bring in the Senecas or any of the Six Nations (though it did not work very hard for their support) was not the only blow to its chances for success. A number of conditions and events delivered severe damage to their cause. Even though the British had "promised" support and had built Fort Miami at the falls of the Maumee just this spring, the Alliance continued skeptical. Although the Shawnee and their allies were unaware that the British had already arrived at a settlement with the Americans, they were not counting on any real help from the Crown.

Secondly, time was against the Alliance. The farther removed the Indians became from their earlier dramatic successes, the more their confidence waned; and as Wayne built forts and continued to advance they could perceive easily enough that this would be a different battle altogether.

Time was against them, too, in the matter of provisions. Simply to keep eleven tribes together, well-fed and equipped, was a major task. By the time of the summer of 1794 many warriors of the lesser tribes had abandoned the resistance and gone home.

Perhaps most hurtful to the cause was the division that occurred within the Alliance. It was dramatized by the war-chiefs Little Turtle and Blue Jacket. Even though the hero of the defeats of Generals Harmar and St. Clair had wiped out one of General Wayne's supply trains at Ludlow, the Miami war-chief Little Turtle failed completely in his assault on Fort Recovery on the last day of June. Wayne's march on the Indian villages along the Maumee River was not slowed. And the General continued to demonstrate, in many ways, that he was intent upon a forward movement. Little Turtle was having second thoughts about another all-out engagement with the American army. At the Great Council convened by the Alliance on August 13, the Miami Chief spoke his piece. He had become steadily more and more impressed by the size and the command of General Wayne's formidable army, and he had *great* respect for its commander, whom he described as "the Chief who never sleeps." Here at this council, as persuasively as he could, he urged caution. In fact, he was arguing for a peaceful settlement. In the heated debate which followed, the Shawnee war-chief Blue Jacket passionately declared for war. The Blue Jacket forces won out. Little Turtle was overruled, and, incredibly, was even accused of cowardice. The council had decided to engage the American army.

Blue Jacket

Chief Little Turtle, who was extremely intelligent (and not without cunning), and was renowned as a strategist and a battle tactician, was promptly replaced as head of the Alliance warriors. Little Turtle would participate in the action, but at the head of the warriors of the Alliance for this battle would be the Shawnee war-chief Blue Jacket.

Although Blue Jacket was probably about the same age as Little Turtle (just a few years older than Cornplanter), his origins are obscure.

He was known among the Shawnee as Weyapiersenwah, and he had achieved his high status as war-chief because of extraordinary courage and battle zeal. He clearly had contributed in large measure to the victories achieved by Little Turtle over Harmar and St. Clair.

And so matters stood. The armies were now assembled. Councils had met. Negotiations had been carried on. Intermediaries had functioned. Some skirmishes through June and July had taken many lives and had provided intimations of the cost to come. But it was plain to all involved that the battle would be fought. Wayne made one more effort. "I have thought proper," he reported to Knox and Washington, "to offer the enemy a last overture of peace; and as they have every thing that is dear and interesting at stake, I have reason to expect they will listen to the proposition mentioned in the enclosed copy of an address, despatched yesterday by a special flag, under circumstances that will insure his safe return, and which may eventually spare the effusion of much human blood. But should war be their choice, that blood upon their own heads. America shall no longer be insulted with impunity. To an all-powerful and just God, I therefore commit myself and gallant army." [30]

And so the battle, so long in the making, was joined at last. It was not the battle that it might have been. The Alliance could bring to the field only 700 warriors (although Wayne reported 2000), far, far fewer than the number that could have contested effectively. In the rout, the retreating warriors sought refuge at Fort Miami. The British refused to admit them.

Anthony Wayne

Eight days after the last shot was fired, and the last scalp taken, General Anthony Wayne penned from his headquarters at Grand Glaize a vivid account for the Secretary of War: "Sir—It is with infinite pleasure that I now announce to you the brilliant success of the Federal army under my command, in a general action with the combined force of the hostile Indians, and a considerable number of the volunteers and militia of Detroit, on the 20th instant, on the banks of the Miamis, in the vicinity of the British post and garrison, at the foot of the rapids." And then he proceeds to provide an account of the battle, rich in details that are now well known.[31]

What the General did not remark on was the well founded rumor that a large body of Senecas had been hovering on his flank, studying the tide of battle apparently. And Seneca runners were ready to return to the villages for warriors if indeed it seemed an Indian victory was possible. Historians are not agreed, but some feel that, Cornplanter notwithstanding, had the western Indians begun to carry the field as they had under Little Turtle against Harmar and against St. Clair, the Senecas would have joined with the Miamis and the Shawnee and the rest.

For the first three days following the battle, Wayne destroyed the Indian crops all over the immediate region. In a dramatic show of force, he marched his army right up to the gates of the British Fort Miami, then abruptly returned to Fort Defiance. Meeting no resistance now, he turned his soldiers over to the destruction of the Indian villages along the upper reaches of the Wabash, and in October built Fort Wayne, which he intended as an announcement that American authority had come to this territory.

In the quiet aftermath the General returned to Fort Greenville "to wait and watch." That November, by the terms of the Jay Treaty which was negotiated, the British agreed to withdraw from its forts in the Northwest territory.

Analysts of history are wont to ponder the "What if?" for the Battle of Fallen Timbers. What would have been the outcome had the Six Nations cast their lot with the Miami and the Shawnee? Doubtless the result would have been the same, but certainly the battle would have raged for a much longer period of time, and the cost to both sides would have been infinitely greater. The futility of resisting the white settlers'encroachment was beginning to dawn on all Indians along the frontier. It had been sensed before the Battle of Fallen Timbers by the warrior Cornplanter, and it had apparently been sensed also by Little Turtle, the skilled Miami war chief who had led the western Indians to impressive victories over the forces of Harmar and those of St. Clair.

XVII

THE CANANDAIGUA TREATY

But Cornplanter was not at the battle of Fallen Timbers. In fact, at the time of the action he was nowhere near. He was organizing a deputation of Senecas to proceed to still another treaty session.

In the fall of 1794, at the "Chosen Spot," on the northern tip of Lake Canandaigua, in the Finger Lakes region of New York State, a little southeast of present-day Rochester, a most remarkable council took place. By this time the Washington administration had settled into a new and very different Indian policy. Timothy Pickering, a fifty-year-old attorney, had been appointed Commissioner of Indian Affairs. He was serving under General Henry Knox, at that time Secretary of War in Washington's cabinet. Pickering, although he was capable of indiscretions, was a very good choice for the handling of the relations between the new United States and the long-time residents of the land, the Native American Indians. He had served during the Revolution in the Continental Army, and as a member of the Board of War. He had been Adjutant General, and for five years (1780-85) Quartermaster General.[1]

In 1785, when he was a resident of Pennsylvania, he was dispatched to the Wyoming Valley to settle disputes between the Connecticut and the Pennsylvania settlers. As noted above, he was enraptured by the great beauty of the region. He had come to understand just why the Indians were so possessive. And by the time of Canandaigua he had accomplished treaty agreements with the Indians many times. When the Six Nations proposed a conference in which they might air their grievances, he generously accepted and promised to audit with a good ear their concerns.

As pointed out by David Swatzler, the administration eventually saw the imperative for changing Indian policy. Finally, it abandoned altogether the wasteful policy of conquest, and came round to a policy (resembling that of William Penn) by which the country would recognize

Timothy Pickering

the hereditary rights of the Indians to their lands, a policy that would require the government to purchase any lands it might desire to acquire.[2] Of course the country was hoping that the Indians would see the need to adopt, perhaps with enthusiasm, the ways of the white man, in which case they would not think of hunting as their existence and not require so much land.

Most enlightening in all of this is a passage contained in a letter written by Commander-in-Chief George Washington, just at the end of the Revolution (dated September 7, 1783). The letter was directed to James Duane, at that time a member of the Continental Congress. It will be seen that the letter does not reflect any great regard for the Indian as a human being, but rather addresses the problem in a most practical way: "Policy and economy point very strongly to the expediency of being on good terms with the Indians," wrote Washington, "and the propriety of purchasing their lands in preference to attempting to drive them by force of arms out of their country which, as have already [been] experienced, is like driving [out] the wild beast of the forest, which will return as soon as the pursuit is at an end. . . . The gradual extension of our settlements will as certainly cause the savage, as the wolf, to retire;

both being animals of prey, though they differ in shape. In a word there is nothing to be obtained by an Indian war, but the soil they live on, and this can be had by purchase at less *expense*." [3]

At Canandaigua in the fall of 1794 the most conspicuous and perhaps the most dramatic expression of this new policy was proclaimed.

First to arrive for the negotiations were the Oneidas, who of course, lived closest to the site, an old Seneca village burned to the ground fifteen years ago by Sullivan. The contingent of Quakers which arrived from Philadelphia found the Oneidas already camped out on the grounds. Next to show up were the Cayuga, the Onondaga, and the Tuscarora. Last, but most certainly not the least, there appeared, on October 14, a company of Senecas 800 strong, with the fifty-four-year-old war-chief Cornplanter at their head. William Savery, a Quaker representative,[4] confided to his journal his great amazement: "Their ceremonial entrance made a terrific and warlike appearance." All told, by the opening of the sessions, there were 1600 Iroquois assembled on the council grounds. This number included but one Mohawk, as the pro-British Mohawks were fairly well content on the land they had been given in Ontario. These council-loving Indians built themselves a village, 300 houses in two days, according to the Quaker records.

Speaking for the Indians, whom he had "adopted," Savery continues his journal record: "Our people made temporary bark shelters in Canandaigua and we sent out hunters. Our hunters were taking as many as 100 [!] deer a day and bringing them back into camp to feed the people that were there. We were fishing and we were hunting water fowl available at that time of the year, the ducks, the geese and those other migratory birds that were on the lake, supplying our people with the food that they needed." [5]

During the preliminaries Pickering addressed the Indians' chief concern, which was the lands taken from them in the Fort Stanwix treaties. It was their continuing hope, of course, that these lands, or at least some portion of them, could yet be restored. Cornplanter was particularly concerned about the land known as the Erie Triangle, which he wanted to recover. As this matter was being taken up, most unexpected news arrived from the West. On October 27, there burst into the camp at Canandaigua a Tuscarora runner with the report of General Wayne's resounding defeat of the western Indians at Fallen Timbers, eight weeks ago, with great loss of life on both sides. Chief Cornplanter, who had participated greatly in the negotiations between

Wayne and the Ohio Indians, received the news with mixed feelings. He must have wondered just how much difference would have been made by Seneca involvement in the battle, and probably appreciated that the outcome could hardly have been much different. He most certainly understood that Wayne's decisive victory would do little to improve the relations between the Iroquois and the Ohio Indians. And he did not need anyone to tell him that the Battle of Fallen Timbers, as it was being called, had done irrevocable damage to the Indians' bargaining power with the Washington administration. This startling news, which naturally caused some interruption in the proceedings, made even more urgent to the Iroquois the need to reach satisfactory agreements here at Canandaigua.

When the negotiations had recovered from this unsettling report, the customary speech exchanges began. Red Jacket was the first Indian to address the assembly. He returned to the "rust" metaphor that he had employed at the German Flats council eighteen years before: "Brother, we the Sachems of the Six Nations will now tell our minds. The business of this treaty is to brighten the Chain of Friendship between us and the fifteen fires [Vermont had become a state on March 4, 1791, and Kentucky had come into the Union on June 1 of the succeeding year.]. We told you the other day it was but a small piece that was the occasion of the remaining rust in the Chain of Friendship." The Quaker Savery seemed to feel that this "rust" represented the Indians' concern over the building of roads: (1) The construction of a four-mile-long portage road that would run along the Niagara River from Fort Schlosser to Buffalo Creek ; (2) the desire to run a four-mile-wide road between the Cayuga Creek and Buffalo Creek. The Indians objected strongly to the proposals, which would mean a big loss of land. This concern was addressed most vigorously by Red Jacket, who, along with Cornplanter, proved to be the most effective in the bargaining. The matter of these two roads was clearly defined, discussed, and settled finally in the wording of Article 5. Pickering, when agreement on the matter was at last reached, concluded by plainly acknowledging a concession: "I confess, brothers, I expected that you would have agreed to my proposal, the Cayuga Creek and the Buffalo Creek road, but as this is not the case, I will give it up, only reserving the road from Fort Schlosser to Buffalo. There has been a mutual condescension, which is the best way of settling business." [6]

Red Jacket

As the Council proceeded, Cornplanter became conscious of some distrust among his people, even supposing that they were suspicious of his motives in the bargaining. He was apparently aware that he was considered to have profited from bribery. And indeed it was well known that both Cornplanter and Little Billy had been handsomely rewarded, each with some $2000 worth of goods at Muskingum, and again at Philadelphia. And he was very sensitive to the popular impression that he was too conciliatory and had made unnecessary concessions of land over the years. And now he was hob-nobbing with Colonel Pickering. With all of this in mind he rose to speak on November 9. He was speaking as a war-chief, and for the warriors. After explaining his role in trying to correct injustices in the time since Stanwix, he now, because of deceit on the part of the commissioners, reports that "I have, therefore, told our warriors not to sign this treaty. The fifteen fires have deceived us; but we are under the sachems, and will listen to what they do. Though we will not sign it, yet we will abide by what they do, as long as they do right. The United States and the Six Nations are now making a firm peace, and we wish the fifteen fires may never deceive them, as they have done us warriors; if they once deceive the sachems it will be bad." [7]

At this point, Cornplanter returned to his council seat, but after a very short and quiet pause, he rose again: "I will put a patch upon what I have spoken. I hope you will have no uneasiness at hearing the voice of the warriors. You know it is very hard to be once deceived; so you must not make your minds uneasy."

From all accounts, Cornplanter's address to the council was received warmly. And indeed, Chief Eel, of the Onondagas, rose to applaud it and to urge a generous reception of its sentiments. But Colonel Pickering, noting the familiar division between the sachems and the warriors, followed with a sharp insistence that the treaty *must* be signed by the warriors. If the document is not signed by the warriors, he said, "I shall have nothing whatsoever to do with it."

And the council proceeded. And it was not long before all parties were feeling pretty good about the agreement that was finally reached. The final document included seven articles, the treaty prefaced by a polite preamble: "The President of the United States having determined to hold a conference with the Six Nations of Indians, for the purpose of removing from their minds all causes of complaint, and establishing a firm and permanent friendship with them; and Timothy Pickering being appointed sole agent for that purpose; and the agent having met and conferred with the Sachems, Chiefs and Warriors of the Six Nations in a general council. Now, in order to accomplish the good design of this conference, the parties have agreed on the following articles; which, when ratified by the President, with the advice and consent of the Senate of the United States, shall be binding on them and the Six Nations."

Article 1, in the familiar treaty way, simply declared that peace and friendship were firmly established. In Article 2, the United States acknowledged the ownership of the lands given to the Oneida, Onondaga, and Cayuga Nations by the State of New York, and promised to honor the Indian claim. Article 3 was the big one. Here the United States made huge concessions, restoring to the Iroquois virtually all of those lands taken from them at Stanwix. The boundaries were sharply defined. In Article 4 the United States pledged never [!] to disturb said lands. Article 5 cleared up the business of the roads. Article 6 provided payments to the Indians and a "quantity of goods" in the value of $10,000.00. It also designated an annuity in the amount of $4,500.00, "which shall be expended yearly forever [!], in purchasing clothing, domestic animals, implements of husbandry and other utensils suited to their circumstances." Article 7 outlawed private revenge or retaliation for injury and required the offended to file a formal complaint to the authorities governing the offender.

The document was signed on November 11, 1794, by 59 sachems and war-chiefs representing the Grand Council of the Six Nations, and by Timothy Pickering. Among the chiefs who signed are many of the familiar names: Little Beard, Little Billy (also known as Green Grasshopper), Farmer's Brother, Red Jacket, Half Town, Big Sky, and the ubiquitous Cayuga known as Fish Carrier. Handsome Lake (*Kon-ne-at-or-tee-ooh*) was the second to affix his X; and Cornplanter (*Kiant-whau-ka*) was next-to-last.

The signing was witnessed by Israel Chapin and Israel Chapin, Jr. Four interpreters were on call throughout the proceedings. Besides Horatio Jones, Joseph Smith, and Jasper Parish was Henry Abeel, the twenty-year-old son of Cornplanter. Henry was not skilled in the English language, but apparently he knew the language well enough for government work. As noted above, Pickering, who was fond of the Iroquois and had been much interested in the boy, had been Henry's sponsor for his schooling in the East.[8]

The treaty was ratified five weeks after the closing of the session, on January 21, 1795, in the city of Philadelphia. The historic document was signed by President George Washington: "Now, know ye, that I, having seen and considered the said treaty, do by and with the advice and consent of the Senate of the United States, accept, ratify and confirm the same, and every article and clause thereof. In Testimony thereof, I have caused the seal of the United States to be hereunto affixed, and signed the same with my hand."[9]

Cornplanter had to feel good about the treaty. He had been taking a lot of heat for concessions made by the Iroquois through a long succession of agreements with the Americans. The Canandaigua Treaty, which people were already calling the Pickering Treaty, was clearly a favorable one for the Indians. It was a make-up arrangement. Almost all of the land lost by the Iroquois in the Stanwix Treaty of 1784, nearly a million acres, was restored here at Canandaigua, only ten years later. Cornplanter's people were particularly lucky. It was agreed that the Senecas should have all the land in New York west of the Phelps and Gorham Purchase, except for a reservation one mile wide along the Niagara River.[10] According to Swatzler, "The acreage in the southwestern angle of New York restored to the Senecas at Canandaigua was four times greater than that permanently yielded to Pennsylvania in the Erie Triangle." And he noted, further, that "the southern two-thirds of the four-mile-wide strip along the Niagara River was also returned to the Senecas—at Red Jacket's insistence."[12] Most pleasing to the Indians was the assurance that this arrangement was "forever." Of course, as is generally the case in the life of the Indian, most of what is welcome is only nervously received.

The council at Canandaigua is significant also in that it marked the very last time that the United States would meet with the Iroquois as a Confederacy.[12] And there was an effect, too, on Jennesadaga. Because of the restoration of the lands, a large number of the Senecas who had been living in Cornplanter Town, on Cornplanter's private ground on the Allegheny, promptly returned to New York State, some in fact returning close to the region of Cornplanter's growing up.

Meanwhile, the Ohio Indians, because of the Battle of Fallen Timbers, had to submit to terms. Organized hostilities were at an end. By the first day of the new year, negotiations had come forward so far that preliminary articles could be agreed to. To Fort Greenville, which he had built as a base from which to launch his Indian campaign,

General Wayne returned, in order to negotiate a treaty with the defeated western Indians. Here he met with some 1100 Indians representing eleven tribes of the Northwest. Delegates began arriving early in June, and General Wayne graciously welcomed each party as it appeared. By the 16th almost all tribes were represented; but Little Turtle, designated to be the chief spokesman for the Western Indians, was late to show up. He finally arrived, together with seventeen Miamis, on June 23. He made no apology, merely observing that he was most happy to see the General (of whom he had always spoken respectfully), and noting that he had nothing in particular to say at this time. He expressed a desire to get his party encamped and out of the bad weather. He did make an early contribution to the conference in declaring that the Miamis were all united with him "in friendly sentiments," and desirous of peace. Wayne replied that he was "pleased to see you," and indicated that the conference had been eagerly awaiting his appearance. As it turned out, Little Turtle did indeed serve as the principal speaker for the Alliance, and he proved most eloquent and compelling. He had his own notions of what was right so far as boundaries were concerned, and he made his points with fervor. He spoke for the 1100 Indians, of eleven tribes, who were present as representatives of thousands of concerned villagers.

The tribes who had dispatched delegates to the treaty sessions were the Delawares, the Shawanese, the Chippewas, the Wyandots, the Ottawas, the Pottawatamies, the Eel River Indians, the Kickapoos, the Piankeshaws, the Kaskaskias, and of course the Miamis. Naturally, not the Senecas, nor any of the Six Nations, were present, as they had nothing to do in all of this.

The council did not break up until the 10th day of August, but the historic agreement was concluded on August 3, and signed by all parties. A jubilant communication from General Wayne to Secretary of War Henry Knox is dated August 9, 1795: "It is with infinite pleasure I now inform you, that a treaty of peace between the United States of America and all the late hostile tribes of Indians northwest of the Ohio, was unanimously and voluntarily agreed to, and cheerfully signed, by all the sachems and war chiefs of the respective nations, on the 3d, and exchanged on the 7th instant." [13]

Thus the 3rd of August, 1795, almost one year to the day from the time of the battle, became an important date in the early history of the young United States and a most consequential date, too, for the centuries-old Indian civilization. By the terms of the treaty the Indians

Henry Knox

were accepting all that had been done at Fort Harmar in January of 1789. The agreement meant the immediate surrender to the United States of the British posts at Detroit, Michilimackinack, Oswego, and Niagara. Most significant was the provision by which all previous treaties ceding land to the United States were recognized, for here for the first time was signed a treaty which acknowledged the Indian claim to lands within the boundaries of the United States. And peace, at long last, had finally come to the Ohio Valley.

The treaty put an abrupt end to Washington's "Indian problem." But it made for a big problem for the Delawares and the Shawnees and the Miamis and the Wyandots, and the members of seven other tribes, for the agreement turned over to the American settlers vast sections of the Ohio Valley (the Old Northwest). The Senecas and Cornplanter were not involved in this arrangement of course, but they were mighty familiar with terms like those agreed to at Greenville.

Wayne made a triumphant return to Philadelphia, but later returned to the West in order to effect the terms of the treaty. He was sailing from Detroit for Presque Isle in Lake Erie, the very last post which it was his duty to visit, when he was cut down by illness. Just the day before he was scheduled to come ashore, on November 17, he suffered a violent attack of the gout. He died one month later, on December 15, 1796, in the very block house that he had built at Presque Isle in 1793. This war-scarred veteran of the Revolution and the Indian wars, a close friend to Washington and to Cornplanter, the patriot hero of a new country, was only fifty-one.

For the struggling colonies Cornplanter had done perhaps his greatest service. He had played a big role in the battle of Fallen Timbers—by staying out of it. He was now prepared to embark upon a new life altogether.

XVIII

CORNPLANTER TOWN

It might be observed that the Seneca Chief Cornplanter lived two lives. In his first life, that of the young and confident warrior (1750-1782), his associations were with Old Smoke and Blacksnake and Little Beard and Half Town and Red Jacket and Joseph Brant and the Butlers and Hiokatoo and Kayahsotha.

In his second life (1782-1836), in which his role for his people was that chiefly of statesman, his association was with Henry Knox, George Washington, Timothy Pickering, Governor Thomas Mifflin, and Timothy Alden; with Generals Anthony Wayne, Richard Butler, and William Irvine; and with David Mead, the Quaker missionaries from Philadelphia and the Seneca people of Cornplanter Town, over which he presided for most of this half-century.

He was born a half-breed, but from the first to the last he was an Indian, a Seneca Indian and a war-chief in the Six Nations. He fought, fiercely as he could, as a warrior, for what he thought was best for his people. By the Sullivan Campaign and by Yorktown and by the Treaty of Paris and by Fallen Timbers he was at last made to see the futility in armed resistance. At the treaty table now, in his Seneca tongue, sometimes passionately but most of the time in reasoned arguments he championed the cause of the Indians. He made concessions, but he slowed the inevitable. With all of his art he continued to fight for what was best for his people. In his late years, painfully aware that the Iroquois culture was to be consumed, he saw the need to adapt to the white man's ways. By this time he had come to appreciate many of the principles of the Quakers. And of course the Quakers had been advocating for over a hundred years a policy based on friendship to the Indians. Naturally, he appealed to the Society of Friends in Philadelphia, who had welcomed him so graciously on his first visit to Philadelphia after war's end. In his last years, while still presenting the rights of the Indian peoples to the State of Pennsylvania and to the heads of the government of the United States, he led the Senecas as best he could, toward education and modern agriculture. With the Senecas thrown into disarray by the Sullivan expedition, and with the War of the Revolution clearly winding down, at least as far as the Indians were concerned, Cornplanter, sometime after 1780, determined on a move. Many Senecas, as above noted, had already been displaced to Fort Niagara. Homeless, their options were few. They could accept the British offer of refuge in Canada, as Brant had done, go to the Seneca settlements on the Allegheny near Pittsburgh, or come here to Niagara. It was plain enough that the latter option, for most, would mean a temporary situation.

Some two or three years after the conclusion of the Sullivan campaign and just before the end of the War of the Revolution, about 1782, together with Handsome Lake and Blacksnake, the Cornplanter Senecas were on the move, by way of Buffalo Creek and Tonawanda, south to the Allegheny country, where Kayahsotha, the powerful Seneca chief, had lived for a long time. Cornplanter certainly was privy to the fact that Kayahsotha was now partial to Americans, and that he was on very good terms with those in the vicinity of Pittsburgh. In any case, whatever the reasons, he clearly preferred this arrangement to resettlement on the Grand River in Canada under Joseph Brant.[1] Kayahsotha, sometimes regarded as the "Ohio Chief" among the Iroquois, had long been considered the Head Man in this territory. He was at this time getting up in years, for he had been born on the Genesee in 1720-25. His family, but without his sister (Cornplanter's mother), moved, when he was quite young, from Ganawaugus in New York State to the region now known as Meadville in Pennsylvania. Almost his entire life had been lived in the Allegheny-Ohio river country where he was reared.[2] At the time Cornplanter arrived in the region, Kayahsotha was living on the Cattaraugus Creek.[3]

He was to enjoy twelve years with his nephew, who had replaced him as head of the Seneca community in the Allegheny region, and with the members of Cornplanter's family. But for most of this time he was in failing health. We know that he was still living on February 1, 1794, for Cornplanter reported at that time to his friend Israel Chapin that "he is alive and that is all." It is presumed that the venerable chief died shortly after that communication and that he died in Cornplanter's house on the Grant. He had always been much revered. Historian Merle Deardorff, for example, esteemed him "able, prudent, and wise."

And from the diary of the Reverend David McClure a Presbyterian missionary to the white settlers of western Pennsylvania, emerges a most arresting and memorable image. The notation is dated August 18, 1772, when Kayahsotha would have likely been in his fifties: "Crossed the Laurel hanning [Lawel-hanna ('middle stream'), Loyalhanna], a pleasant stream which runs through Ligonier, & rode to Col. Proctors.[4] Here we found Kiahshutah, Chief of the Senecas, on his way to Philad[a] & from thence to Sr. Wm. Johnson's, who, as his interpreter Simon Girty informed us, had sent for him, relative to a treaty held some time ago at the Shawaness town. He was dressed in a scarlet cloth turned up with lace, & a high gold laced hat, & made a martial appearance. He had a very sensible countenance & dignity of manners. . . ."[5]

Such impressions must serve as his monument, for no ceremony attended his interment and no stone memorial was erected at his grave site. And although as late as 1935 local Senecas could still point out his grave, there continues great confusion about the actual site of Kayahsotha's resting place. Pittsburgh historian Neville Craig locates it in the Allegany Reservation, and a letter from Cornplanter to George Washington places the grave on the reservation; but others insist that he was buried at "Guyasootha's Bottom," on a farm near Custaloga's town, a village of Senecas on French Creek, near the mouth of Deer Creek.[6]

But from the time of his nephew's arrival in the Allegheny River region, which closely coincided with the formal end of hostilities, both Cornplanter and his uncle Kayahsotha, found themselves in a very different playing field. With the end of the war and the Treaty of Paris, the Indians who lived yet in the region of the "Thirteen Fires" now had to deal with a government being known as the United States of America. Most of the Iroquois had fought on the side of the King, to put down the rebellion. But the rebellion had not been put down, and now they would have to deal with a victorious enemy. These were the same Indians who had been responsible for the blood baths at Oriskany, at Cobleskill, at Wyoming, at Canajoharie, and at Fort Freeland. These were the very warriors who had raided the settlements all along the frontier. The various chiefs, Cornplanter, Red Jacket, Joseph Brant, and Farmer's Brother now had to look in the eye the American Commissioners and ask for their rights!

And it would prove a tough time for the Seneca Chief known as Cornplanter. He would do his best for his people, but he had so strong an impression that their ages-old way of life was doomed that he played a very conciliatory role in the bargaining sessions that followed hard upon the end of the war. And of course the American Commissioners were quick to appreciate that gains could be made through friendship with the Seneca Chief. And indeed Cornplanter was so often given rewards in return for services rendered at negotiations that many of his people, as before noted, wondered whether he was not being bribed and bought off. As the Indian lands were eroded at the treaty table in return for seemingly little, it was natural to place blame somewhere. Could not Cornplanter have done better?

The Senecas, by this time, were in remnants widely dispersed. Some villages remained along Cornplanter's native Genesee, and some Senecas continued to live in the regions close to Niagara and Buffalo. Many were residing in villages similar to that of Cornplanter, along the Allegheny River. But all Senecas were still represented by their venerable war-chief Cornplanter. He had his rivals for prestige in Handsome Lake and in Red Jacket, and promising young men were beginning to appear, but the nation continued to look to Cornplanter, who had by now achieved a reputation for great bravery and sagacity and who was thought a friend of peace. Cornplanter was happy to continue in that role.

In February of 1797, the Chief, now close to fifty years old, once again visited Philadelphia, the capital of the young nation. His mission this time was to pay his respects to President Washington, and to bid him farewell, for the President had announced his retirement from public service. Happily, he secured an audience with Washington, for whom he had great admiration and with whom he had always been on extremely good terms. He made quite an address, and, though he might have done better had he not detailed the familiar grievances on such a tender occasion, he was characteristically sensible and eloquent. And he was deeply concerned, as always, about the future of the Senecas. Fortunately, the speech, for it was that, was preserved in the papers of Thomas Morris, with whom Cornplanter would negotiate the Treaty of Big Tree. Of great interest is what the chief has to say about his abrupt discovery of banking.

Here is the address: "Father! I thank the Great Spirit for protecting us through the various paths which we have trod since I was last at this place [February, 1791]. As I am told you are about to retire from public business, I have come to pay my last address to you as the great chief of the fifteen fires [Actually there were at this time sixteen fires, for besides Vermont (in 1791) and Kentucky (in 1792) Tennessee had been granted statehood just the previous June], and am happy to find that I have arrived here in time to address you once more as father, and to advise with you on the business of our nation. You have always told us that the land which we live upon is our own, and that we may make such use of it as we think most conducive to our own comfort, and the happiness of posterity."

He then spoke of his need "to provide for the rising generation," and for posterity, and asked advice. One thing he wanted to know about was banking: "Father! I am also told that your people have a strong place for their money, where it is not only safe, but that it produces them each and every year an increase without lessening the stock. If we should dispose of part of our country, and put our money with yours in that strong place, will it be safe? Will it yield to our children the same advantages after our heads are laid down, as it will at present produce to us? Will it be out of reach of our foolish young men, so that they cannot drink it up to the prejudice of our children?"

He complained once again about Oliver Phelps and about losing the Ohio Company deed. But in concluding he returned to his chief purpose: "Father! I congratulate you on your intended repose from the fatigues and anxiety of mind, which are constant attendants on high public stations, and hope that the same Great Spirit which has so long guided your steps as a father to a great nation, will still continue to protect you, and make your private reflections as pleasant to yourself as your public measures have been useful to your people." [7]

Cornplanter would have been much distressed had he realized at this time just how very short would prove his dear friend's "intended repose."

The Cornplanter Town, as it was called, was surely the best off of all the Seneca villages in New York and Pennsylvania, which the anthropologist Anthony Wallace has labeled "slums in the wilderness." At least Cornplanter's tract was remote, and the Indians were able to practice a life not much foreign to the life of the forest and the river, which they loved. Cornplanter had chosen this region for its "wilderness" aura. In this land along the Allegheny and deep into the mountains of Appalachia could still be found in great numbers the white-tailed deer without which the Indian could not live the life of the Indian. Here was the forest's biggest bird, the wild turkey, and in abundant flocks, which regularly included gobblers weighing 30-40 pounds! Here also were the black bear and the fur-bearing animals, otter, mink, raccoon, the red fox and the gray fox. And the beaver, who still plied his trade, engineering impressive dams on the tiny mountain streams. Besides, this was the region in which the native Pennsylvania elk was still to be found. In fact, the elk herd was yet large enough as late as1852 to "yard up," which it did along the Clarion River near present Ridgeway, when seven of the animals were killed by Indian trappers, probably Cornplanter's Senecas. The very last elk would be taken in 1867, just east of present-day St. Marys, by an Indian named Jim Jacobs, whose home was the Cattaraugus Reservation in western New York State. And these were the forests, too, which accommodated the incredibly large flocks of passenger pigeons, which fed chiefly on the abundant beechnuts. And there was, too, the bison of the east,[8] an animal sometimes even larger than the plains bison, and a rich source for the Indians for food and robes, and a host of other essentials. In Cornplanter's early years on the Genesee, these animals were fairly numerous; during the first years of his living on the Cornplanter Grant, they were still to be seen in the region of Clarion, not far from the Seneca communities on the Allegheny. But it was not so for long. The lamentable slaughter of the "last herd" is reputed to have taken place in Cornplanter's time, in the winter of 1799-1800. And by the time Cornplanter was seventy years of age, the eastern bison herds had completely vanished.[9] How very numerous were the bison in the Indian lands east of the Mississippi during the eighteenth century is apparent by the hundreds of names, like Buffalo Creek and Buffalo Valley, that continue as names for communities and streams and regions, although, remarkably, the city of Buffalo, New York, may *not* have been named for this animal.

And of course there were fish, trout in the tributaries of the Allegheny, and all kinds of "big fish" in the Allegheny itself. Organized fish drives, as Cornplanter promptly perceived, could be conducted in the summer, when the waters were right.[10]

During the last four decades of his long life, Chief Cornplanter was in occasional association with a young man who was more of a hunter and a woodsman than the most earnest hunter among the Senecas. His name was Philip Tome. He had been born in Dauphin County in 1782, and had come west with his father's family, after two tries, up the West Branch of the Susquehanna to settle finally some six miles from the mouth of Pine Creek. Philip was at this time only nine years old. He became instantly an ardent hunter, intent on the black bear, the white-tailed deer, wolves, foxes, and panthers (Pennsylvania's great cat of the mountains). But his biggest excitement came with the elk hunt, and most especially with the hunt that had as its object the capture of a live, large bull elk. While just a youngster he captained such hunts in the region of the Clarion River, the Kinzua Creek, Pine Creek and Kettle Creek. He had already been successful in such expeditions when, in 1816, while living on the Kinzua Flats, not far from Jennesadaga, he proposed such a hunt to Cornplanter, going to see the Chief "about catching some elk." His experience with Cornplanter on this occasion he described some thirty-five years later: "He said that I could not do it; that no Indian of the Six Nations had done it, or any white man that he knew of. He said that young elk three or four months old had been caught, but no full-grown one could be—they were lords of the forest. I told him that I had caught or assisted in catching and leading in three."

When the Chief asked how he had led them in, young Philip told him. Cornplanter could only marvel:

> *He said he did not know but it was possible, but he did not believe I could take one that winter on the Allegany, as he thought they were larger and wilder than those on the Susquehannah. I told him that if he would show me the track of an elk—I did not care how large—the larger the better; I would willingly wager a small sum of money that I would bring one in alive. He said that he could show plenty of elk-tracks. I told him to find a man that I could hire, and I would employ him. He brought a man who charged a dollar a day, which I agreed to pay him on condition that he would find a track. He said that there was no doubt but that we could find one. There was no rope to be procured except one that belonged to Cornplanter, for which he wanted two dollars, but agreed to refund the money if I returned the rope uninjured. I agreed to his terms, and left the money. As we parted he wanted to shake hands, saying*

> *that he never expected to see me again if I attempted to catch an elk alive.*[11]

Of course, the confident young hunter, did capture a huge animal, "the largest elk I ever saw," according to his partner in the enterprise. And they made a good bit of money out of it too, by exhibiting him in Olean.

Tome, during the time he was living near Jennesadaga, learned what he could from Cornplanter, who had been living in the region for a long time and had a lot of hunting experience to draw on:

> *I asked Cornplanter where he thought the bears, elk, deer, and panthers were the most plenty thirty years previous. He answered that in the year 1786 he found the deer more plenty from the State line to Red Bank [near present-day New Bethlehem], and about twelve miles back from the river, than they were on Pine Creek. But he thought bears were not as plenty, and that panthers were quite numerous on Kenzua Creek and the Tionesta and the country between the head waters of those streams and the Susquehanna river. Elk, he said were not as plenty on the Allegany as they were on Pine Creek; and beaver, otter, and other animals valuable for their fur, he had found more abundant on the Susquehanna than on the Allegany. Bears were found in great numbers from the mouth of Conewango Creek to Chautauqua Lake. They had a crossing place where they passed from the head waters of the Tionesta to the lake. He said his two sons, Henry and John O'Bayle, killed in one summer, fifteen bears on the banks of Chautauqua Lake.* [12]

To capture a live bull elk and lead it back to town was certainly an exciting business, but the bull elk had a rival for providing hair-raising experience. This was the timber rattlesnake. Young Philip, who had had his run-ins with the reptile, was quite curious about the creature. Accordingly, he inquired of Cornplanter about the rattlesnake too:

> *. . . he told me that thirty years previous they had found the snakes as numerous from the place called Red Bank to the State line, as they used to be at Pine Creek. He said all the traveling in summer had to be done in canoes, on account of them. The way they destroyed them was to burn the woods in the same manner that we did. I asked if any of the people were ever bitten. He replied that the men were seldom bitten as they wore woolen socks and leggins, but several of the women and children had been bitten, and it proved fatal in some cases before remedies could be procured. When they were obliged to lie out at night in a place which was infested by snakes, they drove four crotches into the ground, upon which they placed poles, and across these they laid pieces of bark. In this manner they avoided sleeping on the ground. In summer they always kept a fire around the place where they slept, to protect themselves while asleep.*[13]

For these years the village known as Jennesadaga or Cornplanter Town was obviously still a village deep in the wilderness. But great changes were occurring in the life of the Senecas.

For a profile of that community as it was in 1798, we turn to Anthony Wallace, who draws upon the eye-witness accounts as provided by Schenk's history of Warren County, Pa., the history of Cattaraugus County, New York, the informed essays of William Fenton, the Draper manuscripts, the diary of Joshua Sharpless, the journal of the Quaker Henry Simmons, and Halliday Jackson's "Sketch of the Senecas," to provide a beautifully detailed and accurate, very instructive description.

Wallace describes, first, the locale of the Grant, on which most of the Cornplanters had been living for almost two decades now. "A sheltered sliver of bottom land," he presents it, "bounded on the east by the river itself," which at this point was 150 yards across, and not particularly deep. The town was very difficult to approach, tucked in among the cliffs as it was, and accessible only by a torturous, often indistinct, path.

Because of this seclusion, Cornplanter's Senecas, happily, could practice the traditional Indian way of life. The nearest whites in any significant number were living fifteen miles downriver at Warren, once an old Indian town.[14] Meadville was sixty miles to the west of Warren, and no other community was anywhere near.[15]

But Cornplanter Town was not only remote and secluded. It was shrouded in mystery, and the medicine men, much enamored of their "magic," regularly depended upon the strange plants which frequented the forest floor for their marvelous healing powers. The village reposed in a fairyland.

Wallace notes that the town "lay between the banks of the river and a bend of a little stream—Cornplanter Run—that ran down from the cliffs." And "up the river above the narrows was another mysterious spot: a narrow, deep ravine extending straight up the hill." Very strange plants grew here, and were collected by the village herbalist, Handsome Lake.

The Indian way of life was at least partially preserved in hunting of course, and in fishing,[16] and in the springtime maple-sap ritual. The month of March was regularly given over to the tapping of the sugar maples, and the whole village, men and women, boys and girls, would traipse to the woods to sleep for weeks around the kettles in which the collected sap was boiled down to syrup and sugar. And naturally, as the sap ran slowly, and was only very tediously boiled down, the men, with time on their hands, would engage in trapping and hunting during these weeks.[17]

The town at this time (1798) was made up of some forty houses, "scattered in an irregular line in the meadow thirty yards or so from the water's edge." Prominent in the middle of the village stood the statue of Tarachinwagon, where sacrificial rituals were performed. And close to this statue was the most elegant house in the village, Cornplanter's of course, "a pair of cabins joined by a long roofed porch." Almost every Seneca village of that time included a council house. In Cornplanter Town, the Headman's house filled that role.

The dwellings were built of bark and of logs in those days, and each provided only for a single family, perhaps a very large family, perhaps as many as fifteen. At this time, as Wallace notes, there were some 400 Indians living at the old "Burnt House" village site, now Jennesadaga (Cornplanter Town). In the Chief's double house, there lived, generally, fourteen people. Besides Cornplanter's family, which at this time included, besides his wife and himself, five daughters and one son, who "was retarded and was known as 'the idiot,'" it accommodated the family of Handsome Lake. The family of Cornplanter's half-brother numbered probably eight at least (one or both of his daughters, a son-in-law, and grandchildren). Cornplanter's sons Henry and Charles also lived in the village, but not with their father.[18] In the village there lived also a few whites, the long-ago captured Peter Crouse among them.

The houses were modest in size and in appearance. Chief Cornplanter, naturally, enjoyed the largest house, a structure, according to Wallace, sixty-four feet long and sixteen feet wide, with a porch of ten feet in length. The houses were one-room dwellings, with a single entry door, no windows at all, and a hole in the ceiling through which passed the smoke from the cabin fire all the day long.

What made this village seem like a slum to those who were describing it was the manner in which the Indians lived their lives. Although the town was set in a kind of fairyland, with the river on one hand and the wilderness mountains with their deep forests and cold-running streams providing a beautiful backdrop, the people lived in squalor. Wallace explains: "Trash and garbage was simply thrown out of the door into a pile near the house, where it rotted and fed swarms of flies. There were no outhouses or public latrines; people relieved themselves in the privacy of the woods or brush away from the house. There was no soap, and lice infested hair and clothing."

It did not help to make the village a "slum," but the attitude toward women on the part of the braves could hardly be counted a compliment to the life of the Indians. Oft quoted is the statement made by Cornplanter in 1790 that "In the Seneca nation the women have as much to say in council as the men have, and in all important business have equal authority . . . ."[19] But while this was certainly true, as we know from their activity at councils, women continued to be identified with particular menial duties. They were totally responsible for the production of fruits and vegetables, in fact did all of the real work of the village. Women carried wood, kept the fire up, fetched water from the river, hoed the corn and the bean hills, ground the corn, collected the berries, and of course provided the meals. Beyond their hunting and fishing and trapping, men had time only for the occasional house building.

In dress and hygiene the Seneca Indians were at this time, a long way from the practices of the white men and women. In general the life that was lived in Cornplanter Town in many ways was pretty much as it had been in the Indian villages for a long, long time; but more and more frequently there were appearing the implements and tools upon which the white settlers depended, and the customs of the people of Meadville and Warren began to seem less and less strange to the Senecas.

But the Cornplanter Indians, though vaguely appreciating the absolute need to adapt to the white man's ways, continued to hold on as best they could to the life that they had always known and semed genuinely to love. It was with great reluctance that they adopted any change. And a most satisfying connection to the past they steadfastly preserved in their tribal ceremonies and in their age-old rituals.[20] It would be a little while yet before Tarachiawagon would be consigned to the river.

Cornplanter, as Head Man ("mayor") of the town, had *lots* of problems to address. But the most difficult and formidable, by far, could be accounted for in one word. That word was alcohol. For the people liked to drink, and, as Wallace observes, they "preferred not to drink alone but in large, convivial groups," and not only the men of the town but the women as well. Everybody drank, and most of the time much too much.

According to the Quaker Halliday Jackson, who knew the Seneca communities very well, "In the spring, hunters took their peltries to Warren, got drunk by scores, and brought more liquor home with them; at other seasons, they were able to get credit for liquor from the Holland Company factor. Raftsmen taking logs from Cornplanter's sawmill downstream to the white towns as far south as Pittsburgh spent their money on whiskey. Bringing liquor back to the grant, returning travelers sold the whiskey at retail and buyers threw all-night parties where, plied with liquor, groups spent whole nights singing, dancing, drumming, and quarreling. Women could be seen after such routs, lying in stupor beside the paths to their homes. And in the late morning the sodden households woke sometimes to find a member dead, or cut in a brawl, or frozen in the snow outside." [21]

The Quakers, of course, were a huge help to the chief in his passion for temperance. When Cornplanter was lamenting the leaving of the Quaker missionary Henry Simmons in the fall of 1799, he noted to the delegation of Quaker elders who had come to check on the work of Henry Simmons and his fellow missionaries that Simmons "had been useful to him in keeping whiskey and other strong liquor out of their town; that they now drank much less than formerly." He said that the departure of his good friend would hurt him sorely in this matter and declared he would "not be able to prevent [the use of alcohol] as well as he had lately done."[22] In fact, however, in time, chiefly because of the influence of Handsome Lake and his preaching, great inroads into Cornplanter's chief concern seemed to be occurring. Indeed, the Cornplanter Indians did something of a turnaround and for many years became a remarkably sober community.

In the fall of 1816, with Cornplanter now in his sixties, the Reverend Timothy Alden, who had founded Allegheny College in Meadville, and was at this time still President, visited the chief at his village. On his way to the village he stayed overnight at the cabin of the German settler Peter Crouse (Krause), who as a boy had been captured and adopted by the Senecas. Crouse was one of a number of white men (some of them married to Indian women) who were living with the Senecas. In his description of the Cornplanter and his community we are provided some details of interest, additional to those of Wallace, and some changes in the life of the town can be noted:

> *Jennesedaga, Cornplanter's village, is on a handsome piece of bottom land, and comprises about a dozen buildings. It was grateful to notice the agricultural habits of the place, and the numerous enclosures of buckwheat, corn, and oats. We also saw a number of oxen, cows, and horses, and many logs designed for the saw mill and the Pittsburgh market. Last year, 1815, the Western Missionary Society established a school in the village, under Mr. Samuel Oldham. Cornplanter, as soon as apprised of our arrival, came over to see us, and took charge of our horses. Though having many around him to obey his commands, yet, in the ancient patriarchal style, he chose to serve us himself, and actually went into the fields, cut the oats, and fed our beasts. He appears to be about 68 years of age [a very good guess], and 5 feet 10 inches in height. His countenance is strongly marked with intelligence and reflection. Contrary to the aboriginal custom, his chin is covered with a beard three or four inches in length. His house is of princely dimensions compared with most*

> *Indian huts, and has a piazza in front. He is the owner of 1300 acres of excellent land, 600 of which encircle the ground-plot of his little town.* [23]

One would suppose that Cornplanter could live out his last years in the peaceful repose of his village, in the embrace of his family and with the respect due him for some forty years of exhaustive devotion to his people. But that could hardly be.

XIX

THE BIG TREE AND THE SAWMILL

Although the trouble between the Ohio Indians and the administration of Washington, which had occupied Cornplanter through a large portion of his waking hours, as well as his sleeping hours, during a whole decade, was now at an end, the Head Man of the village at Burnt House, was not about to abandon the council fire. From a time just after the battle of Fallen Timbers until the fall of 1826, when the Chief would be seventy-six years old, a steady stream of treaty sessions and conferences seemed to require his presence and very often his active participation.

Certainly the most important of these was the session in which the Senecas sold off—again—the lands that had been pilfered from them by Phelps and Gorham a decade ago. This was the council that is known as the Treaty of Big Tree, held at the tiny village of Big Tree, what is now Geneseo, on the Genesee River, in August and September of 1797. Although the session was conducted under the sanction of the United States, the agreement that was reached was strictly a private affair, between the "financier of the American Revolution," Robert Morris, and the Seneca nation of Indians.

The energetic and able Morris, who had been a member of the Federal Convention of 1787, had just two years prior to the time of this conference completed a term as Senator from Pennsylvania. But he was in big trouble now. Although determined to purchase from the Senecas the right to the land bargained for nine years earlier by Phelps and Gorham, he was operating out of what might be called "house arrest," inasmuch as he feared his appearance would result in debtor's prison (which indeed it did the very next year). Consequently, pleading illness and debilitating age, he appointed his son Thomas, who had made his home some years ago in Canandaigua, to represent him with power of attorney. Red Jacket, and a number of other Seneca leaders, including the powerful Farmer's Brother, very strongly opposed the sale of any land. But Thomas Morris, as early as the previous February, had arranged a meeting in Philadelphia between his father and the influential Joseph Brant and Cornplanter. And the financier had been so much encouraged by Cornplanter's allowing "that it will promote the happiness of his nation to sell at least a part of their lands and place the purchase money in the public funds so as to derive an annual income therefrom" that he determined to go forward. Meanwhile son Thomas, through some hard politicking, finally persuaded the "difficult" Seneca leaders to agree to a conference, and all settled for a time in the middle of August.[1]

Swatzler describes the gifting (bribery) that was customary at such land-buying sessions: "By July wagon loads of supplies and presents for the Indians were en route. Nearly $5,000 of provisions, including beef, flour, whiskey, and tobacco, were shipped to the treaty grounds to feed and entertain the Indian attendees. Also transported were over $15,000 of presents: blankets, cloth, leggings, shirts, kettles, knives, gunpowder and lead shot."[2] Shades of Oswego!

By the contract which was finally signed, September 15, 1797, the Seneca Nation of Indians turned over to Morris most of their remaining lands in western New York, in return for $100,000, to be paid to the nation in vested bank stock. The "treaty" reserved to the Indians twelve designated tracts of land, including Squawkie Hill, Caneadea, and Gardeau (home of Mary Jemison, to whom the Senecas awarded a grant).

Besides the $100,000 which would be paid the Seneca Nation in annuities "for their use," individual big-wigs were awarded special gifts of cash. Red Jacket, who had been the most stubborn in the bargaining was awarded the most ($600); Cornplanter received only half as much. A number of other Seneca leaders were paid $1000, to be divided among them. Cornplanter gained back the difference he had lost to Red Jacket when Morris arranged for a lifetime annuity to him in the amount of $250, Red Jacket receiving a paltry $100, no more than what was awarded to others, including Farmer's Brother and the Young King.[3]

At most of the councils in which he participated over forty years Cornplanter played an important role. He was generally recognized as the head of the Seneca delegation and often as the spokesman for the whole of the Six Nations. But the fact is Chief Cornplanter was a war-chief only. He was not a sachem.[4]

Most of the time of course in the council sessions the sachems and the war-chiefs saw the issue in the same light, but not always. And when there was a difference, Cornplanter was often pointedly reminded that he was *merely a war-chief.* Nowhere perhaps was the difference so pronounced as at the Treaty of Big Tree.

The agreement that finally was reached here did not come easily. Red Jacket at one point exploded in such a rage that he actually put out the council fire. Inasmuch as Red Jacket had the support of most of the sachems, the eruption made for a tense situation. The council returned to fairly peaceful discussion on the following day, only because Morris had won over the women and because Cornplanter, who had "called a secret meeting," had persuaded the warriors to favor the sale.[5] Cornplanter, in anticipation of the division between the warriors and the sachems had as long ago as May called "a general Meeting of all the Warriors and Chiefs of Warriors at which no sachem was to be present." He was determined to persuade the warriors to urge a division of the property and to sell their portion of it. Of all this he had informed Thomas Morris.[6] Actually, it had worked out better than Cornplanter had hoped, as no division had to be made.

Some 1200 Indians, mostly Senecas, participated in the sale. Thomas Morris of course signed for his absent father. Signing for the Indians, all with their X mark, were fifty-two war-chiefs and sachems, including Farmer's Brother, Handsome Lake, Red Jacket, Little Billy, Young King, Little Beard, and Cornplanter. One of the interpreters for the sessions, and serving as a witness, was Cornplanter's son Henry Abeel.

The date was September 15, 1797; and what the contract meant, of course, is that almost all of the Seneca land, except the reservation parcels, would now be open to settlement. Having lost long ago their lands to the east of the Genesee the Indians now surrendered all but some 200,000 acres (311 square miles) of the lands that they had held to the west of the Genesee. These 200,000 acres included eleven reserves, most of them ridiculously small: Canawaugus (Cornplanter's home village), on the Genesee River (two square miles); Big Tree (site of the conference), on the Genesee River (two square miles); Little Beard's Town, on the Genesee River (two square miles); Squawkey Hill, on the Genesee River (two square miles); Gardeau (Mary Jemison's home), on the Genesee River (two square miles); Oil Springs, on Cuba Lake (one square mile); Caneadea, on the Genesee River (sixteen square miles); Buffalo Creek, on Lake Erie, and Tonawanda, on Tonawanda

Creek (together 200 square miles); Cattaraugus, on Lake Erie (42 square miles); and Allegany, on the Allegheny River, adjacent to Cornplanter's private tract (forty-two square miles).[7]

All of this was "Done at a full and general treaty of the Seneka nation of Indians, held at Genesee, in the county of Ontario, and State of New York, on the fifteenth day of September, in the year of our Lord one thousand seven hundred and ninety-seven, under the authority of the United States." [8]

Legend has it that this agreement, by which the Senecas gave up their rights to four million (!) acres of land west of the Genesee, was signed under the Big Tree, a giant oak, which stood on the banks of the river. The tree came to be known as the "Treaty Oak." Sixty years after the conclusion of the council, the tree, at the time an incredible twenty-nine feet in circumference, finally fell. It was toppled by the terrible flood of 1857. Members of the community at the time salvaged portions of the bark, which are to this day on display in Geneseo. As this was the last really significant treaty-agreement reached by the Indians with the colonials, the felling of the Great Tree can be regarded as a symbol for the collapse of an age-old way of life.

And Cornplanter, as Head Man of the village on the property given him by the Quaker State, was steadily leading his people into the ways of the white settlers. Although he labored hard to preserve the hunting and fishing potential of the Allegheny River region, and in that way to continue the traditional life of the Seneca Indian, at the same time he encouraged the adoption of the white man's ways when it came to education and the tilling of the fields. He led his people into the activities of lumbering, and the raising of cattle and the grinding of grain. From the time of his settling there, he was considering the operation of gristmills and sawmills; indeed, by 1795 he had in operation a productive sawmill upriver from Cornplanter Town, near the Pennsylvania-New York State border.[9]

Of course it must be remembered that when we are speaking of the white man's ways, we are not thinking of industry or agriculture by modern standards. It must be kept in mind that "modern" in Cornplanter's day was quite primitive by today's practices. The felling of trees, and the operation of sawmills in Cornplanter's time did not mean power machinery, as it is known today; lumbering meant, at best, broad axes and hand saws. It was still largely manual labor. It was a horse-and-wagon economy. Steam power, though in use, was not practical yet for the sawmill. And this was a time long before electricity or the gasoline engine. It was a time a little before the circular saw and a longer time before the band saw and the very productive gangsaw.

Still, it is plain enough that Chief Cornplanter was enterprising and forward thinking. He was riding a tide. Sawmills were already central to many of the white settlements in New York State. The sawmill, though nothing like the sawmill of today, was in Cornplanter's time a big advance over the older manner of producing boards from logs, which meant laying a log over a "saw pit," with two sawyers working a two-handled saw, one from the pit (the "pitman") and the other from above the log.

Happily for Cornplanter's enthusiasm, lumbering was a natural for his people. They lived in the dense forests which featured varieties of the sturdy oak, the sugar maple, the beech, hickory and three species of ash (black, white, and red). And there was the great American chestnut too. White oak was popular with the sawyers, but the white pine was considered the timber most fit to cut, and indeed it became the wood most commonly used for the building of frame structures. Chestnut and black walnut were particularly useful for fence posts and for rails.

Trees were felled, not by a chain saw, but by chopping with an axe. After they were stripped of their limbs, they were wrestled onto sleds (Cornplanter's men did not have the canting hook or the peavey with which to apply the leverage.) and skidded by teams of oxen or horses to the sawmill or to the river landing from which they could be rafted to the mill. Winter provided the best time for the transport of the logs, naturally, and the Indians would even water down the tram road to provide ice for ease of sledding.

Cornplanter's sawmill, like the others in the early days, was water-powered. The mill would be built in the bed of a stream, or in the race of dammed up water. The water is delivered to the mill by opening the gates of the mill pond; water comes down the sluice to fall upon the millwheel and drive it. The power was such that the saw blade (of an up-and-down saw) could be moved normally as fast as 80-90 strokes per minute, and sometimes as fast as 100 times a minute. In an equal amount of time a mill sawyer could cut into planks as much wood as twenty men working in two-man teams with the pit saw. He might produce 500 boards in a day's time.

Cornplanter's sawmill depended upon what were called "mill irons," which would include the necessary castings for the gig and the bull wheels, etc. It is likely that his mill was constructed with irons brought upriver by canoe from Pittsburgh. His was an early mill, but by 1806, as above noted, his had become only one of seven that were in operation in Warren County. At this time there were only two gristmills in operation. The gristmill, which likewise was water-powered, and crushed the grain (corn or wheat) by applying pressure from a moving flat, round stone to another unmoving stone underneath, proved also to be a big labor-saver for the Indian, who was used to crushing grain with muscle power in a stone handmill.

The boards and posts produced by Cornplanter's sawmill were rafted, normally in the high waters of the spring, to markets in Warren, Franklin, and Pittsburgh. The mill put a lot of the chief's would-be warriors to a very meaningful work. Lumbering, more than farming ever could be, was congenial to them, and there was a big market.

That Cornplanter's sawmill was commercially successful is plain from a letter, dated December 3, 1795, and directed by the chief to Major Isaac Craig, who had served at Fort Pitt for the last three years of the war under General William Irvine. One year after the Treaty of Paris was finally concluded, Craig, together with his friend Stephen Bayard, actually purchased the fort and the land upon which it stood.

At some time in the early winter of 1795, apparently not long after Cornplanter's sawmill began operation, Craig at Fort Pitt was informed by Major Thomas Butler, in command at Fort Franklin, that there was piled up at the sawmill a great quantity of finished boards. Butler, who had been taking Cornplanter's entire output, apparently was already well supplied. He urged Craig to secure what he needed. Major Craig promptly dispatched Marcus Hulings, who was a very able river man, "with three bags of money and some other articles" for whatever that would buy of Cornplanter's lumber. Somehow Major Craig learned the next day that there were others very eager also to purchase the boards. Hastily he prepared a letter explaining that Huling was on his way, and commissioned James Beard to deliver it to Cornplanter posthaste. Happily, Cornplanter had the letter in time and made the lumber available to Beard.

From Jennesadaga on December 3, the Chief sent off a reply to Major Craig, who had served on the artillery unit that fired the cannon balls that so much panicked Cornplanter and his warriors at Newtown some sixteen years ago. It is unknown who it was put the letter into English. It could not have been the chief's son Henry, who at this time was in school in the East. It is most interesting, for many reasons, one of which is the chief's consciousness of age (He was at this time only forty-three years old.), and another of which is his great concern for his son Henry, now twenty-one and at school: "I thank the States for making me such kind ofers. We have made peace with the United States as long as watter runs, which was the reason that I built a mill in order to suport my family by it. More so, because I am getting old and not able to hunt. I also thank the States for the pleashure I now feel in meeting them again in friendship, you have sent a man to make a bargain with me for a sertain time which I do not like to do. But as long as my mill makes boards, the United States shall always have them in preference to any other, at the market price, and when you want no more boards I can't make blankets of them. As for the money you have sent, if I have not boards to the amount, leave it and I will pay it in boards in the Spring."

And he *never* passes up a chance to lash out at his much-hated whiskey:

> *I thank you kindly for the things you have sent me. I would thank Major Craig or Col. Butler to let Col. Pickering and Gen. Washington know that there is a grate deal of damage done in this country by Liquor; Capt. [Joseph] Brant has kiled his son [The son was drunk, not Chief Brant.] and other chiefs has done the same, and when the drink was gone and they began to think of the horid crime they had comited, they resigned their command in the Nation; two Chiefs has been kiled, the one at Fort Franklin the other at Genesee. I have sent a speech to the States conserning the Chief killed at Franklin, and has been waiting all summer to receive pay for him, but can see no sign of its coming. I am by myself to bear all the burden of the people. Now father take pitty on me and send me 40 dollars worth of black Wampum and 10 of white; and I expect to see it in two months and an half, as I must make new Chiefs with it again that time, to help me. I wish to hear from my son and what progress he is making in his learning, and as soon as he is learned enough I want him at home to manage my business for me. I will leave it all to my*

> *father, Gen. Washington, to judge when he is learned enough. My compliments to my father and the United States, and I wish it was possible for me to live forever in the United States.* [10]

The letter is signed "CAPT. O. BEAL" and with his mark "X."

According to Swatzler, Cornplanter's sawmill was constructed at some time between 1791 and 1795, and "predated by at least five years any European-American-owned sawmills on the upper Allegheny River." [11] The significance of the mill needs to be noted, and Swatzler has done that. According to him, the Seneca chief's sawmill "was a genuine cultural innovation, independently initiated by Cornplanter." Swatzler notes that "He employed European-Americans to construct and operate the mill. He negotiated contracts for the sale of boards to the U.S. Army at Franklin and Pittsburgh, which took the mill's entire output for some time.[12] In 1796 the Holland Land Company's storehouse at Warren was constructed of boards purchased from Cornplanter's sawmill. He had the mill reconstructed in 1806." [13] In December of 1790, at the meetings with Washington in Philadelphia, the President had declared to the Seneca delegation that "the only business which will add to your numbers and happiness" is tilling the ground. But for many years now, and increasingly so, lumbering, rather than agriculture, was the chief and most promising profession of the Allegany Senecas. Cornplanter could never have known, of course, but by the time he was seventy-eight years old there would be 31,000 (!) sawmills in operation in the territory known as the United States. He was a real pioneer.

But Cornplanter's sawmill was badly located, as he later acknowledged. Some idea of it is provided by an entry in the journal of Joshua Sharpless under the date of May 21, 1798: "We [the five missionary Quakers] got Cornplanter, his son Henry and three other Indians to embark with us five in a canoe. They put us up the river with setting poles at the rate of 3 miles an hour. In places the river was shallow and ran rapid, in other places the river was from two to six feet deep. In about six miles we came to Cornplanter's sawmill. We stopped at his request and viewed it. The mill is almost new built, on a small stream which, when we were there, was so low that the mill could do very little work. At the time of the year when the stream is pretty full, the river is often so high that it hurts the mill with its back-water." [14]

Cornplanter had hired a Dutchman to run the sawmill for him, which was okay as Cornplanter was half a Dutchman himself. This man who operated the mill in its early life was George Hildebrandt, Sr.,[15] who had served in the rebel forces during the Revolution. Hildebrandt in 1795 would have been forty-two years old, just one year younger than Cornplanter. There continues some confusion about him, partly because his son, who was known as "Jr.," also operated a sawmill. Whether he was indeed "the drunken Dutchman" mentioned so often in the literature of the time, particularly in the Quaker journals, and whether he was truly a "bad influence, who paddled liquor to the Indians"[16] is not certified. He definitely had learned the Seneca tongue pretty well from the time he associated with the Indians, and consequently served as an interpreter for the incoming teachers, notably Samuel Oldham.

In any case, it seems that Hildebrandt left Cornplanter's service in 1806, at which time Cornplanter was having the mill rebuilt by James Morrison.

That Cornplanter was ambitious for money, that "personal wealth" motivated him, and that he was a "shrewd businessman" Swatzler acknowledges, but he goes on to insist that Cornplanter made money to address the needs of his people, and that he was most generous in its distribution. Although he appreciated the necessity to help his people in this way (if he was to continue as Head Man), it is plain that his desire to help was genuine. Noting from an entry in the Sharpless journal, Swatzler provides evidence of the typical Cornplanter, who was constantly bailing his people out of jail. In May of 1798, shortly after the Quaker missionaries had shown up, Cornplanter addressed the council in his characteristic impassioned way. Sharpless recorded the instance: "Cornplanter made a pretty lengthy speech. It did not appear to be directed at us [the Quakers] but [as] our interpreter [Henry Abeel?] informed, was [meant] for an Indian then in the house who had been charged with murdering a white man for which he had been in jail in Pittsburgh, and tried for his life, but being acquitted by the jury, he was now at liberty. The trial and court expenses we understood had cost Cornplanter more than 200 dollars. Though there was not evidence to support the charge yet there was cause to fear it was too true. The chief's speech appeared to be delivered with much earnest and serious expostulation."[17]

All of this brings us to the twilight of the eighteenth century. Jennesadaga and the Senecas of the Allegany Reservation would shortly have their lives much changed by the arrival of their good friends the Quakers of Philadelphia. It would be very difficult to over-value what the genuine interest and enthusiastic tutoring of the Quaker mission meant to the Indians of the Allegheny River region.

XX

THE QUAKER MISSION

The years 1798-99 were momentous for Chief Cornplanter. First there was the follow-up treaty council to the Treaty of Big Tree. The Holland Land Company, which had just acquired most of the land purchased from the Senecas by Robert Morris had now to establish precise boundaries for the parcels which had been set off as reservations. Representing the Senecas at this session at Buffalo Creek were Cornplanter and a number of lesser chiefs. Representing the Holland Land Company was Joseph Ellicott, and serving as supervisor was the Indian Agent, Israel Chapin, Jr., who, it was generally known, had some interest in the Holland Land Company. Although the Quaker missionaries who Cornplanter had hoped could accompany him were not able to attend, Cornplanter proved a hard bargainer, and, according to Swatzler, "acquitted himself with distinction." He apparently made Ellicott and Chapin very conscious of the Quaker interest, even though the Quaker watchdogs were not actually present.[1]

Just a bit earlier, in the middle of May, in response to Cornplanter's steady barrage of requests for aid, there had arrived in the Allegheny River settlement five Quaker missionaries. Their appearance at Jennesadaga is described in the Journal of Halliday Jackson,[2] in his most engaging Biblical style: "Now it was the fifth month on the 17 day of the month that we entered into the Village of Corn-planter, and it was nigh unto the River even the River Oheyu [the Indian name for the Allegheny, as they considered it only the upper Ohio (meaning 'handsome' or 'beautiful' river)], and the name thereof in the Seneca tongue was Je,nuch,ada,dago which being interpreted is Burnt House."

They were received graciously, by the Chief himself: "Howbeit the people spake unto us in a strange Language and we understood them not—nevertheless Corn-planter had a son whose name was Henry, and he had been taught in the Learning of the White people in the Great City [Philadelphia, of course], and the words of his Father made he known unto us—And Corn-planter the Chief spake on this wise, and said unto us 'Brethren—I have heard of your comeing for many days, and rejoice in my heart to see you this day, and am thankful to the Great Spirit for your safe arrival and preservation on the way.'"

The Quakers then presented themselves: "And we spake unto him by the Interpreter, and said, that we were the children of Onas their Brother, come from a far Country to see them, and moreover we desired to have their people collected together that we might speak unto them of the things which we came about—And Corn-planter the Chief spake again unto us & said it should be so, & moreover he sent messengers the self same day, thro' all his Villages to carry the tideings and have the people collected together. . . ."

All in all, it turned out to be quite a reception: "And Cornplanter set before us food to eat such as was convenient." From Mrs. Susannah Wood, who served as a teacher in Tunesassa for some years after 1852, we have an account of this dinner: "Thomas Wistwar was speaking of the first meal Friends took on this reservation. They called at an Indian hut—Cornplanter's I think, and gave them to understand by signs they wanted something to eat. They were invited to help themselves to the contents of the pot which hung over the fire. They, not knowing exactly how to manage, Cornplanter took a stick and drew forth something which proved to be a sort of dumpling boiled in bear's fat. They made a sparing repast." [3]

Halliday Jackson's account continues with a description of how the Chief Cornplanter "brought his wife, & his Sons, and his Daughters, and shewed them unto us—And as we walked in the Field nigh unto the Village, they [the] Women laboured abundantly therein, because it was about the time of planting their Corn and they rejoiced in their hearts, and were merry when they knew we were the Children of Onas come from a far Country to see them. And when the night was come we Slept in the house of Cornplanter, and rested comfortably, because we were weary of the exceeding long Journey."

Next day the reception was carried on in a rather extravagant gaiety: "Now it came to pass on the morrow about the eleventh hour of the day, that they blew the Trumpet and the People collected to the Council, the Chiefs and the warriers and the mighty [In the manuscript the word *wise* is written in above *mighty*.] men and the men of Valour, and they were curiously adorned in fine Apparrel, with breastplates and head bands & earrings, & nose Jewels, & bracelets, and round Tires like the moon, and with Skins of the Wild Beasts of the Forrest, & they prided themselves in the Bravery of their Tinkling Ornaments."

Jackson tells how "they Assembled themselves together at the house of Cornplanter and sat down and mused a little in their own minds and Cornplanter the Chief arose and spoke on behalf of the people and said unto us, 'Men and Brethren, I was rejoiced in my heart when I saw you come out of the bushes Yesterday and thankful to the Great Spirit for preserving you on the way; You told us You had something to say unto us, & behold we are collected together to hear your words.'"

With this invitation the young John Pierce, speaking for the Quaker delegation, addressed the Cornplanter Indians. He presented first the document of introduction and purpose which had been prepared in Philadelphia, which was interpreted for the assembled Senecas. He then added his own explanation, noting for the Indians that the Quakers were come among them to "teach them to Plow to Sow, & to reap that they might eat the Goodly things of the Land." He explained that they were here to teach them how to use the white man's tools and mechanical instruments, that they were here to teach them how better to care for their flocks and for their herds, that they "might have meat in abundance & bread without scarcity."

Cornplanter spoke a little about what the Quakers had said, but declared the Indians would have to meditate. He promised a reply on the morrow. And when the morrow came, and all were assembled in council, the warriors and the men of valor, "Cornplanter the Chief stood up before the people and spake unto us in this wise." He made it plain that the Red people were poor, that many of them were willing to learn how to till the ground and follow the white man's example. But he complained that "we have but very little of all that our forefathers possessed." He insisted that "if you sojourn among us, we desire you to learn our Children to read, and write as you do."

Cornplanter closed out his little speech by noting that two of the Quakers would be going home. He expressed the hope that they would stay in close communication. And the two who would be going home, Joshua Sharpless and John Pierce, assured the Chief that indeed it would be so, and that, besides, there would be much more of the implements of husbandry coming to the villages; and they promised assistance in the building of houses and in the tilling of the fields.[4]

These men, Halliday Jackson, Joel Swayne, John Pierce, Joshua Sharpless, and Henry Simmons, who by the Indian Committee of the

Philadelphia Meeting had been appointed to set up a mission among the Senecas of the Allegheny River region, had of course to establish a residence and had to locate a "model farm." They had felt all along that the farm might be better located apart from Cornplanter's private property, so that on their leaving it could be left to the entire Seneca tribe. Halliday Jackson described for his journal how they settled on Genesinguhta (Oldtown), which was a very small and very old and half abandoned Indian village some ten miles upriver from the principal settlement at Jennesadaga, and how when they explained to Cornplanter what they meant to do, he was much pleased. Indeed, Cornplanter most graciously extended the young Quakers carte blanche: "Men and brethren, the land is all before you. Choose where you please, and ye shall have permission of the Chiefs and Rulers of the people to catch and kill of the wild beasts of the Forest & the Fish that Skim the Surface of the great Deep." [5] That evening the five Quakers returned to Cornplanter's house. A few days later they departed, "with our Horses and baggage and provender, and all that was ours," for Genesinguhta. Here from a woman (whose name was Kiandoxshan) and her daughter, who were laboring in the field, they bought for twenty dollars a house close to the river. It was May the 23rd. Two days later the five of them moved in. Anthony Wallace describes the house they selected as a "typical Seneca house made of unchinked logs, twenty feet long by fourteen wide, with a shed before the door and a bark roof. Two rows of bunks and shelves extended along the sides; deerskins with the hair on served as mattresses." [6]

It had always been understood that Pierce and Sharpless would be staying only long enough to see the mission established; and, in fact, the two did actually depart on June 7, after a little over two weeks of assisting in the organization. The farm that was to serve as a model or a demonstration farm was pretty well into operation by that fall. Known simply as "The Farm," it was intended as an example for the Indians of just what could be done with the land, an operation which could demonstrate for them the white man's techniques in agriculture.

On up the river there was another village, and with some scattered homes outside of Cornplanter Town the total number of Senecas to be served by the mission amounted to something like 400.[7]

One of the three missionaries who remained, Henry Simmons, left the "elegant" two-story house they had just built and in which they had lived only six weeks, and moved into Cornplanter Town in November, in order to provide formal schooling for the Senecas, young and old alike. He began his teaching, in Cornplanter's house, on November 23.[8] Simmons was thirty years old at the time, and he became at once a popular and much sought after friend to the Senecas. Happily, he kept a journal,[9] which, though not a day-by-day account, provides *lots* of information on the events of the year he served the village.

February 3, 1799, which was a Sunday, found him in Cornplanter's home, with the chief's son Henry and "about a dozen other Indians" present. When the company expressed a great interest in the creation of the world and how things were in the beginning, Simmons launched into an account of Genesis, referring to the Lord as the Great Spirit. He recited the story of Cain and Abel, and inquired whether the Indians did "not see it so nowadays—that wicked people envied good ones, and at times were ready to take their lives."

He explained that the Great Spirit had made the world in six days and that then He rested from his labors, so that the seventh day now is intended as a day of rest and worship. He stressed reverence, perhaps unnecessarily. And then he turned to conscience. He spoke of good people and bad. He asked the Indians whether it was not so that when they contemplated the doing of something wrong they would "feel something pricking at their hearts." He reports in his journal entry for this day that "several of the chiefs, including Cornplanter, confessed it was the very truth; they had experienced it so." The young Quaker missionary then declared that it was "the Great Spirit who pricks our hearts and tells us not to do wrong. It is the devil who urges us to do wrong."

Simmons explained on this occasion that one of the great advantages for the person who had learned to read was that he would now be able to peruse "the good book" for himself and sense the truth of it. He spoke at length of the need for education, and was pleased to find that after this meeting the size of his school had increased dramatically. He noted that while some of the Indians were most eager to learn, the instructing is "very tedious." He confided to his journal that "this keeps me faithful in teaching them, so much so that at times I have been almost weary in well doing." [10]

On the Monday eight days later, Simmons reports to his journal: "Cornplanter and two of his sons came up early in the morning, to the house where I lodged. Cornplanter said they had come to talk about something in particular, which was as follows. They had lately received an express from the Buffalo Indians regarding a dream that one of their little girls had had. She had dreamed that the devil was in all white people alike, and that the Quakers were doing no good among them, but otherwise. She had also related that it was not right for the Indian children to learn to read and write." Cornplanter reported to Simmons that after the village had had this news he had convened a council, which had been yesterday, Sunday, February 10. He advised the missionary that while "many of his people were so foolish as to believe the dream was true, for many of them put great confidence in their dreams," [11] he himself did not at all believe it, "and had got very tired of hearing so much noise about their dreams." Simmons remembered that Chief Cornplanter hoped that he (Simmons) would not be discouraged by all of this. He assured Simmons that he fully intended "to make his people do better."

Most interesting is Simmons' response to Cornplanter, as recorded in his journal: "I told him I did not feel at all uneasy about the dream because I thought I knew from whence it had originated. I knew that Farmer's Brother and others of the Buffalo Indians were much injured and set against the Quakers by the instigation of some bad white people at Buffalo. Cornplanter said that was very true."

When Simmons equated the work of the Quakers with the will of the Great Spirit, and lamented that they had to contend with the devil, Cornplanter declared that "some of the white people were as much to blame as the Indians for the devil's frequent interference." He noted for Simmons that "When these white people wanted to get Indian land, they would go to some of the most dissolute and disreputable Indian individuals, and make a bargain with them first, and afterwards apply to the chiefs to honor the deal." Simmons declared that he certainly "believed that to be true" and assured Cornplanter that he would work earnestly to lead these bad men to the Great Spirit, who "would open their eyes and enlighten their understanding."

For the middle of February he reported a decline in the school's enrollment, but was most pleased to discover that by the end of the month it had recovered and then some.

The journal entry for February 27 brings the reader to an altogether new and, for Simmons, a most distressing subject. At this time he is complaining to Cornplanter about the Indians' love of dancing. These dances, which he calls frolics, he finds (not surprisingly) most annoying, because, first, they are "evil" and "wicked," and, because, second, they are terribly disruptive to his school, and because, third, there are *so many* of them. His indignation is disguised not at all. And in great anguish he recorded his feeling in his journal.

This day (Feb. 27), he declared had proved "very trying and painful." The preparation for the "frolic" had interrupted his schooling and the dance itself, with its shouting and wild carrying on was clearly the work of the devil. When he entered Cornplanter's house, in which Henry and most of the family were sitting quietly, he complained vigorously, and expressed the hope that he "might never see any more of it among them." Cornplanter simply said that he could say nothing of it now but would on the next day.

True to his word, Cornplanter did conduct a discussion of the subject the very next morning, and when Simmons arrived at Cornplanter's house on this morning to teach school in that half of the house which was reserved for the sessions, he was asked to wait for the conclusion of the council. "As I sat there, the subject of poor Mordecai, sitting at the king's gate waiting to see how the matter would go, was vividly brought to my remembrance. After a while I was called in, and went with great willingness, though in much fear." With the interpreter present, probably Cornplanter's son Henry, the conclusion of the council was reported to Simmons. It was not perhaps all that the missionary had hoped, but it must have pleased him. Cornplanter, whom Simmons sometimes refers to as "the old chief," let him know that though "they did not all see alike," they had agreed "to quit such dancing frolics." For some of them the chief explained, the dancing had to be considered, like "rum and whiskey and getting drunk," an evil habit, inasmuch as they had learned it from white people. The Indians did determine to continue the twice-a-year play and dance, which was strictly an Indian custom.

On this same day another very delicate subject came up, one that must have excited keen interest in Cornplanter. It was the practice of the mixed marriage. Simmons was asked for his opinion, whether "it was right for Indians and white people to mix in marrying." They reported that one of their women had had a child by a white man who was a resident of Pittsburgh, and they were complaining that he "never came to see anything about his child." All of this must have come sorely home to Cornplanter, whose father had behaved likewise. Simmons answered by noting that it was a very tough question. It might be right for some, he said, but not for me.

Other questions posed for Simmons he answered smartly. To whether white people and Indians arrive at the same place after death, he replied that there were but two places, one for the good and one for the bad, of all nations. To whether the dead would all commune in the same language, he answered in the affirmative, and noted that "They seemed satisfied."

While he had a captive audience, on this last day of the month in the dead of winter, Simmons, through the interpreter, delivered a long lecture, one that lasted into the early evening. He inveighed against many of the customs he considered evil, but "particularly that of dancing and shouting in such a hideous manner." Some of those present had not heard him the evening before, and he thought as he trudged wearily to his lodging that he had done some good this day.

How very much Cornplanter appreciated the presence of the Quakers, and just how much confidence he had in Simmons as a teacher, is apparent from the missionary's journal entry for the very next day, March 1. On this day, the old chief, with two of his sons, probably Charles and William, came to his abode expressly to express their great regard for his teaching and his wholesome influence over the children. "He seemed, in a manner, willing to resign his own commission to me."

Simmons was present when Cornplanter dispatched nine of his men to Buffalo to collect the annuity money that was due them (that provided by the Treaty of Big Tree, September 15, 1797). These men were back in Cornplanter Town in a fortnight with $1560, as well as some materials which were regularly provided by the British in return for the Seneca allegiance during the War of the Revolution. Not long after their return, when the money and goods were being divided, Simmons was asked to attend a council, "because they had something they wanted me to read for them." After he had read as requested, "I was pressed in Spirit to caution them against spending their money for strong drink and other unnecessary articles." Of course Cornplanter, who only rarely partook of alcohol, and would even decline to attend councils at which he expected alcohol to flow, was constantly appealing to them in this way. The *Pennsylvania Archives* contain a letter addressed by the chief to President Washington, and delivered at some time in 1791. For a long time Cornplanter had been disturbed by the way in which alcohol was coming into the life of his village, and he was constantly complaining about this "evil habit" and the place it had in the bartering carried on by whites and Indians. In this letter he applauded the President for endorsing his view, and he declared his support: "And we thank you for the care you have taken to prevent bad men coming to trade among us; if any come without your license, we will turn them back; and we hope that our nation will determine to spill all the rum which shall, hereafter, be brought to our towns." [12]

On Cornplanter's regard for alcohol a letter composed by Judge Samuel P. Johnson of Warren should be of great interest. The letter was inspired by the appearance in the Oil City *Derrick* of an article on the subject of the grant made to Cornplanter of the land on which Oil City at that time was standing (the 400 acres at the mouth of Oil Creek). The article had appeared in the March 2, 1878, issue of the *Derrick.* Judge Johnson was outraged by what he read. In his letter to the editor of the paper, he declared that his "chief object in noticing the article in question is to refute a most atrocious libel upon the memory of [Cornplanter] contained in it." Here is the Judge on the writer of the article:

> *In a sentence composed both of bad English and slang he charges the Cornplanter with getting drunk and losing his land [the Oil Creek tract] in consequence. It reads thus: "Like many of his prototypes of the present day, Cornplanter was addicted to a free indulgence in budge and in one of his drunken frolics, as stated, sold the land which is now so valuable for a mere trifle." Nothing could be more untrue than this. All histories of Cornplanter, tradition and my own personal knowledge of the illustrious chief support the fact that he was the original temperance man of Western Pennsylvania, the life long and persistent enemy of the white man's "fire water," and not only abstained himself but did everything in his power to discourage its use and prevent its introduction among his people. He was the pioneer of total abstinence and even anterior to the present century, appealed to the Governor of the State for aid in the suppression of traffic among his tribe. So far from selling his Oil creek land in a drunken frolic, for a trifle, he sold it for its then full value[13] to two respectable citizens of Venango County, whom I could name and once well knew,[14] who took his deed and gave*

> *him their note for the purchase money, which notes were not paid.* [15]

Although he was not himself certainly a total teetotaler, there really can be no question about Cornplanter's position on alcohol. Time and time again he vented his disgust, even his rage. But Cornplanter and the authorities were virtually helpless to stem the tide much, and in March of this very year (1799), as Swatzler notes, a disappointed Cornplanter registered his extreme displeasure. In a letter dictated to Simmons, which the chief requested him to deliver to the territory's Indian Agent (Israel Chapin of Canandaigua), he censured the Agent for his failure to "suppress that evil habit among them." [16] Alcohol, despite the very helpful influence of the Quakers, was always to remain one of Cornplanter's biggest concerns.

"About the middle of May," as Simmons recalled, "a party of Cornplanter's Indians returned from Pittsburgh with a quantity of whiskey that caused much drunkenness among them, which lasted for several weeks [!] and was the means of some of their deaths [!]. One old woman perished outdoors in the night season with a bottle at her side." Simmons of course was appalled. It was total debauchery, and there was no end to it. "Numbers of them would go about the village, from morning until evening and from evening until morning, in a noisy distracted condition, sometimes fighting each other. They would enter other people's houses in a detestable manner, ready to pull others out of their beds. They even did so in the very house where I myself lodged—and in the dead of the night too!"

The missionaries did not throw up their hands in despair. They were not giving up, but clearly something needed to be done, and the sooner the better. "Their deplorable condition by reason of that destructive article of strong drink," they declared, "greatly augmented our concern and exercise for the promotion of their present and future happiness. So much so, that we were desirous of having them collected in council." Finally, Simmons was able to arrange a date for that sole purpose, and of this he informed his companions (Halliday Jackson and Joel Swayne, who lived at the farm), and all three attended the council. Simmons remembers that "I was—I think—divinely favored to communicate some pertinent and judicious counsel to them on various subjects, to the furtherance of civilization and their future well-being."

The Indians took a number of days to mull over this counsel they had received from their Quaker friends, and by and by another council was convened. By this time Jackson and Swayne had returned to Genesinguhta, but Cornplanter was present and delivered quite a speech. Even though he could not write down a half of it, Simmons was able to record in his journal the chief elements. Cornplanter, noting that the Indians had made inquiry and had "conversed with each other about us," declared that they could not find any fault with the Quaker missionaries. They had agreed that the three were "just and upright" in all their ways and in their proceedings with them. They acknowledged that the fault and the responsibility for bad conduct lay on their (the Indians') side. "They wished us to be easy in our minds, for they would take our advice and try to learn to do better. They had concluded with a resolution not to suffer any more whiskey to be brought among them to be sold." To insure that this resolve would be carried out, "they had chosen two young men as petty chiefs, to have some oversight of their people in the promotion of good among them. They intended to take up work, and do as we said, and would assist their wives and women on the labor of the field." [!]

After the summary remarks by Cornplanter, it became Simmons' turn. Allowing a few minutes to pass, during which he brought order to his thoughts, the young Quaker stood up. It was a dramatic moment. Here, if the Indians were sincere, and if the influence of Cornplanter could be made to count, was a big opportunity to do damage to the devil's arsenal. In the familiar council way, Simmons first declared that he had listened patiently and with great attention to their words and assured them he would remember them for a long time. To his journal he confided that "I felt my heart truly thankful to the Great Spirit for their new resolve. And I felt newly encouraged to persevere in every branch of good instruction to them that I was capable of. Also I had an earnest hope of seeing their own words verified, which would more and more encourage us who were working among them. I told them that if they lived up to their words, it would also encourage our Friends at home, to whom we wrote frequently letting them know what progress is being made among our Indian brethren, etc."

It was a pretty speech, and Cornplanter was happy to hear it. The chief then covered the council fire, and "thus it ended."

Not long after the conclusion of this council, the Indians came together in one of their traditional worship dances. Simmons' description is vivid and most interesting; and certainly he is not critical of *this* kind of dance, which he calls a worship dance, and which Swatzler believes to have been the feather dance, "performed as part of the annual Corn Planting Ceremonial." The dance had at its center the statue of Tarachiawagon, which presided over the arena in front of Cornplanter's house, as we know from Adlum's description and from that of Anthony Wallace. As Swatzler notes, the image, some three years after this occasion, finally surrendered to age, and collapsed to the ground. Cornplanter's son Henry, who was given charge of this sacred relic, consigned it to the waters of the Allegheny River.[17]

Simmons observed the dance from beginning to end:

> *Men, women, and children wearing their best apparel were dancing in a circle around their wooden image, or God. There seemed to be no designated dancers. Those who had a mind to step into the ring, did so, facing toward the image. Two men were seated flat on the ground, face to face within the circle, engaged with musical instruments. Their instruments were gourd shell water turtle, dried with the entrails out, and bullets, shot, or corn in the place thereof. They beat these on a deerskin lying on the ground, making a very great rattle. The men in the circle, always moving round at a slow pace, dance and shout greatly. The women dance chiefly by keeping their feet set close together and moving them sideways, first the toes and then the heels, as they move round with the men. The women, however, remain silent. After they had taken two heats at dance, their minister, who was a very lusty Indian, said it was enough, and thanked them.* [18]

It was not long after, about a week, thinks Simmons, that the Indians assembled for a great feast, out of reverence for the dead of the village. "The present one," writes Simmons, "was being held on account of the old chief's [Cornplanter's] daughter, who had been dead upwards of four months." This daughter must have been the daughter taken very seriously ill about a year before the time of this remembrance feast. Cornplanter, Swatzler reports, had declined to accompany the Quakers John Pierce and Joshua Sharpless on a mission to Buffalo, lamenting "that one of his daughters had been taken very bad, and was likely to die." [19]

All of which brings the reader to another subject, the Seneca's great fear of witches and the practice of witch hunting. It is not clear to just what extent the "old chief" Cornplanter believed in witches, but he apparently did believe that a "bad woman" of the village had been responsible for the death of his daughter the previous winter. And when he heard that this woman had threatened to take the life of one of the children who lived in his house (presumably a grandchild) he either hinted that it would be well to kill her, or he actually ordered her death. The Quaker Halliday Jackson reported that it was Cornplanter's sons (Henry Simmons later used the figure "3") who fell upon the old woman in the fields and with knives slashed her to death:

> *And it came to pass in those days that a certain woman of the Heathen dwelt in the Village of Corn planter whom they suspected to have a familiar Spirrit, because they say she had done much mischief by Poison and by Witchcraft. And there was enmity between her and the house of Corn-planter the Chief, and [here seven words are crossed out] there was a young Child in his house, and the woman of a familiar Spirit threatened to Slay the Young Child [some five words crossed out] and when a messenger came and told these things in the ears of Corn-planter the Chief, his Indignation was raised against the woman, and he commanded his sons, and while she was labouring in the Field [20] they rose up against her and smote [word Aslew" crossed out] her that she died, and they digged a hole in the Earth and put her therein for there was no mourning over her. Now when this thing was noised abroad there was no small stir amongst the People and it came to pass the self same day that the Chiefs and counsellors of the people assembled together concerning this matter, and when they reasoned together they said one unto another that Justice had been done to the Woman because she was found worthy of Death, and in order to do away evil from among the people and put away those of Familiar Spirrits out of the Land.* [21]

Cornplanter's son Henry was at this time twenty-five years old, Charles was nineteen, and William was eighteen.

The council that was held in consequence of the commotion was common practice in such affairs, the old woman receiving trial *after* her death. Cornplanter, not surprisingly, was exonerated by the council, it being concluded that the old woman was a "bad" woman and deserved to die. The date of the murder was June 13, 1799.

When the news of this summary execution reached Henry Simmons, he, strangely, seemed but little disturbed. He was far from faulting Chief Cornplanter: "By command of the old chief, three of his men [He does not say "sons."] took the life of a woman, with knives. They supposed that she was a witch or that she had poisoned others, and that she had threatened the day before to do the like again. This threat reached Cornplanter's ears. However worthy of death she might have been, I know not, but I took her to be a bad woman."[22]

Not very long after this council was concluded, June 15, occurred one of the most momentous events in the long life of Chief Cornplanter, indeed one of the most consequential events in the entire history of the Seneca Nation. It was the "death" and "resurrection" of Handsome Lake.

Handsome Lake (*Sganyadai:yo, Kon-ne-at-or-tee-ooh, Ganiodaio*— "It is a very large lake.") was many years older than Cornplanter. They were born of the same mother, into the Wolf Clan, at Ganawaugus, and had always been very close. Together with Old Smoke and Kayahsotha, they represented the Senecas at the Great Council of Oswego. Together they stood for neutrality, and when the Senecas were drawn into allegiance with the British, they fought fiercely to put down the rebellion for the Crown. Shoulder to shoulder they fought at Oriskany, at Wyoming, and in the raids on Fort Freeland, Canajoharie, and the Schoharie Valley. Handsome Lake, with his family, had accompanied Cornplanter when at some time after 1780, the chief elected to leave Ganawaugus for the Allegheny River and the region of their uncle Kayahsotha. In Cornplanter Town Handsome Lake, with his family, lived in the home of Cornplanter, and served the village as an herbalist. He accompanied Cornplanter to a number of the treaty sessions, including Canandaigua and Big Tree.

But during the years 1780-1799, Handsome Lake was little more than a reprobate, trading pelts in Pittsburgh for whiskey. He gradually surrendered his life to alcohol, and eventually became destroyed by strong drink. He could be found most of the time in a drunken stupor, a dissolute and useless man. Indeed, during the years 1795-1799, he was so wasted away that he lived as an invalid in Cornplanter's home, tended by members of both families, and particularly by his daughter and by her husband. Needless to report, Cornplanter at this time was much disappointed in his half-brother.

Many are the accounts of Handsome Lake's "dying." [23] And while details vary slightly, all accounts have their roots in the versions supplied by Blacksnake, who participated in the drama, and by Henry Simmons, who is a close observer. Blacksnake's account of this astounding event was dictated to his neighbor Benjamin Williams some forty-five years after its occurrence, which was August 8-10, 1799. In it, Blacksnake, who was living in the village at the time, described the dying of Handsome Lake, the intent on his burial, the recognition that the old warrior's heart was beating faintly, and in great detail the vision experienced by Handsome Lake.[24]

What follows in Blacksnake's account is a catalog of the twelve Commandments as Handsome Lake understood them from the visiting angels. These Commandments, the product of his vision, he resolutely determined to preach. And he did so, for the next ten years at Cornplanter Town, and after that for two years at Cold Springs, just upriver from Cornplanter Town, and after that at Tonawanda, for four years.

Now a reformed man, at age sixty-five, he became a passionate and persuasive speaker, urging on his people a new religion. What he taught is sometimes called the Code of Handsome Lake; it is sometimes known as the Longhouse Religion. Its principal tenets were abstinence from alcohol, "the worst of evils," the use of witchcraft for medicinal purposes only, the evil of vanity, the need for family values, and the preservation of the Indian ceremonies and rituals. Handsome Lake in his preaching also encouraged his people to adopt such of the white man's ways as would advance their happiness. He favored formal schooling, for boys anyway; and farming in the white man's fashion.[25]

Henry Simmons had a lot to report to his journal about Handsome Lake's fantastic experience. He tells us how Cornplanter learned of it: "Cornplanter was about three fourths of a mile from his home, where he had men employed to build him a house, and where we were engaged in erecting a schoolhouse. An express came to him that his brother or step brother was dying, who had been on the decline of life for several years. Cornplanter went straightway and found a number of his people convened where his brother had been lying breathless for the space of half an hour. But about two hours later, his brother came to himself again and told Cornplanter how he was feeling and informed him of what he had seen . . . ." As in Blacksnake's account he envisions the three messengers. These advise him that the Great Spirit is much distressed by the drunkenness of the villagers, "and with other gross evils of which they are guilty." The messengers tell Handsome Lake that they "will not charge him with anything except sometimes getting drunk," which he must not do again. They tell him that there are bad people among them and that while one has recently been killed, another, a man, remains. A council must be called.

In fact, a council was called for that very same day. Both Henry Simmons and his companion Joel Swayne attended. During the session, because he felt "the love of God flowing powerfully among us," Simmons felt a call to counsel the Indians. When he had done so, Cornplanter's sister-in-law thanked him for what he had said.

Simmons relates that a fourth messenger later appeared to Handsome Lake, and that this visitor asked the sick man to go with him. After he had dressed, Handsome Lake expressed a desire to see his brother Cornplanter, and Cornplanter came to him and sat with him, "through the course of the day." That evening Handsome Lake fainted dead away, but on awaking, told his brother that he must go with the messenger. He expected to return, but he hoped to see his son, "who had been dead for several years, and Cornplanter's daughter, who had been dead about seven months."

Handsome Lake then "died," and remained lifeless for about seven hours. "His legs and arms were cold; the rest of his body was warm but breathless." When he returned from this state, he related how the fourth messenger had appeared before him as a guide. He appeared "to have a bow and arrow, and was dressed in sky blue." He was advised by the guide to look forward. When he did so, he perceived the two whom he had expected, Cornplanter's daughter and his own son, who were dressed as was the messenger. And then from Handsome Lake's remembrance of his vision emerged this illuminating insight into Cornplanter's family: "Cornplanter's daughter expressed her sorrow that her brother Henry frequently disputed with his father. Sometimes their arguments were so heated [remembers the daughter], that they became very angry at each other. Her brother always thought he knew more than his father, whose advice he would never take. Henry always insisted on having his own way, which was very wrong. The guide then told her to stop because he wanted to say something. He said that she had spoken correctly in describing Henry's abuse of their father, Cornplanter. Henry should obey his father for as long as Cornplanter continued to live."

In the second scene, Handsome Lake is addressed by his own dead son, who (1) expresses great concern over his father's suffering, and (2) laments that his brother, who is still living, does not attend on his father better.

The guide then summarized the message that had been delivered Handsome Lake by the first three angels. He reminded him that the one fault they definitely had to note was his habit of getting drunk. "But they could forgive him because he had now declined liquor for some time and because he had resolved that if he got well, he would never touch the stuff again. However, he must quit all kinds of frolics and dancing, except their worship dance. To dance in worship was right because the people did not make use of any liquor . . . ." The guide urged Handsome Lake to look toward the river, and when he did, "he saw many canoes loaded with kegs of whiskey. [This obviously recalls the mid-May voyage up the Allegheny from Pittsburgh and the one-week drunken rampage in which Handsome Lake was central.] He also saw an ugly fellow, whom [sic] the guide told him was the devil, going about very busy doing and making all the noise and mischief he could among the people."

In Simmons's account the guide next explained to Handsome Lake about dreams and how to respond to them. He next indicated that if the white people wanted to supply schooling that would be all right; and if the Indians preferred to stick to their old ways, "then they had no business drinking whiskey because that belongs to white people and was not made for Indians." The guide then launched into some prophecies, one of which was that Handsome Lake "might soon get well, if his people took good care of him and gave him medicine." He said, further, that Handsome Lake should not expect to see the four messengers again, not until he died.

Having heard all of this, Cornplanter naturally wondered what to make of it. Accordingly he called a council, to which Simmons was invited. Simmons, apparently expecting to be questioned on the validity of Handsome Lake's vision, listened attentively to the retelling of the whole story, and to the discussion which followed. When he was asked whether he believed it all to be true, "I told them there had been instances of the same kind among white people, even among the Quakers. Someone would fall into a trance, and see both the good place and the bad place and many other wonderful sights." He declared that he did indeed believe these visions. "And I told them I could see no reason why it should not be the case with the Indians also, as we are all one of one flesh and blood made by the Great Spirit." Simmons said a little more "to the same purport," and was pleased that the Indians "appeared satisfied."

That afternoon the Indians sacrificed a white dog and ate of it with great delight. There was singing, and lots of shouting too, as they danced around the fire in which the skin of the white dog had been consumed.

When on the next morning Simmons went over to Cornplanter's house, in order to make some notes on the experience, he found the old chief in a talkative mood. While acknowledging that he liked some of the practices of the white man, he continued to like the old ways of the Indians as well. He thought, for example, that the worship dance, which was held twice a year, should be preserved. He thought that since they could not read and had no Scriptures to peruse, the sacred dances provided their best means of worshiping the Great Spirit.

According to Simmons, Cornplanter in the presence of several other Indians "further said it was the white people who had killed our Savior. How he had heard about our Savior, I know not. But, it seems, he had. I told him it was the Jews who crucified, or killed, him, and whether they were white, red, or black or what color they were of, I knew not. Neither did I know but that the Indians were their descendants, for many of the Indians' habits were similar to those practiced by the Jews in former days. Yet I told him that, nevertheless, we were all still crucifying and killing him—whenever we were doing wickedly. He [Cornplanter] said that was very true, very true."

As to the vision of Handsome Lake, Cornplanter was willing to accept what it seemed to imply about the Indians' way of life. Certainly he was strong against alcohol. And he was strong for education. And he was happy to have Handsome Lake allow in his preaching for the adoption of the white man's ways in agriculture. He was okay too at this time with the attitude toward witches that was taught by the Code. For about ten years Cornplanter affirmed the preaching of his half-brother Handsome Lake. In time his enthusiasm would be tempered.

For the remainder of that August, 1799, Simmons records the normal activities of the Indians, their councils and festivals, the corn harvest, the hunting of deer, and the big worship dance of August 30. But he continued unhappy with the grotesque dancing, with the idolatry, and with the conspicuous vanity, which flew in the face of Handsome Lake's moral code. Accordingly, he requested of Cornplanter a council. He hoped to accomplish two things. He wanted to alert the Indians to his leaving, which he expected would occur in a month or two. And he hoped that the farewell could be affectionate and "brotherly." Second, he meant to make the most of the occasion, taking advantage of Handsome Lake's experience, to repeat the advice he had been for almost a year now so free with.

Just before they closed down their two-day lottery game, which likewise displeased Simmons, the Indians sent word to the missionary that they were just about ready to convene a council at which he would be most welcome. As he arrived at Cornplanter's house, the site of all councils, Simmons discovered "about fifty men" standing "in a longitude direction, opposite their wooden image," and firing their guns two or three times upwards "toward the sun."

Then all that could fit therein crowded into Cornplanter's house, leaving great numbers assembled outside. Cornplanter and the Indians' minister each spoke, delivering long but "pretty" addresses. Both urged the Indians to sit still and to listen patiently to what "our friend" has to say. Simmons was most gratified to find the sometimes restless audience "very quiet and solid." In fact, he was much moved. "Indeed, I felt the divine power spread over the gathering, in a very conspicuous manner, to the washing of my face with tears."

But he was blunt with them. "I encouraged them to press forward toward happiness, not only in this life, but in that which is to come. I also set forth my disunity with their vain and idolatrous way of worshiping the Great Spirit. I fully believed that the manner in which they acted was displeasing to him—even though it was their forefathers' custom. I believed there was a loud call to them to come forth and learn better."

When they declared that they thought they should keep up their father's customs, Simmons asked why it was that they were so unwilling to part with some of their customs, at least those which are so obviously injurious, "as that of strong drink." Simmons also referred to their extravagant adornments and superfluous clothes. He suggested that their forefathers were glad "to get skins to cover themselves with." This provoked raucous laughter from some in the crowd, although surely not from the unflappable Cornplanter.

At the conclusion of his remarks, Simmons was accorded a very polite, respectful pause, before various Indians began to speak. They noted that the young missionary had been with them a great while, and they declared they thought him a good man, one who was always willing "to do what was right among them." They thanked him profusely for the service he had done them, remarked how glad they were that he and his companions had been blessed throughout by good health. They "desired that the Great Spirit might conduct me safe home," and they urged Simmons to write to them. "They then took me by the hand and we parted like brothers."

This was September 2. That afternoon Halliday Jackson came down the ten miles from the farm at Genesinguhta, and stayed over with Simmons until the next day.

About a week later, September 11, when Simmons was at his new school building, a company of Friends arrived from Philadelphia, altogether without notice, but in "mutual heartfelt joy." In number these Quaker missionaries were seventeen (!). Among the delegation was William Savery, who had served the Senecas so well at the Treaty of Canandaigua All made their way to the farm at Genesinguhta, where they remained for three days. On September 14, all returned by canoe to Cornplanter Town, "in order to sit with the Indians in council." With all assembled in Cornplanter's house, the old chief and his son Henry both rose to thank the Quakers for coming and to pronounce their readiness to hear what the Friends had to deliver.

There was then read to the Indians the formal "certificate." It was addressed to "the Indians at Genesinguhta and the neighborhood thereof." And it was a most cordial message that was delivered. Presumably Henry Abeel served as interpreter: "Brothers, it is now a considerable time since three of our young men settled among you. They came here because of a desire to be serviceable to you, to instruct you in farming and such other useful ways of the white people as would enable you to live comfortably on the lands which the Good Spirit has permitted you to enjoy. To do this, they left behind their comfortable homes, kind and beloved connections and friends. They came here to live with you in the wilderness."

And then, "Brothers, to see how our young men fare and what progress you make in learning from them, our Friends, Joshua Sharpless, Isaac Coats, Thomas Stewardson, and James Cooper, propose visiting you now, Brothers. As these our brethren are true men, beloved by us, and have your welfare much at heart, we hope you will receive them as such and attend to what advice they may give you."

The document was signed "on behalf of the people called Quakers of Pennsylvania, New Jersey, etc. By your Friends and Brothers."

A second address was delivered to the Indians: "Brothers, you have now heard that our coming here was to see how you and our young men, who live among you, are getting along. We are glad the Good Spirit has favored us to meet you in health, and [has] given us the opportunity of taking you by the hand, and brightening the chain of friendship. Now brothers, we should like to hear from your own mouths whether or not you are entirely satisfied with our young men being among you. They came here with a hope of being useful by instructing you in a better way of managing your land and providing for yourselves and your cattle. We desire you to speak freely."

Then the delegation, who had been going about the town and the model farm, in their address took note of the progress that they had observed, remarking on the cleared land, the warmer houses, the increase in the number of cattle, and the new fencing, and providing some advice on the harvesting of corn, the clearing of even more land, the need to plant wheat (which provides straw), etc.[26]

And of course it could not have been a sufficient lecture without some mention of the evils of hard drink. Here they heard again what they had been hearing constantly from Henry Simmons for a year now: "Brothers, we understand you are desirous to discourage whiskey from being brought among you, with which we are much pleased, and should be glad you could entirely keep it away. For, to get whiskey, you give your money, which you should use instead to buy clothes and to buy oxen and plows with which to work your land. And, besides, the whiskey does not do you any good."

Before any real reply was made to the delegation, the Indians wondered whether Simmons might be persuaded to stay on. The missionary explained that as it was right for him to come among them it was right for him to return home; but all will be determined by the Friends who are here with us now. The Indians assembled for the council then reported that they had talked among themselves about the Quaker mission, and "could not find fault against us. Rather, we were always doing what was right among them, etc." Cornplanter himself was quick to speak up. He declared that "I [Simmons] had been a great help to him, particularly in endeavoring to prevent so much whiskey from coming into their town." He complained that "if I went away he would have nobody there to help him."

During a recess the members of the delegation consulted with Simmons on his plans to return home, and it was agreed that if he felt it his duty to depart then he should do it. To the Indians who remained it was announced by Joshua Sharpless that Simmons would indeed be leaving. Cornplanter, obviously disappointed, said that he would not plead against the decision, and then expressed his desire to "accompany me through the Indian settlements as far as Canandaigua." He was happy with the business that had been accomplished. "So we took each other by the hands, all around."

The Friends returned to Genesinguhta that same day and after three more days at the farm set out for Canada "to visit the members of our Society scattered there."

It was time too for Henry Simmons to say goodbye. October the 6th was a Sunday: "Today I took my final farewell of many of the Indians at Cornplanter's village, some of whom appeared very sorry about my departing from them. I set forward in a canoe up the river about nine miles to Genesinguhta, our settlement, where my companions resided. Some of the principal men came there to see me start in the morning." And next morning, Henry Simmons, after more than a year among the Senecas of Cornplanter's community, took "solemn leave" of his two companions, Halliday Jackson and Joel Swayne, and bade farewell to the Indians who had come to see him off. "I set out with Cornplanter and several others. . . ." [27]

Cornplanter, who was committed to a meeting with Israel Chapin, then serving as Superintendent of Indian Affairs in the administration of John Adams, had agreed to accompany Simmons as far as Canandaigua, where Chapin was headquartered. And this he did, much to the pleasure of the young Quaker, who always saw Cornplanter most respectfully as "the old chief." Cornplanter had always hoped for much from the Quakers, whose character, with its passion for the humane and the right, he admired and respected immensely. He had hoped for schooling for his people, both in their villages and in the East; he had hoped for instruction in agriculture and in "the useful arts of the white people"; he had hoped for support at the treaty and bargaining sessions; and he had hoped for protection from exploitation by the unsavory characters and the wheelers and dealers, who frequented Pittsburgh and Wheeling. Now, as he said goodbye to his young friend, who had been through so much with him, he was deeply moved. In Henry Simmons he saw all that he expected of the Quaker.

Swatzler quotes a letter that Cornplanter, in the Canandaigua sessions, dispatched via Chapin to the Indian Committee of the Philadelphia Yearly Meeting. In it he voices his great regard for Simmons and his fellows, and expresses his gratitude for their conscientious service: "I thank the Great Spirit for his protection in preserving me and my Friend whom I have accompanied to this place. I hope the Great Spirit will still preserve my Friend on his journey to Philadelphia, and every evening when night shall overtake him, that the Great Spirit will spread over him the curtain of safety, that he may again meet the Society that sent him among us for the purpose of teaching us the useful arts of the white people. And that he may return to them my kind thanks for the kind offices they are disposed to bestow on us. I cannot omit this favorable opportunity to inform Friends that I believe the young men placed at the Allegheny have discharged the trust committed to them in endeavoring to do the best they could for our advantage." [28]

XXI

HANDSOME LAKE AND RED JACKET

Not long after the death of Cornplanter's daughter, the chief suffered another similar crisis. This event concerned his daughter Jiiwi, and it excited an incredibly perilous situation between the Cornplanter Senecas and the Munsees (Muncys) of the Cattaraugus region.

Apparently, if long-lived legend can be believed, a young Munsee chief named Silver Heels (In some versions of the story he is John Logan.) was the precipitator. Silver Heels was a member of the Munsee band of hunters which, with Cornplanter's customary permission, had been hunting in the Allegheny River basin, considered Allegheny River Seneca hunting grounds. Silver Heels, who for perhaps as much as two weeks altogether was lodged, both going and coming, in Cornplanter's house, apparently became intimate with Jiiwi. The result was (1) pregnancy, and (2) a mysterious illness that assaulted the young woman just after the birth of her child, in the fall of 1800.

Handsome Lake, who had been prevailed upon by Cornplanter to divine the cause of her illness, failed miserably both in diagnosing the condition and in arresting its progress. Not surprisingly, as the young mother grew steadily more ill, he hinted at witchcraft. It was enough for a community that had been hearing a lot lately about witchcraft. A Munsee chief was promptly taken prisoner, held as a hostage, and threatened with death should Jiiwi die. To what extent Cornplanter himself was responsible for this action is not known, but certainly it could not have happened without at least his tacit approval. What he appreciated only too late was that blaming the Munsee people for the illness of his daughter and declaring a life for a life could only antagonize the Munsee nation. Indeed, as the Chief was made to recognize, the prospect of war between the Allegheny Senecas and the Cattaraugus Munsees loomed very real.

Anxious now, not only about Jiiwi, but about the consequences if she were to die and the Munsee chief were to be killed in retribution, he called a council. The consensus was expressed in concern; and the Seneca leaders determined to seek advice from Cussawaga (Meadville), and particularly from David Mead, the community's founder. Cornplanter had visited with the Meads frequently from the time they first arrived in the region and was very close to David Mead. Happy with the Council's decision, the Chief promptly (This is in April.) addressed a very long letter to his longtime friend. "To David Meads and others of the respectable inhabitants of Cussawageh" he carefully detailed the whole story, and closed with, "Therefore we intreat you to Consider our difficulty and remember former friendships, and send us your answer as soon as covenant (convenient)."

The letter then is signed by eleven principals of the community, Cornplanter first, and Henry Abeel last. It was witnessed by Joseph Gray, of Warren County, and William Wilsib, and signed finally by Henry York, who must have provided the English language.[1]

Mead's response was prompt and curt, and very plain. He insisted that peace *must* be maintained. "Do not kill the hostage."

Not long after, on April 11, after the Muncy Indians had seen Mead's reply to Cornplanter's letter, the Muncy Nation filed with David Mead or Samuel Lord, esqs, an "Application of the Chieftains of the Muncy Nation of Indians for a friendly interposition of the Governor between them and the Seneca Nation." The letter comes from Cattaraugus and is addressed to David Mead and other friends: "Brothers, We have Reciv[d] your letter directed to CORNPLANTER & other chiefs and warriors of the Seneca Nation: We learn you was appointed by your people to carry the CORNPLANTER'S letter to the Governor of Pennsylvania [Thomas McKean] with the string of wampum a full account of the dispute with our Nation." Then the Muncy chiefs declared their intent for peace, and urged Mead's help in settling the dispute and making us all Brothers once again.

The letter is signed by two principal chiefs of the Muncy Nation and thirteen altogether, including White Seneca, Old Fish, Old Snake, and Big Snake. The letter was certified by Henry Johnston, who served as interpreter. It was followed with a postscript: "Gentlemen we hope you will furnish our Runner with Provisions to Car[r]y him back to this Place again. As Brother you Know it is to[o] hard for a man to carry Provisions to your town & Back to this place."

Just how fragile and tense and perilous was the situation is apparent from the relay letter to the Governor which enclosed the Muncy chiefs' appeal. It is dated April 24, and is addressed to His Excellency Thomas McKean, Governor of the State of Pennsylvania, who was then in Lancaster, and was composed by Henry Baldwin[2] and William Wallace. In drawing attention to the very critical nature of the dispute, Baldwin and Wallace offered the Governor some advice: "It may be proper also to state that accounts have been received here that a number of Indians of the Muncey and other tribes to the amount of about two hundred are collected in New Connecticut [present Ohio] near the line of Pennsylvania, that they have left their families behind and are prepared for war waiting to join Great Britain in case the existing dispute should not be amicably settled." [3]

Fortunately, Jiiwi's happy recovery relieved the chief and the headmen and the Governor of any decision. It was a crisis that ended without loss of life, and with no real damage done. But it could have erupted into war, and could have been very, very costly to all involved. And the episode hardened the relationship between the heretofore friendly Munsees and the Senecas of the Allegheny. The Munsees, not surprisingly, declined Cornplanter's invitation to continue their hunting in the Tionesta Creek and the Allegheny River region, and eventually, when they determined to withdraw from Cattaraugus, it was not to Chief Cornplanter and his people, but to the Mohawk Joseph Brant, and the Iroquois whom he had led to the Grand River of Ontario, that they went.[4]

Cornplanter remained active in the ceaseless bargaining councils. Although he did not participate so much in the sessions, speaking less, and twisting fewer arms, his presence seemed to mean a lot to both the Senecas and the negotiating parties. What the Senecas were doing now was engaging in the sale of the only lands they had left, the properties designated "reservations." One such conference occurred on June 30, 1802, at Buffalo Creek. The meeting brought together several Seneca headmen with the land speculators Oliver Phelps, Isaac Bronson and Horatio Jones, under the supervision of a Commissioner "appointed by the President of the United States." Called simply the Buffalo Creek Treaty, it was held under the authority of the United States government, though it was simply a private sale. What happened here was the sale by the Indians of Little Beard's Reservation (two square miles, or 1280 acres), which was on the Genesee River and Little Beard's Creek, next the Big Tree Reservation.

Cornplanter (as Koeentwahka) signed the sales agreement. Among other Senecas agreeing to the sale were Young King, Red Jacket, and Farmer's Brother. The document was ratified by the United States Senate February 7, 1803.

Not long after the departure of Henry Simmons from Jennesadaga and increasingly through the years 1801-1804 a division between Cornplanter and his older half-brother Handsome Lake began to occur. The Senecas had been much moved by Handsome Lake's vision, and were much impressed, too, by his subsequent, very compelling preaching. Consequently, the prophet, as he was being called, despite criticism of his witch hunting, assumed an ever and ever larger place among them. Handsome Lake, not altogether unhappy with his newly acquired status, began to oppose some of Cornplanter's ideas of what was good for the Indians. At a council called for Buffalo Creek on the subject of witches, Handsome Lake opined that there was no need for the Indian children to learn to read and to write; and he insisted, too, that they should not sell the produce they produced but share it with one another. When Henry Abeel, who had been at the council with his half-brother Charles, returned to Jennesadaga, he expressed his disappointment in the council. He declared to his father that he felt "it would be much better for them to hold Councils about making fields than about witchcraft and dances & such things." [5]

Because of pressure from the Quakers, who were urging the teaching of reading and writing, there was convened that October another council on that subject, and the larger subject of the white man's ways. Cornplanter here spoke strongly for education. Handsome Lake, who could sense the opinion of the majority, went along for obvious political reasons. And he did not oppose either the decision of a council held at the Genesee in November, by which the Senecas agreed to the exchange of certain small parcels of land in return for adjustment in the way their annuities were paid and for more oxen, pigs, sheep, and cows—and farming equipment.[6]

Henry Abeel

Cornplanter had been for twenty years at the head of the Seneca delegation to most councils, and at most of these served as the principal speaker, representing more often than not the entire Six Nations. But in January of 1802, it was not Cornplanter but his half-brother Handsome Lake who was made head of the delegation that set out for the nation's new capital in Washington. The Senecas had addressed to the President of the United States a letter in which they requested an audience, not expressly to air grievances, but to present a formal request for more farming and spinning equipment.[7] And when President Thomas Jefferson promptly responded with a "cordial invitation," the company was organized. It included representatives of all the Six Nations (excepting the Mohawk) and the Delawares. The celebrated Tonawanda Chief Blue Sky was a member, and a number of warriors accompanied the chiefs.

Handsome Lake, however, as Anthony Wallace points out, took advantage of this occasion to promote his own station among the Senecas. He opened his address to the President with the customary ingratiations, then proceeded to some self-aggrandizement. "The Great Spirit," he said, "has appointed four Angels and appointed me the fifth to direct our people on Earth. I thank the Great Spirit that the Great Chief of my white Brother is well and hearty. This is the first year since the Great Spirit appointed me to guide my people and give them knowledge, good from bad. He directed me to begin with my own people first and that is the Reason why I have been so long in coming to my white Brother."[8]

After impassioned reference to the problem of alcohol and complaint about the white people's seizure of the Indian lands, he reminded the President that he was to "negotiate only" with those persons appointed by him as "the 'fifth angel' and the director of mankind."[8] The closing of his speech is typical of Handsome Lake's preaching. It is impressive for its passion and includes an interesting observation about Cornplanter. Of course it is not without a dig at the demon rum.

After declaring that he has been appointed by the four angels to direct the people on earth, and that he has been empowered to relieve any man of any wickedness (though he can do nothing for one who is fond of liquor) he speaks of "My Brother Captain Cornplanter," whose place he has assumed:

> *He is cried down by the Sachems of Buffalo Creek which you very well know. But it is not my wish for I very well know that he has done his Endeavour for the benefit of our nation. He is a Sober man and endeavours to make all our young men Sober and good—the Sachems at Buffalo Creek are all drunken men and dislike him. I, who am now Talking to you, would wish you to know, that half of my Spirit is here on Earth yet, and the other half is with the Great Spirit above and I wish you to consider my Business and my Nation well, that we may Continue friends and Brothers and when that takes place I will be thankful to the Great Chief of my white Brothers and to the Great Spirit above us all. We will be good friends here and when we will meet with the Great Being above we shall have bright and happier Days. Dear Brother, that is all I have got to say because I know you have got the Word of the Great Spirit among you.*[9]

This speech was delivered on March 7. Three days later, the Secretary of War, General Henry Dearborn, delivered to the assembled Indians the reply of the President. Like Washington's Secretary of War, Henry Knox, Henry Dearborn[10] had served in the Continental Army

Henry Dearborn

throughout the Revolution. He was made a prisoner-of-war during the ill-fated Quebec campaign of General Richard Montgomery and Colonel Benedict Arnold. Like Knox, he had been at the siege of Boston, had suffered the incredible cold of Valley Forge and the terrific heat of Monmouth, and attended the surrender of Cornwallis at Yorktown. He had learned a good bit about Indians from his service as one of General John Sullivan's officers on the campaign against Cornplanter and Brant and Little Beard in the summer of 1779.

The President's response was largely just what Handsome Lake had hoped to hear. In his remarks, Jefferson applauded Handsome Lake for his good counsel, and declared that he had no doubt that if the Indians traveled his path they would become "sober, honest, industrious and good." He noted for the chiefs and warriors that Congress was at that very time considering the writing of a law which would make it a crime for Indians to use alcohol. And of course he promised protection for their land.[11]

Whereupon, on March 12, Handsome Lake launched into a second address. Here he framed the Indians' request for "separate deeds" for each reservation; and he requested for himself the deed to the Oil Springs Reservation, which was ten miles square, "for the exclusive use, benefit and comfort of myself." The President's response to this speech was also delivered by Secretary Dearborn. He pledged protection "forever" of the Indian lands, and he declared he would look into the Oil Springs matter.[12]

By the time the Indians had returned to their homes they were feeling pretty good about their reception, most especially as each had been given provisions for the trip, some money, a shirt, an axe, and a hoe.[13] Of course it was not long before the persistent concerns over alcohol and the security of their land made them anxious again. And at some time that summer Handsome Lake dispatched a letter to President Jefferson, in which he made troubled note of these problems. Dearborn responded at once, and Jefferson himself eventually dictated a long letter, dated Washington, November 3, 1802. It was addressed to Handsome Lake. The letter reviewed some history of land settlements, and was full of assurances and expressions of confidence in a happy future for the Indians. It is not without advice. Here again the problem of alcohol was front and center. Jefferson blames Indians and whites alike, and notes that every single soul "must be the guardian of his own health and happiness." He reminds Handsome Lake that no sale of land is to be made to any individual, and that even selling to a state must be done under the supervision of the United States government. The letter ends with Jefferson's vision of a bright future for the Indian nation, which he regards as separate from the United States (Cornplanter was in the habit of speaking of "one nation."). Writes the President:

> *Go on, then, brother, in the great reformation you have undertaken. Persuade our red men to be sober and to cultivate their lands; and their women to spin and weave for their families. You will soon see your women and children well fed and clothed; your men living happily in peace and plenty, and your numbers increasing from year to year. It will be a great glory to you to have been the instrument of so happy a change, and your children's children, from generation to generation, will repeat your name with love and gratitude forever. In all your enterprises for the good of your people you may count with confidence on the aid and protection of the United States and on the sincerity and zeal with which I am animated in the furthering of this humane work. You are our brethren of the same*

land; we wish your prosperity as brethren should do. Farewell! [14]

Cornplanter's last thirty years, though not without their satisfactions, and even some genuinely happy moments, were years of torment and disappointment. There was, in the first place, the continuing and sometimes unpleasant rivalry between the chief and Red Jacket, between the chief and Handsome Lake. There was, second, a continuing anxiety about their land, their reservation lands, which were to have been theirs "forever." There was the disappointment over his son Henry, who had experienced drinking problems, and had, it was generally observed, made poor use of his education. There was a continuing problem with the schools. There was the division among his people occasioned first by the War of 1812 and second by the arrival of the Christian missionaries. He did not need all of this. He was not a young man any more. Sometimes he felt a little tired.

Cornplanter had always stood first among his people, as a warrior and as a champion of Indian rights. But he had seen his popularity and his influence steadily diminish because of his seeming willingness to surrender lands. Now his half-brother had usurped his place, and the "northern" Seneca Red Jacket was clearly capitalizing on his unpopular stance with respect to the lands. Cornplanter did not disguise his resentment, and he must have been pleased when Handsome Lake, upset over Red Jacket's stand on the proposed sale of a strip of land known as the Black Rock Corridor,[15] took advantage of the Senecas' universal belief in witchcraft to bring charges against Red Jacket. At a great council held at Buffalo Creek, Red Jacket was publicly denounced. So serious were the accusations that the chief suddenly found himself on trial for his life. Rising to the occasion, the most critical of his eventful career, the artful orator, in a passionate address to the convening council that lasted a good three hours, spoke most impressively in his defense. Not surprisingly, he won an acquittal. And another very damaging blow had been dealt the reputation of Chief Cornplanter.

The Trial of Red Jacket

In 1801 a Buffalo Creek council of the Iroquois had made Handsome Lake "the supreme leader of the Six Nations." [16] This election made natural the removal of the council fire from Buffalo Creek to Jennesadaga and in 1803, with Handsome Lake presiding, that move was made official. The chief had lots of support at this time, including that of his nephew Henry Abeel (who was made one of the council's official interpreters), and his nephew Charles, and his brother Cornplanter.[17] But, naturally, not everybody was happy. Some continued to prefer Buffalo Creek for the council fire; and some, notably Joseph Brant (now in Ontario), insisted that the fire burned still at Onondaga. Because the move had been to the home of Cornplanter, some chiefs were made suspicious, and wondered whether the whole thing was not designed to return Cornplanter to his former status.[18]

The 1803 council included a meeting with the Quakers who had made a request to move from Jennesadaga to Tunesassa. Their proposal was discussed. Halliday Jackson had left Genesinguhta in June of 1800, but two young Quakers, Jonathan Thomas and Jacob Taylor, who had had some experience among the Oneidas, had arrived in May, and these, with Joel Swayne felt the move would be a good one. What Taylor and Swayne[19] wanted to do was to buy land off the reservation, but still fairly near to it. On August 30 the council granted their wishes, but reluctantly, and Handsome Lake expressed the hope that their move would not take them far; and so did Cornplanter. And in fact, the Quakers did remain close. They moved to Quaker Bridge, New York, just off the reservation lands, and continued there for a hundred years.[20]

But at some time in 1804, when Cornplanter was in his mid-fifties, he experienced a difference with his half-brother Handsome Lake, who had been living in the Cornplanter household now for over a decade. Although Handsome Lake had clearly, because of his vision and because of his influential preaching, emerged as a political rival to Cornplanter, and had actually usurped his place, Merle Deardorff insists that "no clear evidence of an open personal break at any time between Cornplanter and Handsome Lake appears."[21] The trouble, such as it was, was rooted in many community problems.

And it all begins with the sawmill! Cornplanter had been experiencing big problems with the mill, for it could not operate at all times. Sometimes the stream was too high, and sometimes it was too low. Finally he had to admit that he had made a mistake in its location. He now proposed to the community to move it to a more advantageous site, so that he could attend it more profitably. What he wanted to do was to place the mill on the reservation, lease it to a skilled operator, as before, and, hopefully, pocket substantial profits. Well, the community was not about to buy this, and the people were quick to say so. When he met resistance from the Senecas, who did not think it proper for him to use reservation land for his own personal gain, he erupted. He had for a long time felt that the people did not appreciate sufficiently his willingness to let them live on his private property. Now he repeated his earlier expressed determination to lease out portions of his private property to the settlers coming from the east. That proposal naturally did not sit well with the Senecas, most of whom really did not appreciate that they resided on the Grant at the pleasure of the owner. And, then, in a seemingly thoughtless action, the enraged chief removed his permission for the Indians to plant on his property.

The reaction was not surprising. Those who had led the uprising were now made influential members of the council; Cornplanter was reduced in the community from Head Man to a common warrior. And, marvelously, they actually turned over Cornplanter's intended sawmill site to one of the chief's millwrights in return for 60,000 board feet of lumber, to be paid yearly—to the tribe. This was competition that Cornplanter did not need.[22] In disgust, he ordered everybody off.

The consequence of all this fuss was (1) the removal of Cornplanter from his office as Head Man, and (2) the withdrawal of almost everybody, except the chief's own close family, from the Cornplanter Grant. And the troublesome sawmill never did arrive on the reservation.[23]

Exactly when Chief Cornplanter was deposed is not really clear. We know from the Quaker John Philips, who visited Cornplanter in 1806, that in September of that year Cornplanter was still "displaced." Halliday Jackson in his record for the following year noted: "This fall Cornplanter was again restored to his former station as chief; and from the disposition he had always manifested to the object of the Friends, there was reason to expect his renewed influence in their councils would be useful."[24] So Cornplanter was "out of office" from some time in 1804 until the fall of 1807, when he was restored to his position as a member of the Chiefs' Council, and apparently to Head Man status. The Quakers were apparently very happy to have him back at the head of the community.

In consequence of all this turmoil, a great many Senecas over these three years in a huff steadily departed the village, most of them in a real huff. Indeed, very nearly everybody vacated the Cornplanter Town. Among these were not only Handsome Lake and his family, but the Chief's son Henry,[25] who took up residence at the Cold Spring area of the Allegany Reservation, which was on the west bank of the Allegheny River, ten miles upstream from Genesinguhta, some twenty miles from Cornplanter Town, and east of Lake Chautauqua.[26] The settlement was about three miles above the mouth of Tunesassa Creek (now called Quaker Run). The Allegany Reservation, which had been created by the Canandaigua Treaty of 1794, was totally within New York State. It lay on both sides of the Allegheny River, stretching for a mile or a little less in each direction. It reached for thirty-five miles north and east into New York from Pennsylvania. At its southernmost limit, it included the village of Cold Spring. It was here that Blacksnake had been living, in the house next to that of his translator, the young English-speaking Seneca Benjamin Williams. This village got quite a boost from the alienated Cornplanter Grant people. Within two years Halliday Jackson was able to report the construction in Cold Spring of about 100 new houses, many of them well shingled, the establishment of a wholly new town.[27] As Anthony Wallace notes, "The removal to Cold Spring and the deposing of Cornplanter are described in three letters from Friends at Tunessassa [often Tunesassa] to the Indian Committee in Philadelphia, dated March 24, June 9 and Aug. 29, 1804." [28] The houses, he reports, were "modern," as the bark house had long ago disappeared, and the log house (with its bark roof) was now disappearing. A number of families, including Cornplanter's son Henry, settled not in the main community but rather "out of town," in a little village of their own. Henry, it was noted, had a "neat little house on a hill" there, where he lived with his wife Hannah, who had married Henry when she was sixteen.

Handsome Lake became the head of this sudden colony. He continued here the preaching he had begun in Cornplanter Town, and became steadily more influential. He continued, too, in his witch hunting (from which Cornplanter had become disenchanted). It was not that long ago, and while he was yet living in Cornplanter's home, that he had accused Red Jacket of witchcraft and very nearly had him executed! [29] Here at Cold Spring he was responsible for at least three executions during his residence there, 1804-09.

Indeed, at Cold Spring, though Chief Handsome Lake experienced a great many very serious problems, surely the biggest was occasioned by this relentless witch hunting. Very strong reaction was expressed to the extremely cruel and grisly torture-execution of an Onondaga woman, which was carried out by zealous followers of Handsome Lake. Charged with witchcraft, she had been tried at Cold Spring. When Cornplanter heard of the affair, he "privately told people that he disapproved of it." [30] And certainly Cornplanter's son Henry was also offended. He voiced his opinion in no uncertain terms, much more indignantly even than had his father. In a total rejection of Handsome Lake's policy, he declared vehemently that "witchcraft . . . does not exist." [31] Before long, Handsome Lake had fallen almost completely out of favor, even with members of his family. After five years at Cold Spring, he abruptly took leave of the community, and with a few of the most ardent members of his following set out for the reservation at Tonawanda, near Buffalo.[32] As he was able to persevere in his preaching, and seemed to have had enough of witch hunting, he was not unhappy there. And during the last years at Cold Spring and early in his time at Tonawanda, Cornplanter's half-brother continued active in the councils. Indeed, in the late summer of 1808, having been oft invited, he headed up a delegation of chiefs of the Six Nations in a visit to the still restless western Indians. He was joined in this mission by Cornplanter, Red Jacket, and "eight other distinguished chiefs from various reservations and a large number of warriors." At Sandusky they urged peace between the western Indians and the United States.[33]

In 1809, as he presided over a council meeting, the seventy-four-year-old (?) Handsome Lake presented to William Allinson quite a picture: "Old Conudiu had a blaze of vermillion from the Corner of each Eye—his ears were cut round in their manner & extended a considerable length, on each Ear were two silver quills, one about 3 and one-half & the other 2 inches. The erect one having a tuft of Red Feathers tuck[ed] in the lower end—part of his forehead & on big Crown were also painted red & being nearly bald & a very grave countenance, he looked venerable—on his arms were wide silver bracelets—his leggings were of Red Cloth & his covering a Blanket over all—which he threw off in Council & took up his long Pipe . . . ." [34]

At Tonawanda he lived out his last years. He had experienced some visions in which his death seemed to figure, and he had had intimations that his end was near. While on a journey to Onondaga, near Syracuse, New York, he was struck by a sudden illness, possibly a stroke. He died on August 10, 1815.[35]

At about the same time as the mass exodus from Cornplanter Town, or just a little earlier, the Quakers moved also (as they had proposed in the 1803 council), the entire mission withdrawing from Genesinguhta to a new farm on property they had bought outside the reservation. This property, some 700 acres, included a portion of what was then known as Tunesassa Creek and is today Quaker Run. On this stream, at some time in 1804, they constructed a gristmill.[36] This was okay with the Senecas and with Cornplanter, who did not have a gristmill. The Quakers, as expected, permitted the Indians to use the mill. And, as noted by Swatzler, for the first two years the Quakers "ground all of the Indians' grain for free . . . and charged a nominal fee thereafter." [37]

But the Quakers also built a sawmill on the stream, and though they accommodated the Senecas with generous fees, the Indians were not happy with the competition. Cornplanter's sawmill, after all, had been in operation since probably 1795 at least. Four years later, however, the Quakers, with Indian labor, constructed a sawmill expressly for the use of the Senecas; and the Indians operated it off and on, with widely varying production, until some time in 1820.

Division between Red Jacket and Cornplanter had been growing steadily. Cornplanter was determined to put an end to liquor among the Indians. Red Jacket could have no problem with that. But Cornplanter was determined, too, to bring the Senecas ever closer to the white man's ways. He was encouraging the men to build farms and to plow the land; he urged the women to spin and weave. He was hoping that everybody, beginning with the children, could learn to read and to write. He was constantly promoting the construction of sawmills and gristmills. But Red Jacket, who was the chief influence among the Senecas at Buffalo Creek, and the head sachem, was resisting all of that, vigorously. He had little desire to learn or to practice the white man's ways. He declared that it would be a matter of "great time before the Indians gave up their beloved ancient customs and became educated and civilized." [38] The breach between the two was widened when Red Jacket accused Cornplanter of concocting a fraud in order to make his half brother a prophet. He intimated that Cornplanter hoped to make capital out of Handsome Lake's prestige, in order to regain his own former status. He declared the whole business of visions just one grand scheme. He even insisted that Cornplanter's sons Henry and Charles, as well as his nephew Blacksnake, were in on it.[39] He didn't believe any of it, not for one minute.

But there was some good time for the old chief too. One of Cornplanter's happy moments during his last years was provided by a visit he made in 1810 to his father's home in Fort Plain on the Mohawk River just north of Cherry Valley. He had been here thirty years ago of course during the raid on Canajoharie, when he had captured and released his father. Now, as he returned, it was not to see his father, who he knew had died more than a dozen years ago, but to visit with members of the family, and in this way at least make a connection, which he clearly longed for. He was just a wee bit uneasy as he set out, for though the great war had ended a long time ago, trouble on the frontiers continued, and white settlers were still suspicious of and wary of Indians. Cornplanter wondered just what sort of reception he would receive here at Fort Plain.

John (Johannes) Abeel had settled in the region about 1748. According to the Montgomery County history, he eventually was able to secure "several hundred" acres of land from the Bleecker (Blucker) patent. Having built a fine stone house atop a little knoll, not far from the river and above the flats, he felt comfortable in proposing marriage to a young German girl of the neighborhood. On September 22, 1759, he married Mary Knouts. It was this home that he brought her to which, together with a church nearby and the house of William Seeber, was burned by the Indians in the raid of August, 1780. It was at this time, as above described, that Cornplanter recognized his captured father, and released him, clearly understanding that he would never see him again.

At some time after the war's end John Abeel constructed another house on the same site, and it was to this home that his warrior son (now sixty years old) came in 1810.

The chief was accompanied by a number of other Senecas "of dignified rank." As they were all attired in their native dress and adorned with gaudy bracelets and ear rings and extravagant ornaments, they must have presented quite a picture. In any case, the company was most graciously welcomed by the relatives of John Abeel, some of whom would therefore be blood relatives of the famous chief as well. The County History records that first the company was escorted to the home of Peter J. Wagner, who was a grandson of John Abeel, on Mary Knouts' side. Next they were taken to the house of Nicholas Dygart, whose wife was a sister to Joseph Wagner's wife. Here they were "richly entertained."

Cornplanter, with his entourage, was then led to the home of Jacob Abeel,[40] who was living with his widowed mother on the old homestead. Everywhere the Indians were received with enthusiastic and generous hospitality. The villagers knew enough about Cornplanter to know that they were in the presence of a most extraordinary personage, a noble and celebrated Seneca warrior. Consequently the visit, which for Cornplanter, who always enjoyed being fussed over, was a most happy one and extended over many days.[41]

XXII

THE WAR OF 1812

It was not long after this trip into his father's country that a crisis emerged for the young United States and for the Seneca nation of Indians. This was the War of 1812. The trouble had been building for some time. Many influential Americans, notably James Calhoun and Henry Clay, had never given up their designs on Canada; and the British had long been in violation of the Treaty of Paris. They continued to hold forts in the United States. There occurred all kinds of disputes about shipping, with embargos and the British impressment of American sailors causing lots of trouble. That the difficulties were extremely serious was recognized in the Declaration of War against Great Britain on June 18, 1812. And that the war would go forward was assured when a small American vessel, loaded with salt, was captured by an organized force of Canadians out of Fort Erie. The date was June 27, 1812. The war, which pitted Americans against the British once again, did not unite the members of the Six Nations but instead this time divided them. In the course of the fighting, warriors fought on both sides. The Seneca Nation, including Cornplanter, was much involved.

The Iroquois had been approached by the western Indians, particularly the Shawnee, who were quick to perceive in the conflict an opportunity (by allying themselves with the British) to recover their lands. They had no luck with Handsome Lake, who throughout would play the role of "peace prophet." And they certainly got nowhere with Cornplanter, whose allegiance to the Americans was avowed and heartfelt. He called a council early in the summer, to be held at Jennesadaga. At this meeting, Cornplanter and Handsome Lake, speaking as one, assured the people of Warren and Meadville that they were determined on peace.[1]

And neutrality was the position taken by the two influential Seneca chiefs Captain Strong and Little Billy (Green Grasshopper). Strong warned the Iroquois of the forked tongue of the British, and insisted that his people would "take no more notice" of the king. Little Billy pointed out that it was not their quarrel. We mean nothing to either the Crown or the Americans. Let us not needlessly endanger our homes and our families.[2] But Cornplanter early reneged on the pledge that he had made. With 200 warriors he had assembled he marched to Fort Franklin, and proudly presented his company to Colonel Dale, who at that time was putting together a regiment from Crawford and Venango Counties to go to the defense of Erie. The chief was much disappointed when he was turned away, his service declined. Cornplanter, who was sixty years old at this time, had been eager to fight in the defense of what he was calling "my country." He was much distressed.

The *Buffalo Gazette* for September 29, 1812, reported that "about 140 warriors of the Seneca nation from Alleghany River arrived in town last week and are encamped near the village." As they proved a little disorderly and troublesome, the white officers persuaded them to "go home." And for a while the Americans saw no need to enlist Indians. But with the war going badly, the Americans had second thoughts. Before the Indians got thoroughly discouraged and disinterested, the American forces discovered they could be of valuable service. After the Seneca warriors had been ordered up twice and then ordered home, the young men, Henry Abeel among them, registered some effective complaints. And because the Mohawks of Joseph Brant had enlisted in substantial numbers in the British forces, the United States Army decided to accept Indian volunteers. Even though Handsome Lake protested vehemently, and even though a council was convened at Onondaga (where Mohawk influence was strong) to voice opposition, the U. S. Army announced its willingness to have the service of the Indians.[3]

One of the first episodes of the war to involve the Senecas in significant numbers was the affair at Black Rock, near Buffalo, where there had been established an American supply depot. The American agent for the Six Nations in Buffalo at this time (summer of 1813) was Erastus Granger. According to one historian of the war, Granger had been asked by Henry Dearborn to recruit warriors for Fort George (present-day Niagara-on-the-Lake). And when Granger learned somehow that the British were preparing to assault the depot at Black Rock, he perceived an opportunity to get the Indians into the war. He hurriedly sent out an invitation to the Seneca chiefs whom he knew well, urging them to visit him at his home, which was just two miles from the depot. Among the forty warriors who showed up were Red Jacket, Farmer's Brother, and Young King. Inspired by Farmer's Brother, who appeared to be in command of the warriors and who delivered a rousing, war-whooping speech, the Senecas attacked the British forces which had sacked the depot in the wee hours of the morning. Because the warriors fought valiantly and effectively, the result was a complete rout of the British. The date was July 11, 1813.[4]

At a council at Buffalo Creek just two weeks later, the Senecas and other Iroquois more formally took up the hatchet. Of course they were not pledging unconditional support for the Americans, far from it. They made it clear that they expected to be provided for and paid. Red Jacket defined their position: "The part we take in this war is not voluntary on our part; you have persuaded us into it . . . . Your voice was for us to sit still when the war began, but you have beat us—you have got us into the war." [5] And Cornplanter, at the same council, added his insistence. Addressing the Americans, he declared, in his compelling voice, "You must pay well. You must open your purse. You must pay some now, and do not let your taverns supply our warriors with spiritous liquors." And then he added, probably with Black Rock in mind, "We feel some anxiety that there is no provision made for the families of our men who fell in the war."[6] Henry Abeel picked up on his father's reference to hard drink. He urged the same caution: "We can not stand [it] in battle. You can [not] drink and fight. Our forefathers fought without liquor."[7]

Before long, Indians were enlisting in significant numbers, and for the two years 1812 to 1814, the muster rolls showed the names of 600 Iroquois officers and men. Of the Allegany Senecas, some twenty were given commissions.[8] Where the influence of Handsome Lake was most strong at this time, the enlistments were slow, the Allegany and Tonawanda reservations producing only seven warriors by the summer of 1813.[9]

It was immediately after the Black Rock success that Indians were accepted for service in substantial numbers. In fact, a volunteer company of Iroquois (not only Senecas) was formed. Some 143 chiefs and warriors were assembled. Among these were some of the familiar figures of the Revolution, now thirty-five years older. Historian Carl Benn reports that four Senecas received commissions: Farmer's Brother was made a captain at $40 per month; Little Billy and Captain Pollard were appointed lieutenants at $30; and Blacksnake was commissioned an ensign at $20. Besides these commissions, as Benn notes, four chiefs were made sergeants (at $11 per month) and 135 warriors were enrolled as privates, at $8 per month. And because, not long after that, so many

Iroquois warriors had enlisted, a real battalion could be organized. These 400 men were placed under the leadership of Farmer's Brother, now promoted to colonel.[10]

There had been lots of war activity in the vicinity of Jennesadaga. Ammunition wagons lumbered by, and the Indians from time to time could study the lines of prisoners in forced marches. Runners with dispatches were constantly on the move. Keelboats loaded with freight for Erie were headed up French Creek for Fort Le Boeuf. The war swirled around the Seneca villages.

On July 12, 1813, a town meeting was called for Meadville. Colonel Joseph Hackney, Major J. W. Farrelly, and David Mead had been appointed to visit the Indians on the Allegany Reservation to provide for them an explanation of the war, and to secure from them some reaction. The council was actually held at Jennesadaga, and was extremely lively, even slightly unruly. There was a *lot* of talk, and Cornplanter did most of it for the Senecas. He addressed the deputation in his customary way, deferentially, but plainly. His remarks included this passage: "Brothers—We are very glad to see you today. Our forefathers made an agreement which we hoped would be lasting. If any bushes grow up in the road we will cut them down . You have now come forward to renew our friendship. We made this agreement with the United States [Pickering Treaty of 1794] that we should have our lands together and should always be friends as long as the sun shines and the water runs."[11]

Eventually taken into service, besides Cornplanter's close friend New Arrow (Captain Strong), was also Cornplanter's son Henry, at this time thirty-nine years old. At the time his service was accepted he was simply a private, and probably in the Seneca company commanded by Captain John Littlebeard. This company was active on the Niagara River frontier. It is known that Henry Abeel was in service in the mid-summer of 1813; and it is known that he participated in the action at Fort George, for he was commended for that by General John Parker Boyd. In his report of August 28, 1813, Boyd singled out Major Henry O'Bail for special praise. Henry, as he had assumed the rank of Major, was apparently one of the chiefs at the head of the warriors in the fighting.[12]

Exactly one month after the affair at Black Rock, when it was clear that the "southern Iroquois" were now allied with the Americans, the Ontario Iroquois, mostly Mohawks, convened a council, at which they declared the New York and Allegheny Iroquois the "enemy." Most naturally in all of this the Canadian Iroquois sided with the British, and the Senecas and other New York State and Allegheny River Iroquois elected to fight for what they now regarded "my country." On August 17 and 18, at Ball's Farm, near Niagara, the Iroquois warriors fought each other in significant numbers for the first time. And it was a bloody business, carried on in hand-to-hand combat with scalping knives and tomahawks. There were Indian casualties on both sides.[13] In fact, not only in the fighting at Ball's Farm but at Fort George and elsewhere as well, the Indians began to recognize that they were being thrown into the forefront of the action. It seemed to them, and justifiably so, that the regular army soldiers were letting them do most of the fighting. Naturally the chiefs complained.

And they had more to complain about too. Their pay was tardy, and when it came it rarely came in the full amount. The Indians declared that they would no longer serve without their promised reimbursement. Loudest among the voices that were raised in this complaint were those of Cornplanter and Red Jacket and Blue Sky. As Benn points out, some of the chiefs, notably Little Billy, Farmer's Brother, and Young King, seemed a little more understanding of the economic problems faced by the army.[14]

In any case, the majority of the Senecas, chiefs and warriors both, gradually grew disenchanted with the war. Because of the bloodshed and the feeling that they were being offered up as sacrifices, and the delinquent pay, they began to reconsider their role in the conflict. Under the influence of Cornplanter chiefly, and Blue Sky and Red Jacket as well, the southern Iroquois, and the Senecas particularly, began to question their decision to fight in this war.[15] Most had only the dimmest idea of just what the quarrel was all about, and many were now of the opinion that their fighting should be only in some obvious defense of their homeland. On July 25, 1814, Red Jacket,[16] Blue Sky, and some other chiefs, announced that they were opposed to further Indian participation. Even Cornplanter endorsed the position. Now close to death, Handsome Lake, of course, insisted, as he always had, that "We must remain at peace." [17]

Of course by this time it was all academic, as the war was limping to a wearisome close, with nobody gaining much of anything. Certainly, the United States did not achieve the conquest of Canada; and certainly the British made no advance to the south. There were some appreciable effects, however. And one of these concerned the remaining Indian lands.

After the conclusion of the War of 1812, white settlement westward stepped up dramatically. There occurred a big surge in lumbering, and the reservation lands became steadily less and less sacred. White people even grazed their cattle on reservation lands. They built gristmills and sawmills. There occurred lots of encroachment on Indian lands. And even though the adoption of the white man's ways was accelerating, trouble was inevitable.

XXIII

LAST YEARS

One of Cornplanter's biggest problems during these troubled years concerned the attitude of the Indians toward the land the Senecas owned in reservation. At some time after the conclusion of the War of 1812, this problem came to a head. The Quakers had for many years been urging private ownership of the land, feeling of course that private title to a lot would result in a greater reverence for the land. Swatzler has noted that "the Ogden Land Company—holders of the preemptive right to the Allegheny Reservation land"—put great pressure on the Senecas to sell their land, which influenced the Quakers to press the Indians further toward private ownership.[1] The Quakers argued that this would be a better move than simply to sell the reservation outright, which was precisely what was happening to the reservations in New York State. Cornplanter agreed. He was strong against selling the reservation wholesale, and thought that one way to discourage the sale of the reservation would be to abandon the communal system of living, and divide the land into lots identified with private owners and secured through certified deeds. This, to his way of thinking, would be in tune with improved farming and lumbering. But the proposal did not sit well with the women, who pointed out that their garden plots were widely scattered; at the same time many of the young men objected because they felt that there would be more timber available from the tribal lands.

Although a council convened for the Seneca Nation entertained the subject at Cattaraugus in 1817, and reached approval of the lot division, at least to the extent of surveying, the Allegheny Senecas bolted. As explained by Swatzler, they requested the Quakers to secure for them, from President James Monroe, official title to their reservation. At the same time they urged the Quakers to test the President's regard for the Quaker program of divided private lots. Cornplanter had by this time changed his mind, and was prepared to take the matter into his own hands. Swatzler reports on the consequence: "In August of 1818, when the surveyor showed up on the Allegany Reservation to start laying out the individual lots, he was met by Cornplanter and some other chiefs who firmly refused to allow the survey to proceed." [2] They politely asked the surveyor and Jonathan Thomas, the Quaker missionary accompanying him, to leave the reservation.

By June of the next year, the Indians had an opinion from President Monroe. He was recommending the Quaker plan. But a difficulty appeared in the fact that there was no title or deed for the reservation, and by this time the Allegany Senecas had split into two factions over the issue of dividing the reservation into individual lots. Those opposed ultimately prevailed. [3]

In February of 1822, Cornplanter, now at least seventy years old, felt compelled to provide the Quaker State an autobiography, which meant of course a history of the Seneca Nation for the last half-century. But all of that was only a vehicle from which to voice his continuing concerns. He complains about the abuse of the Indians by the whites: encroachment on the Indian land, the determination of the whites to "destroy all wolves," taxes, alcohol, the many violations of the provisions of the Treaty of Fort Stanwix. He points out that the American Revolution occurred out of the impression of unjust taxation. He knows about unjust taxation. To Governor Joseph Hiester, who had entrusted the Indians to Cornplanter's care, he dictated and dispatched quite a speech. It opens with the now well known account of the young Indian lad's visit to his father, quoted earlier, and continues, "I grew up to be a young man, and married me a wife, and I had no kettle nor gun. I then knew where my father lived, and went to see him, and found he was a white man, and spoke the English language. He gave me victuals while I was at his house, but when I started home, he gave me no provisions to eat on the way. He gave me neither kettle nor gun, neither did he tell me that the United States were about to rebel against the government of England."

He then declares to those who are in session of the Legislature of Pennsylvania, that "the Great Spirit has made known to me, that I have been wicked; and the cause thereof has been the Revolutionary war in America. With respectful references to General Rufus Putnam, he speaks of the causes of the Revolution and of the aftermath, which included the Fort Stanwix treaty session, and of receiving the grant of land, and of the constant erosion of the Indian lands and of the effects of liquor.

Joseph Hiester

Then he turns to a current personal problem, one which could be hurtful to all Indians:

> *Another circumstance has taken place which is very trying to me, and I wish for the interference of the Governor. The white people who live at warren called upon me some time ago, to pay taxes for my land, which I objected to, as I never had been called upon for that purpose before; and [I] having refused to pay they became irritated, called upon me frequently, and at length brought four guns with them, and seized our cattle. I still refused to pay, and was not willing to let the cattle go. After a time of dispute, they returned home, and I understood the militia was ordered out to enforce the collection of the tax. I went to Warren, and to avert the impending difficulty, was obliged to give my note for the tax, the amount of which was forty-three dollars and seventy-nine cents. It is my desire that the Governor will exempt me from paying taxes for my land to white people; and also to cause that the money I am obliged to pay, be refunded to me, as I am very poor. The Governor is the person who attends to the situation of the people, and I wish him to send a person to Allegheny, that I may inform him of the particulars of our situation, and be authorized to instruct the white*

> *people in what manner to conduct themselves toward the Indians.*

He then reminds Pennsylvania of its promise: "The government has told us, that when difficulties arose between the Indians and the white people, they would attend to having them removed. We are now in a trying situation, and I wish the Governor to send a person authorized to attend thereto the forepart of next summer, about the time that the grass has grown big enough for pasture."

He felt it imperative that the Indians be provided very real help: "The Governor formerly requested me to pay attention to the Indians, and take care of them. We are now arrived at a situation in which I believe the Indians cannot exist, unless the Governor should comply with my request, and send a person authorized to treat between us and the white people the approaching summer. I have now no more to speak." [4]

On the tax episode, Warren County historian Merle Deardorff has an account. According to him, when the sheriff arrived at Cornplanter's home, with a company of armed men, to collect the delinquent taxes, "He was received in silence . . . . Around the walls stood thirty of the chief's young men, each with a rifle. No word was said; but the sheriff was a smart man and could take a hint." [5] In another version, Cornplanter escorted the sheriff to another room in which there could be easily perceived a stack of rifles in number of perhaps 100. The Chief made it plain that at his call there would appear one warrior for each rifle.[6]

But the appeal that Cornplanter made to Pennsylvania Governor Joseph Hiester,[7] with whom he was on pretty good terms, did not fall on deaf ears. In fact, Cornplanter could not have had a more gratifying response. Not only did the Pennsylvania Legislature order the state treasurer to pay off the tax notes and meet all taxes due, the Grant was exempted from any kind of taxes so long as Cornplanter or his heirs held the land. Besides that, the Commonwealth of Pennsylvania announced that it was now prepared to hit with heavy penalties anyone found trespassing on the Cornplanter property. Just to be sure that Cornplanter understood all that was happening here, the Governor authorized the appointment of commissioners "to explain it all to him." [8]

When these two commissioners arrived in Warren, July 6, 1822, the aged chief met them on the steps of the Warren County Courthouse, and made it quite plain that he did not require an explanation. Instead he took advantage of the occasion to give some advice to the Commonwealth. In a typical Cornplanter address he made his points: He repeated, first, his insistence that the Commonwealth of Pennsylvania prohibit white men from giving liquor to Indians. Interestingly, he noted, second, that the Great Spirit had made the white people and the Indians to be separate, and that he had not made the Indians to keep the seventh day. Finally, he urged the white people to take better care of their own affairs, and to leave the Indians alone.[9]

Chief Cornplanter was a great one for doing "what is right." Despite his tendency to exaggerate his exploits, and to wander around when asked about his age, he had a great reverence for the truth, and would bristle if ever it were suggested that he was departing from it. In the courts of law of course the truth gets lots of testing. Chief Cornplanter was not in court often, but one occasion is of great interest in this regard. He was involved in a case which had come to the Venango Court. When it was suggested by an attorney that he might be lying, Cornplanter (as soon as he understood it from the interpreter) declared vehemently and "with much energy of expression, that he had never been 'guilty of lying in my life,' even in private conversation." Certainly he would not lie under oath. "Nay," said he, pointing a finger of scorn at the lawyer, "I would not be guilty of it for all you are worth, or ever will be." [10]

And he thought the world of General William Irvine,[11] who "is one white man I can trust." General Irvine, who had served with distinction in the Continental Army and at war's end was Head of the Western Department with headquarters at Fort Pitt, was after the war in the region north of Pittsburgh to take charge of the surveying of the lands. He and Cornplanter had become very good friends, and visited back and forth. There is a story that on one occasion, when the General felt his life threatened by hostile Delawares, Cornplanter dispatched a number of his own warriors to keep watch on that particular party of Indians. Cornplanter was heard many times to declare that General Irvine was "one of the few white men who spoke the truth." [12] But truth, if operating at all, did little for the Indians' great problem. The bigger land concerns of course continued. By 1817, so great was the concern for their holdings and the security of the reservations, the Senecas seriously considered selling all of their lands and moving west to join the tribes beyond the broad Ohio. And indeed some twenty years later some did exactly that.

In 1821 part of the Oneida Reserve was lost. And another costly sale of the same kind occurred some two years later, on September 3, 1823.

William Irvine

It was the sale known as the Treaty of Moscow (now Leicester, New York). The land given up by the Senecas on this occasion was the largest part of that tract known as Gardeau. For $4286 the land speculators Henry Gibson and John Grieg acquired this property, almost twenty-eight square miles, from a group of Seneca leaders. A small parcel of a little over 1200 acres, apparently that plot to which Mary Jemison with her family had fled at the approach of Sullivan's troops and on which she was to live until 1831, continued in the possession of the Seneca nation.

Nathaniel Gorham reappears here. He was at the time Superintendent of the State of Massachusetts, and served as a witness. Cornplanter was presumably not present, as he did not sign. His son Charles Cornplanter was among those who agreed to the sale. Also signing the contract were Young King, Red Jacket, Little Beard, Little Billy, Blacksnake, and Mary Jemison.

On the last day of August, 1826, after nearly sixty years of negotiating, the history of these land sales by the Senecas finally came to an end. It had been a long and eventful history of bargaining, very costly of course to the Senecas and all of the Six Nations. The treaties which cost the Senecas most dearly were those made at Fort Stanwix in 1784, at Big Tree in 1797, and here at Buffalo Creek in 1826. The Treaty of Buffalo Creek terminated the existence of the Genesee Valley Reservations, and ended the Seneca claim to almost all of the land that had ever been theirs, excepting the Allegany Reservation on the

Allegheny River (forty-two square miles) and the private tract belonging to Cornplanter.

By this agreement, the Seneca Nation of Indians surrendered their rights to the reservations known as Big Tree (two square miles), Canawaugus (two square miles, including Cornplanter's birthplace), Caneadea (sixteen square miles), Squawkie Hill (two square miles), the little bit of land that remained at Gardeau (two square miles), and large portions of the reservations at Buffalo Creek, Cattaraugus, and Tonawanda, west of the Valley of the Genesee.

These lands were sold to Robert Troup, Thomas L. Ogden, and Benjamin Woolsey Rogers, a group of New York City investors (the Ogden Land Company), for $48,260 "lawful money paid in hand" to the sachems, chiefs, and warriors of the Seneca Nation of Indians.

The agreement was made firm through the signatures of forty-seven Senecas. John Abeal (Cornplanter) signed with his mark X. So did his son Charles (here Charles Obeal), and Young King, Little Billy, Blacksnake, and Red Jacket. Horatio Jones, who was one of the purchasers in the Buffalo Creek Treaty, served as interpreter.

In 1838, after the death of Cornplanter, the Senecas in a treaty arrangement agreed to pull out of New York, to emigrate westward. They had their sights set on the territory known as Kansas. And in fact, as noted earlier, some, perhaps as many as 200, did go. Regretfully, nearly half of those who set out for the west died en route. The survivors returned. Under new agreements reached in 1842, the Senecas retained possession of the Allegany, the Cattaraugus, and the Oil Creek reservations.[13]

Another cross that Chief Cornplanter had to bear came floating into his mind as the image of a tiny, one-room schoolhouse. He had had from the time of his first acquaintance with the Quakers in Philadelphia high hopes for schooling for the Seneca children, as we know from his letter of 1791. And when the Quakers showed up at Jennesadaga in 1798, the very first order of business for him was the establishment of a school. The first school was opened on November 23, 1798. It was fairly easy to open, as it was one section of Cornplanter's double house. The second schoolhouse was the specially constructed log building provided by Henry Simmons not far from Cornplanter's home.

From 1798 until 1815, first at Jennesadaga and later at Genesinguhta, the Quakers conducted school.[14] But the schooling was sporadic. If the weather was bad, the teacher could expect a full house. When the weather was good . . . ! And there were other difficulties. Sometimes, because of the threat of war with the Delawares, the children were kept out of school, and the school would be closed down. Besides, there was the very difficult Seneca language to negotiate. Teachers, only a few of whom were Indians,[15] were not easy to enlist. Consequently, the school was sometimes closed for long periods. Although both Handsome Lake and Cornplanter were genuinely keen about schooling, and both felt that it was most desirable for the youngsters to learn to read and write, they were not sure that it was good for *all* of the children. The history of the schooling provided in the early days of the reservation and in Jennesadaga is a story of constant interruption, on again and off again. At some time in the summer of 1801 a decision was reached to move the school from Jennesadaga to Genesinguhta, where the Quakers were living. In a letter to the Committee in Philadelphia, dated August 3, 1801, the Quaker Mission reported that the Indians had agreed "it was the most centrable place for the whole of the settlements to keep it." [16] But for much of the time after the departure of Henry Simmons, the Quaker school was closed. Cornplanter's repeated requests that the school be re-opened often had no result.[17] And on one occasion when the school did re-open it was not long before Cornplanter closed it, dismissing the Quakers on the grounds that they did not teach the youngsters to respect their elders!

Some suppose that it was because he was miffed at the Quakers for complaining about his drinking that he dismissed the teachers. In 1814 (some say it was 1815), Cornplanter appealed to the Western Missionary Society to set up a school on the Grant. He asked the Presbyterians to send him a man. And in that year indeed the Society did establish a school at Jennesadaga.

Philip Tome, in his *Pioneer Life*, recalls the arrival of the preacher-teacher the Reverend Samuel Oldham, who had come to teach both whites and Indians at Cornplanter's request: "Soon after our conversation [about the rattlesnakes and the numbers of bear and elk, etc.] I again saw Cornplanter and he told me that he had learned, by a letter from the Presbyterian Society, of Pittsburgh, that they intended to send a preacher to establish a school at Cornplanter's Town, and he asked me to send my children, as there was no school or place of instruction near us." He reports then the arrival of the Presbyterian Samuel Oldham and his wife from Virginia, and recalls that after two days he went to see Cornplanter about enrolling his children in the school. Cornplanter promised to help.

Most interesting is what Cornplanter had to say about the Quakers when Tome asked him why it was the Quakers had left the community about fours years previous: "He said the Quakers did not keep the Sabbath, and he thought that was very wrong; and they taught the children that he was no wiser or better than any other man, and ought not to be considered so. This displeased him very much, as he wished to be considered the wisest and best of his tribe, and he told the Quakers that they might go, as the tribe did not wish to have them on their ground, or to have their children taught in that manner." When Cornplanter asked Tome what *he* thought of the Quakers, the hunter replied that he liked them very much, "as they were a very sober people, and did not drink or swear." Cornplanter, Tome remembered, "did not coincide with me in my favorable opinion of them."

Tome was also curious to know just how the Chief felt about the exodus of the older Indians, about their withdrawal into Cattaraugus County, New York. "I asked him if he did not regret to have them all leave him." Cornplanter seemed unoffended. He replied that he "was not sorry to have them go, as they were better situated on their own land, and the young men who were left would soon be grown up to take the places of those who had gone." And then the Chief added that since they were not willing to be ruled by him, he was "quite willing that they should leave." [18]

When the Reverend Timothy Alden visited the community in 1816, he found Oldham teaching away; when he returned two years later, he found Oldham teaching away "with missionary zeal." The Oldham school was in a log house, and according to a sketchy history apparently the schoolmaster taught off and on in the building for fifteen years.

At about the same time that Oldham arrived in Jennesadaga, the Quaker Joseph Elkinton came to teach, not only at Jennesadaga but at the other towns upriver. He had been teaching, apparently with much success and satisfaction for five years when, in February of 1821, Cornplanter abruptly ordered him to close the Quaker school and "go home." [19] Except for what Philip Tome has noted, it is quite difficult to account for Cornplanter's sudden expressions of disappointment in the Quakers. Merle Deardorff insists that it was not son Henry's experience in the Quaker schools in Philadelphia that provoked such action.[20] In any case, the school was soon opened again, at the request of the Indian parents.

But the schools in this way provided the opening wedge for evangelism, for the teachers invited often turned out to be more inclined

Timothy Alden

to preach than to teach. They were bringing the word of God to the heathen.

In 1816, when the Reverend Mr. Timothy Alden, representing the Society for the Propagation of the Gospel among the Indians of North America, visited Cornplanter's Town and the school there, he was "pleased" with what he found. And "next year, when Alden returned to preach in Cornplanter's house, with Henry O'Bail as interpreter, he found that the schoolmaster was holding religious services every Sunday." Cornplanter told him that Christians must be right "because you have the words of the Great Spirit written in a book."[21] In 1818 Alden was again at Jennesadaga, as one stop on a circuit that included Cold Spring on the Allegany Reservation, Buffalo Creek, and Cattaraugus. In 1820 he returned to Cattaraugus and also took in the Reservation at Tonawanda.[22] During his visits to the reservations he perceived much evidence of the evangelistic fervor.

And it was this evangelism which posed still one more problem for Cornplanter, as well as for Red Jacket and his sachems. It turned out to be very divisive. The invitations to the missionary societies to "come and teach" had opened the doors for an evangelism which was energetic and, for Cornplanter, disconcerting.

By the end of the century's second decade, the Senecas, indeed all of the Iroquois, were split sharply, between two kinds of believers. There were first the unconverted, those who continued to believe in the Great Spirit and worshiped in their traditional tribal religious ceremonies. These, historians are wont to call pagans, that is non-Christian. Blacksnake, and of course Handsome Lake, headed up the resistance to Christianity on the Allegany Reservation, where some 180 Senecas, including five chiefs, could be identified as Christians.[23] They continued to preach the Handsome Lake Code, and to insist on the preservation of the traditional Iroquois ritual and ceremony.[24]

But those who were converted to Christianity, by the Presbyterian ministry chiefly and by others, although the Quakers were not much for proselyting, were numerous, and included many chiefs. As Handsome Lake was the leader of the southern Seneca pagans, Red Jacket was the leader of the northern. Under Red Jacket the Buffalo Senecas barred the evangelists from any activity among them. And so aggressive was he that his wife, who had embraced the Gospel, left him, or he left her (though they were later reconciled);[25] and the Christian chiefs, who were numerous, were able to have him deposed as chief sachem of the Wolf clan. The evangelists had lots of support from those who were already offended by Red Jacket's stout opposition to the selling of the land. This action occurred on September 15, 1827. The decision was overthrown one month later.

Cornplanter was in the habit of welcoming everybody, including the Presbyterian and Congregational preachers whom the Missionary Society of Pittsburgh was sending to him annually. But with all the missionary activity, and the Quaker schools, and Handsome Lake's teachings, Cornplanter was betwixt and between. In 1833 he explained to the evangelical missionaries who were showing up regularly at Jennesadaga that he had "tried the Christian religion and could not get along with it at all." [26] And for a while he actually turned against the Quakers, giving as his reason that they made no attempt to convert the natives! [27] In 1818, in a move they had come to expect, the Chief rudely closed down the school, declaring that he had enough of preaching and would "hear no more."

At some time in the year 1827, when he was in his seventy-fifth year, the troubled chief, noting that he had heard a "voice," explained to the Reverend Timothy Alden the belief he had finally accepted. A disappointed Alden reported it this way: "He seems to have re-adopted his earlier opinions, which, for a length of time, were magnanimously abandoned, and to be settled down under the idea that, although the gospel might be suitable for the white population, the religion taught him and his red brethren and fathers, as he supposes, by Nauwenneyu, or the Great Spirit, is the best adapted to the circumstances and character of Indians." [28]

Certainly, as Anthony Wallace notes, "Cornplanter was not a convert. His joining the Quakers in their worship was more an expression of courtesy and interest than an act of religious conviction. Many Senecas even today [1952] see no inconsistency in participation in both Indian and Christian services." [29]

When the Reverend Timothy Alden, visited Jennesadaga in 1816, he found the community consisting of "about a dozen buildings." He observed some livestock and a number of logs that appeared to be intended for Cornplanter's mill. When Alden returned two years later he found little change. He was alarmed, however, when he learned that the old chief had not been all that well for several months. In fact, Cornplanter had been to Pittsburgh, it is not known how many times, for medical advice and treatment. An unsigned letter, dated February, 1846, is most interesting. It includes this paragraph: "I distinctly recollect him, in the winter of 1817, when he visited Pittsburgh for medical advice, as he suffered exceedingly from rheumatism of the head, which he imputed to witchcraft." [30]

Clearly, from a time shortly after the close of the War of 1812 until some time in 1826 or 1827, Cornplanter was in poor health. His behavior during these years led to suspicions of mental disorder. His condition was so bad that some thought him mad, completely out of his mind, deranged. In truth, he was experiencing what is best regarded as acute melancholia or severe depression, attended by prophetic dreams and visions. It was not unlike the experience suffered by President Abraham Lincoln during the darkest hours of the War Between the States, some forty years later. The difference was that Lincoln had a sense of humor, which helped to bail him out. Lincoln could joke about even the most frightening of his dreams. Cornplanter had no sense of humor whatsoever.[31] None. Whatever he might ever have had was now long extinguished by pain and anxiety.

What had reduced him to this condition? Cornplanter himself, when he was recovered sufficiently to reflect on the illness, attributed it all, as we know, to "witchcraft." Actually, this melancholy was the result, most probably, of great weariness, of discouragement and painful disappointment. It is the kind of illness that comes to one who is very proud, is *very* conscious of obligation, and has for a long, long time borne the weight of great responsibility. It extinguishes every spark of energy. It can lead to irrational rage, to bitterness, even to suicide of course. As early as December1795, in his letter to Major Craig, Chief Cornplanter had lamented "I am by myself to bear all the burden of my people."

It was natural, and very easy, for Cornplanter to blame the whites for the calamity that had befallen the Seneca Nation. Nothing much had happened lately, and nothing was happening now, to relieve the impression that he had been betrayed by the American and Pennsylvania commissioners, as well as by unscrupulous private interests. But deep, very far back, in the recesses of his once nimble mind there lurked the gnawing sense that he, Chief Cornplanter, the leader of the people, had failed. He could not help thinking that perhaps from the very beginning he had been all wrong.

Of course the old chief did not suffer from this melancholy every hour of every day. He had his bright moments. One of these must be brought into this context, as it occurs in 1822. Cornplanter had been called to the Warren County Courthouse, as above described, to receive an explanation from the Commonwealth Commissioners on his taxes. He was invited to speak, and did so, with his characteristic vigor and compelling personality. He did not seem a man suffering from *any* kind of illness. The date is July 6. The theme is a familiar one:

> *Brothers: Yesterday was appointed for us all to meet here. The talk which the Governor sent us pleased us very much. I think that the Great Spirit is very much pleased that the white people have been induced so to assist the Indians as they have done, and that He is pleased also to see the great men of this state and of the United States so friendly to us. We are much pleased with what has been done.*
>
> *The Great Spirit first made the world and next the flying animals, and found all things good and prosperous. He is immortal and everlasting. After finishing the flying animals He came down to earth and there stood. Then He made different kinds of trees and weeds of all sorts, and people of every kind. He made the Spring and other seasons and the weather suitable for planting. These He did make. But stills to make whiskey to be given to Indians He did not make. The Great Spirit bids me tell the white people not to give Indians this kind of liquor. When the Great Spirit had made the earth and its animals, He went into the great lakes, where He breathed as easily as anywhere else, and then made all the different kinds of fish. The Great Spirit looked back on all He had made. The different kinds He made to be separate, and not to mix with and disturb each other. But the white people have broken His command by mixing their color with the Indians. The Indians have done better by not doing so. The Great Spirit wishes that all wars and fighting should cease.*

He next told us that there were three things for our people to attend to. First, we ought to take care of our wives and children. Secondly, the white people ought to attend to their farms and cattle. Thirdly, the Great Spirit has given the bears and the deer to the Indians. He is the cause of all things that exist, and it is very wicked to go against His will. The Great Spirit wishes me to inform the people that they should quit drinking intoxicating drink, as being the cause of disease and death. He told us not to sell any more of our lands, for He never sold lands to anyone. Some of us now keep the seventh day; but I wish to quit it, for the Great Spirit made it for others, but not for the Indians, who ought every day to attend to their business. He has ordered me to quit drinking any intoxicating drink, and not to lust after any woman but my own, and informs me that by doing so I should live the longer. He made known to me that it is very wicked to tell lies. Let no one suppose this I have said now is not true.

I have now to thank the Governor for what he has done. I have informed him what the Great Spirit has ordered me to cease from, and I wish the Governor to inform others of what I have communicated. This is all I have at present to say.[32]

Of this address, Merle Deardorff, Warren County's much esteemed and energetic historian of the Indians, had this to say: "The most eloquent speech that Warren County has ever heard, I am sure." And Chester Hale Sipe, author of *The Indian Chiefs of Pennsylvania*, who thought Cornplanter's speech moving and spirited, declared it to be "eminently characteristic of himself and his race."

Although some strange reasoning appears, as when on mixed marriages he declares the white people have done wrong to mix with Indians, but the Indians have not been guilty in this way, certainly it was not the speech of a man deranged. And, some years before, when Alden returned to Meadville from his 1818 visit to Jennesadaga, though he expressed a continuing concern to a friend, he perceived great improvement: "The aged chief had been under a mental derangement, for several months, but was, to appearance, nearly recovered, when I saw him. He still expresses his desire of religious instruction, and his interest in the prosperity of the school, which continues, but under some discouragements."[33] Alden did remember seeing on this occasion the sword and medals and the Chief's uniform, none of which he perceived in 1827. It was his impression in 1827, when the Chief would be at least seventy-five years old, that these things "had been destroyed several years since." And by this time it seems that the old condition had returned. Alden was most dismayed to find Cornplanter again evidently, to a certain extent, "under some derangement of intellect . . . ."[34]

Most interesting and illuminating is the Reverend Timothy Alden's long letter composed in New York City on June 8, of this same year, 1827. The letter was addressed to a fellow minister, the most distinguished Reverend Abiel Holmes, Doctor of Divinity, and father of the poet-essayist Oliver Wendell Holmes (who was named for Abiel's second wife's father, Oliver Wendell), and grandfather of the man who would one day be Supreme Court Justice Oliver Wendell Holmes. Dr. Holmes is in Cambridge, Massachusetts. Apparently the two pastors have not been in communication for a long time. Alden's letter reveals just how terribly concerned he is about the aging chief, his good friend of many years, and how saddened he is to see this heroic figure in such a state of decline. It could be more than melancholia now. *Madness* may be too strong a term for the condition described by Alden, but clearly there is evidence here of mental instability or of the confusion that can be attributed to senility. Certainly the dramatic rescue of his father, which Cornplanter narrates with such relish, never did happen. The old warrior-chief has confused the details of the actual capture of his father at Canajoharie with an imagined, heroic rescue, perhaps a longed-for event.

Alden notes that he has had a recent opportunity to visit the celebrated Seneca chief at Jennesadaga. "I found him in good health, apparently glad to see me, and for a man of eighty-four [actually seventy-five to seventy-seven] years of age, active, and intelligent . . . yet, evidently, to a certain extent, under some derangement of intellect."

But he notes that Cornplanter has forsaken the Christian religion, and reveres only the Great Spirit. The supernatural voices which he says he hears have told him that "as he was advanced into the vale of years, it was time to lay aside everything calculated to excite ideas of war; and that there were several things in his house, which, to this end he must destroy, that he might have nothing, in the way, to prevent

Abiel Holmes

him from studying and promoting the blessings of peace. The Great Spirit he says, specified, for his definite information, a sword, which General Washington gave him; a gold laced hat, which was a donation from Governor Mifflin; also a French flag and superb belt of wampum, trophies of valour, which had been retained, for several generations, in honour of some of his wife's ancestors, who won them in battle, perhaps two hundred years ago."

And the chief, "conscientiously regarding the injunction, made a large log heap, put the sword upon it, set fire to it, early in the morning and stood by it, all day, till the pile was reduced to ashes, and of that venerated implement of war scarcely a relic remained. At other times, he committed to the flames the gold laced hat, the French flag, and the belt of wampum, which with the sword were once, in his estimation, the most precious articles in his cabinet."

At the suggestion of Henry York of Cattaraugus, Cornplanter determined to prepare his supernatural communications for publication, and Alden, who got to see the manuscript, describes it for Holmes:

> *It commences abruptly with an account of the origin of the human race. A man is said to have dug a hole through the upper world and to have compelled a*

> *woman to sit on its margin with her feet suspended in it. The man then went behind her, gave her a kick, and she fell through to this lower world. The birds, witnessing the descent of this heavenly stranger, flew to her aid, or she would have fallen into a lake. In process of time, she had two children, and, when arrived at old age, told them, that she would die, and designated the spot, where they were directed to bury her. From her grave, white corn, squashes, ground nuts, and tobacco, grew. These, Cornplanter says, were not brought over the big water by white men.*

Alden continues with "further evidence of some mental disorder," reporting that "this noted chief made a speech, of considerable length, at a late council, when, instead of delivering it, in his accustomed manner, he sung it, from the beginning to the end, in a tune of his own invention, to the great amusement and astonishment of his hearers. At the close of this musical performance, he gravely stated, that the Great Spirit had commanded him, for the future, to sing all his speeches."

Then he recites for Dr. Holmes an anecdote which he regards as a credit to the character of the venerable chief:

> *At a certain period of the revolutionary War, Cornplanter ascertained that his father, whom he had not seen for many years, had fallen into the hands of an enemy, and was to be put to death. At the imminent hazard of his own life, he rushed into the midst of the savage foe, with wonderful prowess and strength, rescued his father from the vengeance of the tommahauk and scalping knife, conducted him, in haste, a considerable distance, from the Indian camp, made himself known to him as his son, told him that he would proceed with him no further—that he could do nothing more for him, and that, if he fled, in a certain direction, with the utmost speed, he might possibly escape, as he actually did, with his life.*

He closes out with an apology for the great length of his letter, and a lament for what has happened to his dear friend: "Perhaps you may think that I have written too much of this hero of the forest. The past celebrity of his character is the only apology I offer. Cornplanter, once the terrour of his enemies and the glory of his tribe; at a subsequent period, in the full exercise of his strong mental powers, nobly exerting himself for a knowledge of religious truth, and cordially yielding to its dictates, so far as brought to his understanding, seemed, for a season, to be destined, in providence, to become a burning and shining light to his people; but the all wise God has been pleased to frustrate the expectations of the Christian community, and is suffering his sun to go down in a cloud."

Your brother in the gospel,

Timothy Alden [35]

There comes a time in the life of every man, every man in whom the conscience is active, when he must take the measure of his years. Gaiantwaka had been born a half-breed, but he was ever a Seneca, in every drop of his rich red blood. His god was Nauwenneyu; his home was the wilderness home that for centuries and centuries had been provided for the people he was born to. He had risen to prominence among them, to war-chief and Head Man, to incalculable influence and power. Now, at the end of a long life he was compelled, as every honorable man is, to take stock. The question that reached out to him from the impenetrable darkness was "Did I do right by my people?"

In the end he could not say so. He could only rationalize that he was betrayed by the British commissioners who simply used him to squelch a rebellion; that, with the success of the rebellion, he was betrayed by the American commissioners, who had used him simply to acquire land for a hungry nation. As he reviewed his life, he found a lot he could feel very good about, but there was a lot also to regret. There were mistakes, there were failures. Some of these he could blame on his own inadequacies; some disappointments he could blame on his naivete, or on misplaced trust. The terrible cruelties practiced by the warriors for whom he was responsible he could ascribe to the war situation or justify as a response to hurts received. But such thinking did not quiet his conscience. His was a soul tormented. He was haunted by the vanishing of the land, which Cornplanter as warrior had slowed but little, which Cornplanter as statesman had slowed but little.

Gaiantwaka, he who was the leader of his people, had he done right? Had he not merely followed the easy way, followed the road that had been made comfortable for him, with "rewards for services." Would it not have been better to have declared, for all to hear, "Our land is our land, and death only will separate it from us!" Why was it that among his own people he walked in fear of his life?

That Chief Cornplanter, as he felt his long life coming to its end, was a tortured soul, there can be no question. When he destroyed the cherished mementoes of his career, as he watched them slowly disappear in the enveloping flames, he was engaged in a symbolic act, there can be no question. It may very well have been an expression of disappointment in the people of the "thirteen fires," who had professed friendship and concern, as the generations to follow have presumed. But it may indeed have been an act of shame, a confession that he, the leader of the Seneca Nation, had been bought off, had betrayed the people that he loved.

Either way, he did not desire to be remembered in death. He did not desire to have his life applauded. He longed only for peace with Nauwenneyu.

But Cornplanter's last years were not lived in total darkness. A little excitement came into his life in the spring of 1830. The *Pittsburgh Gazette* of May 28 reported the passage of a strange new vessel on the river. "She left Pittsburgh . . . on the 14th of May, 1830, with sixty-four passengers and twenty-five or thirty tons of freight, and arrived at Warren at nine o'clock on the 19th,—three and one-half days' running time,—and on the same evening she departed from Warren for Olean." This was the steamboat *Allegheny,* making the first-ever steamboat voyage of the upper Allegheny.[36] The boat had been built chiefly by Archibald Tanner of Warren and David Dick of Meadville, although apparently designed by a "Mr. Blanchard of Connecticut." [37] It was ninety feet long and thirteen feet wide. It was powered by two stern wheels, which extended about twelve feet behind the stern. Its maximum speed was three miles per hour.

According to the *Gazette,* "The trip was made to the amusement of the 4,697 inhabitants of the county as witnessed the spectacle and the utter astonishment of the native Senecas." The brothers James and Lewis Follett, of Warren, served as pilots.

The newspaper story reported that "We arrived in Warren, a beautiful village, situated at the outlet of Connewango Creek, at 9:00 on the 19th of May, 200 miles above Pittsburgh." The trip so far had required three and one-half days. These 200 miles normally required keel boats and canoes, manned in the most expert fashion, eighteen to twenty-five days to negotiate.

On the morning after she left Warren, at 9:00, the riverboat put into the bank at Cornplanter's village, which at the time consisted of eight or ten houses at most, accommodating some fifty members of Cornplanter's immediate family. "Here a deputation of gentlemen waited on this ancient and well known Indian King, or Chief, and invited him on board this new and to him wonderful visitor, a steam boat." The newspaper accounts continue: "This venerable old chief was a lad in the French war in 1744 [!], and is now nearly one hundred [!] years of age. He is a smart, active man, seemingly possessed of all his strength of mind, and in perfect health, and retains, among his nation, all that uncontrolled influence he has ever done. Cornplanter's wife and her good mother, one hundred and fifteen years of age [!] are in good health."[38]

Here at Jennesadaga the boat took aboard the old chief, his son Charles, who was sixty years old at this time, and, by some accounts, the chief's son-in-law. According to the report, Cornplanter and Charles and the unnamed son-in-law, having delighted in the trip, departed the steamboat after about six miles, and returned home by canoe. *Most* interesting, especially because of what it reveals of Cornplanter's health, is the account given of the Chief and his house at that time. The deputation which called upon him found him "in all his native simplicity of dress and manner of living, lying on his couch, made of rough pine boards, and covered with deer skins and blankets. His habitation, a two-story log house, was in a state of decay, without furniture, except a few benches, and wooden bowls and spoons to eat out of. He was a smart, active man, seemingly possessed of all his strength of mind and [in] perfect health."[39]

The *Allegheny* docked at Olean Point on the 21st of May, 300 miles upriver from Pittsburgh. The first person to go ashore was Mr. David Dick of Meadville, the principal owner of the boat. The vessel was back in Pittsburgh at 4:00 p.m. on May 24.[40]

In his last years the aged Chief Cornplanter was definitely a bitter man, disillusioned and discouraged. Although he was much disappointed in his eldest son Henry, with whom his relationship had been much strained from time to time, Merle Deardorff insists that Henry "was not disowned by his father, as some have thought." His bitterness "had nothing to do with Henry." And when in 1832 Henry, because of excessive drinking, was killed in an accident, the father was much grieved. No, it was not disappointment in Henry that turned Chief Cornplanter finally against everything of the white people.[41] It was the larger disillusionment he suffered as he reviewed the history of the treatment of his people by the whites. Or, as suggested above, it was the acute consciousness of his own failure to preserve the Indian lands and culture. As Reverend Timothy Alden reported to Dr. Holmes, Chief Cornplanter had had a vision. He had informed Dr. Alden that the Great Spirit had appeared to him with a message—to reject all that had come to the Senecas from the whites. And surely it was this dream that caused him to burn the much cherished mementos of his long career: the sword which had been presented to him by Washington, the gold-laced hat which was a gift from Governor Mifflin, his beautiful wampum belt, and the flag of France.[42] That he was taking it all personally, that he was blaming himself, is suggested by his changing of his name, from Gaiantwaka (which suggests growth and vitality) to Nonuk, which means "Cold" or "Dead," which is how he saw himself.[43] And in his last years he simply faded away, as old warriors sometimes do, unnoticed and unacclaimed.

On February 18, 1836, the long and vigorous life of Pennsylvania's most notable Indian finally came to a close. The great Seneca Indian chief, known first as Cyantwahia or Gaiantwaka and later as Cornplanter, who had allied his people with the British in their effort to squelch the rebellion in the colonies, and who had after the Treaty of Paris, worked zealously for peace along the frontier, was laid to rest, in the backyard of his home, here where he had lived out the last fifty-six years of his long life, near the great river he had always loved. The very moving and respectful ceremony that was befitting the great chief did not occur. There was delivered no stirring eulogy. Indeed, there was present no official representative of the Seneca Nation, which he had labored to preserve. There was no representative of the infant United States, whose character he had helped to form. There was no representative of the Quaker State, whose early history he had helped to write. In the way that old warriors often simply fade away—that was the way with the great chief.

How he was received by the Great Spirit was touchingly described by one of the few present: "I was there and saw him buried. They had just a rough box nailed together. Four men carried him to the grave a short distance from the house. They went ahead and the Indians came next, marching in Indian form, single file; then the squaws the same way. They went by a path back of his house in the woods. There they had a hole dug in which they placed him and covered him up. Not a word was said by any of them. They did not know what to do. They went back to the house as they came out in single file, and there they sat down, mute and no talking, all quiet, not the least mark left to tell where he was buried, only the fresh dirt that did not last long."[44]

And it was in this way that the great chief preferred to pass from his people. Embittered and cruelly tormented, broken in body and spirit, the aged warrior in his last years had requested an unmarked grave, known only to *Nauwenneyu.* But that could be the case for only a short time.

In fact, only thirty years after his interment, the Commonwealth of Pennsylvania, at the urging of the Pennsylvania Historical Commission, elected to establish a monument to his memory, and in 1866, by the Legislative Act of January 25, there was erected at this grave site,[45] by the direction of Samuel P. Johnson, Esq., of Warren (at a cost of $550) a beautiful Vermont marble shaft, eleven feet in height. It has been regarded ever since as the first monument ever erected to an American Indian.

And the tardy ceremony finally took place. A very long and laudatory dedicatory address was delivered by James Ross Snowden. The principal war-chief of the Senecas, and their chief statesman as well, was celebrated for his great courage, but he was esteemed, too, for his sagacity, for the power of his speech, for his forward looking, and for his desire for peace. The three surviving children were present, and so was one of his better known grandsons, Solomon O'Bail, as well as a great many other descendants. Snowden's remarks, which amount to a mini-biography, were repeated, on request, to a joint session of the Pennsylvania House and Senate on March 14, 1867. And the speech was published in an edition of 1000 copies by order of the Legislature.[46]

Because of so much weathering the old monument, which had to be moved because of the Kinzua Dam, has been replaced by an exact replica (except granite for marble) and in the same place, at the

Riverview-Corydon Cemetery, in Elk Township, Warren County. It was dedicated at 2 p.m. on Sunday, October 18, 1998.

Gyantwahia
The
Cornplanter
John
O'Bail
Alias

Cornplanter
Died
At Cornplanter Town
Feb. 18 AD 1836
Age About 100 Years

Upon another side it is noted that the monument has been "Erected by Authority of the Legislature of Pennsylvania By Act Passed Mar.

AD 1866." On a third side there is acknowledged the service rendered by the Boy Scouts in the restoration and preservation of the monument. A "Good Deed," declares the inscription, "Chief Cornplanter Council Boy Scouts of America." And the replica is dated "1998."

Upon the remaining side there is provided a capsule account of the life and character of Cornplanter: "Chief of the Seneca tribe and a principal Chief of the 6 nations from the period of the Revolutionary War to the time of his death distinguished for talents, courage, eloquence sobriety and love for his tribe and race to whose welfare he devoted his time, his energy and his means during a long and eventful life."

The beautiful monument presides over the waters to which the noble chieftain was steadfastly devoted, the lovely Allegheny, backed up now to include a lake, a lake that the Chief was never to see.

There are other monuments too. The famous chief is immortalized all over the northwestern region of the Quaker State. At least three wilderness streams go by the name Cornplanter Run. One of course is the brooklet that flows into the Allegheny at the site of the Cornplanter Tract; another is a tributary of Buffalo Creek; the third emerges from the Allegheny forest to swell Oil Creek a little.

In Forest County the Chief is remembered in the Cornplanter Forest District and in a 1256-acre section of the District called the Cornplanter State Forest. In Venango County can be found Cornplanter Township, which includes Oil City, and which is served by the Cornplanter Volunteer Fire Department. Warren County is home to the very active Chief Cornplanter Council of the Boy Scouts of America, the same which has so much helped to preserve the cemetery monument.

But surely the monument that the "Old Chief" would cherish the most is to be perceived in the healthy lives of the members of his big family. It would please him to know that his name continues in those who descend from his children's children. It would please him to know that there is a Cornplanter Descendants Association, that it is alive and well, and that it prints and distributes a bonding newsletter and sets aside the first Saturday in August each and every year for a happy get-together in a Cornplanter family picnic.

Afterword

Of all the colonies, surely Pennsylvania, because of William Penn and the Quakers, who felt a special kinship to the native peoples they found living there, was the most sympathetic and friendly and helpful to the Indians. It is somewhat ironic, then, that today in the Keystone State there are only a very few Indians living. And there is no reservation, no land that can be called Indian land. The Indians of the northeast live in New York State, in Quebec and Ontario.

The Seneca Nation of Indians, which is a federally recognized tribe, came into being some twelve years after the death of Cornplanter, when it put an end to the old "Chief" system and endorsed a constitution which required elected officials. The Senecas consider themselves a sovereign, independent nation, but actually in their government they are closely and well coordinated with local, New York State, and federal agencies. The Nation holds title to three reservations in the western region of New York State, all established by the Pickering Treaty of 1794, which Cornplanter signed. These are Cattaraugus, Oil Springs, and Allegany.

The Cattaraugus Reservation embraces 21,680 acres, and is located across the three counties of Erie, Chautauqua, and Cattaraugus, in the region of Irving, New York. This reservation extends along the Cattaraugus Creek from Gowanda to the shore of Lake Erie.

The Allegany Reservation is located north from the Pennsylvania-New York border upriver to Vandalia, New York, and is entirely in Cattaraugus County with some 20,468 acres (almost forty-four square miles). If the area inundated by the Kinzua Dam is included, the total area is almost 31,000 acres. The reservation is a narrow strip of land lying along both banks of the Allegheny River, and including an oxbow bend in the river. It was at one time some forty-two miles long, but is now only thirty miles long. It averages about 1.5 miles in width. Included within the Allegany Reservation is the city of Salamanca, recognized as the only city in the states to be on a reservation. A portion to the south carries the name of Jimersontown. Also accommodated by the reservation are the villages of South Valley, Cold Spring, Great Valley, Red House, Allegany, Kill Buck, Vandalia, and Carrolltown.

The Oil Springs reservation, located near Cuba, New York, is very small. It was originally surveyed to encompass a mile square around the natural oil springs that the Seneca used to cure illness. There are but a few businesses located on this reservation.

A few acres remain of the original acreage designated the "Cornplanter Grant" in Pennsylvania, south of the New York State border on the west bank of the Allegheny River.

About fifty per cent of the people living on these three reservations are Native Americans. The Indians are primarily Senecas of course, but a number of Cayugas abide here as well. The current tribal membership is approximately 6400, half of whom live on the reservations. The Seneca people also reside on a number of other reservations and in urban areas in the United States and on the Grand River in Ontario. The Tonawanda band of Senecas occupies the Tonawanda Reservation near Akron, New York.

The total number of Senecas living on the several reservations of New York State, Quebec, and Ontario is probably close to 25,000.

Chief Cornplanter in his long life as war-chief and Head Man and principal negotiator for the Iroquois suffered a great many hurts to his people. But one of the biggest blows of all he missed out on. It was a pain that he was spared.

On March 24, 1789, the Quaker State awarded Cornplanter 1600 acres of land at four sites in the region of the Allegheny River. In 1794, by the Treaty of Canandaigua, the United States awarded the Seneca Nation a reservation, called Allegany, 31,000 acres, upriver from the Cornplanter Grant. These lands were given to Cornplanter and to the Seneca people in perpetuity, theirs "forever."

President George Washington in his December 29, 1790, Proclamation to a delegation of Senecas headed by Cornplanter, declared from the capital in Philadelphia: "Your great object seems to be the security of your remaining lands, and I have therefore, upon this point, meant to be sufficiently strong and clear. That in the future you cannot be defrauded of your lands; that you possess the right to sell and the right of refusing to sell your lands."

Four years later, while representing the United States at the Canandaigua treaty sessions, which established the Allegany Reservation,

Timothy Pickering declared to Cornplanter and the attending Senecas: "This [Treaty of November 11, 1794] is a new and important security against your being cheated; and shows the faithful care which the United States now means to take for the protection of your lands."

And the Canandaigua Treaty contains this passage: "Now the United States acknowledges all the land within the aforementioned boundaries, to be the property of the Seneca Nation, and the United States will never claim the same, nor disturb the Seneca Nation."

In 1908 a proposal to build a dam on the upper Allegheny River was sounded. Over a period of fifty years this proposal steadily became more and more attractive. As it was taken more and more seriously, controversy raised its ugly head.

In the ensuing arguments four good reasons for the construction of the dam were presented. The greatest value of the proposed dam of course was its capacity for flood control. The community of Warren and towns down the river all the way to its confluence with the Monongahela, and including the city of Pittsburgh itself, would be protected.

Advocates pointed out also that a second value lay in the recreational opportunities the dam would make possible. They envisioned a vast lake which would provide for boating, fishing, hiking, camping, canoeing, and water skiing. And a third good reason for constructing the dam was drought relief. Not only could the dam back up potential flooding water, the reservoir could provide water in time of need. There was a fourth value, too: hydroelectric power.

And there was no good reason *not* to build the dam, was there? Oh, yes, there was one. The proposed structure would necessarily displace the people living on the lands that would be inundated by the backed up water. Was that a problem?

Turned out it was a problem.

As the dam began to look more and more like a possibility, controversy grew. As the dam began to look more and more like a probability, the controversy heated up. As the situation became understood all across the country, the prospect of a dam on the upper Allegheny inspired outrage.

The Indians living on the Grant, Cornplanter's descendants chiefly, and those whose homes were on the threatened portion of the Allegany Reservation, not surprisingly, voiced strong and passionate opposition. Indeed, the Seneca resistance was massive and bitter. And the natives had their influential supporters in people like United States

Congressman John Saylor of Cambria County, Pennsylvania,[1] who, very much concerned about the Senecas, felt that other sites might be considered. He was put off by the great expense too, and by doubt that the dam might be so effective as its engineers supposed.

In nearby Warren, Merle Deardorff, long a genuine and devoted friend of the Senecas, got into the debate. Deardorff pointed out that federal authorities had concluded that "insofar as the United States was and is concerned this [Cornplanter] reservation is individual property over which the United States has no jurisdiction."[2] In the winter of 1969 (after the dam was completed) in a letter to Dr. Sylvester Stevens of the Pennsylvania State Museum, he declared "I am the original Pennsylvania white involved in this Dam business in the Indians' behalf from the beginning . . . ."

Even the celebrated country-western singer Johnny Cash got in on it, recording with much feeling the plaintive ballad "As Long As the Grass Shall Grow," which was composed by Peter La Farge as a lament for the plight of the Seneca people.

Those opposed to the dam were constantly pointing out that the Army Corps of Engineers had not considered alternate sites. Arthur Morgan, a hydraulic engineer invited by the Indians to find an alternate site, did so. In fact, he identified several, including some which he insisted would serve much better than the proposed Kinzua site.

Opponents, taking their cue from Saylor, constantly referred to the terrific cost of the project, and raised questions about the dam's effectiveness in preventing floods. But most disturbing, and most consequential for the arguments of the opposition, was the displacement of the people from their homeland. The Pickering Treaty was always out front.

Powerful forces were assembled to support the effort to halt construction of the dam. A number of lawsuits were filed. On behalf of the Seneca Nation the Society of Friends, ever a genuine and helpful friend to the Indians of the Quaker State, filed in the courts a suit against the breaking of the Pickering Treaty, by which the United States had guaranteed *perpetual* ownership of the land to the Senecas. The case was carried all the way to the United States Supreme Court, where it lost out to the right of eminent domain.

In fact, all suits were ultimately dismissed.

And the way was cleared. Actual construction of the dam, which had been authorized by the Flood Control Acts of 1936, 1938, and 1941, was begun, by the Army Corps of Engineers, in 1960.

When the dam was finally completed, in 1965, what did the people of Pennsylvania and New York have?

As the reservoir filled, the rising waters inundated virtually *all* of the habitable land of the Cornplanter Grant. As Deardorff noted, the dam "did leave about 168 acres of the high land thereon 'as is,' so that there is still a piece of Indian land in Pennsylvania, a pathetic remnant left to the people who once owned it all. Let's see how long it will be before this, too, is taken under one pretext or another."[3]

The rising waters flooded as well 10,000 acres of the Allegany Reservation in New York State, one third of the reservation, cemeteries and all. The Allegany Reservoir was created, an impressive body of water, called Kinzua Lake, twenty-five to twenty-seven miles long, and very deep.

Another 20,000 acres of Seneca land was rendered virtually useless, inasmuch as the waters would rise and fall over these lands bordering the central reservoir.

Cornplanter's grave and his monument of course were imperiled. Everybody agreed that the chief's remains and the monument should be removed before the dam was completed, but there occurred lots of confusion and disagreement about where to re-locate. Owing much to the efforts of Merle Deardorff, the monument, together with Cornplanter's remains was moved in time to escape the inundation. It was the same monument and continued to overlook Cornplanter's beloved Allegheny. Because it suffers so much from time and weather, of course it has required refurbishing from time to time. It had a really good overhaul in 1977, and not long ago was entirely replaced by a replica carrying a new inscription together with the slightly varied originals. It stands now in the Riverview-Corydon Cemetery high above the waters of the Kinzua Dam, several miles to the north of the Grant. For forty-five years now the Cornplanter monument, as well as the many other graves of the cemetery, has had the tender, loving care of eighty-eight-year-old Harry Tome of the Bradford area. Harry, who proudly declares he is the great great grandson of Philip Tome, the elk-hunter and "sometime interpreter" for the Chief, has long been with the Riverview Cemetery Association and is currently the President.

But besides Cornplanter's remains, the dam displaced almost 700 people (some 130 Indian families), 230 descendants of Chief Cornplanter and 400 Senecas of the Allegany Reservation. These Indians lost their homes. They lost their church. They lost their tribal hunting and fishing grounds. The last Indian school[4] to be found anywhere in Pennsylvania surrendered to the enveloping waters. Indeed the proud and richly storied Seneca Nation vanished completely and probably forever from the Quaker State of William Penn.

It took some time, but eventually the Senecas were compensated, by the United States government, which provided the Nation fifteen million dollars for the lost land and the costs of relocation.

Was it right to build the Kinzua Dam? Judged strictly from moral and ethical standards, probably not, although even there it can be argued that for displaced people hundreds of lives have been saved. Judged from a practical point of view the answer would seem to be yes.

So what have the people of the Allegheny watershed got?

The Kinzua Dam was built at a cost of 108 million dollars (by some accounts, 114 million). It is located on the Allegheny River, six miles east of Warren and almost 200 miles above the confluence of the Allegheny and Monongahela Rivers, which form the Ohio. The reservoir that is produced by the dam spans the Pennsylvania-New York border. It is located in Warren and McKean Counties, Pennsylvania, and in Cattaraugus County, New York.

The project area is 26,541 acres. The breast of the dam reaches to a height of 179 feet above the streambed. The length of the lake when water is considered "normal" is close to twenty-five miles.

The portion of the reservoir in Pennsylvania is completely surrounded by the Allegheny National Forest (500,000 acres). In New York State the lake is embraced by the Allegany State Park (65,000 acres). The Kinzua Lake can boast nearly 100 miles of forested shoreline.

Almost the entire portion of the New York State shoreline is bounded by the Allegany Indian Reservation of the Seneca Nation.

The dam controls drainage on a watershed of 2180 square miles (twice the size of Rhode Island). This size means that the Kinzua Dam is the largest dam in this country east of the Mississippi. And the lake that is formed is Pennsylvania's deepest. And the lake is getting larger! It is estimated that the shoreline has eroded seventy to ninety feet over the past forty years. Even the Riverview-Corydon-Cornplanter Cemetery is imperiled.

Has the Kinzua Dam proved effective in flood control? The answer has to be a resounding yes. It has provided protection for the community of Warren, and has effectively discouraged flooding in the villages downstream and in Pittsburgh. It has been estimated that during the floods of June, 1972, which were in consequence of tropical storm Agnes, damages that would have reached 247 million dollars were prevented.

What about hydroelectric power? The generating power plant is operated by the First Energy Corporation. It reports a peak capacity of 400,000 kilowatts per hour, a significant contribution to the energy pool.

And of course the dam, since the water is stored in such great quantity, is well prepared to relieve drought at any time.

Recreation? Here is a very deep lake twenty-five miles long, surrounded by deep forests. It affords matchless opportunity for outdoors and nature recreation year round. All of the water sports, as well as camping and hiking, are provided for the public.

So what of the Indians who were displaced fifty years ago? Well, to speak generally, these families appear to be well adjusted. They suffered trauma in the loss of their beloved homestead, but that has been put behind them.[5] By all accounts the Senecas, many of whom reside today on the Allegany reservation, or close to it, while assimilated and comfortable in the white man's modern world, keep alive the Iroquois customs, and the Iroquois culture which is their precious heritage.

It is not known just how many children Cornplanter had. In fact, it is not known how many wives he had, or how many at one time. According to his son Charles, who was interviewed by Lyman Draper,[6] Cornplanter's son Henry was born of one mother and he, Charles, of another. Henry we know was born in 1774, when Cornplanter was probably twenty-two years old and living at Ganawaugus; Charles was born in 1778, in the year before the arrival of the Sullivan expedition. Early historians report Cornplanter showing up in Warren and Pittsburgh with "wives." The *History of Warren County*, for example, reports that "Cornplanter with his two wives, his children, and a following of many others of his band . . . became permanently established." But clearly he had only one wife at the time of the Quakers' arrival at Jennesadaga in 1798, and for the rest of his life.

By at least two wives, Cornplanter had *at least* ten children, five daughters and four sons and a child who died at the time Cornplanter was participating in the Fort Stanwix conference in October of 1784.

For three sons (Henry, Charles, and William) and three of the daughters (Polly, Esther, and Ja-wah-a-joh), thanks to the tireless genealogical work of Jack Ericson, we have lots of information.

Five daughters, according to Anthony Wallace in his *Death and Rebirth of the Seneca*, were living with their father at Cornplanter Town in 1798. One of these died in January or February of 1799. A son named John is remarked on by Philip Tome in his *Pioneer Life* (1854), but there is no other record of him. To another (?) son, referred to always as "the Idiot," Cornplanter was apparently much devoted, but there is little record of him.[7]

Apparently only five children were living at the time of their father's death in 1836. Henry had died in an accident at Tonawanda on April 25, 1832. Charles, William, Polly, Esther, and *Ja-wa-joh* survived their father. For a long time after Cornplanter's death his estate was held undivided by the several heirs. Merle Deardorff reports that at the request of the heirs, "The Pennsylvania legislature in 1871 authorized partition of the Cornplanter lands and stipulated that control of the land must always remain in Seneca hands. The heirs met and agreed on their several interests. On August 21 of that year, 1871, a meeting was convened in the schoolhouse. Presiding were three Quaker commissioners, appointed by the Warren County Orphans Court. All of the heirs were represented at the meeting. The commissioners recognized six children of Chief Cornplanter, all dead except Polly (Polly O'Bail Logan). One-sixth share in the lands was allotted the heirs of each of Cornplanter's three identifiable sons—Henry, Charles and William; and one-sixth to [the heirs] of each [of the daughters], Esther, Polly, and a third daughter dead so long ago that only her Indian name, Ja-wa-joh, was remembered. Polly died December 7, 1871, soon after completion of the division in October of that year." [8]

The legislative act, passed May 21, 1871, made property awards to these heirs: Hannah Silverheels, wife of James Cooper; Jonathan Pierce, a descendant of Esther; Polly Logan; Solomon O'Bail, Henry's son; Emily O'Bail Hotbread, daughter of Henry; Betsy O'Bail Thompson, granddaughter of Henry; Esther Abrams; Henry Abrams; Lucy Thompson, daughter of Henry; Eleanor Jacobs; Lucinda Pierce, granddaughter of Esther; Wallace Pierce, grandson of Esther; James Pierce, grandson of Esther; Marsh Pierce, son of Esther; Allen Jacobs; Caroline Plummer Jimison; George Titus; James Blacksnake; and David Gordon.[9]

Charles and William Abeel

By 1940 only about forty of the Cornplanter heirs were still living on the Grant, but, as Deardorff notes, perhaps as many as 550 were interested in the property.[10]

Although much confusion continues over birth dates and death dates and marriages and children, a helpful genealogy (which follows the line of Henry chiefly) is available from the Seneca Library at the Seneca Museum in Irving, New York, and a more complete genealogy may be had from Cornplanter family historian Jack Ericson of Westfield, New York. According to the Ericson family tree, Henry, Cornplanter's eldest child, was twice married and had three children, two daughters (Emily and Julia) and the firstborn, a son named Solomon. Less is known about the second son, Charles, but he appears to have been a man of spotless reputation and married to a fine and devoted wife, who bore him four daughters. About another son, known only as "the Idiot," very little is known, except that Cornplanter cared for him tenderly.

A little more is known about daughter Polly. She was married to a Cayuga named John Logan. Like her father, she lived a long life, dying shortly after the estate was divided. Cornplanter's son William was married and the father of three daughters. One of these, Esther, was married to Moses Pierce and had four children, Marsh, Jonathan, Susan, and another daughter for whom we have no name. Jawajuh (Jawajoh, Jiiwi), Cornplanter's youngest daughter, who died young, was the mother of Abraham (Abram) Silverheels.

Cornplanter's grandson Marsh Pierce, son of Esther and Moses Pierce, was educated by the Quakers and became a builder by trade. He married Cassandry Silverheels, and by her had nine sons and two daughters.

Among other descendants of Cornplanter are Mrs. George Lee, granddaughter of Jenny Blacksnake, who was the granddaughter of Chief Cornplanter. She lived a lifetime on the Grant and reared two daughters, Nellie and Harriet. Leonard Lee, who was a son of Elizabeth Dowdy Lee and great-great grandson of Cornplanter, also lived on the Grant. He was an artist. Two descendants, Mrs. Harriett Pierce and Merrill W. Bowen, in May of 1973 filed claim to the "one-mile square" property deeded to their great-great-great grandfather at Marietta on February 9, 1789.

Henry's grandson Solomon O'Bail in 1957 claimed all the land along Oil Creek, on which Oil City is now located. He petitioned Harrisburg and won a hearing, but the Pennsylvania Legislature did not find the claim substantiated. Jesse J. Cornplanter, who by some is thought to be a fifth-generation descendant, and by others is thought only to have taken the name, died in March of 1957, at his home on Council Road, on the Tonawanda Reservation near Akron, New York. He was sixty-seven years old. A son of Chief Edward Cornplanter, he had been producing sketches since he was seven years old. He wrote *Legends of the Longhouse* and made frequent appearances at Seneca ceremonials. He had fought in World War I and was wounded.

The descendants of Cornplanter are of course well scattered by now, almost 180 years beyond his death, but many continue to live on or near the Allegany Reservation, some near the Kinzua Dam, and some close enough to the old Cornplanter Grant to feel a special kinship.

It is the city of Salamanca which is now at the heart of the Seneca Nation. Here in the city, which is completely within the Allegany Reservation, or in nearby Irving, are to be found the Seneca Nation Museum and the Seneca Library. Director of the Museum, which opened August 1, 1977, is Ms. Jaré Cardinal. In the Museum can be found many of the principal features of the Iroquois culture, and a tour of the exhibits (conducted generally by Josh Johnnyjohn) brings one close to the life

led by the Senecas in times long ago. Not much of Cornplanter is here, but there is a cane which is supposed to be the Chief's "magic" cane. On one wall are displayed the memorable, plaintive words from the speech made by Red Jacket at Buffalo Creek in May of 1811: "In making up our minds we have looked back, and remembered how the Yorkers purchased our land in former times. They bought them piece by piece for a little money paid to a few men in our nation, and not to all our brethren; our planting and hunting grounds have become very small, and if we sell these we know not where to spread our blankets."

Head of the library, which is next door to the museum, is Pam Bowen, a great-great-great-great granddaughter of Cornplanter. She will graciously supply you whatever book about the Iroquois you care to see, or impart whatever information about the history of the Senecas you desire to have.

Seneca children attend the public schools, which do offer training in the Seneca tongue. There is also on the Allegany Reservation, west of Salamanca, an Immersion School for Senecas through the twelve grades.

When Cornplanter built his sawmill on the upper Allegheny he was setting aside a moment in history. He did not know that he was doing this. But it was a dramatic event. For the sawmill was the very first venture into business by a Seneca, or perhaps by any Indian anywhere. With this sawmill the Chief delivered his people from one way of life to another. Nowhere is "assimilation" more evident than in the white man's world of business, where today the Senecas are very active. Yet these First Americans cling tenaciously to the culture of their ancestors. The Seneca Nation is composed of a proud people. They have their history.

They have their heroes. It is altogether fitting and proper that their roots should be nourished, that their story should be preserved, as their land could not, for the time now and the time to come.

Image Credits

Cornplanter Monument, photo by Tom Betts, July 22, 2010.

Cornplanter (Gyantawanka), portrait by Frederick Bartoli (1796). Collection of New-York Historical Society.

Mary Jemison monument, Letchworth State Park. Photo by Tom Betts,1995.

Sir William Johnson, from a portrait in the State Library at Albany, that was copied from an original owned by Sir John Johnson.

Peter Gansevoort, portrait in oil on canvas by Gilbert Stuart (ca.1794). Courtesy the Munson-Williams-Proctor Art Institute, Utica, New York, 54.88.

Joseph Brant (Thayendanegea), portrait by Charles Willson Peale, from life, 1797. Independence National Historical Park.

Nicholas Herkimer, courtesy of Oneida County (N.Y.) Historical Society, Utica, New York.

Oriskany Battlefield Monument, courtesy of Oneida County (N. Y.) Historical Society, Utica, New York.

John Sullivan, portrait by A. Tenney, after portrait by Ulysses Dow Tenney, developed from 1790 pencil sketch by John Trumbull. Collections of the State of New Hampshire, Division of Historical Resources.

James Clinton, courtesy of Florida Center for Instructional Technology.

Allegheny River at Redbank, photo (1995) by Thomas Betts.

David Ramsay, from the original portrait by Rembrandt Peale. Independence National Historical Park.

Arthur St. Clair, portrait by Charles Willson Peale, from life, 1782-84. Independence National Historical Park.

Thomas Mifflin, portrait in oil by Charles Willson Peale, 1783-84. Independence National Historical Park.

Josiah Harmar, portrait by Raphaelle Peale, from an engraving by John Sartain. Courtesy of the Ohio Historical Society, Columbus, Ohio.

Little Turtle (Michikinkna), portrait by an unknown artist at an unknown date. Courtesy of the Ohio Historical Society, Columbus, Ohio.

Richard Butler, portrait by John Trumbull. Courtesy Butler County (Pa.) Historical Society.

Blue Jacket (Weyapiersenwah). Courtesy of Shelby County (Ohio) Historical Society.

Henry Knox, portrait by Charles Willson Peale, from life, ca.1784. Independence National Historical Park.

John Graves Simcoe, portrait, oil on canvas, by George Theodore Berthon, ca. 1881. Courtesy of Governor Simcoe Branch, United Empire Loyalists Association of Canada.

Red Jacket, from "The Indian Tribes of North America," photographer unknown. Courtesy of National Museum of the American Indian, Smithsonian Institution.

Anthony Wayne, portrait by James Sharples, Sr., from life, 1796. Independence National Historical Park.

John Adlum, courtesy of The State Museum of Pennsylvania, Pennsylvania Historical and Museum Commission.

Image Credits

Timothy Pickering, portrait by Charles Willson Peale from life (1792-93). Independence National Historical Park.

Henry Abeel, portrait, ca. 1827, by Charles B. King. Original in National Museum, Copenhagen. Courtesy of Warren County (Pa.) Historical Society.

Henry Dearborn, portrait, from life, by Charles Willson Peale (1796-7). Independence National Historical Park.

Red Jacket, "The Trial of Red Jacket," portrait by John Mix Stanley. Gift of George M. Stanley (grandson of the artist) and family. Copyright American Art Museum. Courtesy of Smithsonian American Art Museum.

Joseph Hiester, Wikipedia.

William Irvine, portrait from an oil painting by B. Otis, after one by Robert Edge Pine, an eminent English artist who came to America in 1784. The original was taken in New York City, when Irvine (at age 48) was a member of Congress. Courtesy of Archives and Special Collections, Dickinson College, Carlisle, Pa.

Timothy Alden, Allegheny College Archives, Wayne and Sally Merrick Historic Archival Center, Pelletier Library, Allegheny College, Meadville, Pa.

Abiel Holmes, portrait from the Archives, courtesy of First Church in Cambridge, Congregational, UCC, Cambridge, Mass.

Cornplanter monument, photo by Tom Betts, 2010.

Charles and William Abeel, photograph taken prior to 1868. Courtesy of Warren County (Pa.) Historical Society.

Seneca Iroquois National Museum, author photo, 2006.

Works Consulted

Primary Materials

Abler, Thomas S., ed. *Chainbreaker: The Revolutionary War Memoirs of Governor Blacksnake As Told to Benjamin Williams* (Lincoln: University of Nebraska Press, 1989).

Alden, Reverend Timothy, *An Account of Sundry Missions Performed among the Senecas and Munsees: In a Series of Letters* (New York: J. Seymour, 1827).

Alden, Timothy, The Timothy Alden Papers, Allegheny College, Meadville, Pa.

Allinson, William, The Journal of William Allinson, 1809 (at Haverford College, Haverford Pa.).

American State Papers: Documents, Legislative and Executive, of the Congress of the United States, Indian Affairs, ed. Walter Lowrie, et al. (Washington, D.C.: Gales and Seaton, 1832-61). 2 vols.

Blacksnake, *Chainbreaker's War: A Seneca Chief Remembers,* ed. Jeanne Winston Adler (Hensonville, N. Y.: Black Dome Press, Inc., 2002).

Brodhead, Daniel, "Daniel Brodhead Papers," in Lyman C. Draper Collection, Series F, vols. 16-18; Series H, vols. 1-3; Series S, vols. 1-9 (Madison: Historical Society of Wisconsin).

Colonial Records of Pennsylvania (Minutes of the Supreme Executive Council) (Harrisburg, Pa.: Theodore Fenn, 1853).

Cook, Frederick, ed. *Journals of the Military Expedition of Major General John Sullivan against the Six Nations of Indians in 1779, with Records of Centennial Celebrations* (Auburn, N. Y.: Knapp, Peck, and Thomson, 1887).

Cornplanter File, Warren County Historical Society, Warren, Pa.

Denny, Ebenezer, "Military Journal of Ebenezer Denny," *Memoirs of the Historical Society of Pennsylvania*, VII (Philadelphia, 1860), 345-353.

Draper, Lyman C., *Draper Manuscripts* (Madison, Wisconsin: State Historical Society of Wisconsin). 25 vols.

Fitzpatrick, John C., ed. *The Diaries of George Washington* (Boston: Mt. Vernon Ladies' Association, 1925).

Fitzpatrick, John C., ed. *The Writings of George Washington, 1744-1799* (Washington, D.C.: United States Government Printing Office, 1931-1944). 39 vols.

George Morgan Letterbooks (1775-79), 3 vols. Carnegie Library, Pittsburgh, Pa.

Harris, Benjamin, "History of the Harris Family," unpublished letters (Harrison Smith Morris and Amos Harris), April 21, 1850.

Henry Simmons Journal (1799), with the Friends Historical Library, Swarthmore College, Swarthmore, Pa. Printed in David Swatzler, *A Friend among the Senecas*, pp. 257-278.

Hollister, Isaac, *A Brief Narration of the Captivity of Isaac Hollister, Who Was Taken by the Indians, Anno Domini, 1763* (New London, Ct.: (Printed and Sold at the Printing Office in New London, 1767).

Jackson, Halliday, "A Short History of My Sojourning in the Wilderness, 1798-1800." Printed in "Halliday Jackson's Journal to the Seneca Indians, 1798-1800," ed. by

Anthony F. C. Wallace, *Pennsylvania History*, XIX, No. 2 (April, 1952), pp. 117-147; No. 3 (July, 1952), pp. 325-349.

Jackson, Halliday, "Halliday Jackson's Journal of a Visit Paid to the Indians of New York (1806)," ed. by George F. Snyderman, *Proceedings of the American Philosophical Society*, CI, No. 6 (December, 1957), 565-599.

Johnson, William, *The Papers of Sir William Johnson,* ed. James Sullivan, et al. (Albany: Prepared for publication by the Division of Archives and History, The University of the State of New York, 1921-1965). 14 vols.

Kirkland, Samuel, The Samuel Kirkland Papers (Journal for 1846), at Hamilton College, Clinton, New York.

Lincoln, General Benjamin, "Journal of a Treaty Held in 1793, with the Indian Tribes North-West of the Ohio, by Commissioners of the United States," *Collections of the Massachusetts Historical Society*, Series 3, V (1836), 109-176.

Meginness, John Franklin, ed. *Journal of Samuel Maclay, While Surveying the West Branch of the Susquehanna, the Sinnemahoning and the Allegheny Rivers, in 1790* (Williamsport, Pa.: John F. Meginness, 1887).

O'Reilly Collection, New York Historical Society.

Parrish, Joseph, The Joseph Parrish Papers, at Vassar College, Poughkeepsie, New York.

Pennsylvania Archives, First Series, ed. Samuel Hazzard (Philadelphia: J. Stevens, 1852-56); Second Series, ed. John B. Linn and William H. Egle (Harrisburg, Pa.: 1896); Fourth Series, ed. George E. Reed (Harrisburg, Pa.: 1900); Eighth Series, ed. Gertrude MacKinney (Philadelphia: B. Franklin and D. Hall, vols. I, II, and III, 1752, 1753, 1754 respectively; vols. IV, V, and VI, 1774, 1775, and 1776 respectively).

Philadelphia Yearly Meeting Archives (Indian Committee; John Pierce Journal (1801); Joseph Elkinton Journals (1810-1828).

Proctor, Thomas, "Narrative of the Journey of Col. Thomas Proctor to the Indians of the North-West, 1791," *Pennsylvania Archives,* Second Series, vol. IV (1876), pp. 465-524.

Savery, William, *A Journal of the Life, Travels, and Religious Labours of William Savery*, ed. Jonathan Evans (London: Charles Gilpin, 1844).

Sharpless, Joshua, "A Visit to Cornplanter in 1798: Extracts from the Diary of Joshua Sharpless," Published in 1930 in Warren, Pa. *Times-Mirror* (original manuscript in possession of W. T. Sharpless of West Chester, Pa.). Reprinted in *Record of a Quaker Mission to Cornplanter Tribe.*

Sharpless, Joshua, *Some Account of a Journey I Took into the Indian Country 1798.* The journal in manuscript is with Friends Historical Library at Swarthmore College, Swarthmore, Pa.

Sullivan, John, *The Letters and Papers of Major General John Sullivan,* ed. by Otis G. Hammond, New Hampshire Historical Society Collection (Concord, N.H.: New Hampshire Historical Society, 1930-39). 3 vols.

Transcript of the Records of the Western Missionary Society, Pennsylvania Historical Commission.

Secondary Materials

Abler, Thomas S., Cornplanter, *Chief Warrior of the Allegheny Senecas* (Syracuse, N.Y.: Syracuse University Press, 2007).

Abler, Thomas S., "Iroquois Cannibalism: Fact Not Fiction," *Ethnohistory*, XXVII (1980), 309-316.

Abler, Thomas S., "Red Jacket, Chief of the Senecas," *American National Biography* (Oxford University Press, 1999).

Abrams, George H., "The Cornplanter Cemetery," *Pennsylvania Archaeologist*, XXXV, No. 2 (1965), 59-73.

Agnew, Daniel, *A History of the Region of Pennsylvania North of the Ohio and West of the Allegheny River* (Philadelphia: Kay and Brother, 1887).

Albert, George Dallas, ed. *History of the County of Westmoreland, Pennsylvania, with Biographical Sketches of Many of Its Pioneers and Prominent Men* (Philadelphia: L. H. Everts and Co., 1882).

Albert, George Dallas, *The Frontier Forts of Western Pennsylvania* (Harrisburg: C. M. Busch, state printer, 1896).

Albert, George Dallas, and others, eds. *Report of the Commission to Locate the Sites of the Frontier Forts of Pennsylvania* (Harrisburg: C. M. Busch, state printer, 1896).

Aldrich, Lewis Cass, ed. *History of Clearfield County, Pennsylvania* (Syracuse, N. Y.: D. Mason and Co., Publishers, 1887).

Armstrong, William H., *Warrior in Two Camps: Ely S. Parker, Union General and Seneca Chief* (Syracuse, N. Y.: Syracuse University Press, 1978).

Ashe, Thomas, *Travels in America, Performed in 1806, for the Purpose of Exploring the Rivers Alleghany, Monongahela, Ohio, and Mississipi* (London: Richard Phillips, 1808).

Aupaumut, Hendrick, "A Narrative of an Embassy to the Western Indians," *Memoirs of the Historical Society of Pennsylvania*, II (1827), 61-131.

Babcock, Louis L., *The War of 1812 on the Niagara Frontier* (Buffalo, N.Y.: Publications of the Buffalo Historical Society, 1927).

Barton, Lois, *A Quaker Promise Kept: Philadelphia Friends Work with the Allegany Senecas, 1795-1960* (Eugene, Oregon: Spencer Butte Press, 1990).

Beauchamp, William M., *A History of the New York Iroquois*, New York State Museum Bulletin 78 (Albany:1905).

Beauchamp, William M., ed. *Moravian Journals Relating to Central New York, 1745-66* (Syracuse, N.Y.: Onondaga Historical Association, 1916).

Beck, Harold Thomas, *Cornplanter Chronicles* (Custer City, Pa.: Mountain Laurel Publishing Co., 1998). 3 vols.

Bell, Herbert C., "The Revolutionary Period," pages 99-142 in Herbert Bell, ed. *History of Northumberland County, Pennsylvania* (Chicago: Brown, Runk and Co., 1891).

Belue, Ted Franklin, *The Long Hunt, Death of the Buffalo East of the Mississippi* (Mechanicsburg, Pa.: Stackpole Books, 1996).

Benn, Carl, *The Iroquois in the War of 1812* (Toronto: University of Toronto Press, 1998).

Betts, William, W., Jr., *Bombardier John Harris and the Rivers of the Revolution* (Westminster, Md.: Heritage Books, 2006).

Bilharz, Joy A., *The Allegany Senecas and Kinzua Dam, Forced Relocation through Two Generations* (Lincoln: University of Nebraska Press, 1998).

Boyd, Thomas, *Mad Anthony Wayne* (New York and London: Charles Scribner's Sons, 1929).

Boyd, Thomas, *Simon Girty and the White Savages* (New York: Minton, Balch and Co., 1928).

Brick, John, *Captives of the Senecas* (New York: Duell, Sloan and Press, 1964).

Bristow, Archie, *Old Time Tales of Warren County* (Meadville, Pa.: Tribune Press, 1932).

Broshar, Helen, "The First Push Westward of the Albany Traders," *Mississippi Valley Historical Review*, VII (1920-21), 228-241.

Brush, Edward Hale, *Iroquois Past and Present, including brief sketches of Red Jacket, Cornplanter, and Mary Jemison by Edward Dinwoodie Strickland* (New York: Ams Press, Inc., 1901; reprint of edition published by Baker, Jones of Buffalo, N.Y., 1901).

Butterfield, Consul Willshire, ed. *Washington-Irvine Correspondence* (Madison, Wisc.: David Atwood, 1882).

Campbell, William W., *Annals of Tryon County; or the Border Warfare of New-York, During the Revolution* (New York: Harper, Ellis, 1831).

Canfield, Wiliam Walker, ed. *The Legends of the Iroquois, Told by "The Cornplanter"* (New York: A. Wessells Co., 1904).

Carroll, John Alexander, and Mary Wells Southworth, completing the biography by Douglas Southall Freeman, *George Washington* (New York: Charles Scribner's Sons, 1957). 7 vols.

Carter, John H., *Early Events in the Susquehanna Valley* (Northumberland, Pa.: Northumberland County Historical Society, 1981).

Carter, John H., "Indian Incursions in Old Northumberland County During the Revolutionary War, 1772-1782," pp. 63-380 in Charles F. Snyder, ed. *Northumberland County in the American Revolution* (Sunbury: Northumberland County Historical Society, 1976).

Carter, John H., "New Light on the Battle of Fort Freeland," pp. 147-162 in Charles F. Snyder, ed. *Northumberland County in the American Revolution* (Sunbury: Northumberland County Historical Society, 1976).

Cartwright, Richard, *Life and Letters of the Late Honorable Richard Cartwright* (Toronto: Belford Bros., 1876).

Chazanoff, William, *Joseph Ellicot and the Holland Land Company: The Opening of Western New York* (Syracuse, N. Y.: Syracuse University Press, 1970).

Cleland, Hugh, *George Washington in the Ohio Valley* (Pittsburgh: University of Pittsburgh Press, 1955).

Code of Handsome Lake, the Seneca Prophet (Albany: New York State Museum Bulletin 163 (1913).

Coe, Stephen Howard, "Cornplanter (Kaiiontwakan), ca. 1750-1836, Seneca Chief," Master's thesis for the American University, Washington, D.C., 1962 (in Cornplanter File, Warren County Historical Society).

Coe, Stephen Howard, *Indian Affairs in Pennsylvania and New York, 1783-1794*, Ph.D. Dissertation, American University, Washington, D.C., 1968.

Congdon, Charles E., *Allegany Oxbow: A History of Allegany State Park and the Allegany Reserve of the Seneca Nation* (Little Valley, N.Y.: Straight Publishing Company, 1967).

Copway, George, *The Life, History and Travels of Kah-ye-ga-gah-bowh* (Albany, N.Y.: 1847).

"Cornplanter Monument Rehabilitated," in *Stepping Stones*, II, No. 4 (March, 1957), p. 1.

Cornplanter, Edward, version of Handsome Lake's Code, in *The Code of Handsome Lake, the Seneca Prophet,* ed. Arthur C. Parker, New York State Museum Bulletin 163 (Albany: 1913).

Cornplanter, Jesse J., *Legends of the Longhouse* (Port Washington, N.Y.: Ira J. Friedman, 1963).

Cotterill, R. S., *The Southern Indians: The Story of the Civilized Tribes Before Removed* (Norman: University of Oklahoma Press, 1954).

Craft, David, *The Sullivan Expedition, An Address Delivered at the Seneca County Centennial Celebrataion in Waterloo, N. Y., Sept. 3, 1879* (Waterloo, N.Y.: Observer Book and Job Printing House, 1880).

Craig, Neville, ed. *The Olden Times* (Pittsburgh: Dunmars and Co., 1946).

Cribbs, George Arthur, "The Frontier Policy of Pennsylvania," *The Historical Society of Western Pennsylvania*, II (1919), 5-35, 72-106, 174-198.

Cruikshank, General E. A., collected and ed. *The Correspondence of Lieutenant-Governor John Graves Simcoe, with Allied Documents Relating to His Administration of the Government of Upper Canada*, Vol. I (1789-93) (Toronto: Ontario Historical Society, 1923-31). 5 vols.

Cutcliffe, Stephen H., "Colonial Indian Policy a Measure of Rising Imperialism: New York and Pennsylvania, 1700-1755," *Western Pennsylvania Historical Magazine*, LXIV (1981), 237-268.

Dahlinger, Charles W., "Old Allegheny," *Western Pennsylvania Historical Magazine*, I (1918), 161-223.

Dailey, R. C., "The Role of Alcohol among North American Indian Tribes as Reported in the Jesuit Relations," *Anthropologica*, X (1968), 45-59.

Day, Sherman, *Historical Collections of the State of Pennsylvania* (Philadelphia: G. W. Gordon, 1843).

Dearborn, Henry A. S., "Journals of Henry A. S. Dearborn," ed. Frank H. Severance, *Publications of the Buffalo Historical Society,* VII (1904), 33-225.

Deardorff, Merle H., "Chief Cornplanter," *Historical Pennsylvania Leaflet No. 32* (Harrisburg: 1972).

Deardorff, Merle H., "Henry O'Bail, 1774-1832: The Young Cornplanter," *Stepping Stones*, XIV, No. 3 (Sept., 1970), 411-416.

Deardorff, Merle H., "The Cornplanter Grant in Warren County," *Western Pennsylvania Historical Magazine*, XXIV (1941), 1-22.

Deardorff, Merle H., "The Religion of Handsome Lake: Its Origin and Development," *Bureau of American Ethnology Bulletin*, CIX, No. 5 (1951), 77-107.

Deardorff, Merle H., "Zeisberger's Allegheny River Indian Towns: 1767-1770," *Pennsylvania Archaeologist*, XVI, No. 1 (Jan., 1946), 2-19.

Deardorff, Merle H., and George S. Snyderman, eds. "A Nineteenth-Century Journal of a Visit to the Indians of New York," *Proceedings of the American Philosophical Society*, C, No. 6 (Dec., 1956), 582-612.

Delbanco, Andrew, *Melville: His World and Work* (New York: Alfred A. Knopf, 2005).

Democratic Arch, The, Franklin, Pa., 1830.

Densmore, Christopher, *Red Jacket: Iroquois Diplomat and Orator* (Syracuse, N.Y.: Syracuse University Press, 1999).

Dillin, John Grace Wolfe, *The Kentucky Rifle* (York, Pa.: George Shamway, 1967).

Donehoo, George P., *A History of the Indian Villages and Place Names in Pennsylvania with Numerous Historical Notes and References* (Harrisburg: Telegraph Press, 1928).

Downes, Randolph C., *Council Fires on the Upper Ohio: A Narrative of Indian Affairs in the Upper Ohio Valley until 1795* (Pittsburgh: University of Pittsburgh Press, 1940).

Drake, Samuel Gardner, *Indian Biography* (Boston: Josiah Drake, 1832).

Drake, Samuel Gardner, *The Aboriginal Races of North America; comprising biographical sketches of eminent individuals . . . .* , 15th edition, rev., with valuable additions, by H. L. Williams (New York: Hurst and Co., 1880).

Eckert, Allan, *That Dark and Bloody River* (New York: Random House, 1996).

Egle, William Henry, *The First Indian Massacre in the Valley of Wyoming, Fifteenth of October, 1763, An Address Delivered at the Wyoming Monument on July 3, 1889* (Harrisburg: Harrisburg Publishing Co., 1890).

Eccles, W. J., "The Fur Trade and Eighteenth-Century Imperialism," *William and Mary Quarterly*, Third Series, XL (1983), 341-362).

Ellis, Edward S., *The Indian Wars of the United States* (New York: Cassell Publishing Co., 1892).

Ellis, Joseph J., *His Excellency, George Washington* (New York: Alfred A. Knopf, 2004).

Ericson, Jack T., *Cornplanter Descendants Association Newsletter* (Salamanca and Westfield, New York: August, 1994 - present).

Evans, Griffith, "Journal of Griffith Evans, Clerk to the Pennsylvania Commissioners at Fort Stanwix and Fort McIntosh, 1784-85," *Pennsylvania Magazine of History and Biography,* LXV (1941), 202-233.

Feigert, Don, "Cornplanter: Seneca Chief," *Pennsylvania Game News*, August, 1944, pp. 21-27.

Fenton, William N., *An Outline of Seneca Ceremonies at Coldspring Longhouse* (New Haven: Yale University Publications in Anthropology, 1936). Rptd. by Human Relations Area Files Press.

Fenton, William N., "Fish Drives among the Cornplanter Senecas," *Pennsylvania Archaeologist,* XII, No. 3 (July-Oct., 1942), 48-52.

Fenton, William N., "Iroquois Suicide," *Bureau of American Ethnology Bulletin*, CXXVIII (1941), 80-137.

Fenton, William N., "Place Names and Related Activities of the Cornplanter Senecas," *Pennsylvania Archaeologist*, XV, No. 2 (April, 1945), 42-50; XV, No. 3 (July, 1945), 88-96; XVI, No. 2 (April, 1946), 42-57.

Fenton, William N., "Seneca Indians by Asher Wright (1859)," *Ethnohistory,* IV (1957), 302-321.

Fenton, William N., *The Great Law and the Longhouse: A Political History of the Iroquois Confederacy* (Norman: University of Oklahoma Press, 1998).

Fenton, William N., ed. "The Hyde de Neuville Portraits of New York Savages in 1807-1808," *New York Historical Society Quarterly*, XXXVIII (1954), 119-137.

Fenton, William N., and Merle H. Deardorff, "The Last Passenger Pigeon Hunts of the Cornplanter Senecas," *Journal of the Washington Academy of Sciences*, XXXIII, No. 10 (Oct., 1943), 289-315.

Ferguson, Russell J., "A Cultural Oasis in Northwestern Pennsylvania," *Western Pennsylvania Historical Magazine*, XIX (1936), 269-280.

Fischer, Joseph, *A Well Executed Failure: The Sullivan Campaign Against the Iroquois, July-September, 1779* (Coumbia, S.C.: University of South Carolina Press, 1997).

Fitzpatrick, John C., ed. *The Diaries of George Washington,1748-1799* (Boston and New York: Houghton Mifflin Co., 1925). 4 vols.

Fitzpatrick, John C., ed. *The Writings of George Washington, from the Original Manuscript Sources, 1745-1799* (Washington, D.C.: United States Government Printing Office, 1931-1944). 39 vols.

Fornance, Joseph Knox, *The Pennymite Wars, Address before the Society of Colonial Wars in the Commonwealth of Pennsylvania, March 13, 1941* (Harrisburg: Printed

by Historical Publications of the Society of Colonial Wars in the Commonwealth of Pennsylvania, Vol. VI, No. 1, 1941).
Francello, Joseph A., *The Seneca World of Ga-no-say-yeh (Peter Crouse, White Captive)* (Washington, D.C.: University Press of America, 1980).
Frothingham, Washington, rev. and ed. *History of Montgomery County, New York* (Syracuse, N.Y.: D. Mason and Co., 1892).
Ganter, Granville, ed. *The Collected Speeches of Sagoyewatha, or Red Jacket* (Syracuse, N.Y.: Syracuse University Press, 2006).
Godcharles, Frederic Antes, *Chronicles of Central Pennsylvania* (New York: Lewis Historical Publishing Co., 1944). 4 vols.
Godcharles, Frederic Antes, *History of Fort Freeland* (Williamsport, Pa.: n. pbl.,1922).
Godcharles, Frederic Antes, "The Battle of Fort Freeland," pp. 131-145 in Charles F. Snyder, ed. *Northumberland County in the American Revolution* (Sunbury, Pa.: Northumberland County Historical Society, 1976).
Godcharles, Frederic Antes, "The First Expedition Against the Indians of the Six Nations," in Charles F. Snyder, ed. *Northumberland County in the American Revolution* (Sunbury, Pa.: Northumberland County Historical Society, 1976).
"Governor Blacksnake as a Young Man: Speculation on the Identity of Trumbull's >The Young Sachem,'" *Ethnohistory,* XXXIV (1987), 329-351.
"Governor James Adopted into Seneca Nation at Interesting Ceremony on Cornplanter Reserve—Highly Praises Indians in Ceremonial Talk," *Pennsylvania Archaeologist,* X, No. 4 (October, 1940), 78-83.
Graymont, Barbara, *The Iroquois* (New York and Philadelphia: Chelsea House Publishers, 1988).
Graymont, Barbara, *The Iroquois in the American Revolution* (Syracuse, N.Y.: Syracuse University Press, 1972).
Harper, Josephine L., *A Guide to the Draper Manuscripts* (Madison: State Historical Society of Wisconsin, 1893).
Harpster, John W., ed. *Crossroads, Descriptions of Western Pennsylvania, 1720-1829* (Pittsburgh: University of Pittsburgh Press, 1938.
Hassler, Edgar W., *Old Westmoreland, A History of Western Pennsylvania during the Revolution* (Pittsburg: J. R. Weldin and Co., 1909).
Headley, Joel Tyler, *Washington and His Generals* (New York: Charles Scribner's Sons, 1875).
Heckewelder, John Gottlieb Ernestus, *Account of the History, Manners and Customs of the Indian Nations Who Once Inhabited Pennsylvania and the Neighboring States* (Philadelphia: The Historical Society of Pennsylvania, 1876).
Heckewelder, John Gottlieb Ernestus, *Thirty Thousand Miles with John Heckewelder,* ed. Paul A. W. Wallace (Pittsburgh: University of Pittsburgh Press, 1958).
Hertzberg, Hazel W., *The Great Tree and the Longhouse: The Culture of the Iroquois* (New York: Macmillan, 1966).
Hill, Henry Wayland, ed. *Municipality of Buffalo, New York, A History, 1720-1923* (New York and Chicago: Lewis Historical Publishing Co., 1923). 4 vols.
History of Cattaraugus County, New York (Philadelphia: L. H. Levers, 1879).
Horsman, Reginald, *Expansion and American Indian Policy, 1783-1812* (Lansing: Michigan State University Press, 1967).
Hough, Franklin B., ed. *Proceedings of the Commissioners of Indian Affairs* (Albany: Joel Munsell, 1861). 2 vols.
Hubbard, John Niles, *An Account of Sa-go-ye-wat-ha, or Red Jacket and His People, 1750-1830* (Albany: J. Munsell's Sons, 1886).

Hulbert, Archer Butler, *The Ohio River, A Course of Empire* (New York and London: The Knickerbocker Press, 1906).

Hulbert, Archer Butler, and William N. Schwarze, *David Zeiberger's History of the Northern American Indians* (Columbus: Ohio State Archaeological and Historical Society, 1910).

Hunt, George T., *The Wars of the Iroquois: A Study in Intertribal Trade Relations* (Madison: University of Wisconsin Press, 1940).

Ibbotson, Joseph D., "Samuel Kirkland, the Treaty of 1792 and the Indian Barrier State," *Proceedings of the New York State Historical Association,* XXXVI (1938), 374-391.

Irving, Washington, *Life of George Washington* (New York: G. P. Putnam's and Sons, 1855-59). 5 vols.

Jackson, Halliday, *Civilization of the Indian Natives* (Philadelphia: Marcus T. C. Gould, 1830).

Jackson, Halliday, *Sketch of the Manners, Customs, Religion and Government of the Seneca Indians in 1800* (Philadelphia: Marcus, T. C. Gould, 1830).

James, Sydney V., *A People among Peoples: Quaker Benevolence in Eighteenth Century America* (Cambridge: Harvard University Press, 1962).

Jemison, G. Peter, and Anna M. Schein, and Irving Powless, eds. *200 Years of Treaty Relations between the Iroquois Confederacy and the United States* (Santa Fe: Clear Light Publisher, 2000).

Jennings, Francis, *The Ambiguous Iroquois Empire: The Covenant Chain Confederation of Indian Tribes with English Colonies from Its Beginnings to the Lancaster Treaty of 1744* (New York and London: W. W. Norton and Co., 1984).

Jennings, Francis, *The History and Culture of Iroquois Diplomacy: An Interdisciplinary Guide to the Treaties of the Six Nations and Their League* (Syracuse: Syracuse University Press, 1985).

Johansen, Bruce E., and Donald A. Grinde, Jr., eds. *The Encyclopedia of Native American Biography* (New York: De Capo Press, 1997).

Jordan, John W., "Biographical Sketch of Colonel Thomas Hartley, of the Pennsylvania Line," Pennsylvania Magazine of History and Biography, XXV (1901), 303-306.

Kappler, Charles J., *Indian Affairs, Laws and Treaties* (Washington, D.C.: U.S. Government Printing Office, 1904). 3 vols.

"Kayahsotha," in *Dictionary of Canadian Biography* (Toronto: University of Toronto Press, 1979), vol. IV, pp. 408-410.

Kelsay, Isabel Thompson, *Joseph Brant, 1743-1807, Man of Two Worlds* (Syracuse, N. Y.: Syracuse University Press, 1984).

Kelsey, Rayner Wickersham, *Friends and the Indians, 1655-1917* (Philadelphia: The Associated Executive Committee of Friends on Indian Affairs, 1917).

Kent, Donald H., *Iroquois Indians I: History of Pennsylvania Purchases from the Indians,* Vol. I (New York: Garland Publishing, 1974).

Kent, Donald H., and Merle H. Deardorff, eds. "John Adlum on the Allegheny: Memoirs for the Year 1794," *Pennsylvania Magazine of History and Biography,* LXXXIV, Nos. 3 and 4 (July, 1960) 265-324; (Oct., 1960), 435-480.

Ketchum, William, *An Authentic and Comprehensive History of Buffalo* (Buffalo, N.Y.: Rockwell, Baker, and Hill, 1864). 2 vols.

King, Samuel A. and Helen H., *Cornplanter's Kingdom,* 4th edition, Map of the Allegheny National Forest and the Kinzua Country (DuBois, Pa.: 1920).

Knopf, Richard C., ed. *Anthony Wayne, A Name in Arms* (Pittsburgh: University of Pittsburgh Press, 1960).

La Farge, Oliver, *A Pictorial History of the American Indian* (New York: Crown Publishers, Inc., 1956).

Lenski, Lois, *Indian Captive: The Story of Mary Jemison* (Philadelphia: Lippincott, 1941)

Lossing, Benson, John, *The Pictorial Field-Book of the Revolution* (New York: Harper & Bros., 1859. 2 vols.. Republished (Rutland, Vt. And Tokyo, Japan, 1972). 2 vols.

Lowenthal, Larry, ed. *Days of Siege: A Journal of the Siege of Fort Stanwix in 1777* (New York: Eastern Acorn Press, 1983).

Malinowski, Sharon, ed. *Notable Native Americans* (New York: Gale Research, 1995).

Mancall, Peter C., *Deadly Medicine: Indians and Alcohol in Early America* (Ithaca, N.Y.: Cornell University Press, 1995).

Manley, Henry S., *The Treaty of Fort Stanwix, 1784* (Rome, N.Y.: Rome Sentinel Co., 1932).

Markowitz, Harvey, consulting editor, *American Indians* (Pasadena: Salem Press, 1955).

Marshall, Peter, "Sir William Johnson and the Treaty of Fort Stanwix, 1768," *Journal of American Studies*, I (1967), 149-179.

McConnell, Michael N., *A Country Between: The Upper Ohio Valley and Its Peoples, 1724-1774* (Lincoln: University of Nebraska Press, 1992).

McKnight, William James, *A Pioneer History of Jefferson County, Pennsylvania* (Philadelphia: J. B. Lippincott, 1898).

McKnight, William James, *A Pioneer Outline History of Northwestern Pennsylvania* (Philadelphia: J. B. Lippincott, 1905).

Meginness, John Franklin, *Biography of Frances Slocum, the Lost Sister of Wyoming* (Williamsport, Pa.: Heller Bros., 1891).

Meginness, John Franklin, *Otzinachson, A History of the West Branch of the Susquehanna* (Philadelphia: H. B. Ashmead, 1857).

Merrill, Arch, *A River Parable: Saga of the Genesee Valley* (Rochester, N.Y.: L. Heindl and Sons, 1943).

Meyers, Wilbur A., ed. *The Book of the Sesqui-Centennial Celebration of the Battle of Wyoming, July 1st-4th, 1928* (Wyoming Valley, Pa.: A Wyoming Valley Publication, 1928).

Mickley, Joseph J., *Brief Account of Murders by the Indians and the Cause Thereof, in Northampton County, Pennsylvania* (Philadelphia: Thomas William Stuckey, 1875).

Miner, Charles, *History of Wyoming, in a Series of Letters from Charles Miner to His Son William Penn Miner, Esq.* (Philadelphia: J. Crissy, 1845).

Mohawk, John C., "Cornplanter," pp. 135-137 in Frederick E. Hoxie, ed. *Encyclopedia of North American Indians* (Boston and New York: Houghton Mifflin Co., 1996).

Mohr, Walter Harrison, *Federal Indian Relations, 1774-1788* (Philadelphia: University of Pennsylvania Press, 1933; London, H. Milford, Oxford University Press, 1933).

Monette, Richard, "Treaties," pp. 643-646 in Frederick E. Hoxie, ed. *Encyclopedia of North American Indians* (Boston and New York: Houghton Mifflin Co., 1996).

Montour, Ted, "Handsome Lake, pp. 230-231 in Frederick E. Hoxie, ed. *Encyclopedia of North American Indians* (Boston and New York: Houghton Mifflin Co., 1996).

Moore, H.N., *Life and Services of General Anthony Wayne* (Philadelphia: John B. Perry, 1845).

Morgan, Lewis H., with Ely S. Parker, *League of the Ho-de-no-sau-nee or Iroquois* [1851] (New York: Dodd, Mead and Co., 1902).

Morison, Samuel Eliot (with Henry Steele Commager), *The Growth of the American Republic* (New York: Oxford University Press, 1930).

Morse, Jedidiah, *A Report to the Secretary of War of the United States on Indian Affairs, comprising a narrative of a tour performed in the summer of 1820* (New Haven: 1822).

Murray, Elsie, "Hartley's and Sullivan's Expedition against the Iroquois," pp. 129-130 in Charles F. Snyder, ed. *Northumberland County in the American Revolution* (Sunbury, Pa.: Northumberland County Historical Society, 1976).

Nelson, Larry L., *A Man of Distinction among Them: Alexander McKee and British-Indian Affairs along the Ohio Country Frontier, 1754-1799* (Kent, Ohio: Kent University Press, 1999).

Nerburn, Kent, ed. *Wisdom of the Great Chiefs: the Classic Speeches of Chief Red Jacket, Chief Joseph, and Chief Seattle, selected with chapter introductions* (San Rafael, Cal.: New World Library, 1994).

Nester, William R., *The Frontier War for American Independence* (Mechanicsburg, Pa.: Stackpole Books, 2004).

Newton, J. H., ed. *History of Venango County, Pennsylvania, and Incidentally of Petroleum, together with accounts of the Early Settlement and Progress of Each Township, Borough and Village, with Personal and Biographical Sketches of the Early Settlers, Representative Men, Family Records, etc. By an able corps of Historians* (Columbus, Ohio: J. A. Caldwell, 1879).

New York Division of Archives and History, *The Sullivan-Clinton Campaign, Chronology and Selected Documents* (Albany: The University of the State of New York, 1929).

Norris, Major, "Journal of Sullivan's Expedition," *Buffalo Historical Society Publications*, I (1879), 217-252.

Norton, Thomas Eliot, *The Fur Trade in Colonial New York, 1686-1776* (Madison: University of Wisconsin Press, 1974). 2 vols.

O'Callaghan, E. B., ed. *Documents Relative to the Colonial History of the State of New York* (Albany: Weed, Parsons and Co., 1853-1857). 15 vols.

O'Reilly, Henry, *Papers Pertaining to the Six Nations* (New York Historical Society, owned and filmed by Microfilmed, 1948). Vol. VIII includes letters of Secretary of War Henry Knox; Vol. XIII includes letter by John Pierce.

Parker, Arthur C., "An Analytical History of the Seneca Indians," in *Researches and Transactions of the New York State Archaeological Association,* Rochester, N.Y., VI, Nos. 1-5 (1926).

Parker, Arthur C., "Notes on the Ancestry of Cornplanter," Lewis H. Morgan Chapter of the New York State Archaeological Association, Rochester, N. Y., Vol. V, No. 2 (1927), pp. 1-22.

Parker, Arthur C., *Parker on the Iroquois*, ed. and with an introduction by William N. Fenton (Syracuse, N.Y.: Syracuse University Press, 1968).

Parker, Arthur C., *The Code of Handsome Lake, the Seneca Prophet* (Albany: New York State Museum, Bulletin 163, 1913).

Parker, Arthur C., *The History of the Seneca Indians,* Empire State Historical Publication XLIII (Port Washington, N.Y.: Ira J. Friedman, Inc., 1967).

Parker, Arthur C., "The Indian Interpretation of the Sullivan-Clinton Campaign," *Rochester Historical Society Publication Fund Series,* VIII (1929).

Parker, Arthur C., "The Senecas in the War of 1812," *Proceedings of the New York State Historical Association*, XV (1916), 78-90.

Parkman, Francis, *History of the Conspiracy of Pontiac and the War of the Northern American Tribes against the English Colonies after the Conquest of Canada* (Boston: Little, Brown, 1851).

Peck, George, *Wyoming: Its History, Stirring Incidents, and Romantic Adventures* (New York: Harper and Bros., 1958).

Peckham, Howard H., *The Colonial Wars, 1689 -1762* (Chicago: University of Chicago Press, 1965).

Phillips, Paul Chrisler, *The Fur Trade* (Norman: Oklahoma University Press, 1961). Vol. I.

Preston, David L., *The Texture of Contact* (Lincoln, Nebraska and London, England: University of Nebraska Press, 2009).

Prucha, Francis Paul, ed. *Documents of United States Indian Policy*, 2nd edition (Lincoln: University of Nebraska Press, 1990).

Rafert, Stewart, "Little Turtle," pp. 342-344 in Frederick E. Hoxie, ed. *Encyclopedia of North American Indians* (Boston and New York: Houghton Mifflin Co., 1996).

Rankin, Hugh F., "War on the Frontier," Chapter 15 (pp. 213-219) of Hugh F. Rankin, *The American Revolution* (New York: G. P. Putnam's Sons, 1964).

Reynolds, John Earle, *In French Creek Valley* (Meadville, Pa.: The Crawford County Historical Society, 1938).

Richter, Daniel K., *Ordeal of the Longhouse: The Peoples of the Iroquois League in the Era of European Colonization* (Chapel Hill: University of North Carolina Press, 1992).

Richter, Daniel K., "Red Jacket," pp. 532-533 in Frederick E. Hoxie, ed. *Encyclopedia of North American Indians* (Boston and New York: Houghton Mifflin Co., 1996).

Richter, Daniel K., and James H. Merrell, eds. *Beyond the Covenant Chain: The Iroquois and Their Neighbors in Indian North America, 1600-1800* (Syracuse, N.Y.: Syracuse University Press, 1987).

Rossman, Kenneth R., *Thomas Mifflin and the Politics of the American Revolution* (Chapel Hill: University of North Carolina Press, 1952).

Russell, Carl P., *Guns on the Early Frontiers: A History of Firearms from Colonial Times through the Years of the Western Fur Trade* (Berkeley, Cal.: University of California Press, 1957).

Russell, Eber L., "The Lost Story of the Brodhead Expedition," *New York History*, XXVIII (1930), 252-263.

Shannon, Timothy J., *Iroquois Diplomacy on the Early American Frontier* (New York: Penguin Books, 2008)

Schenck, J. S., assisted by W. S. Rann, ed. *History of Warren County, Pennsylvania, with illustrations and biographical sketches of some of its prominent men and pioneers, etc.* (Syracuse, N.Y.: D. Mason and Co., 1887.

Scott, John Albert, *Fort Stanwix and Oriskany* (Rome, N.Y.: Sentinel Co., 1927).

Seaver, James E., ed. *A Narrative of the Life of Mrs. Mary Jemison* (Canandaigua: J.D. Bemis and Co., 1824). Rptd. New York: Corinth, 1961.

Severance, Frank H., ed., ANarrative of the Early Mission Work on the Niagara Frontier and Buffalo Creek," *Publications of the Buffalo Historical Society,* VI (1903).

Severance, Frank H., *Old Trails on the Niagara Frontier* (Buffalo: n.pbl, 1899).

Shimmell, Lewis Slifer *A History of Pennsylvania* (New York: Charles E. Merrill Co., 1900).

Shimmell, Lewis Slifer, *Border Warfare in Pennsylvania During the Revolution* (Harrisburg: R. L. Myers, 1901).

Simms, Jeptha R., *History of Schoharie County and Border Wars of New York* (Albany: Munsell and Tanner, 1845).

Sipe, Chester Hale, *Indian Wars of Pennsylvania* (Harrisburg: The Telegraph Press, 1931).

Sipe, Chester Hale, *The Indian Chiefs of Pennsylvania* (Butler, Pa.: The Ziegler Printing Co., 1927). Rptd. in 1998 by Wennawoods Publishing of Lewisburg, Pa.

Smith, Robert, ed. "The Friend," Vol. XVIII (Philadelphia: Joseph Kite and Co., 1845). Vols. 1-24 (1838-50) are on microfilm at the University of Michigan, Ann Arbor.

Smith, Robert W., *History of Armstrong County* (Chicago: Waterman, Watkins and Co., 1883).

Smith, Samuel Robert, *The Story of Wyoming Valley* (Kingston, Pa.: S. R. Smith, 1906).

Snowden, James Ross, *The Cornplanter Memorial: An Historical Sketch of Gy-ant-wa-chia, The Cornplanter, and of the Six Nations of Indians* (Harrisburg: Singerly and Myers, 1867). Published in an edition of 1000 copies by order of the Pennsylvania Legislature.

Snyder, Charles F., "Additional Data Concerning the Battle of Fort Freeland," in Charles F. Snyder, ed. *Northumberland County in the American Revolution* (Sunbury: Northumberland County Historical Society, 1976).

Snyder, Charles F., ed. *Northumberland County in the American Revolution* (Sunbury: Northumberland County Historical Society, 1976).

Snyder, Charles M., ed. *Red and White on the New York Frontier: A Struggle for Survival; Insights from the Papers of Erastus Granger, Indian Agent, 1807-1819* (Harrison, N.Y.: Harbor Hill Books, 1978).

Snyderman, George S., *Behind the Tree of Peace* (dissertation for the University of Pennsylvania, Philadelphia, Pa., 1948).

Stevens, Sylvester K., *Pennsylvania, Birthplace of a Nation* (New York: Random House, 1964).

Stone, Rufus B., "Brodhead's Raid on the Senecas," *Western Pennsylvania Historical Magazine,* VII, No. 2 (1924), 88-101.

Stone, William Leete, *Life of Joseph Brant, Thayendanegea* (New York: George Dearborn and Co., 1836). 2 vols.

Stone, William Leete, *The Life and Times of Sa-Go-Ye-Wat-Ha, or Red Jacket* (New York and London: Wiley and Putnam, 1841). Includes mini-biographies of Farmer's Brother (pp. 409-419); Cornplanter (pp. 423-456); and Henry O'Bail (pp. 456-458).

Stone, William Leete, *The Poetry and History of Wyoming: Containing Campbell's Gertrude and the History of Wyoming from Its Discovery to the Beginning of the Present Century* (Albany: J. Munsell, 1864).

Sublett, Audrey, J., "The Cornplanter Cemetery: Skeletal Analyses," *Pennsylvania Archaeologist*, XXXV, No. 2 (August, 1965), 74-92.

Sugden, John, "Joseph Brant," in Frederick E. Hoxie, ed. *Encyclopedia of North American Indians* (Boston and New York: Houghton Mifflin Co., 1996).

Swartz, Roger G., *Fields of Honor, The Battle of Fort Freeland, July 28, 1779* (Turbotville, Pa.: Warriors Run-Fort Freeland Heritage Society, 1996).

Swatzler, David, *A Friend among the Senecas, the Quaker Mission to Cornplanter's People* (Mechanicsburg, Pa.: Stackpole Books, 2000).

Swigett, Howard, *War Out of Niagara, Walter Butler and the Tory Rangers,* Empire State Historical Publications XX (Port Washington, N.Y.: Ira J. Friedman, 1963).

Sword, Wiley, *President Washington's Indian War: The Struggle for the Old Northwest, 1790-1795* (Norman: University of Oklahoma Press, 1985).

Thorn, James Alexander, *From Sea to Shining Sea* (New York: Ballantine Books, 1984).

Thwaites, Reuben Gold, and Louise Kellogg, eds. *The Revolution on the Upper Ohio, 1775-1777* (Madison: State Historical Society of Wisconsin, 1908).

Tome, Philip, *Pioneer Life, Or, Thirty Years a Hunter, Being Scenes and Adventures in the Life of Philip Tome, Fifteen Years Interpreter for Cornplanter and Gov. Blacksnake,*

Chiefs on the Allegany River [Buffalo, 1854] (Harrisburg: Privately printed by the Aurand Press, 1928). Reprint of the scarce edition of 1854.

Trelease, Allen W. *Indian Affairs in Colonial New York: The Seventeenth Century* (Ithaca, N.Y.: Cornell University Press, 1960).

Trippe, M. F., "Historical Facts Concerning Peter Crouse the Captive, His Wife Rachel, Their Descendants and Their Times," William M. Fenton Holdings.

Turner, Orsamus, *History of the Pioneer Settlement of Phelps and Gorham Purchase* (Rochester, N.Y.: William Alling, 1851).

Twohig, Dorothy, ed. *The Journal of the Proceedings of the President, 1793-1797* (Charlottesville, Va.: University Press of Virginia, 1981).

Van Every, Dale, *A Company of Heroes, the American Frontier, 1775-1783* (New York: Morrow, 1962).

Vaughan, Alden T., general editor, *Early American Indian Documents: Treaties and Laws, 1607-1789*, Vol. XVIII ("Revolution and Confederation") ed. Colin G. Calloway (Bethesda, Md.: University Publications of America, 1994).

Wallace, Anthony F. C., with the assistance of Sheila C. Steen, *The Death and Rebirth of the Seneca* (New York: Alfred A. Knopf, Inc., 1970).

Wallace, Paul A. W., *Indians in Pennsylvania* (Harrisburg: The Pennsylvania Historical and Museum Commission, 1961).

Wallace, Paul, A. W., *The White Roots of Peace* (Port Washington, N.Y.: Ira J. Friedman, 1968).

Wallman, Carl, *Who Was Who in Native American History* (New York: Facts on File, 1990).

Walton, William, *A Narrative of the Captivity of Benjamin Gilbert* (Philadelphia: Cruickshank, 1784).

Warren Centennial, *An Account of the Celebration at Warren, Pennsylvania . . . 1895* (Warren, Pa.: Warren Library Association, 1897).

Whitsel, Gary, "The Cornplanter Senecas: A Study in Social Disintegration," Master's Thesis submitted to the Kent University Graduate School, July, 1969.

Whittemore, Charles P., *A General of the Revolution: John Sullivan of New Hampshire* (New York: Columbia University Press, 1961).

Whittemore, Henry, *The Abeel and Allied Families* (New York, privately printed, 1899).

Wildes, Harry Emerson, *Anthony Wayne, Trouble Shooter of the American Revolution* (Westport, Conn.: Greenwood Publishers, 1941).

Wilhelm, Samuel Alfred, "History of the Lumber Industry of the Upper Allegheny River Basin," Master's Thesis (1953), in Cornplanter File as "Cornplanter and His Sawmill."

Wilkinson, Norman B., "Robert Morris and the Treaty of Big Tree," *The Mississippi Valley Historical Review,* XL, No. 2 (Sept., 1953), 257-278.

Williams, Benjamin G., *Life and Speeches of Cornplanter*: *Once Chief of the Seneca Nation of Indians* (Warren, Pa.: Warren Ledger, 1883).

Wilson, Edmund, *Apologies to the Iroquois* (New York: Farrar, Straus, and Cudahy, 1960).

Witthoft, John, *Indian Prehistory of Pennsylvania* (Harrisburg: Pennsylvania Historical and Museum Commission, 1965).

Wrenshall, John, "The Manuscript Autobiography of John Wrenshall, Early Pittsburgh Merchant, Trader and Methodist Leader, in 1803," *Western Pennsylvania Historical Magazine*, XXV (1947), 81-83. The original autobiography of John Wrenshall, Pittsburgh merchant, is in the custody of the Historical Society of Western Pennsylvania.

Works Consulted

Wright, John Ernest, and Doris S. Corbett, *Pioneer Life in Western Pennsylvania* (Pittsburgh: University of Pittsburgh Press, 1940).

Notes

Chapter I

1. Norton, pp. 36 and 41.
2. Cornplanter File (CF hereafter), Binder One. Or, as Blacksnake suggests, Gah-hon-no-neh (Draper Manuscripts—DM hereafter—4-S-68).
3. Parker, "Notes on the Ancestry," p. 13.
4. Stone, *Life of Brant,* I, 434.
5. Ibid., I, 424.
6. DM, 16-F-227.
7. Newton, p. 76.
8. Alden, who was born in Yarmouth, Massachusetts, earned his Doctorate from Harvard in Classical and Oriental Languages. After serving as pastor and teaching in various girls' schools, he came to Meadville and established Alleghany College, which welcomed its first class on July 4, 1816. He resigned the presidency on August 2, 1831. He visited the Cornplanter community many times, and befriended the chief in his late years. Alden died near Pittsburgh, and is interred in the Greendale Cemetery in Meadville.
9. McKnight, 653.
10. Ibid., pp. 563-564; printed also in Sipe, pp. 470-471.
11. Deardorff and Snyderman, p. 600.
12. Although his birth date is now authoritatively established at 1750-52, confusion over the date of Cornplanter's birth has been constant from the first commentary on his life right down to the present day, the chief's birth date given as early as 1719 (!). Even the New-York Historical Society continues to accompany the Borzoi portrait with dates 1732/40-1836.
13. Dillin, p. 156.
14. Ibid., pp. 43 and 159.
15. Ibid., p. 154.
16. Dillin, p. 155.
17. Ibid., p. 156.
18. Parker, "Notes on the Ancestry," p. 7.

Chapter II

1. Swatzler, p. 259.
2. It has been suggested that Edward Cornplanter was not actually a descendant, but simply chose the name (see genealogy in "Afterword").
3. Parker, "Notes on the Ancestry," p. 3.
4. Ibid., p. 22.
5. Ibid., p. 13.
6. Peckham, p. 168.
7. L. S. Everett, in Seaver, pp. 145-149.
8. Seaver, p. 56.

9. A. Wallace, p. 116; Peckham, pp. 224-225; Parkman, pp. 374-376; Abler, *Chainbreaker,* p. 31.
10. Abler, *Chainbreaker,* p. 20.
11. DM 4-S-13; quoted by Abler, *Chainbreaker*, p. 17.
12. Kent, p. 453.
13. DM 4-S-81.
14. Deardorff and Snyderman, p. 604.
15. See Abler's *Chainbreaker* for an accessible Blacksnake.
16. DM 4-S-60.
17. Ibid.; quoted by Abler, *Chainbreaker*, p. 32.
18. A. Wallace, p. 116.
19. Parkman, p. 376n; quoted by Abler, *Chainbreaker*, p. 32.

Chapter III

1. The fort is today a national monument. The city of Rome was laid out at some time in 1786 at the site of the fort.
2. The fort was rebuilt again in 1777 and defended in August of that year by patriot forces under the command of Colonel Peter Gansevoort.
3. Molly was twenty-two years old when in 1758 she took up with Johnson. She moved into Johnson's fieldstone mansion (which, built in 1764, is still standing and is now a museum) and became a renowned hostess. Before the end of the Revolution, she was obliged to flee to Canada, and after the end of the war she removed with her family permanently to Kingston, Ontario.
4. The final section of this new boundary line was not completed until some five years later. Called the "Purchase Line" by historians, it was accepted by representatives of the Six Nations at that spot in present-day Indiana County, Pa., where the West Branch of the Susquehannah is given its beginning by Cush Cushion Creek. By the Indians it was called Canoe Place; it is today Cherry Tree.
5. Swatzler, p. 108.
6. For a map see Swatzler, p. 107; for an explanation of the boundary line segment, see Swatzler, pp. 104-111.
7. Swatzler, pp. 108-109.
8. Sometimes spelled Caustrax.
9. See O'Callaghan, VII, 111-137 for the proceedings and the document.
10. Abler, *Chainbreaker*, pp. 46-48.
11. Ibid., pp. 50-51.
12. Guy Johnson, Sir William's nephew, had also been born in Ireland. He married William Johnson's daughter in 1763. Toward the war's end, in 1782, he was succeeded in the post by Sir William Johnson's natural son John Johnson.
13. Abler, *Chainbreaker*, p. 36.
14. Stone, *Life of Brant*, I, 102.
15. Graymont, *Iroquois in the American Revolution,* pp. 71-74; Abler, *Chainbreaker,* p. 36.
16. Mingo was the term employed for those Senecas who had left their homes in New York State to settle in the Ohio Valley.
17. A. Wallace, p. 129.
18. Thwaites and Kellogg, pp. 31-32.

19. Nester, p. 356, note 34; George Morgan Letter Book (GMLB hereafter), July 6, 1776, pp. 37-39. For Kayahsotha's remarks see GMLB, 1776, pp. 43-49. See A. Wallace, p. 130.
20. For a chronology of these conferences see Abler, *Chainbreaker*, pp. 35-45.
21. The Albany-born General Philip Schuyler is one of the most fascinating figures of the entire Revolution. One of Washington's four major generals, and a member of the 1st Continental Congress, he was a man of incredible courage and selflessness. He is credited with saving the life of the young Ethan Allen, as well as with saving his own a number of times.
22. Graymont, *Iroquois in the American Revolution*, p.106.
23. For the entire speech see Abler, *Chainbreaker*, appendix, pp. 229-237.
24. Abler, *Chainbreaker*, pp. 40-45.
25. See Mohr, pp. 122-126; Stone, *Life of Brant,* II, 3-4n; and A. Wallace, pp. 131-132.

Chapter IV

1. Godcharles, *Chronicles*, p. ix.
2. Wright and Corbett, p. 117.
3. Ibid. pp. 117-118.
4. Ibid., p. 52.
5. Ibid., p. 62.
6. Idem.
7. Wright and Corbett, pp. 62-63.
8. Ibid., pp. 71-72.
9. Mickley, pp. 11-37.
10. For a copy of the letter, see Mickley, p. 22.
11. Meginness, *History of the West Branch*, pp. 111-119.
12. Day, pp. 196-197.
13. Seaver, pp. 104-105.
14. Godcharles, *Chronicles,* p. ix.
15. Carter, "Indian Incursions," pp. 363-380.
16. Meginness, *History of the West Branch*, p. 215.
17. Godcharles, *Chronicles*, p. 135.
18. Sipe, *The Indian Chiefs*, pp. 449-451; reprinted from Meginness, *History of the West Branch.*
19. Brady was an experienced scout and soldier. He had crossed the Delaware with Washington. He did not like Indians, and records of his life bristle with accounts of fierce encounters and miraculous escapes.
20. But there was another Bald Eagle, a Seneca, who lived among the Delawares at Salt Lick Town. He was a most friendly Indian, could speak English well, was known as a good hunter and as a "very kind, good man." During the winter of 1774 he was brutally murdered.
21. Graymont, *Iroquois in the American Revolution,* pp. 245, 253-254.

Chapter V

1. The Rangers, like the Queen's Own Rangers, fought the entire war in green uniforms. They devastated the New York frontier. Butler's Rangers fought at Oriskany and led the raid against Wyoming. After the Revolution John Butler retired to Canada, on a pension from the government. He died in Niagara in 1794.
2. Abler, *Chainbreaker*, pp. 46-49.
3. Ibid., p. 38.
4. Ibid., pp. 49-54.
5. Ibid., p. 39.
6. Graymont, *Iroquois in the American Revolution,* p. 102. The Iroquois activity during the Revolution is carefully and fully documented by Graymont.
7. Abler, *Chainbreaker,* pp. 39-40.
8. Farmer's Brother (*Ho-na-ye-wus*) was closer in age to Kayahsotha than to Cornplanter. He was a war-chief and had been present at the Devil's Hole massacre. He would participate in the Council at the Glaize on Sept. 30, 1792, and at the Big Tree Treaty sessions. He would fight for the United States in the War of 1812.
9. A. Wallace, pp. 131-132.
10. Peck, p. 32.
11. Kirby, p. 55.
12. A. Wallace, p. 132.
13. Stone, *Life of Brant,* I, 228.
14. William Leete Stone, in his *Life of Brant* (which was composed while Cornplanter was yet living), appended a note to Colonel Willett's account of this "incident." Stone has his information from his conversation with Dr. Jonathan Eights of Albany, who was a member of the tavern party in which this shooting was discussed. As Stone understood it from Dr. Eights, Brant had been in Albany in 1797 in the company of Cornplanter and "two or three other sachems," to discuss the Mohawk sale of lands to New York State. Brant would be probably fifty-four years old at this time, and Cornplanter forty-five. According to the account provided by Dr. Eights, when the party arrived in the evening at Canajoharie, Brant determined to call upon a very good friend of his, Major Hendrick Frey. Frey, like the Butlers, had cast his lot with the British when the war broke out, but at the close of the hostilities had returned to his native county. He was very glad to see Joseph Brant, the meeting, according to Dr. Eights, occurring "like that of two brothers." "The party," the doctor reported "adjourned to a tavern, where they had a merry time of it during the live-long night." It seems that the Indians, together with Major Frey, were enjoying their recollections of episodes of the war. One of these included a duel that was fought by Frey, with Brant serving as his second. As their exploits were being reviewed, "Corn-planter acknowledged that [it was] he [who had] shot the girl who was gathering berries in the neighborhood of Fort Stanwix." As Dr. Eights remembered it, Cornplanter described how he was "lurking about the fort," apparently determined to take a prisoner. When he was discouraged in that hope, he fired upon the girl. As there were, according to Colonel Willett's account, two girls killed, one wonders about the second. In any case, most interesting is the account of the reaction of the inn-keeper to Cornplanter's telling of the murder. Dr. Eights, who was a witness to it all, described for William Stone how the landlord, whose name he remembered as Rolfe, and who had been living near Fort Stanwix at the

time the girls were shot, immediately erupted in almost uncontrollable anger. As Dr. Eights remembered the scene, the man "could hardly be restrained from doing violence upon Corn-planter." (Stone, *Life of Brant*, II, 411n)

15. Irondequois is an Iroquois term meaning "where the two waters meet."
16. There is *great* confusion over not only the actual site but the number of conferences. And the dates. Graymont does not accept Oswego as the site (pp. 120-121); Blacksnake seems confused, but Abler thinks the site is Oswego. Mary Jemison reported Oswego.
17. Graymont, *Iroquois in the American Revolution,* p.120.
18. Ibid., p. 123.
19. Kayahsotha's Indian name, which translates as "It sets up a cross," has been rendered over the years in some 30-40 spellings.
20. There is some confusion over the date of the Indian raid on the fort. The William Johnson Papers report (IV, 165) that the fort "was attacked June 18 by a large body of Senecas." But in another place the Johnson Papers report that "Venango probably fell June 16." June 16 is the commonly accepted date. Venango was the name of the old Delaware/Munsee Indian village. The stockade first built there was constructed by the French and called Machault. When this fort was utterly destroyed, the British built a new one (in 1760) and called it Fort Venango. After it was burned by the Senecas under most probably Kayahsotha, in 1763, it was rebuilt by the Americans as a military post. It was constructed by Captain (later Major) Jonathan Heart (or Hart), who had widened the Indian path (always known as the Venango Trail) in order to bring in materials. The new fort was located on the south bank of French Creek, and maintained a garrison, sometimes as large as 100, but normally much smaller, until 1796. Nothing remains now.
21. Accounts vary some in details. In one version printed in the Johnson Papers, the Indians "put the garrison to death, except 2 officers whom they made prisoners and the Sentinel at the gate, who while they were murdering the garrison, got into one of the Indian canoes and made his escape down the River." In this version the two officers were killed in the woods by the Indians, who beat them and abused them as they were marched along. See The Johnson Papers Ms, Historical Collections of Pennsylvania, and see *The Papers of William Johnson* published by the Division of Archives and History (Albany, New York), IV, 165n., 169, 171, 182; X, 767-769.
22. See *History of Venango County,* pp. 29-31. Allan Eckert dramatizes this episode in *The Wilderness Empire,* volume II of his *Winning of America* series.
23. DM 4-S-61; quoted by Abler, *Chainbreaker*, p. 30.
24. Such was Kayahsotha's reputation that for a long time the chief was also given credit for the burning of Hannastown, near present-day Greensburg, Pa., in 1783. But it is thought now that the Seneca Chief Farmer's Brother led that war party.
25. Cleland, p. 258.
26. Graymont, *Iroquois in the American Revolution,* p.123.
27. See Abler, *Chainbreaker*, pp. 59-63.
28. Ibid., p. 75.
29. Seaver, p. 66. For accounts of the council, see Stone, *Life of Brant*, I, 186-188; A. Wallace, pp. 132-134; and Graymont, *Iroquois in the American Revolution,* pp. 120-124.
30. Seaver, pp. 66-67.
31. DM 4-S-17; Abler, *Chainbreaker*, pp. 66-67.
32. Graymont, *Iroquois in the American Revolution,* p. 124.
33. Ibid., p. 158.

34. Ibid., p. 134.
35. DM 11-U-196-197, 200, 215-217; see Abler, *Chainbreaker*, pp. 86-90 and 128-130; and see Graymont, *Iroquois in the American Revolution,* p. 135.
36. Blacksnake has the losses at 30, Mary Jemison reported 36.
37. DM 4-S-24- 25; Abler, *Chainbreaker*, p. 88.
38. DM 4-S-25-26; Abler, *Chainbreaker*, p. 89. For a good account of the battle, see Stone, *Life of Brant*, II, 209-246.
39. Abler, *Chainbreaker*, p. 90.
40. Seaver, p. 68. Quoted by Abler, *Chainbreaker*, pp. 90-91.
41. Seaver, p. 68.
42. Peter Gansevoort was distinguished not only in his eventful military career, but also as the grandfather of Herman Melville, and as the subject of one of President Lincoln's favorite poems, Ralph Waldo Emerson's "The Last Leaf." See Delbanco. He named his second son Stanwix in memory of the fort he had defended so stoutly. For the siege of Fort Stanwix, see Graymont, p. 143; and Abler, *Chainbreaker*, p. 90.
43. See Abler, *Chainbreaker*, pp. 93, 96.

Chapter VI

1. Myers, p. 13.
2. Idem.
3. Egle, p. 22.
4. Miner, p. 54.
5. Swiggett, p. 126.
6. Blacksnake Conversations, DM, 4-S-27-28.
7. Peck, p. 29.
8. Sam Smith, p. 34.
9. Graymont, *Iroquois in the American Revolution,* pp. 168-169.
10. DM 4-S-29; Abler, *Chainbreaker*, p. 101.
11. Graymont, *Iroquois in the American Revolution,* pp. 169-171, but see Graymont's note # 29.
12. Sam Smith, p. 40.
13. Abler, *Chainbreaker*, p. 136.
14. Sam Smith, p. 40.
15. Idem.
16. Sam Smith, p. 41.
17. Ibid., p. 45. Stone (*History of Wyoming*, p. 219) reports that one powerful man, named Hammond, in a desperate effort broke free and was able to burst through the circle and escape.
18. Abler (*Chainbreaker,* p. 101) cites Blacksnake's absolute denial of the Queen Esther tomahawking. And see Stone, *History of Wyoming*, p. 208.
19. Sam Smith, p. 45.
20. Swiggett, p. 129.
21. Ibid., p. 127.
22. Carter, p. 367.
23. Idem.
24. Mohawk, p. 136.
25. Walton, p. iv.

26. It is thought that Butler's conduct in the sacking of Wyoming cost him the honor of knighthood.
27. Stone, *The Poetry and History of Wyoming*, p. 213n. For a vivid and highly detailed account of the capture of Forty Fort and the barbarities of Wyoming, see Stone, pp. 197-229.

Chapter VII

1. Thomas Hartley was born in Reading, Pa., on September 7, 1748. During the war he served in the Pennsylvania House of Representatives and after the war he represented Pennsylvania in the U. S. House. He died in York, Pa., on December 21, 1800, at age fifty-two, and is interred in St. John's Churchyard. See Jordan, "Biographical Sketch."
2. *Pennsylvania Archives (PA* hereafter), First Series, VII, 5. Quoted by Abler, *Chainbreaker*, p. 102.
3. *PA*, First Series, VII, 5.
4. Wyalusing is an Indian name meaning "at the dwelling of the ancient warrior."
5. The Indian Hill Battlefield historical marker is today located four miles east of present-day Wyalusing on Route 6.
6. DM 4-S-148-150; see Abler, *Chainbreaker*, p. 138.
7. *PA,* First Series, VI, 773, and VII, 7-8.
8. Idem.
9. Walter Butler, son of John, was killed in 1781 (at age twenty-nine) by a patriot troop commanded by Marinus Willett.
10. DM 4-S-33.
11. Graymont, *Iroquois in the American Revolution,* pp. 184-187; but see her notes #52-54.
12. Ibid., p. 186.
13. DM 4-S-31.
14. Graymont, *Iroquois in the American Revolution,* p. 186; but see her note #60.
15. Ibid., p. 187.
16. Paul Wallace, *Indians in Pennsylvania,* p. 139.
17. Seaver, pp. 107-108.
18. Fitzpatrick, XIV, 198-201.
19. Craft, p. 10.
20. Ibid., p. 9.
21. Often spelled McDonnel, sometimes McDonald.
22. Graymont, *Iroquois in the American Revolution,* p. 202.
23. DM 4-S-33; Abler, *Chainbreaker*, p. 106; Sipe, p. 502.
24. Godcharles, "The Battle of Fort Freeland," p. 132.
25. Idem.
26. Some accounts report thirty men.
27. See Wolfinger in Egle's *History of Pennsylvania* and Meginness in *Otzinachson.*
28. Seaver, p. 107.
29. Godcharles, "The Battle of Fort Freeland," p. 136.
30. Seaver, p. 107.
31. Godcharles, "The Battle of Fort Freeland," p. 137.
32. Ibid., p. 136.
33. *PA*, First Series, VII, 597; Sipe, p. 502.

34. Seaver, p. 107.
35. Godcharles, "The Battle of Fort Freeland," p. 145.
36. Paul Wallace, *Indians in Pennsylvania,* p. 141.
37. Cartwright, p. 37.
38. *PA*, First Series, VII, 610.
39. *PA*, Second Series, XV, 260.
40. Ibid., pp. 264-265.
41. Ibid., pp. 265-266.
42. There is some confusion over the number of boats, some historians reporting numbers as low as twenty; but Proctor, writing on March 23, 1791, in his Journal , recollects, "I had the command of 214 vessels on the Susquehanna, taking with me provisions and stores of 6000 men." (*PA*, Second Series, IV, 557).
43. For a most poetic expression, see Headley's journal, in Cook, pp. 193-194.
44. Cook, p. 155.
45. James Clinton, elder brother of George Clinton, "the father of New York State," had fought in the French and Indian Wars, and had during the Revolution just two years ago heroically defended Fort Clinton (near Kingston, N.Y.) against the British forces of Sir Henry Clinton, who were moving up the Hudson River Valley. There is a General Clinton Park at Bainbridge, New York, and on each Memorial Day weekend the Sullivan-Clinton Campaign is commemorated with a Canoe Regatta here.
46. Cook, p. 124.
47. Colonel Proctor later declared that he was carrying provisions for 6000 men.
48. Journal of Lt. Col. Adam Hubley, Cook, p. 156.
49. Cook, p. 94; Fischer, p. 89.
50. Fischer, p. 89.
51. Cook, pp. 127-128.
52. Cook, p. 128.
53. Cook, pp. 127-128.
54. Trussell, *The Pennsylvania Line,* p. 208 and 208n.
55. Cook, p. 183.
56. Cook, p. 197.
57. DM 4-S-36.
58. DM 4-S-36-37; Abler, *Chainbreaker*, p. 109.
59. Stone, *Life of Joseph Brant,* II, 35.
60. Cook, p. 130.
61. The Reverend John Breckenridge, as quoted by Stone in *The Life and Times of Sa-Go-Ye-Wat-Ha*, p. 22.
62. Graymont, *Iroquois in the American Revolution,* p. 216.
63. Ibid., p. 217.
64. Idem.
65. Cook, p. 32.
66. Mary Jemison would live seventy-five years with the Senecas, marry two different warriors, and die at age ninety.
67. Seaver, pp. 72-73.
68. Cook, p. 365; Codman, p. 304. Washingtonville is today in Montour County. Boyd's birthplace has been given as Derry, Pa., but that seems to be in error. There has been erected a Boyd-Parker Memorial. It is located a little to the east of Cuylerville in Livingston County, New York, in the Genesee State Park.
69. Cook, p. 369.

70. The later Seneca villages known as Big Tree and Little Beard's Town at the site of the old Genesee Castle (Swatzler, pp. 279-280).
71. *PA,* Second Series, XII, 105.
72. Brodhead's very long letter to Washington, dated September 16, 1779, which details the expedition, is printed in Cook, pp. 307-309. The detailed report of the mission can be found in *PA*, Second Series XII, 155, and in *The Magazine of History and Biography,* III, 649.
73. Ibid., p. 308.
74. Abler, *Chainbreaker*, pp. 141-142.
75. Ibid., pp. 142-143.
76. Brodhead's account is in Cook, pp. 307-308.
77. This episode has inspired a great deal of confusion, in time and in place, in number of participants; some historians mistakenly identify the escaping swimmer as Cornplanter.
78. Abler, *Chainbreaker*, p. 117.
79. Hassler, p. 101
80. Cornplanter speech in 1790 to Congress in Philadelphia. Graymont, *Iroquois in the American Revolution,* p. 192; Fischer, p.7.
81. Abler, *Chainbreaker*, p. 112; Craft, pp. 70-71.
82. A. Wallace, p. 144.
83. Unpublished John Harris family letters.
84. *PA*, Second Series, XV, 757.
85. A. C. Flick, New York State Historian, in Cook, p. 16.
86. Cook, p. 16.
87. Cook, pp. 8, 12-13, 49, and 244; and Abler, *Chainbreaker*, p. 113.

Chapter VIII

1. DM 4-S-44-45; Abler, *Chainbreaker*, p. 120.
2. Graymont, *Iroquois in the American Revolution,* p. 236.
3. Stone, *The Poetry and History of Wyoming*, p. 127.
4. Seaver, pp. 77-78; see also Stone, *The Poetry and History of Wyoming*, pp. 425-426.
5. Seaver, pp. 77-78. Stone follows her, but Abler notes that later scholars (A. Wallace, *Death and Rebirth*, pp. 145-146, and Graymont, *Iroquois in the American Revolution,* p. 236) follow the Blacksnake narrative as recorded in the Draper manuscript (DM 4-S-44-45).
6. Seaver, p. 78.
7. DM 4-S-43-45.
8. Graymont, *Iroquois in the American Revolution,* p. 237; and "Blacksnake Conversations," DM 4-S-45; Abler, *Chainbreaker*, pp. 120-121.
9. A. Wallace, pp. 145-146.
10. Abler, *Chainbreaker*, pp. 121-122.
11. Stone, *Life of Brant,* II, 124; DM 4-S-56; Abler, *Chainbreaker*, p. 122.
12. A. Wallace, pp., 145-146.
13. Graymont, pp. 238-239; Abler, *Chainbreaker*, pp. 122-123.
14. Graymont, p. 238; and Blacksnake in the Draper MSS, 4-S-46-56.
15. Fort Niagara enjoys quite a history. Regarded as the oldest continuously active military site in all of North America, the fort was established by the French in 1679,

and was known then as Fort Conti. The renovated structure, a National Historic Landmark, now serves as a New York State Park and Museum.

16. Graymont, *Iroquois in the American Revolution,* p. 22.

Chapter IX

1. Deardorff, "The Cornplanter Grant," p. 8.
2. Kent and Deardorff, p. 269.
3. NYHS, O'Reilly Collection, vol. VIII; A. Wallace, p. 168.
4. Hough, I, 165; A. Wallace, p. 163.
5. A. Wallace, pp. 174-175.
6. On treaties and land agreements, see Richard Monette, "Treaties," in the Hoxie Encyclopedia, pp. 643-646.
7. Aldrich, p. 43.
8. Idem.
9. Ibid., p. 44.
10. Ibid., p. 45.
11. Ibid., pp. 44-45.
12. Idem.
13. Idem.
14. Hulbert, p. 86.
15. Morison, pp. 196-197.
16. Idem.
17. Idem.
18. Swatzler, p. 122.
19. Thomas Mifflin of Pennsylvania was the third President of the United States to be elected under the Articles of Confederation.
20. Swatzler, p. 123.
21. For an account of this session and a very thorough explanation of the treaty session which was to follow, see Graymont, *Iroquois in the American Revolution*, pp. 270-284, and Swatzler, pp. 117-126.
22. Swatzler, p. 125.
23. Idem.
24. For a good account of the proceedings at Fort Stanwix see Graymont, *Iroquois in the American Revolution,* pp. 270-284.
25. *PA*, First Series, XI, 509.
26. Oliver Phelps was born at about the same time as Cornplanter, in 1750, in Windsor, Ct. In 1792, four years after his purchase of the Seneca land, he built the first framed house in Canandaigua. He died there on February 21, 1809.
27. An older man than Phelps, by twelve years, Nathaniel Gorham enjoyed a *most* distinguished career in public life, serving his native colony (state) of Massachusetts and the United States as a member of Congress. Under the Articles of Confederation he was actually (as President of the Congress) the "President of the United States" for one year. He was a member of the Convention which framed the Constitution of the United States. He died June 11, 1796, at age fifty-eight.
28. Hough, I, 110-128; 160-163; A. Wallace, p. 170.
29. Mohawk, p. 136.
30. A. Wallace, p. 217.

Chapter X

1. During the Revolution the capital of the United States, which was simply the meeting place of the Continental Congress, was moved eight times.
2. Abler notes that Blacksnake had informed Lyman Draper that the four besides himself were *Kog-ga-do-wa,* of Tonnewanda (Towanda), *Che-wah-ya*, *To-doin-jo-wa* (Split World), and *Jo-nah-hah*, of Cattaraugus (DM 4-S-22; Abler, *Chainbreaker*, p. 159).
3. Blacksnake calls the interpreter Joseph Dickinson. He surely meant Joseph Nicholson. But Abler (*Chainbreaker*, p. 162) believes that General Richard Butler served as the interpreter on this journey.
4. Passages from Blacksnake's narrative are from the Draper manuscript via Abler, *Chainbreaker*, pp. 171-174.
5. Deardorff, "The Cornplanter Grant," p. 9.
6. *Independent Gazetteer*, April 22, 1786. Philadelphia's *Independent Gazetteer* or *The Chronicle of Freedom* was published daily, except Sunday, from April 13, 1782 until January 9, 1790.
7. The only portrait of Cornplanter that exists is the one done by Bartoli, which was probably painted in 1796 after Bartoli arrived in New York City from London.
8. Deardorff, "The Cornplanter Grant," p. 9.
9. The *Pennsylvania Evening Herald*, May 6, 1786. Philadelphia's *Pennsylvania Evening Herald*, a pro-Irish newspaper, was published by Matthew Carey and appeared semiweekly. Its first edition was March 26, 1785. It was much occupied with the political proceedings and debates of the Pennsylvania General Assembly.
10. Abler, *Chainbreaker*, pp. 170-176.
11. The Articles had been submitted to the thirteen states for ratification on November 7, 1777, but the document was not ratified by all thirteen (Maryland the last) until March 1, 1781.
12. Ramsay, in Hancock's stead, served as President pro tem from November 23, 1785 to May 12, 1786. Hancock served as President (before the Articles of Confederation) May 24, 1775, to October 29, 1777, and again (under the Articles) from November 23, 1785, to June 5, 1786.
13. Ramsay was one of the most accomplished figures of the Revolutionary War years. A student of medicine, he graduated from Princeton at the age of sixteen and became a physician, and a surgeon during the war. He became a close friend of Dr. Benjamin Rush. He was a most prolific writer, turning out medical treatises, biographies (including a life of Washington and a eulogy for Rush), and histories (including a chronicle of the Revolution). He was twice married, the second time to Martha Laurens, the daughter of Henry Laurens, who served as President of the United States under the Articles of Confederation from Nov.1, 1777 to Dec. 9, 1778, a critical time of the war. Martha Laurens was a most exceptional person in her own right, extremely active in the cause of the needy and a big help to her husband in his literary production.
14. Abler, *Chainbreaker*, p. 160.

Chapter XI

1. *PA*, First Series, XII, 371.
2. Kelsay, pp. 424-425.

3. Eckert, p. 492. Eckert's note: "This is the present Indian Run, which empties into the Muskingum River two miles above the Ohio River. The major encampment of the Indian delegates was directly across the Muskingum River from the present Washington County Fairgrounds."
4. Butler had been one of the three commissioners (Oliver Wolcott and Arthur Lee were the others) who negotiated the purchase of northwestern Pennsylvania from the Iroquois at Fort Stanwix four years earlier.
5. Eckert, p. 492.
6. Idem.
7. Eckert, p. 493.
8. A. Wallace, p. 156.
9. Kelsay, p. 425.
10. Deardorff and Snyderman, p. 583.
11. A. Wallace, pp. 158-159.
12. Idem., and Swatzler, p. 129.
13. Swatzler, p. 129.
14. Kelsay, p. 426.
15. Idem.
16. Stone, *Life of Brant*, II, p. 427; Newton, p. 80.
17. Newton, p. 80, from Ohio Company Records, p. 54.
18. A. Wallace, p. 171. See also Deardorff, "The Cornplanter Grant," p. 8. Deardorff's affectionate and informative essay was read by Deardorff himself at a meeting of the Historical Society of the Cornplanter Indians Committee of the Pennsylvania Federation of Historical Societies.
19. Schenck, pp. 100-101.

Chapter XII

1. One of the most distinguished figures of the American Revolution, Thomas Mifflin, though a Quaker, became an energetic and ardent patriot, and was appointed Quartermaster General of the Army in August of 1775. Considered the first Governor of Pennsylvania, Thomas Mifflin has been honored by the Commonwealth in the names of many city streets and avenues, in the name of one of her sixty-seven counties, and in the names of three communities, none of which is in Mifflin County: Mifflintown (Juniata County), Mifflinburg (Union County, and Mifflinville (Columbia County).
2. Schenck, p. 96.
3. Ibid., p. 70.
4. Ibid., pp. 97- 98.
5. Meginness, *History of the West Branch*, p. 364.
6. *PA*, First Series, XI (1786-1790), 709-10.
7. *PA*, First Series, XII (1790), 321. The letter is also included in Newton's *History of Venango County,* p. 80.
8. Brigadier General Josiah Harmar was at this time (1790) thirty-seven years old. It was he who had carried to Paris (with greatly detailed instructions and the blessing of President Thomas Mifflin), after it had been ratified by Congress, the treaty ending the Revolutionary War. In October of 1785 he built Fort Harmar, at the point where the Muskingum River enters the Ohio, in order to discourage settlement in the Ohio Valley. Ironically, because it seemed to afford protection, the fort

only invited settlement. His conduct during the Indian wars in Ohio came under investigation, and he was accused of wrongdoing during the campaign, including being drunk on duty. The court-martial that was convened in 1791 to try Harmar finally exonerated him of all charges. But he shortly thereafter, on January 1, 1792, retired from the Army. When he returned to his native state, he soon became the Adjutant-General of Pennsylvania, serving until 1799. He was dismissed from the Jefferson administration for his opposition to statehood for Ohio. He died August 20, 1813. He had had his portrait painted by Raphael Peale, the artist son of Charles Willson Peale.

9. Kent, p. 452.
10. Pa. MSS, Indian Affairs, 1734 (Pennsylvania Historical Commission, Harrisburg).
11. Brackenridge (1748-1816) had his master's degree from the College of New Jersey (now Princeton), where he had been good friends with the poet Philip Freneau and a promising young man named James Madison. With them Brackenridge helped to form the American Whig Society. By the time of Cornplanter's trip to Philadelphia, he had become the most important and influential citizen of the community. In 1786, he founded the *Pittsburgh Gazette*, still printed today, as the *Pittsburgh Post-Gazette.* In that same year he was elected to the Pennsylvania State Assembly, in which he became an ardent spokesman for the federal constitution. Just three years before his meeting with Cornplanter, he helped to secure a sufficient endowment to establish the Pittsburgh Academy (presently the University of Pittsburgh). He was largely responsible for the organization of Allegheny County, and in 1799 he was made a justice of the Pennsylvania Supreme Court. He died in 1816 in Carlisle, Pa., the home of Molly Pitcher and Brigadier General William Irvine and General John Armstrong. Best known of his many writings is the comical *Don Quixote*-like satirical narrative *Modern Chivalry.*
12. Colonel John Gibson (1740-1823), a landowner and trader, was a pioneer settler of Beaver County. During the French and Indian Wars, in 1763, he was captured by the Indians while canoeing downriver on the Ohio. He was scheduled for theIndians' favorite torture, but because one of the old women of the village took a fancy to him and insisted on "adopting" him (as often happened), he escaped the burning at the stake. Like Brackenridge, he had come from the east to the frontier. He served the rebel cause during the Revolution, as a Colonel of the 13th Virginia Regiment; and he assumed temporary command of the Western Department (including Forts Pitt, McIntosh, and Laurens). At the time of Cornplanter's trip to Philadelphia, Gibson was a member of the convention which was drafting the Constitution of Pennsylvania, which would be adopted in January of 1791. He was well known to President Mifflin.
13. *PA*, First Series, XI (1786-90), 732-733.
14. Ibid., p. 733.
15. Schenck, pp. 97-98.
16. Joseph Nicholson had been a trader on the frontier. He early became the chief interpreter for the Iroquois in their dealings with the British and the American commissioners. It was Nicholson who served as William Johnson's interpreter at the treaty sessions held at Fort Stanwix in 1768.
17. The speech is printed entire in *Colonial Records* (hereafter *CR*), XVI, 501-506; also in Schenck, pp. 96-105.
18. *PA*, First Series, XI (1786-90), 740.
19. The text of the Council's response is printed in *Colonial Records*, XVI, 507.

20. For an account of Cornplanter's session with Mifflin and Pennsylvania's Executive Council, see Schenck, pp. 96-103.
21. The first capital of the United States under the Constitution was New York City (March 4, 1789-Aug. 12, 1790). The capital was transferred to Philadelphia during the fall of 1790, and became officially the capital on Dec. 6, 1790. It would be the capital until March 14, 1800, with Congress accommodated in the Philadelphia County Building (Congress Hall). The capital was moved again in the summer of 1800, and Washington City (later Washington, D. C.) became officially the capital on November 17, 1800.
22. Newton, p. 18. General Erastus Root once remarked to Red Jacket's biographer William Leete Stone that he considered John Randolph and Red Jacket "the two most perfect orators whom he had ever heard." (Stone *Life and Times of Sa-Go-Ye-Wat-Ha,* p. 25).
23. These speeches by Cornplanter at the Philadelphia Conference are included in the *American State Papers, Indian Affairs* (hereafter *ASP,IA)* and in the *Pennsylvania Archives*, Second Series, IV, 527-537.
24. *ASP, IA*, I, 142.
25. *PA,* First Series, XII (1790), 322.
26. For the complete text of the speeches delivered at the 1790-91 conference with Washington, see *American State Papers, Indian Affairs*, I, 140 ff.
27. *PA*, Fourth Series, IV (Papers of the Governors), 164-165.

Chapter XIII

1. Schenck, p. 102.
2. Ibid., p. 101.
3. *PA*, Second Series, IV (1794), 555.
4. Ibid., p. 554.
5. *PA*, First Series, XI (1786-1790), 562-563; *CR*, XVI, 36.
6. See *CR*, XVI, 86, and *PA*, First Series, XI (1786-1790), 562.
7. Schenck, p. 103.
8. Deardorff, AThe Cornplanter Grant," pp. 10-11.
9. Swatzler, pp. 132-133.
10. It is not known just how many wives Cornplanter had, or how many at one time, It is very clear that at the time of the Quakers' arrival in Cornplanter Town he had only one. But his uncle Kayahsotha apparently for some of his life had two wives at the same time. The eminent historian William Leete Stone, who lived among the Iroquois for many years, observed many instances of polygamy.
11. *PA*, Ninth Series, II, 956-958; Deardorff, "The Cornplanter Grant," pp. 1-22.
12. Schenck, p. 103.
13. This letter is reproduced in the hand of Joseph Nicholson as the frontispiece to Lois Barton's *A Quaker Promise Kept*, and again, in type, on page 1. See also Deardorff and Snyderman, p. 584; and Newton, p. 81.
14. *PA*, Second Series, IV (1794), 555.
15. Ibid., p. 556.
16. Ibid., p. 557. Brady, a scout for Brodhead, was a celebrated Indian fighter, famous for miraculous escapes and a vengeful nature.
17. CF. These letters are with the Burton Historical Collection, Detroit, Michigan. On microfilm at the Pennsylvania Historical and Museum Commission, Harrisburg.

18. *PA*, Second Series, IV (1790-96), 569-570.
19. Ibid., p. 570. And see A. Wallace, *Death and Rebirth*, pp. 163-164, 169.
20. Reynolds, pp. 60-61.
21. A sketch of his sawmill and gristmill dates from 1795. See Reynolds, p. 32.
22. Reynolds, pp. 33-34. For Mead's account of his settlement and the anxious years 1790-94, see Reynolds, pp. 33-41.
23. Reynolds, p. 37.
24. Idem.
25. Reynolds, p. 39.
26. Ibid., p. 61.
27. Ibid., pp. 61-62.
28. This letter is on file with the Pennsylvania Historical Society. Dr. W. A. Irvine of Warren County procured a copy of it and made it available to the historians of Venango County. It is printed in Newton, pp. 90-91. Bears Oil is not identified. He should not be confused with Mahkeemeetew, who was a Monomonie chief, and an outstanding leader and orator serving under the direct command of Tomah. He was chosen as the Speaker for the Chiefs after Tomah's death. He was the chief negotiator for the 1831 and 1832 Treaties with the New York Indians. He was rigidly devoted to the Indian way ("The forest is our life . . . we do not like to part with it—or any part of our land."). He died in 1834.

Chapter XIV

1. Ellis, p. 212.
2. Ibid., p. 213.
3. Boyd, *Mad Anthony Wayne*, p. 237.
4. Ibid., p. 238.
5. Moore, pp.167-168.
6. The Miami war-chief Michikinikwa, known as Little Turtle, was born in 1752 (some historians give the date as early as 1747) on the Eel River (Kenapocomoco). He was a most courageous and able warrior, but like Cornplanter he foresaw the need to bury the hatchet. After the Treaty of Greenville, he became an apostle of peace, and began to lead his people, as Cornplanter was doing for the Senecas, toward peaceful living with the white settlers. He urged them, as did Cornplanter, away from alcohol and into farming. During the last three years of his life he lived at his village west of Fort Wayne on the Eel River. Little Turtle met with Washington in the last year of the President's second term. He had his portrait painted by Gilbert Stuart. He died in Fort Wayne on July 14, 1812. It was in this same year that the village in which he had been born and reared, on the Eel River, as well as two other Miami villages, was destroyed by American troops. Most members of the tribe were removed from Indiana by 1845.
7. His name is sometimes spelled "Procter." Washington spelled it both ways.
8. *PA*, Second Series, IV, 552.
9. Ibid., p. 610.
10. CF, Binder Four. This letter is on microfilm with the Pennsylvania Historical and Museum Commission.
11. Deardorff and Snyderman, p. 584. Much of the correspondence between the Quakers and the Indians is housed in the Department of Records, etc., in Philadelphia, Box 1 and ff.

12. Swatzler, p. 7.
13. See Rafert, p. 343, and Moore, pp. 168-169.
14. Irving, V, 108-109.
15. The Ireland-born Butler had been a friend of George Washington and a friend also of Lafayette. When at the turn of the century, eight new counties were formed out of Allegheny County, he was honored in the name of the one immediately north of Allegheny. It was Richard's brother William who as a Lieutenant Colonel of the 4th Pennsylvania Regiment conducted the revenge expedition from Schoharie which destroyed the Indian settlements of Unadilla and Anaguaga in the aftermath of the Wyoming massacre. A second brother, Thomas, won a commendation from Washington for his valiant fighting at the Brandywine, and later received a commendation from General Anthony Wayne for his heroics at Monmouth. Thomas was also with St. Clair at the time of the Ohio disaster. He was in command of a Pennsylvania battalion from Carlisle. He was wounded, but was one of the few officers to survive the battle.
16. Knopf, pp. 302-303.
17. A. Wallace, p. 201.
18. Carroll, VII, 14-15.
19. Abler, *Chainbreaker*, p. 183.
20. *ASP, IA*, I, 229; Kelsay, p. 464; Abler, *Chainbreaker*, p. 183.
21. Abler, *Chainmbreaker*, pp. 189-190.
22. Ibid., p. 176.
23. Ibid., p. 190.
24. Ibid., p. 192.
25. Chapin (1740-95) was the first Indian Agent appointed by Washington for the Six Nations. He had served as a general under Washington during the War of the Revolution. About the time of the Phelps and Gorham Purchase (1788) he had come, with his four sons, to Canandaigua and took up land, and when that settlement became a town, in 1791, Chapin was made its first supervisor.
26. *ASP, IA*, I, 229-233.
27. Carroll, VII, 14-15.
28. *AS , IA*, I, 229.
29. Coe, p. 317.
30. Abler, *Chainbreaker*, p. 193.
31. Ibid., pp. 193-195.
32. The England-born Simcoe, who had obtained a commission in the 35th Regiment of Foot, had participated in the evacuation of Boston and in the battles of Long Island and the Brandywine. After Brandywine he assumed command of the already famous Queen's Rangers, which was composed of Loyalist volunteers who wore green uniforms throughout the war. Simcoe attained the rank of Lieutenant Colonel, was wounded three times, was captured in 1779 at Perth Amboy, New Jersey, and was returned through prisoner exchange to England in 1781. Under his command the much feared Queen's Rangers never lost an engagement. The unit operated out of Philadelphia during the British occupation of that city, and Simcoe was responsible for the massacre at the Hancock House in Salem, New Jersey, March 21, 1778 (See Betts, pp. 289-290). After the close of the American Revolution, the province of Upper Canada (the region of southern Ontario plus the shoreline of the Georgian Bay and Lake Superior) was created by the British under the Constitutional Act of 1791. Simcoe was named its first Lieutenant Governor, and served until 1796. He founded the city of York (now Toronto), and, most notably,

put an end to slavery in Upper Canada, long before the British Empire abolished slavery. The town of Simcoe in southwestern Ontario, s well as Simcoe County and a number of streets and roads, is named for him. Lake Simcoe, at present-day Barrie, Simcoe himself named for his father.

33. Alexander McKee, like Cornplanter, was a half-breed. He was the son of a western Pennsylvania trader and a Shawnee mother, who may have been a white captive. As he was, like Simon Girty, much accomplished in the Indian dialects, he served as an intermediary throughout the frontier territory. He was a trader and owned land at the mouth of Chartiers Creek, and he had served as a justice in both Bedford and Westmoreland Counties. He served as a British Indian Agent at Fort Pitt and with "the shot heard round the world" he remained loyal to the Crown. He was held prisoner for a time in Pittsburgh, but with the notorious Simon Girty, and some other renegades (including Matthew Eliot), on the 28th of March, 1778, he fled Pittsburgh to join the Indians who had become allied with the British. As he had been won over to the British cause, he was much reviled by the Americans, and, with Girty, could be numbered among the most hated men of the late Revolution and post-war years. Colonel John Proctor, in a letter to the President of the Supreme Executive Council of Pennsylvania, Thomas Wharton, Jr., dated April 26, 1778, expressed his dismay: "Sir, I am able to inform you that Capt. Alexander McKee with sevin other VILONS is gon to the Indians, and since there is a Serjt. And twenty od men gon from Pittsburgh of the Soldiers, what may be the fate of this Country? God alone knowes, but at Prisent it wears a most Dismal aspect." It was thought that McKee energetically engaged in stirring up the Indians, and it was well known that he was constantly making promises to them on the part of the British, promises he must have known would never be fulfilled. Certainly he was hurtful to the rebel cause. During the turbulent decade following the war, he served as an official in the British Indian Department, regularly in the capacity of Indian Agent. It was McKee who in 1790 negotiated the treaty with the Indian tribes that opened up much of southern Ontario to settlement by the whites. For a biography, see Larry L. Nelson's *A Man of Distinction among Them: Alexander McKee and British-Indian Affairs along the Ohio Country Frontier.*

34. Quoted in Stone, *Life of Brant*, II, 333; and in Kelsay, p. 476.

35. Kelsay, p. 463.

36. The village of Hardin, in Shelby County, Ohio, is named for Colonel Hardin; so is Hardin County, Kentucky, which was formed in this very year, 1792. A memorial marker has been erected at the site of the murders, which is at the center of the village of Hardin, on SR 47. (David Lodge, Shelby County Historical Society website, 1997).

37. Kelsay, p. 444 and p.707, note 77.

38. Isabel Kelsay notes that there were three rivers called "Miami." "The Great Miami and the Little Miami," she explains, "emptied into the Ohio near Cincinnati. The Miami of the Lake, now called the Maumee, emptied into Lake Erie. By the Treaty of Fort Finney [also known as the Treaty at the Mouth of the Great Miami, Jan. 31, 1786] the Americans obtained the mouth of the Great Miami, up the river, and across to the Wabash. By the Treaty of Fort Harmar they also claimed most of the east side of the Great Miami. The Americans did not claim the mouth of the Maumee." (Kelsay, page 77, note 80).

39. Kelsay, p. 477.

40. Newton, p. 81.

41. Council, Oct. 4, 1792, *Simcoe Papers*, ed. by Cruikshank, I, 222. Quoted by Kelsay, p. 479.
42. Council, Oct. 2, 1792, *Simcoe Papers*, ed. by Cruikshank, I, 220. Quoted by Kelsay, p. 478.
43. Idem.
44. For Red Jacket's oration see *ASP,IA*, I, 323-324.
45. *ASP, IA,* I, 337.
46. Idem.
47. Carroll, VII, 14-15.
48. Kelsay, p. 480.
49. Cruikshank, I, 295.
50. Major General Clarke had arrived in America in 1776. He was Brigadier General for the British in command at Savannah, 1778-79. For a time after the Revolution (1782-90) he served the Empire as Governor of Jamaica. He became the Lieutenant Governor of the Province of Quebec on October 8, 1790; he became Lieutenant Governor of the Province of Lower Canada on December 26, 1791. In his later years he would serve the British Empire in India and in South Africa.
51. Cruikshank, I, 308.
52. Ibid., I, 317.
53. Ibid., I, 355.
54. *ASP, IA*, I, 356.
55. Abler, *Chainbreaker*, p. 187.
56. A. Wallace, pp. 164-165.
57. Sugden, p. 85.
58. Idem.
59. Richter, p. 532.
60. Stone (*Life and Times of Sa-Go-Ye-Wat-Ha*, p. 18) has Red Jacket born about 1750, at a place called Old Castle, some three miles west of present-day Geneva, "at the foot of Seneca Lake."
61. Red Jacket did fight valiantly for the Americans during the War of 1812.
62. Richter, p. 532.
63. Idem.
64. Richter, p. 533.
65. Idem.
66. Kelsay, p. 508.
67. Ibid., p. 558.
68. Ibid., p. 589. But see her note # 97!
69. *PA*, Second Series, VI, 710.
70. Moore, p. 170.

Chapter XV

1. For the complete text, see Kent and Deardorff, "John Adlum on the Allegheny," pp. 440-48
2. Samuel Maclay, born June 17, 1741, Lurgan Township (present Union County) was the brother of William Maclay.
3. A farmer turned surveyor, he led a very distinguished life, serving in the Revolution, and representing Pennsylvania in both the Unites States House of Representatives

and the Senate. He kept a journal of the surveying he did in northeastern Pennsylvania in 1790, which was published in 1887 by John Meginness.

4. Kent and Deardorff, "John Adlum on the Allegheny," pp. 273-274, 294-302
5. Ibid., pp. 435 and 302-303.
6. *Journal of Samuel Maclay*, pp. 32-34.
7. Wallis Papers, microfilm, HSP; Kent and Deardorff, p. 296.
8. See Kent and Deardorff note, p. 301.
9. Ibid., pp. 301-302.
10. Ibid., pp. 303-307.
11. Ibid., pp. 312-317.
12. Ibid., p. 438.
13. Ibid., p. 437.
14. Kent and Deardorff explain that the Senecas in the opening ceremonies of their councils traditionally provide a recapitulation of all that has gone before, regardless of how well known it may be to all.
15. It was the custom among the Iroquois to consume on the premises only a token amount of food. (Kent and Deardorff, p. 453).
16. Kent and Deardorff, pp. 451-453.
17. Ibid., p. 456.
18. Ibid., pp. 458-460. In a letter to Wilkins, dated September 17, Adlum reported that "the Cornplanter said that before they attacked us they would give notice to clear the frontiers. That the Indians did not intend to make War upon Women and Children, but against men . . . ."
19. Kent and Deardorff, pp. 460-461.

Chapter XVI

1. Knopf, p. 48.
2. Ibid., p. 98.
3. Ibid., p. 100.
4. Ibid., pp. 114-115.
5. Ibid., p. 119.
6. Ibid., pp. 121-122.
7. Eckert, pp. 585-586.
8. Ibid., p. 742n.
9. Twohig, p. 23.
10. Knopf, p. 132.
11. Ibid., p. 135.
12. Ibid., p. 141.
13. Ibid., pp. 143, 148.
14. Ibid., p. 151.
15. Ibid., p. 191.
16. Twohig, p. 64.
17. Knopf, p. 192.
18. Carroll, VII, 14-15.
19. Knopf, p. 194.
20. Ibid., pp. 195-196.
21. Ibid., p. 202.
22. Knopf, p. 203, and Twohig, p. 105.

23. See Boyd, p. 256.
24. Sipe, *The Indian Chiefs*, p. 465. See also Stone, *The Life and Times of Sa-Go-Ye-Wat-Ha*, p. 444.
25. Knopf, p. 230.
26. Wildes, pp. 391-392.
27. Knopf, p. 251.
28. Wildes, p. 394.
29. Newton, p. 82.
30. Moore, p. 189.
31. Ibid., pp. 190-197. For an historian's account of the Battle of Fallen Timbers, see Boyd, *Mad Anthony Wayne,* pp. 237-322.

Chapter XVII

1. Pickering served as Postmaster General, 1791-95, and as Knox's successor as Secretary of War, before becoming Secretary of State under President John Adams.
2. Swatzler, p. 128.
3. Manly, p. 47; Horsman, p. 9; Prucha, p. 2. These remarks are quoted by Swatzler, p. 129.
4. The Quakers, mostly to insure that the rights of the Indians were not violated, had got into the habit of attending these councils. Other Quakers attending at Canandaigua were James Emlen, David Bacon, and John Parrish, who had been invited by both the Americans and the Indians. (See Swatzler, p. 135.).
5. Savery, p. 100.
6. Ibid., pp. 145-147.
7. Jonathan Evans, p. 92. Stone, *Life and Times of Sa-Go-Ye-Wat-Ha*, p. 139. For a fine account of the Canandaigua proceedings see Stone, *Life and Times of Sa-Go-Ya-Wat-Ha*, Chapter V, pp. 109-143.
8. Henry Abeel had been born in 1774, in Ganawaugus, of a Seneca mother. While still a very young man he had his training in the language in schools in Philadelphia, Woodbury, New Jersey, and New York City, and, as Swatzler notes, was at the time the Quaker missionaries arrived in Jennesadaga, in 1798, the only person present "who could speak both Seneca and English." He had become a professional interpreter, serving first the Quakers and later the famous Red Jacket. When only nineteen years old he served Pickering and Edmond Randolph and a party of Quaker observers as a guide for their 1793 journey to the general council with the western Indians. Even though the mission proceeded only as far as Detroit and had to turn back, Henry was commended by John Parrish, one of the Quakers, who recorded in his diary that Henry was an extremely good guide. "In the woods," he noted, "Henry was in his element, and most useful." (Deardorff, "Henry O'Bail," p. 412) By early 1794 he was back in the East, enrolled, at Pickering's request, in the Reverend Dr. Hunter's school at Woodbury, New Jersey. On February 1 of that year Cornplanter wrote General Chapin, the Indian Agent at Canandaigua, to ask about "my son in Philadelphia, whether he is alive or not." Actually, the boy "was not too happy" there and by letter promptly informed Pickering. (For this letter, see Deardorff, "Henry O'Bail," p. 412.) Again, on July 4, Cornplanter, while at a Buffalo Creek council, inquired of Chapin for news of Henry. (*PA*, Second Series, V, 736) Henry was back home in time to serve as an interpreter at the Canandaigua Treaty proceedings in November. And in the next year, he could be found, as Chapin observed, "stealing horses from the whites and holding them for

ransom." Chapin noted that the young man was "very little respected by his own or the white people." (Deardorff, "Henry O'Bail," p. 412) He fought for the United States during the War of 1812, serving first as a private and then with the rank of major among the Indian forces. He died in 1832, four years before his father, of injuries suffered in an alcohol-related accident. His half-brother Charles, during his interview with Lyman Draper, reported that Henry "while drunk, fell and hurt himself at Tonawanda, New York, in 1834 or 1836, and died there." But his widow, when applying for a pension gave the date as 1832. Henry's son Solomon was a conspicuous figure in the Warren area, and is accounted for in Deardorff's essay on Henry ("Henry O'Bail," p. 415).

9. The complete treaty is printed in *PA*, Second Series, VI, 799-802.
10. Schenck, p. 100.
11. Swatzler, p. 126.
12. Schenck, p. 122.
13. *ASP,IA,* I, 564.

Chapter XVIII

1. Kent and Deardorff, p. 269.
2. Ibid., pp. 298 ff.
3. A. Wallace, p. 168.
4. John Proctor, first Sheriff of Westmoreland County.
5. Harpster, pp. 117-118.
6. See Kent, p. 300; and see CF, Binder One.
7. Newton, pp. 89-90.
8. Called the wood or woods buffalo in Canada.
9. See Ted Belue, *The Long Hunt.*
10. On the fish harvesting, see Fenton, "Fish Drives," pp. 48-52; and Swatzler, pp. 155-156.
11. Tome, p. 53. Philip Tome hired an Indian by the name of George Silverheels in November of 1817 to assist in the capture of a live elk. This could be the brother of the Silverheels who had taken up with Cornplanter's daughter Jiiwi.
12. Tome, p. 35.
13. Idem.
14. Schenck, p. 332. (A. Wallace's note, p. 220).
15. "The history of early frontier settlement in the Allegheny Mountains area surrounding the Cornplanter grant is derived from a number of local histories, particularly those concerned with Warren County, Pennsylvania, and Cattaraugus County, New York. See in particular Schenck, 1887; *Cattaraugus County,* 1879; and *Warren Centennial,* 1897." (A. Wallace's note, p. 184).
16. W. N. Fenton, "Fish Drives among the Cornplanter Senecas," 48-52. (A. Wallace's note, p. 185).
17. "A detailed description of place names and related activities of the Cornplanter Senecas is in Fenton, 'Place Names . . . .' *Pennsylvania Archaeologist,* volumes XV and XVI." (A. Wallace's note, p. 187).
18. "The names and reputations of most of the chiefs, warriors and leading women of the Allegany Senecas at this time are provided principally by Adlum, 1794 (as edited and annotated by Kent and Deardorff, pp. 435-480); by John Decker in his recollections for Draper, preserved in the SHSW DC, 4 S; and by the Quaker

diarists of 1798 and thereafter, particularly MHD, Sharpless, 1798; SC, Simmons; the several Jackson journals at SC and CCHS; and Jackson, 1830a." (A. Wallace's note, p. 190).

19. Kent and Deardorff, p. 456. See also Paul A. W. Wallace, *Indians in Pennsylvania,* pp. 91-92.
20. On the Seneca rituals, see A. Wallace, pp. 49-59.
21. "A detailed description of the houses, the economy, the diet, the religious beliefs and observances, and the alcoholic excesses of the Allegany Seneca in 1798 is given in MHD, Sharpless, 1798; SC, Simmons Letter Books, 1798-99; and in Jackson's 1830 Sketch of the Manners, Customs, Religion and Government of the Seneca Indians in 1800. Their accounts are based on personal observations during visits to the town in 1798 and 1799." (A. Wallace's note, p.194). David Swatzler's recent *A Friend among the Senecas* is invaluable. On the Quakers at Cornplanter Town, see, besides Swatzler, A. Wallace, pp. 220-236. For the impression of Cornplanter Town given above, see A. Wallace, pp. 184-194. Reproduced here by the kind permission of Random House, Inc.
22. Jackson, *Civilization of the Indian Natives,* p. 37.
23. Sipe, *The Indian Chiefs*, p. 467.

Chapter XIX

1. Swatzler, p. 140.
2. Idem.
3. For a thorough account of the Big Tree council, see Chazanof, pp. 18-23; Swatzler, pp.137-144; A. Wallace, pp. 179-183.
4. Sachems had their status through hereditary right, and most, though not all, were men. In any sachem serving in the Six Nations was reposed undisputable civil authority. He, or she, was responsible for the government of the village: the administration of justice, the delegation of property, the organization of festivals and ceremonies, and the reception of guests or emissaries. The sachem was regarded as superior to any war-chief, whose sole responsibility was the conduct of battle or of raiding operations. The sachem would also be given a special name (an official title).
5. Swatzler, pp. 143-144.
6. A. Wallace, p. 181.
7. Ibid., p. 183.
8. For a record of these treaties and sales, see *ASP, IA, Laws and Treaties.*
9. Sipe, *The Indian Chiefs*, pp. 465-466; A. Wallace, p. 356, note 44. The Warren Centennial (1897) pointed out that the first sawmill operated by white people in Warren County was built on Jackson Run in 1800 and that the first raft of lumber floated down the Allegheny was sawed there. Cornplanter's mill was farther upstream.
10. Sipe, *The Indian Chiefs,* pp. 465-466.
11. David Mead, of course, had had both a sawmill and a gristmill in operation on French Creek, in what is today Crawford County, as early as 1790, the sawmill actually dating from 1787. For a sketch see Reynolds, p. 32.
12. Sipe, *The Indian Chiefs*, pp. 465-466.
13. Swatzler, p. 48.
14. *Stepping Stones*, III, No. 1, p. 86.

15. Hildebrandt was born in Lancaster County in 1753. He died in Washington County, Ohio, in 1827 and is interred in the Mound Cemetery at Marietta. His wife was Mary Kinsley (sp.?), and his son Jesse became a decorated officer in the Civil War. Another son, George Hildebrandt, Jr., was operating a mill on the Brokenstraw in 1808, as is known from the tax register. (CF, Binder Four).
16. CF, Binder Four.
17. Sharpless, *Some Account of a Journey.* See Swatzler, pp. 48-49, and note 49, p. 283.

Chapter XX

1. Swatzler, pp. 18-19, 34.
2. Jackson's journal is fascinating to read, because of its quaint Biblical style and because it provides so much detail about life as it was lived in the Cornplanter villages. For the text of the journal, see, "Halliday Jackson's Journal to the Seneca Indians, 1798-1800," ed. A. Wallace, in *Pennsylvania History,* XIX (1952), 117-147, 325-349.
3. Barton, p. 32.
4. Jackson, "Halliday Jackson's Journal," pp. 126-129.
5. Ibid., p. 130.
6. A. Wallace, p. 204.
7. Swatzler, p. 23. See Swatzler's *A Friend among the Senecas* for a complete and very informative account of the Quaker mission during the years 1798-1806.
8. Jackson, "Halliday Jackson's Journal," p. 141.
9. Henry Simmons' 1799 Journal is reproduced in Swatzler, both in its original form and in Swatzler's edited version, pp. 257-278.
10. Quotations from Simmons' Journal, here and following, derive from Swatzler's edited text, pp. 257-278, and are reproduced here with the kind permission of David Swatzler and Stackpole Books.
11. On dreams among the Senecas, see A. Wallace, pp. 59-75.
12. *PA*, Second Series (1896), IV, 537; see also Hough, p. 171. Quoted by Swatzler, p. 4, and see his note 8, p. 279.
13. Deardorff ("The Cornplanter Grant," pp. 11-12) has the figure at $2120.00.
14. Deardorff ("The Cornplanter Grant," pp. 11-12) identifies the two men as William Connolly of Venango County and William Kinnear of Centre County.
15. Newton, p. 91; and Deardorff, "The Cornplanter Grant," pp. 11-12. That Cornplanter did not resolutely and totally abstain from the firewater is known from the number of toasts that he proposed (as at Fort Harmar, and with General Wayne), from the expressed dismay of the Quakers, and from the account of Dr. Jonathan Eights of the tavern party enjoyed with Joseph Brant and Major Hendrick Frey in Canajoharie.
16. Swatzler, p. 4 (from PA RG 5, Kent Barnard Collection, Series 3, general correspondence, LC Boxes 3 and 4, 1799-1824).
17. Swatzler, pp. 178-179.
18. Ibid., pp. 265-266. On the Seneca and Iroquois dances, see Swatzler, Chapter Eight.
19. Swatzler, p. 196 and notes 1 and 2, p. 298.
20. A. Wallace reports that the scene was "in full view of the community" (*Death and Rebirth*, p. 236).
21. Jackson, "Halliday Jackson's Journal," p. 127.

22. Swatzler, p. 266. On the Senecas' great dread of witches, see Swatzler, Chapter Nine, pp. 196-207.
23. See especially A. Wallace, passim; Abler, *Chainbreaker*, pp. 207-218; Swatzler, pp. 1-6, 35, 216-225, 266-272; and Montour, pp. 230-231.
24. Abler, *Chainbreaker*, pp. 210-211.
25. Besides the Journal of Henry Simmons, see Montour, pp. 230-231; Paul Wallace, *Indians in Pennsylvania*, pp. 168-170; A. Wallace, pp. 3-18, 275-285, 303-318; Swatzler, pp. 300-311. For Edward Cornplanter's version of the Code of Handsome Lake, see Parker, *The Code of Handsome Lake.* One of the best accounts of Handsome Lake and his religion is to be found in Merle Deardorff, "The Religion of Handsome Lake: Its Origin and Its Development."
26. By 1801 a fence two miles long enclosed Cornplanter's Town. And the Indians were into rail splitting and road building within a year later. By the end of 1803, they had built a road connecting Jennesadaga to the upper settlement. The highway was twenty-two miles long.
27. The above passages from the 1799 Journal of Henry Simmons are from Swatzler's edited version, pp. 257-278, and are reprinted here with the kind permission of David Swatzler and Stackpole Books.
28. Swatzler, p. 254.

Chapter XXI

1. 1 CF, Binder Four.
2. Henry Baldwin is the Connecticut-born Pennsylvania attorney who commenced practice in Pittsburgh in 1801 and later had a home in Meadville. In this year of all the trouble, he would have been twenty-one years old. He was elected to the Fifteenth, Sixteenth, and Seventeenth sessions of the United States Congress as a Representative from the Commonwealth of Pennsylvania.
3. CF, Binder Four.
4. Jackson, *Civilization*, pp. 43, 57; Fenton, "Place Names," p. 54; A. Wallace, p. 261. For a complete account of the drama, see Swatzler, pp. 203-205.
5. John Pierce Journal, D 10 A; A. Wallace, p. 265.
6. PYM, Indian Committee, Box for March 9, 1802; O'Reilly Collection: Cotterillo, p. 226; A. Wallace, p. 266.
7. A. Wallace, p. 267.
8. Idem.
9. Logan Papers, XI, 74. See A. Wallace, p. 268.
10. Dearborn, a New Hampsherite, had been a member of Congress and was Secretary of War for both terms in Jefferson's administration. While he was Secretary of War, the fort built at the mouth of the Chicago River (1803) was named for him. He participated in the War of 1812.
11. A. Wallace, p. 269.
12. Idem. As Anthony Wallace notes, the Oil Springs reservation "was secured to the Seneca."
13. Ibid., p. 270.
14. Daniel Parker Papers, Box 2. For a draft copy of the letter, see A. Wallace, pp. 270-272; also Stone, *The Life and Times of Sa-Go-Ye-Wat-Ha*, 447-449.

15. This is ironic as Red Jacket actually favored the sale. (A. Wallace, p. 285) For an account of the trial, see Stone, *Life and Times of Sa-Go-Ye-Wat-Ha*, pp. 165-168. As Stone points out, there is a little irony here, as Red Jacket is known to have executed at least one "witch."
16. A. Wallace, p. 285.
17. Logan Papers, IX, 74; A. Wallace, p. 285.
18. Stone, *The Life and Times of Sa-Go-Ye-Wat-Ha*, II, 408-429, and Appendix, pp. 39-44; A. Wallace, pp. 285-286.
19. Joel Swayne was still with the community of Senecas in 1814, having married Mary Bell of nearby Ceres (CF, Binder One).
20. Deardorff and Snyderman, p. 591; and Deardorff in CF, Binder One.
21. Deardorff and Snyderman, p. 593.
22. A. Wallace, pp. 287-288.
23. Swatzler, p. 240; A. Wallace, pp. 287-288; Barton, pp. 7-8.
24. Jackson, *Civilization*, p. 53.
25. Henry, "now a sober man," apparently had been living in the neighborhood of Genesinguhta, and was owner of "eleven horned cattle." (A. Wallace, p. 214).
26. Jackson, *Civilization*, p. 49.
27. Jackson, 1806 Journal, ed. George Snyderman.
28. PYM, Indian Committee, Box 2.
29. Richter, p. 532.
30. A. Wallace, pp. 292-293.
31. William Allinson Journal, Book 2, p. 15.
32. Parker, *The Life of Ely S. Parker*, p. 47.
33. Schenck, p. 136; Babcock, pp. 23-25.
34. William Allinson Journal, Book 2, p. 44. No painting or sketch of Handsome Lake has ever appeared.
35. On the death of Handsome Lake, see Parker, *The Code of Handsome Lake*, pp. 79-80; Jasper Parrish Papers (E. Granger to J. Parrish, Aug. 27, 1815); *Buffalo Gazette*, Oct. 13, 1815; A. Wallace, pp. 318-320.
36. Jackson, *Civilization*, pp. 46-47, 49.
37. Swatzler, p. 239.
38. A. Wallace, p. 167.
39. Ibid., pp. 290-291.
40. The *Montgomery County History* does not further identify this Jacob Abeel. Some of Abeel's descendants by his second wife (Mary Knouts) continue to live in Montgomery County.
41. Frothingham, p. 233.

Chapter XXII

1. Schenck, pp. 136-137.
2. Benn, p. 40.
3. For detail on all of this, see Ketchum, II, 419-435.
4. Benn, p. 128.
5. Ibid., p. 131.
6. Charles M. Snyder, p. 66, Council Minutes; Benn, p. 131.
7. Charles M. Snyder, p. 67, Council Minutes.
8. Jasper Parrish Collection, No. 23, Military Census of February 14, 1814.

9. Ketchum, II, 422.
10. Benn, p. 130.
11. *The Daily Tribune Republican* of Meadville, Pa., Centennial Edition, May 12, 1888. (See Reynolds, pp. 212-213.).
12. Deardorff, "Henry O'Bail," p. 414.
13. Benn, p. 138.
14. Ibid., p. 148.
15. Ibid., p. 166.
16. It should be noted that Red Jacket during the war erased once and for all his earlier reputation as a coward. For he fought valiantly for the Americans, most notably in the battles waged at Fort George in August of 1813 and at Chippewa almost a year later. See Abler, "Red Jacket, Chief of the Senecas."
17. Deardorff, "Henry O'Bail," p. 414.

Chapter XXIII

1. Swatzler, p. 250.
2. According to Anthony Wallace, it was not Cornplanter but two other chiefs who halted the surveying (*Death and Rebirth*, p. 170).
3. Swatzler, from Indian Committee Collections of Philadelphia Yearly Meeting, and from Jackson, *Civilization*, pp. 72, 74, 77.
4. Newton, p. 90.
5. Deardorff, "The Cornplanter Grant," p. 13.
6. Coe, pp. 91-92.
7. Hiester was born in perhaps the same year as Cornplanter, perhaps in the same month, perhaps on the same day. He served fourteen years in the Congress and as Governor of the Quaker State from December 19, 1820, until December 16, 1823. Born in Berks County into a Pennsylvania-German family, he was known as "Old German Grey," and spoke with an accent. He energetically raised troops at the outbreak of the Revolution, but he was captured by the British during the fighting in Long Island and was treated cruelly while confined on the prison ships. By prisoner exchange he was returned to the Continental Army in time to fight at Germantown, where he suffered a wound to the head. He presided at the dedication ceremonies for the first state capitol building in Harrisburg. He died on June 1, 1832, and is interred in the Charles Evans Cemetery of Reading, Pa. Today on the campus of the Pennsylvania State University stands a residence hall named in his honor.
8. Deardorff, "The Cornplanter Grant," p. 13.
9. Coe, p. 92.
10. CF, Binder One.
11. Colonel, later Brigadier General William Irvine, a Carlisle, Pennsylvania, physician, had raised a Pennsylvania company at the outbreak of the war, and had participated in the invasion of Quebec. Captured, he was returned in time to fight at Monmouth. He was Commander of the Western Department from 1781 until the very end of the war.
12. Sipe, *The Indian Chiefs*, pp. 464-465.
13. A. Wallace, p. 324.
14. On the early schools, see Barton, pp. 13-24.

15. One of these Indian teachers was the aunt of the highly esteemed historian Dr. Arthur C. Parker of the Rochester Municipal Museum. (Deardorff, "The Cornplanter Grant," p. 17).
16. Barton, p. 113.
17. A. Wallace, p. 280.
18. Letter of Frances Ramsay, dated April 13, 1961 (CF, Binder One). See also Tome, pp. 35-36. Philip Tome's *Pioneer Life* includes (Chapter XX) some "Reminiscences of Cornplanter." The profile that is offered there is fairly accurate, except for the persistent insistence on Cornplanter's very early birth and his presence at the defeat of Braddock. Tome recalls (pp. 36-37) a time in the year 1817 when, as he was going down the Allegheny from New York State (where they had been at work) in a canoe with Cornplanter and his son Henry, he inquired of Henry whether it might be all right to ask Chief Cornplanter about battles in which he had been engaged. When Henry insisted that his father liked to talk of such things, Tome began his questioning. Cornplanter, according to Tome's remembrance, declared that his first battle was at Braddock's defeat, when he was then seventeen years of age. And his details make the story quite convincing.
19. Deardorff, "The Cornplanter Grant," p. 18; Coe, p. 90.
20. Deardorff, "Henry O'Bail," p. 413.
21. For Reverend Timothy Alden's experiences in the schools and missions, see his *An Account of Sundry Missions Performed among the Senecas*.
22. A. Wallace, p. 322.
23. Severance, p. 269; Morse, pp. 83-84.
24. For a good account of the effects of the evangelism among the Senecas, see A. Wallace, *Death and Rebirth*, pp. 322-325.
25. This was Red Jacket's second wife, Awaogoh. He had ten children by his first wife, Aanjedek, before they were separated. When Red Jacket married Awaogoh, she was a widow, her husband, Two Guns, having been a casualty of the fighting at Chippewa, where Red Jacket fought bravely. (Abler, "Red Jacket, Chief of the Seneca," *American National Biography*, Oxford University Press, 1990).
26. CF, Binder Two.
27. Deardorff, "Henry O'Bail," p. 414.
28. Alden, p. 140.
29. Jackson, "Halliday Jackson's Journal," p. 129.
30. Alden, p. 69; Coe, p. 89.
31. The present writer is aware of only three instances when Cornplanter was "obliged" to laugh. One was on the occasion in which the plundering Indians in the raid on Canajoharie mistook lime for flour; another is reported by the hunter Philip Tome, who heard the Chief laugh at one point as he recited his eventful history; and the third is noted by William Leete Stone in his life of Red Jacket (p. 20): Cornplanter and Joseph Brant are laughing as they recall the story of the "cow killer" in the presence of Red Jacket, all the while pretending that they do not know to whom the term refers.
32. Sipe, *The Indian Chiefs*, pp. 468-469.
33. Craig, II, 95; Coe, p. 89.
34. Alden, p. 139; Coe, pp. 88-90.
35. CF, Binder Four, from Alden's *Missions*, 1827.
36. This was the boat's third trip on the river, but its first this far up.
37. Reynolds, pp. 291-292.
38. *Crawford Weekly Messenger*, June 15, 1830, from *Pittsburgh Gazette*.

39. *Pittsburgh Gazette*, May 28, 1830; Sipe, *The Indian Chiefs*, pp. 469-470; Reynolds, p. 292.
40. For accounts of the boat's trip up the river and of the subsequent celebrations on July 4, at Conneaut Lake, see Reynolds, pp. 285-295.
41. Deardorff, "Henry O'Bail," p. 413.
42. In the custody of the Seneca-Iroquois Museum on the Allegany Indian Reservation at Salamanca, New York, are Cornplanter's personal wampum belt, which reveals a pattern of mysteriously missing beads, and his "magic" cane. (CF, Warren County Historical Society).
43. A. Wallace, pp. 327-329; Benn, p. 183.
44. Williams, p. 12.
45. In order to make positive identification, Cornplanter's coffin had been opened. (Abrams, p. 63).
46. Deardorff, "The Cornplanter Grant," p. 18.

Afterword

1. Saylor, for his loyal support, was made an honorary member of the Seneca Nation on September 15, 1962, before the dam was completed. He joined Pennsylvania Governor Arthur James, who was adopted by the Seneca Nation on August 26, 1940, and by the Wolf Clan mother was baptized *O-dahn-goht* ("Sunlight"). At these ceremonies, attended by 400 Senecas, Governor James had high praise for Cornplanter.
2. Deardorff, "The Cornplanter Grant," p. 15.
3. Deardorff, "Henry O'Bail," p. 415.
4. Pennsylvania's last Indian School, the school in the Cornplanter Grant, Corydon Township, Warren County, closed forever on the last day of 1953. It was a red brick building one hundred yards from the river. The last teacher, Ms. Lucia E. Browne, was completing her 24th year as "the Indian teacher."
5. For an account of the forced relocation and the effects of the dam, see Bilharz.
6. DM 4-S-117-124.
7. Joseph Elkinton, a Quaker schoolmaster, on May 14, 1821, recorded in his journal (Quaker Collection, Haverford College) that he had been informed by some Indians that a son of Cornplanter had just passed away. This *may* have been the son known as "the Idiot."
8. Deardorff, "Henry O'Bail," p. 415.
9. CF, Binder Four. For genealogy and information on Cornplanter's descendants, see issues of the newsletter produced by Jack Ericson, historian for the Cornplanter Descendants, Fredonia, New York.
10. Deardorff, "The Cornplanter Grant," p. 22.

Index

A

Aanjedek, 382
Abeel, Charles, 21, 112, 116, 266, 287, 293, 306, 312, 317, 331, 346, 357, 358, 360
Abeel, Christoffel, 4
Abeel, Emily, 360
Abeel, Hannah, 315
Abeel, Henry, 20, 116, 143, 192, 211, 239, 252, 263, 266, 272, 275-276, 277, 278, 280, 284, 286, 291, 293, 295-296, 299, 304, 306, 311, 312, 314, 315, 317, 320, 321, 322, 335, 346-347, 357, 358, 359-360, 398
Abeel, Jacob, 318
Abeel, John (Johannes), 1-5, 10-13, 16, 107-110, 317-318
Abeel, William, 287, 293, 358, 360
Abler, Thomas, 20, 47, 48, 62, 103
Abraham (Tyahanesera), 29, 31
Abrams, Esther, 359
Abrams, Henry, 359
Adams, John, 301
Adams, John Quincy, 211
Adlum, John, 182, 216-219, at Cornplanter Town, 220-229; 291
Akron, N.Y., 352
Albany, 1-2, 3, 6, 10, 12, 27, 29, 32, 46, 48-49, 58, 65, 78, 99, 107, 121, 211
alcohol, 115, 267, 276, 278, 287-290, 293-294, 296-297, 300, 308, 309, 310, 317, 321, 327, 329, 339
Alden County, 199
Alden, Ichabod, 73-79
Alden, Timothy, 7, 170, 256, 268-269, 334-344, 347, 379
Alexander, Robert, 4-5
Aliquipiso, 2, 5
Allanawissica, 30
Allegany, 273, 351
Allegany Reservation, 258, 278, 314, 321, 322, 331, 332, 335, 336, 351, 352, 353, 355-356, 361, 362
Allegheny (steamboat), 345-346
Allegheny College, 7, 170, 268
Allegheny Mountains, 36, 121, 180
Allegheny River, 7, 8-9, 28, 36, 44, 51, 52-53, 82, 98, 99-103, 112, 116, 117, 118, 123, 130, 144, 145, 149, 150, 164, 165, 169, 170, 171, 180, 183, 185, 201, 208, 216, 219, 253, 257, 258, 259, 261, 262, 273, 277, 279, 280, 283, 291, 303, 305, 314, 320, 331, 350, 351, 352, 353, 356, 362
Allegheny (Allegany) Senecas, 325-326
Allen Town, 38
Allinson, William, 316
Ambridge, 232
American State Papers, 155
Amherst, Jeffrey, 22
Anaguaga, 394
Appletown (see Kendaia)
Arcadia, 68
Armstrong, John, 180
Arnold, Benedict, 64-65, 98
Articles of Confederation, 124, 135
Athens, Pa., 90
Atlee, Samuel, 125-128
Au Glaize Council, 199, 202-205, 208, 232
Au Glaize River, 199, 200, 203, 205, 232
Aupaumat, Hendrick, 197, 199
Avis, 146
Avon, 2, 27, 28, 47, 103
Awaogoh, 405
Awl-breaker (see Blacksnake)

B

Babb Creek, 146
Bald Eagle, Chief, 44-45, 381
Bald Eagle, Delaware Indian, 45
Bald Eagle Creek, 39, 44
Baldwin, Henry, 305, 402
Baldwin, Isaac, 190
Baldwin, Waterman, 190-193
Ball's Farm, 323
Bartoli, Frederick, 363
Barton, William, 89
Bayard, Stephen, 275
Beard, James, 275
Bears Oil, 179
Beatty, Erkuries, 96-97, 99
beaver, 11-12, 14

Beaver Creek, 232
Beaver River, 36
Beaver Valley Indians, 172
Benjamin family, 39
Benn, Carl, 321-322
Berry, Jack, 110
Big Cross (see Gyasota)
Big Knife, 30, 151
Big Sky, 183, 252
Big Snake, 304
Big Tree (Great Tree, Stif-knee), 117, 141, 144, 149, 150, 152, 154, 155, 156, 159, 161, 162, 163, 164, 183, 196, 236, 237
Big Tree (Treaty Oak), 273
Big Tree (village), 270
Big Tree Reservation, 306, 331
Black Chief, 183, 221
Black Rock, 320-321, 322
Black Rock Corridor, 311
Blacksnake, 6, 19-22, 27-31, 44, 47-48, 51-65, 68-73, at Wyoming, 66-74; 77, defends against Sullivan, 81-106; 107, 109-112, first trip to Philadelphia, 130-137; 141, 149, 155, 197-198, 200, 225, 256, 257, 294-295, 314, 317, 321, 331, 336
Blacksnake, James, 359
Blacksnake, Jenny, 360
Blake, Thomas, 99
Bleeker patent, 318
Blockhouse Creek (see Little Pine Creek)
Blue Jacket (Weyapiersenwah), 174, 194, 199, 240-242
Blue Sky, 307, 323
Board of War, 245
Book of Common Prayer, 210
Boone, Daniel, 85
Boone, Hawkins, 84-85
Border Wars, 35-46
Boston Tea Party, 123
Boswell, James, 210
bounties, 37-38
Bouquet, Henri, 52, 54
bow and arrow, 10-12, 14
Bowen, Merrill, 360
Bowen, Pam, 361
Bowman's Creek, 69
Boyd, John Parker, 322
Boyd, Thomas, 96-99
Brackenridge, Hugh, 142, 149, 391
Braddock, Edward, 16, 21, 35, 36, 52
Brady, James, 42-45
Brady, Samuel, 44-45, 172, 381
Brady's Beaver Blockhouse, 117
Brady's Bend, 44
Brandywine, battle of, 182, 215
Brant, Joseph (Thayendanegea), 25, 38, 46-48, 50, at Oswego, 52-65; 74, at Cherry Valley, 78-80; resists Sullivan Expedition, 81-106; 107, 110, 117, 130, 138-139, 141, 182, 190, 197, 201, 206, 207, 208, 209-213, 232, 256-258, 271, 276, 305, 309, 312, 320
Brant, Molly, 25, 60, 380
Bries, Margarita, 4
Bristol, 119
Brodhead, Daniel, 82, 99-104, 116, 152, 165, 170
Brodhead Expedition, 99-104, 165
Brokenstraw Creek, 101-102
Broken Tree, 144
Bronson, Isaac, 305
Brown, Christian, 65
Brown, Enoch, 38
Browne, Lucia E., 406
Brownsville, Pa., 36
Browntown Mountains, 76
Buckley Farm, 39
Buckloons (Buckaloons), 100
Bucks County, Pa., 119
Buffalo, 119, 130, 184-185, 186, 187, 259, 320
Buffalo Creek, 126, 128, 159, 173, 174, 186, 187, 199, 206, 211, 213, 223-224, 226, 230, 235, 239, 250, 257, 261, 272, 280, 305, 306, 312, 361
Buffalo Creek Mission Cemetery, 211
Buffalo Creek Reservations, 331, 335
Buffalo Gazette, 320
Buffalo Historical Society, 211
Buffalo Valley, 261
Bunker Hill, 19
Burgoyne, John, 49, 58, 65, 75, 201
Burnt House, 102, 103, 170, 185, 231, 265, 270, 280
Bushy Run, 52, 60
Butler, John, 47, 49, at Oswego, 52-65; at Wyoming, 66-74; 96, resists Sullivan, 81-106; 128, 188, 206, 256

Butler, Richard, 124, 132, 138, 142, 153, 167-168, 195-196, 256, 276, 394
Butler's Rangers, 47, 49, 60, 68, 70-74, 91, 96-106
Butler, Thomas, 275
Butler, Walter, 77-78, 256
Butler, Zebulon, 69, 73, 77, 181, 188

C
Cadaraqua, 79
Calhoun, James, 319
Campbell, Michael, 41
Camp Fatigue, 87
Campfield, Jabez, 99
Campus Martius (Marietta), 142
Canada Creek, 26
Canajoharie, 6, 107-112, 114, 258, 293, 317, 341
Canajoharie Creek, 107
Canandaigua, 96, 245-253, 270, 289, 301, 302
Canawaugus Reservation, 331
Caneadea, 271-272
Caneadea Reservation, 331
Canoga (Gah-noh-geh), 211
Captain Cass, 177, 230
Captain Clayton, 67
Captain David, 80
Captain, Denny, 175
Captain Hendricks, 231
Captain Hughes, 231
Captain Loudon, 191
Captain Pipe, 30
Captain Pollard, 321
Captain Smoke, 187
Captain Strong (see New Arrow)
Carahaderra, 183
Cardinal, Jaré, 361
Carrolltown, 351
Carrying Place, 26
Carter, John, 40
Cartwright, Richard, 73
Cash, Johnny, 354
Catfish, 143
Catherine's Town, 72, 76, 93, 95, 103, 105
Cattaraugus, 53, 130, 173, 187, 264, 272, 303, 304, 305, 325, 342
Cattaraugus County, 333, 351, 356
Cattaraugus Creek, 112, 257
Cattaraugus Reservation, 261, 331, 332, 335, 351
Cayuga Indians, 34, 65, 68, 82, 84, 87, 107, 110, 124, 126, 130, 210, 211, 247, 251, 352
Cayuga Lake, 106, 211
Centre County, 44
Chainbreaker (see Blacksnake)
Chambers, David, 41
Chapin, Israel, 177, 198, 213, 232, 240, 252, 257
Chapin, Israel, Jr., 252, 280, 289, 301, 302
Charles Evans Cemetery, 404
Charles II, 118
Chartiers Creek, 395
Chateaugay, 158
Chatham, John, 147
Chautauqua County, 351
Chautauqua Lake, 140, 263
Chelsea Hospital, 50
Chemung, 76, 78, 91-92, 100, 192
Chemung River, 91
Chemung Valley, 90, 190
Cherry Tree, 66
Cherry Valley, 78-80, 86, 107, 114, 209, 317
Chesapeake Bay, 66
Chester County, 214
Cherokee Indians, 25, 53, 54, 122, 203
Cherokee River (Hogahee), 26
Chickasaw Indians, 11
Chief Eel, 251
Chief Redeye, 98, 101-103
Chinuchahangutho, 204, 205
Chippewa (Ojibwa) Indians, 138, 236, 254
Chittiawdunk (see Hummingbird)
Cincinnati, 230
Clarion River, 261, 262
Clark, John S., 92-94
Clarke, Alured, 206-207, 396
Clay, Henry, 319
Clayton, Captain, 67
Clinton, George, 110, 124, 159-160
Clinton, Henry, 386
Clinton, James, 82, 91-92, 386
Coats, Isaac, 299
Cobleskill, 65, 258
Code of Handsome Lake (Longhouse Religion), 294-296, 336
Cohocton (see Painted Post)

Cold Spring, 103, 294, 314, 315, 351
Colonel Dale, 320
Conawaugus (see Ganawaugus)
Conewango, 100, 231 (see Warren, Pa.)
Conewango Creek, 140, 170, 176, 187, 263, 345
Congress Hall, 154
Conneat, 179, 190
Connecticut, 25, 67-68, 245
Conneuesut, 25, 67-68, 245
Cooper, James, 299, 359
Cornplanter (Gaiantwaka), birth, 2-13; boyhood, 14-16; his name, 15; pre-war councils, 26-35; at Oswego, 51-65; at Wyoming, 66-74; Cherry Valley, 78-80; defends against Sullivan, 81-106; battle of Newtown, 91-95; rescue of Redeye, 101-103; Canajoharie, 107-112; captures and frees his father, 107-109; Fort Stanwix (1784) Treaty, 123-129; journey to Philadelphia and New York City, 130-137; Tammany Society, 130-134; carriage accident, 134-135; Fort Harmar Treaty, 138-143; meets with Thomas Mifflin, 144-153; addresses President Washington, 153-154; as orator, 155-156; Ohio Indians, 29, 180-190, 203-216; receives John Adlum, 220-229; Anthony Wayne, 230-244; Canandaigua Treaty 245-253; Cornplanter Town, 9, 14, 114-115, 183-184, 260-279; Washington's retirement, 259; Treaty of Big Tree, 270-273; the sawmill, 273-278; receives Quaker mission, 280-302; Handsome Lake's vision, 306-316; dealings with Red Jacket, 311-317; War of 1812, 319-324; illness, 337-344; destroys trophies, 340, 342, 344-345, 347; death and burial, 347-348
Cornplanter Descendants Association, 350
Cornplanter, Edward, 15, 360, 379
Cornplanter Grant (Tract), 102, 112, 114, 153-154, 180, 167-170, 352, 353, 355
Cornplanter, Jesse J., 360
Cornplanter Run, 183, 265, 350
Cornplanter State Forest, 350
Cornplanter Town, 9, 14, 114-115, 183-184, 260-279
Cornplanter Township, 350
Cornplanter Volunteer Fire Department, 350
Cornwallis, Charles, 35, 96, 309
Council Road, 360
Covenhoven, Robert, 43
Cox, Ebenezer, 60-61, 63
Craig, Isaac, 275-276, 338
Craig, Neville, 258
Crawford County, 320
Crawford, William, 121
Creek Indians, 122
Crooked Creek, 171
Crouse, Peter, 266, 268
Cuba Lake, 272
Cussawaga (Meadville), 145, 149, 166, 172, 173-174, 176, 304 (see Meadville)
Custaloga, 258
Cuyaratta, 189
Cuylerville, 386
Cyentwokee (see Cornplanter)

D

Dahg,ya,doh (see Blacksnake)
Dah-wah-de-ho (Fish Lapper), 62
Dah-gon-wa-sha (Twenty Canoes), 68
Dansbury (East Stroudsburg), 99
Dauphin County, 262
Dearborn, Henry, 106, 309-310, 320, 402
Deardorff, Merle, 9, 114, 133, 257, 313, 328-329, 335, 340, 346, 354, 355, 358, 359
Deckard rifle, 11
Deckart, John, 149, 152, 162
Deer Creek, 258
Defiance, 199, 203
Dehgewanus (see Mary Jemison)
Delaware Indians, 22-26, 29, 37-38, 67, 75, 78, 80, 100, 113, 116, 120-121, 124, 138, 166, 182, 186, 203, 207, 254, 307, 330, 332
Democratic Arch, 7
Dennison, Nathan, 69, 73
Detroit, 177, 199, 201, 207, 243, 255
Devil's Hole, 16-21
Dey-og-oh-kah-heh, 2
Dick, David, 345-346
Dickinson, John, 127
Dickinson, Joseph, 389
Dinwiddie, Robert, 52
Dog Barker, 144

Donation Island, 169
Doughty, Major, 138
Doyle, 147, 154
Draper, Lyman, 19-20, 51, 62, 82, 357
Draper Manuscripts, 21, 112, 198, 264
Duane, James, 247
Dygart, Nicholas, 318

E

Eagle Dance, 224
Earl of Dunsmore, 122
Easton, 36, 76, 86, 99, 100, 111
Eaton, S. J. M., 53
Eckert, Allan, 139
Edge Hill, 52
Eel River, 254
Eights, Jonathan, 382
Eleventh Pennsylvania Regiment, 88
Eliot, Matthew, 395
Elkinton, Joseph, 335
Ellicott, Andrew, 175, 176, 178
Ellicott, Joseph, 280
Elmira, N. Y., 91
Elmore, Samuel, 58-59
Ericson, Jack, 359
Erie, 53, 322
Erie County, 351
Erie Triangle, 140-141, 168, 209, 248, 253
Ernest, Matthew, 166-167
evangelism, 335-336

F

Fallen Timbers, 115, 179, 196, 225, 230-244, 245, 248, 253, 255, 256, 270
Farmer's Brother, 34, 40, 48, 68, 78-80, 82, 84, 107, 110, 187-189, 206, 207, 234, 252, 258, 271, 272, 285, 306, 320-322, 382
farming, 159-163, 197, 277, 283
Farm, the, 283
Farrelly, J. W., 322
Fenton, William, 264
Findley, William, 171
Finger Lakes, 82, 95, 117, 245
First Reformed Church of Albany, 4
Fish Carrier, 68, 87, 96, 106, 183, 188, 189, 252
Fishing Creek, 36
Fitzpatrick, John, 81
Fleming, Robert, 147
Flood Control Acts, 355
Fogg, Jeremiah, 92
Follett, James, 345
Follett, Leavis, 345
Forbes, John, 52
Forest County, 169, 350
Forest County (Cornplanter) Tract, 169
Forest Lawn Cemetery, 212
Forts: Armstrong, 36, 100; Augusta, 83-84; Bedford, 36; Boone, 83-85; Burd, 36; Clinton, 386; Conti, 388; Crawford, 100; Davis, 110; Detroit, 209, 255; Duquesne, 35, 52, 121; Erie, 53, 188, 319, 320; Finney, 395; Forty, 69-70, 74, 88; Franklin, 52-53, 145, 148, 166, 172-179, 185, 186, 190, 192, 220, 223, 224, 228, 230-232, 275, 276, 320; Freeland, 41-42, 82-86, 114, 218, 258, 293; George, 58, 320, 322-323; Greenville, 243, 253; Hamilton, 203; Harmar, 117, 138-143, 157, 181-182; Hunter, 109; Jenkins, 69, 73; Jefferson, 194, 203; Laurens, 391; Le Boeuf, 16, 52-53, 175-178, 322; Machault, 52-53; McIntosh, 36, 100; Miami, 240, 242; Muncy, 41, 76, 83; Niagara, 9, 22, 27, 34, 48, 111-113, 115, 188, 209, 255, 257, 387; Pitt, 27, 28, 36, 45, 46, 48, 100-101, 138, 143, 150, 152, 165-167, 175, 190, 275, 330; Presque Isle, 16, 53-54; Recovery, 194, 241; Saint Clair, 203; Schlosser, 18, 250; Stanwix, 22-28, 49-52, 58-65, 157, 196, 380; Ticonderoga, 65, 215; Venango, 16, 52-54, 383; Washington, 164, 199, 202, 239; Wayne, 243; Wintermoot(e), 69-72, 88
Fort Plain, 317-318
Fox Indians, 236
Franklin, 16, 116, 275, 277
Franklin, Benjamin, 38, 86, 122
Franklin, John, 73
Freeman, Justice, 148
French and Indian Wars, 35, 52
French Creek, 27, 52-53, 101, 130-131, 145, 175-178, 258, 322
Freneau, Philip, 391
Frey, Hendrick, 382
Friendship Hill, 175

Fulton County, 36
fur trade, 10-13

G
Gahgeote (see Half Town)
Gah-ko-on-den-oi-ya, 68
Gahnasqua, 18
Gaiantwaka(e) (Gyantwahia), 2-13, 14-15, 16, 26, 117, 141, 142, 344, 347 (see Cornplanter)
Galbraith, Robert, 150
Galeton, 146
Gallatin, Albert, 175
Ganawaugus (Conawaugus), 1-13, 18, 19, 26, 27, 29, 47, 48, 56, 62, 98, 103, 106, 112, 127-128, 211, 257, 272, 293, 357
Gansevoort, Peter, 50-51, 58-66, 384
Gardeau, 271-272, 330-331
Gardeau Reservation, 331
Gardner family, 69
Gates, Horatio, 65, 81
Genesee, 20, 109, 112, 116, 130, 139, 159, 211, 232, 257, 259, 261
Genesee Castle, 97-99, 112
Genesee River, 2, 18, 27, 28, 46, 51, 57, 97, 100, 103, 107, 117, 118, 183, 238, 270, 272-273, 306
Genesee Valley Reservations, 331
Geneseo, 270, 273
Genesinguhta (Old Town), 283, 290, 299, 301, 312, 314, 316, 332
Genesis, 284
Geneva, 96
Genishau, 18, 99
Georgia, 215
Germain, George, 49
German Flats, 27, 31-33, 46, 48, 250
Germantown, battle of, 182, 215
Gettysburg, 17
Gibson, Henry, 330-331
Gibson, John, 150, 214
Gilbert, Benjamin, 74
Girty, Simon, 30, 201, 258
Glade Run, 36
Godcharles, Frederic, 40
Goh-no-dunk, 53
Gordon, Andrew, 188
Gordon, David, 359
Gordon, Francis, 52
Gore, Obadiah, 93-94
Gorham, Nathanial, 127-129, 157, 331, 388
Gospel of St. Mark, 210
Governor Blacksnake (see Blacksnake)
Gowanda, 351
Grand Canyon of Pa., 146
Grand Glaize, 243
Grand River, 210, 212-213, 257, 305, 352
Granger, Erastus, 320
Gray, Joseph, 304
Graymont, Barbara, 51, 69, 109, 111
Great Island, 85
Great Keeper, 190
Great Lakes, 201
Great Runaway, 35, 177
Great Sheshequin Path, 36
Great Spirit, 14, 203, 226, 260, 281, 282, 284, 285, 290, 295, 297-299, 302, 307, 308, 327, 329, 335-339, 342, 343, 347
Great Swamp, 87
Great Trail, 2, 12
Great Tree (see Big Tree)
Great Valley, 351
Greendale Cemetery, 379
Green Grasshopper (see Little Billy)
Green Mountain Boys, 65
Greenville, Pa., 176
Greensburg, 150
Gregg, Andrew, 172
Grieg, John, 330-331
Griffin, Edmund, 66
Guthrie, Major, 167
Guyasootha's Bottom, 258
Guyasuta (see Kayahsotha)
Gyasota (Big Cross), 141

H
Hackney, Joseph, 322
Hah-no-gwus (Grease-Skimmer), 62
Half Town, 68, 78-80, 103, 141, 144, 149, 150, 152-156, 159, 161-164, 167, 176, 183, 220-221, 224, 252-256
Hamilton, Alexander, 234
Hamilton, James, 38
Hammond, 41
Hancock House, 394
Hancock, John, 135
Hand, Edward, 81, 86, 88
Handsome Lake (Hiadeoni), 3, 16, 19, 29, 48, 51, 68, 78, 82, 84, 107, 109-112,

115, 252, 257, 259, 265, 266, 268, 272, "death" and "resurrection," 293-297; 303, 306-316, 317, 319, 320, 321, 323, 332, 336
Hannastown, 383
Hardin County, 395
Hardin, John, 201-202
Harding massacre, 69
Harmar, Josiah, 138-139, 148, 158, 160-161, 173, 181-182, 193, 201, 203, 205, 208, 209, 219, 223, 241-244, 390
Harvard University, 7
Hasquesahah (Axe Carrier), 62
Hawken rifle, 11
Heap-of-Dogs, 128
Heckewelder, John, 202
Henry rifle, 11
Herkimer, Nicholas, 59-62
Hiester, Joseph, 3, 6, 326-329, 404
High Hill (see Guastrax)
Hildebrandt, George, 278, 401
Hildebrandt, George, Jr., 278
Hildebrandt, Jesse, 401
Hill, Aaron, 127
Hiokatoo, 6, 17, 21, 39-40, 44, 68, 80-85, 97, 107, 256
Hobson's Choice, 215, 230, 239
Hogahee River, 226
Holland Land Company, 218, 267, 277, 280
Holmes, Abiel, 341-343, 347
Holmes, Justice Oliver Wendell, 341
Holmes, Oliver Wendell, 341
Honanadaganius (see George Washington)
Honayewus (See Farmer's Brother)
Hohnogwas, 78
Hotbread, Emily O'Bail, 359
Howe, William, 49, 65, 209
Hubley, Adam, 88-90
Hubly, Bernard, 147
Hudson, Jem, 162
Hudson River, 2, 22, 49, 215
Hudson, Thomas (Telenemut), 95
Hulings, Marcus, 275
Hummingbird (Chit-ti-aw-dunk), 222
Hung Face, 110
Hunter, Adam, 79
Hunter, Samuel, 83-84
Huntingdon Valley, 36
Huron Indians, 231
Hutchins, James, 149, 152

I
Indian Camp Run, 138
Indian Hill, 77
Indian Queen Hotel, 133
Indian Run, 390
Iontonkque (Cornplanter), 134 (see Cornplanter)
Irondequois Bay, 51
Irondequois Creek, 51
Iroquois, 10, 22, 28-30, 46-65, 75, 80
Iroquois Confederacy, 51, 111, 117, 120-121, 141, 158
Irvine, Mrs. M. A., 53
Irvine, Pa. 101
Irvine, W. A., 393
Irvine, William, 76, 175, 256, 275, 330
Irving, N. Y., 359, 361
Irving, Washington, 195
Irwin, John, 174

J
Jack Berry, 68, 78, 82, 84, 107, 110
Jackson, Andrew, 211
Jackson, Halliday, 264, 267, 280, 281-283, 289-290, 299, 301, 314-315
Jackson Run, 400
Jacobs, Allen, 359
Jacobs, Eleanor, 359
Jacobs, Jim, 261
James, Arthur, 406
Jeffers, John, 145-146, 148, 149, 166, 173, 174
Jefferson, Thomas, 234, 307-311
Jemison, Mary, 17-19, 37-40, 44, 57, 62-63, 80-81, 84-85, 97-98, 108-109, 271, 331
Jenkins family, 69
Jenkins, John, 81
Jennesadaga (Cornplanter Town), 6, 114, 170, 172, 178, 191, 192, 193, 214, 220, 253, 262-265, 268, 275, 278, 280, 283, 306, 312, 319, 322, 332-333, 335, 336, 337, 340, 342, 346, 358
Jennings, 214
Jersey Shore, 118, 146
Jeskaka, 68 (see Little Billy)
Jimersontown, 351

Jimison, Caroline Plummer, 359
Johnson, Guy, 28, 380
Johnson, John, 60, 107, 109-110, 210
Johnson, Samuel, 210
Johnson, Samuel P., 288, 348
Johnson, William, 9, 19, 21-26, 28, 46, 50, 52, 58, 122, 258
Johnston, Francis, 125-128
Johnston, Henry, 304
Jones, Horatio, 183, 252, 305, 331
Juniata River, 36

K
Kanadaseaga (the Grand Village), 96
Kanadaseaga Creek, 96
Kanaghsaws, 96
Kanassee (see New Arrow)
Kaskaskie Indians, 254
Kaweaweatinen, 124
Kayahsotha, 16, 19, 22, 29-30, 38, 48, at Otsego, 51-65; 112, 116, 130, 200, 222, 230, 231, 236, 237, 256-259, 293, 383
Kayenthoghke (Seneka Abeal), 125
Keepers of the Western Door, 46
Kekionga, 193
Kelsay, Isabel, 202, 203, 205, 213
Kendaia (Appletown), 19, 27, 95
Kendarindgon, 125
Kenightie, 30
Kentucky long rifle, 11
Kettle Creek, 262
Kiandoxshan, 283
Kickapoo Indians, 254
Kientwoughko (Cornplanter), 144
Kightoi, 30
Kill Buck, 351
Kilpatrick, James, 171-172
King, Charles Bird, 211
King George III, 48, 67-68, 88, 210
King, Jacob, 37
Kingston, Ont., 381
King, Mrs. William, 41
King Tammany, 132
King, William, 41
Kinsley, Mary, 401
Kinzua Creek, 183, 262, 263
Kinzua Dam, 348, 351, 352-357, 361
Kinzua Flats, 262
Kinzua Lake, 355-356
Kirkland, Samuel, 197
Kittanning, 26, 36, 100, 171
Knouts, Mary, 13, 318
Knox, Henry, 141, 159, 163-164, 166, 172, 173, 182-183, 186, 191, 192, 197, 201, 202, 205, 221-222, Wayne expedition to battle of Fallen Timbers, 230-244; 245, 256, 309
Kowatz, Colonel, 76

L
La Farge, Peter, 354
Lafayette, Marquis de, 124-125
Lake Canandaigua, 245
Lake Champlain, 49
Lake Chautauqua, 314
Lake Conneaut, 176
Lake Erie, 27, 52, 53, 131, 168, 175, 182, 187, 199, 205, 255, 272, 273, 351
Lake George, 19
Lake Oneida, 58
Lake Ontario, 22, 29, 51, 57, 111, 128, 183
Lake Otsego, 91
Lancaster, 11, 305
Lancaster County, 62
Land Office, 169
Large Tree (see Big Tree)
Laurens, Henry, 389
Laurens, Martha, 389
Lear, Tobias, 195-196
Lee, Arthur, 124
Lee, Elizabeth Dowdy, 360
Lee, George (Mrs.), 360
Lee, Harriet, 360
Lee, Leonard, 360
Lee, Nellie, 360
Legends of the Longhouse, 360
Legionville (Legion Ville), 196, 202, 205, 215, 230, 232, 233, 236, 237
Leicester, N. Y., 97
Leni Lenape, 120
Letchworth State Park, 18
Lexington/Concord, 27, 104, 182, 211
Lieutenant Prior, 233
Ligonier, 258
Lima, 199
Lincoln, Benjamin, 177, 239
Little Beard, 68, 78-80, 82, 84, 89, 96-99, 107, 110, 112, 183, 184, 186, 252, 272, 306, 309, 331

Littlebeard, John, 322
Little Beard's Creek, 306
Little Billy, 68, 78-80, 128, 250, 252, 272, 319-320, 321, 331
Little Crow, 225
Little Meadows, 16
Little Muskingum River, 200
Little Pine Creek (Blockhouse Creek), 146
Little Turtle (Michikinkna), 174, 181-184, 193-195, 201, 208, 240-242, 253, 393
Liverpool, 119
Livingston County, 18
Livingston, John, 127-128, 157, 160
Livingston Lease, 127
Lock Haven, 85
Logan, John, 303, 360
Logan, Polly O'Bail, 358-360
Logstown, 52
London, 119
Longhouse Religion, 306-316
Lord Dunmore's War, 22
Lord, Samuel, 304
Lossing, Benton, 73
Loyalhanna, 258
Loyalsock, 39, 42
Ludlow, 241
Lycoming, 41
Lycoming County, 42
Lycoming Creek, 39, 41, 76, 80

M

Maclay, Samuel, 218-219
Maclay, William, 83, 86, 125-128, 218
Madison, James, 124
Mahican (Stockbridge) Indians, 197
Mahoning, 100
Mahusquechikoken, 101
Marietta, 138-140, 233, 360
Markham, William, 119
Marsh Creek, 17, 146
Matlack, Timothy, 159, 163
Matthews, Elijah, 173
Maumee Conference, 207
Maumee River, 138, 148, 161, 181, 199, 201, 203, 205, 240, 241
Maxwell, William, 86, 88
May, William, 231
McClure, David, 95, 258
McCully, George, 174
McDonnell, John, 82-86, 92
McDowell, Alexander, 169
McGuire, Captain, 172
McKean, Joseph, 7
McKean, Thomas, 304-305
McKee, Alexander, 201, 395
McKnight, James, 83
McKnight, Mrs., 41-42
McKnight, W. J., 7
McNeill, Samuel, 105
Mead, Darius, 176
Mead, David, 173-177, 191, 256, 322
Meadville, 7, 52, 131, 176, 191, 257, 267, 268, 304, 319, 322, 340
Meginness, John, 41, 42
Meigs County, 54
Miami Indians, 115, 116, 124, 138, 148, 182, 186, 188, 189, 190, 193-195, 199, 207, 225, 236, 253-255
Michikinkna (see Little Turtle)
Middle Brook, 82
Mifflin, Thomas, 124, 142-154, 161, 164, 167-169, 170, 172, 174-175, 178, 183, 213-214, 256, 347, 390
Milesburg, 44
Millville, 36
Millyard Tract, 128
Milton, Pa., 83
Minden, 13
Miner, Charles, 67-68
Mingo Indians, 29-30, 52-53, 138
Missionary Society of Pittsburgh, 336
Mohawk Castles, 78
Mohawk Indians, 25-26, 28-29, 34, 124, 125, 130, 138, 247, 307, 322
Mohawk, John, 73
Mohawk River, 12, 22, 25, 32, 36, 49, 58, 62, 78, 82, 107, 109, 317
Mohawk Valley, 25, 31, 46-48, 107-110, 116
Molly Pitcher, 391
Monmouth, battle of, 215, 309
Monongahela River, 16, 28, 36, 52, 200, 353, 356
Monroe, James, 325-326
Montgomery County, N. Y., 13, 317
Montgomery, Richard, 58, 98
Montour, Catherine, 95
Montreal, 22, 109
Mordecai, 286
Morgan, Arthur, 354

Morgan, Daniel, 65, 201
Morris, Robert, 129, 270-271, 280
Morris, Robert Hunter, 37
Morris, Thomas, 259, 270-273
Morrison, James, 278
Morristown, 111, 182
Mound Cemetery, 401
Mount Vernon, 135
Muncy, 36
Muncy Hill, 36, 83, 86
Municipal Museum, Rochester, 3
Munsee (Muncy) Indians, 39, 186, 303-305
Muskingum, 138, 143, 146, 250
Muskingum River, 3, 138

N
Nauwenneyu, 337, 344, 345, 348
Nephew, The (see Blacksnake)
Nescopek, Gap, 36
New Arrow, 141, 144, 166, 170, 183, 185, 186, 187, 189-190, 196, 198, 202-205, 216, 224, 231, 232, 236, 237, 239, 319, 322
New Bethlehem, 263
New Connecticut, 305
Newkirk, William, 109
New London, 46
Newtown, battle of, 91-95, 114, 182, 183, 275
New Wales, 118
New York and Genesee Land Company, 127
New York City, 31, 49, 130, 132, 206, 239, 259, 323
Niagara, 2, 10, 12, 28, 68, 86, 103, 206, 239, 259, 323
Niagara Genesee Company, 128
Niagara-on-the-Lake, 320
Niagara River, 16-21, 111, 250, 253, 322
Nicholson, Joseph, 130, 143, 144, 152, 153-154, 156, 159, 162, 163, 171, 191-192, 391
Nonuk, 347
Northampton County, 36, 38
North Branch, Susquehanna, 66, 76-78
Northumberland, 41, 66, 86, 147
Northumberland County, 40, 75, 76, 98, 106, 176

O
O'Bail, Charles (see Abeel)
O'Bail, Esther, 358
O'Bail, John, 3
O'Bail, Polly, 358
O'Bail, Solomon, 348, 359, 360
O'Bail, William (see Abeel)
Odongot, 23
Ogden Land Company, 325, 331
Ogden, Thomas, 92, 331
Oghkwaya, 78
O'Hara, James, 138
Oheadarighton, 125
Ohio (Western) Indians, 115, 124, 131, 158, 161, 163-164, 166, 172-173, 175-180, 182-190, 193-216, 222
Ohio Land Company, 142
Ohio River, 26, 29, 36, 122, 138, 139, 200, 205, 207, 215, 232, 236, 237, 356
Oil City, 169, 288, 350, 360
Oil City Derrick, 288
Oil City Tract, 169
Oil Creek, 288, 350, 360
Oil Springs, 185, 272
Oil Springs (Creek) Reservation, 310, 332, 351-352
Ojibwa Indians, 54
Old Castle, 396
Old Fish, 304
Old German Grey, 404
Oldham, Samuel, 268, 278, 333, 335
Old Hickory, 211
Oldnews, 144
Old Smoke (Sayenqueraghta), 20, 22, 34, 38, 45, 52-65, at Wyoming, 70-74; 77-79, resists Sullivan, 81-106; 107, 110, 256, 293
Old Snake, 304
Olean, 263, 345
Olean Point, 346
Onas, 30, 170, 281
Oneida Indians, 49, 56, 57, 60, 82, 123-126, 247, 251, 313
Oneida Reserve, 330
Onogwendahonji, 125
Onondaga, 28, 48, 120, 173, 312, 315, 316, 320
Onondaga Indians, 33-34, 56, 57, 65, 68, 78, 91, 111, 124, 247, 251
Onondaga Lake, 110

Onongadakas, 78
Oriska, 60
Oriskany, 20, 45, 61-65, 77, 209, 258, 293
Oriskany Battlefield Monument, 62-63
Oriskany Creek, 60
Oswego, 27, 28, 50-65, 271, 293
Otetiania (see Red Jacket)
Otsego Lake, 78
Ottawa Indians, 29, 52, 54, 138, 199, 236, 254

P

Paducah, 26
Painted Post (Cohocton), 183
Paoli, 215
Parish, Jasper, 252
Parker, Arthur, 3, 15
Parker, Captain, 65
Parker, Michael, 96-99
Parker, Robert, 94
Parkman, Francis, 21
Parrish, John, 397-398
passenger pigeon, 188-189, 261
Paxtang, 167
Pemetamah, 30
Penn, William, 118-120, 132, 246, 351, 356
Pennamite Wars, 67-68
Penn's Creek, 35, 37
Pennsylvania Gazette, 38, 67
Pennsylvania Historical Commission, 348
Pennsylvania State Museum, 354
Pepy, Joseph, 30
Petain, Marshal, 114
Phelps, Oliver, 127-129, 151, 157, 160, 260, 305-306, 388
Philadelphia County, Building, 154
Phile, Eliza, 134
Philips, John, 9, 314
Piankeshaw Indians, 254
Pickering, Timothy, 66, 116, 159, 199, 224, 226, 239, 245-253, 256, 276, 353
Pierce (Cornplanter descendants): Esther, 360, Harriet, 360, James, 359, Jonathan, 359-360, Lucinda, 359, Marsh, 359-360, Moses, 360, Susan, 360, Wallace, 359
Pierce, John (Quaker missionary), 282, 283, 291
Pine Creek, 36, 39, 116, 118, 146-149, 151, 154, 160, 161, 262-264
Pioneer History, 7
Pioneer Life, 268
Pittsburgh, 17, 27, 29-30, 36, 47, 82, 115, 116, 117, 130-131, 147, 149, 165, 174-175, 215, 230, 232, 235, 238, 275, 277, 301
Pittsburgh Gazette, 345
Planter's Field Tract, 169
Plunket, Dr., 42
Point Pleasant, 22
Polhemus, John, 178
Pollard, Captain, 74
Pontiac, 25, 29, 52
Poor, Enoch, 86, 92-94
Portland, Maine, 148
Potawatamie Indians, 138, 236, 254
Potter County, 118, 146
Presque Isle, 175, 177, 208, 213, 240, 255
Presbyterian Society, 333
Price, 109
Princeton, battle of, 182
Proctor, John, 395
Proctor, Thomas, 86, 88, 89-91, 92-94, 153, 163, 166, 182-190, 191, 216, 221, 229, 233, 234, 235
Purchase Line, 381
Putnam, Rufus, 202, 327

Q

Quakers, 9, 14, 115, 118, 132, 151, 170, 191-192, 247-250, 256, 267, 277-278, 279, at Cornplanter Town, 280-302; 306, 312, 314, 316-317, 325-326, 332-333, 336, 351, 358
Quaker Bridge, 20, 313
Quebec, 58, 61, 98, 352
Quedor, 32
Quaker Run (see Tunesassa Creek)
Queen Esther, 72-74, 77, 87, 95
Queen's Own Rangers, 381

R

Ramsay, David, 135-138, 139
Ramsay, Frances, 405
Randolph, Beverley, 239
Randolph, Edmund, 234
Randolph, John, 392

Reading, Pa., 175
Red Bank (Redbank), 101, 263, 264
Redeye, Chief, 98, 101-103
Red House, 351
Red Jacket (Sagoyewatha), 19, 27-28, 33, 47-48, 56, 60, 68, 69, 77, 79, 89, 94-96, 103, 107, 110, 115, 117, 123, 128, 155, 156, 183, 187-189, 198, 203-204, 209-212, 232, 249-250, 252-253, 256, 258, 259, 270-272, 306, 311-312, 315-317, 320-323, 331, 335-336, 361
Reed, Joseph, 83, 104
Richland Tract, 169
Ridgway, 261
Rifle, 10-12
Riverview-Corydon Cemetery, 348, 355, 356
Rochester, 51, 245
Rogers, Benjamin Woolsey, 331
Rogers, William, 87-88
Rolfe, 382
Rome, N.Y., 22, 49, 62, 123-126
Root, Erastus, 392
Rosencrantz, Nicholas, 204-205, 231-233, 236
Royal Greens, 60, 77
Royal Proclamation of 1763, 121, 122, 180
rum, 10, 31, 57-58, 74, 115, 120, 189, 286, 288, 308
Rush, Benjamin, 389

S

Sac Indians, 236
Sagoyewatha (see Red Jacket)
Sagwarithra, 68, 78-80, 107, 110
St. Clair, Arthur, 138-142, 163, 173-174, 186, 190, 193-197, 201, 203, 205, 208, 209, 214, 219, 223, 242-244
St. Leger, Barry, 49, 50, 58-65
St. Marys, Pa., 261
Salamanca, N. Y., 351, 361, 362
Salt Lick Town, 381
Sandusky, 103, 316
Sandusky River, 208
Saratoga Campaign, 65, 75, 201
Savery, William, 247-250, 299
Sawmill, 313-314, 316-317, 362, 400
Sayenqueraghta (see Old Smoke)
Saylor, John, 354, 406
Schenectady, 110
Schoharie Creek, 109
Schoharie Valley, 65, 107, 109, 114, 209, 293
Schuler, Catalyna, 4
Schuyler, Philip, 31-33, 381
Schuylkill River, 133
Scioto River, 138, 148
Scott, Charles, 192
Scovell, Elisha, 69
Seaman, Walter, 268
Seaver, James, 18-19
Seeber, William, 318
Seneca Billy, 149, 152
Seneca Indians, passim
Seneca Lake, 19, 95
Seneca Nation of Indians, 351, 352, 361, 362
Shade River (Guyun Run), 54
Shade, The, 30
Shades of Death, 87
Shamokin, 37, 40, 120
Shamokin Path, 36
Sharpless, Joshua, 264, 277-278, 282, 283, 291, 299, 301
Shawnee Indians, 17, 22, 29, 38, 45, 54, 115, 116, 120, 124, 138, 148, 151, 172, 182, 190, 199, 200, 203, 236, 254, 255, 319
Shelby County, 202
Shenango, 176
Sheninjee, 18
Shesequin Path, 76
Shinneshangotha, 173
Shippensburg, 148
Shreve, Israel, 88
Silverheels, Abraham (Abram), 360
Silverheels, Cassandry, 360
Silverheels, George, 399
Silverheels, Hannah, 359
Silverheels, Jawajuh, 360
Simcoe, John Graves, 200-201, 206-207, 209, 212-213, 239, 394
Simmons, Henry, 9, 14, 264, 267, 282-302, 306, 332
Simpson, Michael, 98
Sinnemahoning, 219
Sipe, Charles Hale, 42, 340
Six Nations, 8, 15, 22-26, 229-32, 38, 46-65, 83, 87, 100, 104, 106, 116, 120,

124-128, 130, 138, 140, 145, 156, 159, 161, 176-177, 183-186, 197
Slocum, George, 183
Smalley, William, 202
Smith, Jonathan Bayard, 134
Smith, Joseph, 189, 252
Smith, Matthew, 84, 98
Smith, Michael, 41
Smith, Mrs. Peter, 41
Smith, Peter, 41-42
Snodgrass, 41
Snowden, James Ross, 348
Society of Friends, 256, 302, 354
Souetdo, 78
South Mountain, 17
South Valley, 351
Squakey (spelled variously) Indians, 183, 189
Squawkie Hill, 183, 221, 271-272
Standing Stone, 45
Stanwix, John, 22, 58
Stephenson's Tavern, 147
Stewardson, Thomas, 299
Stewart, David, 172
Stevens, Sylvester, 354
Stif-knee (see Big Tree)
Stockbridge Indians, 197
Stone, William Leete, 50, 73, 95, 108-109
Stony Point, 215
Street, Samuel, 128
Struthers, John, 6, 8
Struthers, Thomas, 6, 7
Stuart, Gilbert, 393
Stump Foot, 183
sugar camps, 185, 265
Sullivan Expedition, 35, 81-106, 109, 110, 114, 157, 183, 190, 228, 256, 257
Sullivan, John, 81-106, 184, 247, 309
Sullivan, John, Jr., 230
Sunbury, 36, 42, 43, 76, 88
Supreme Executive Council (Pa.) 75, 83, 85, 127, 143, 144, 147, 152-154, 160
Susquehanna Company, 25
Susquehanna River, 12, 36, 40, 66, 68, 73, 87-106, 109, 122, 262
Swatzler, David, 246, 253, 271, 277-278, 280, 289, 291, 302, 316
Swayne, Joel, 282, 289-290, 295, 301, 313

T
Tammany Society, 132-134
Tanner, Archibald, 345
Tarachinwagon, 245, 267, 291
Tayagonendagighti, 125
Taylor, Jacob, 9, 312-313
Tegunteh, 139
Tehonwaeaghrigagi, 125
Telenemut (see Thomas Hudson)
Ten Broeck, Abraham, 109
Tetepuska, 30
Thaosagwat, 96
Thayendanegea (see Joseph Brant)
"The Gift," 169
Thomas, Jonathan, 312, 326
thunder trees, 90
Tice, Gilbert, 63
Tin-nes-hau-ta-go (see Jennesadaga)
Tioga, 76, 78, 79, 90-91, 95, 100, 105, 127, 183
Tioga Conference, 159
Tioga Point, 72
Tionesta, 169, 263
Tionesta Creek, 305
Titus, George, 359
Tome, Harry, 355
Tome, Philip, 262-264, 333, 335, 355, 358, 405
Tonawanda, 116, 257, 272, 294, 316, 358
Tonawanda Creek, 272
Tonawanda (Towanda) Reservation, 315, 321, 331, 335, 352, 360
Tonawanda Senecas, 352
Torture Tree, 98
Touighnatogen, 125
Towanda *Republican*, 73
Town Destroyer, 104, 155, 156
Treaties: Big Tree, 129, 211, 259, 270-273, 280, 287, 293, 331; Buffalo Creek (1826), 211, 305-306, 331; Fort Finney, 395; Fort Harmar, 129, 138-143, 146, 162, 255; Fort McIntosh, 140; Fort Stanwix (1768), 116, 122-123, 204, 248, 251; Fort Stanwix (1784), 113-116, 124-129, 130, 140, 142, 161, 162, 180, 248, 251-252, 326, 331, 358; Greenville, 35, 129, 255; Hard Labour, 122; Jay, 243; Moscow, 330-331; Paris, 35, 113, 117, 130, 135, 144, 157, 171, 181, 209, 256, 258,

275, 319; Pensacola,, 122; Pickering (Canandaigua), 129, 245-253, 293, 299, 314, 322, 351, 352-354
Treaty Oak (see Treaty of Big Tree)
Troup, Robert, 331
Trueman, Alexander, 201-202
Tunesassa (spelled variously), 281, 312, 315
Tunesassa Creek (Quaker Run), 314, 316
Turkey Run, 42
Turtle Clan, 2, 51, 211
Turtle Creek, 147, 202
Tuscarora Indians, 49, 56, 57, 68, 78, 87, 107, 110, 123-126, 247, 248
Twenty Canoes, 78
Two Guns, 405

U
Ulysses, 146
Unadilla, 394
Underwood, Thomas, 232, 236-237

V
Valley Forge, 99, 182, 309
Vandalia, N. Y., 122, 351
Vandalia Company, 122
Vaness, Jerome, 43
Van Horn, Cornelius, 191
Van Rensselaer, Robert, 110
Venango, 166, 172, 175, 177
Venango County, 7, 288, 320, 329, 350
Venango Road, 100
Vermont, 250
Vichy, 114

W
Wabash Indians, 182, 202
Wabash River, 193-195, 202, 243
Wait, Jason, 92
Wagner, Peter J., 318
Walker, Benjamin, 147-149, 154
Walker Captain, 83
Walker, Henry, 147-149, 154
Walker, Joseph, 147-149, 154
Wallace, Anthony, 21, 109, 110, 139-140, 196, 208, on Cornplanter Town, 264-267; 268, 283, 291, 307, 315, 337, 358
Wallace, William, 305
Wallis, John, 220
Wapakoneta, 199
Ware, Jesse, 19
War of 1812, 19-20, 115, 311, 319-324, 325, 337
Warren County Orphans Court, 358
Warren, Pa., 100, 103, 170, 265, 267, 275, 277, 288, 319, 327, 329, 345, 348, 353-357
Warrior (Warrior's) Run, 36, 41-42, 82-85
Washington, George, 6, 16, 20, 31, 52, 54, 58, 66, 76, 80-82, 100, 103, 115, 121-123, 126, 129, 131-135, 139, 142, 144, 149, meets with Cornplanter, 153-163; 166-167, 170, 172-173, 175, 180, his 1790 Proclamation, 180-181; concern over Ohio Indians, 180-190, 192, 194-195; receives Cornplanter delegation in Philadelphia, 197-199; 203, 204, 214-216, 219, 223, 224, Fallen Timbers, 230-244; 245, 247, 252, 255, 256, 258, 259-260, 276-277, 287, 342, 352
Washington County, 143
Washington, D.C., 175, 212, 307
Washingtonville, 98
Waterford, Pa., 53
Wayne, Anthony, 178, 196, 200, 202-208, 213-215, 219, 228-229, Fallen Timbers, 230-244; 248, 253-256
Wegenpiersenwah (see Blue Jacket)
Wells family, 80
Wells, Robert, 79
Wemple, Abraham, 109
West Branch of Pine Creek, 146
West Branch of the Susquehanna, 37, 39, 66, 82-85, 118, 146, 219, 262
Western Confederation, 173
Western Department, 165, 192, 193, 330
Western Missionary Society, 268, 333
Westfield, N.Y., 359
West Hickory, 169
Westmoreland, 69
Westmoreland County, 100, 101, 166-167, 214
Wetzel, Lewis, 139
Wewelatimiha (Shawnee chief), 30
Weyenpiersenwah (see Blue Jacket)
Wheeling, Va., 45, 143, 233, 301
White Eyes, 29
White Seneca, 304

Wighalousing, 67
Wilkins, John, Jr., 148, 169, 174, 175, 178
Willett, Marinus, 49-50, 61, 64, 382
Williams, Benjamin, 19-20, 32, 56, 135, 197, 294, 314
Williams, Elias, 42
Williams, Peter, 42
Williamsport, Pa., 41, 66, 85
Wilsib, William, 304
Wilson, James, 218
Winganum, 30
Wintergreen Park, 107
Wistwar, Thomas, 281
witchcraft and witch hunting, 115, 292-293, 294, 306, 315, 337
Wolcott, Oliver, 124-125
Wolf Clan, 2, 211, 293, 336
Wood Creek, 26
Wood, Susannah, 281
Wren, Christopher, 50
Wundungohteh, 78
Wyalusing, 77, 86
Wyalusing Path, 36
Wyandot Indians, 29, 54, 116, 124, 138, 140, 186, 188, 199, 207, 236, 254, 255
Wyoming, 36, 44, 45, 49, 58, 66-74, 75-81, 86-89, 99-100, 105, 107, 114, 183, 246, 258, 293
Wyoming Path, 36

Y

Yahrungwago, 100
York, Henry, 304, 342
York, Pa,, 11
Yorktown, 35, 215, 256, 309
Young King, 198, 272, 306, 320, 331
Youngsville, 101
Youngwoman's Creek, 39

Z

Zeigler, David, 138